GEOFFREY MOORHOUSE

Geoffrey Moorhouse's books, which have been translated into several languages, have covered topics ranging from monasticism and Indian history, to accounts of his 2,000 mile journey by camel across the Sahara, and the year he spent working as a fisherman on the Banks off North America. His CALCUTTA is regarded as a classic study of that city, and was described by the late Paul Scott as 'the best book on modern India I have read', while TO THE FRONTIER won the Thomas Cook Award for the best travel book of 1984. Geoffrey Moorhouse is a Fellow of the Royal Society of Literature. He lives in a hill village in North Yorkshire.

'He has the knack of reducing a large subject to manageable proportions without draining it of life and idiosyncrasy . . . the book's overall assessment of New York is commendably balanced'
John Gross in The New York Times

'Written with enormous grace and great insight . . . A superb delineation of a city'
Kirkus Reviews

'In his fluent and masterly way, Mr Moorhouse has hit the gong'
Daily Telegraph

'A welcome reminder that people still can and do write books'
The Times

Geoffrey Moorhouse

IMPERIAL CITY
The Rise and Rise of New York

First published in Great Britain in 1988 by Hodder and Stoughton Ltd

Sceptre edition, 1989

Sceptre is an imprint of Hodder and Stoughton Paperbacks, a division of Hodder and Stoughton Ltd.

British Library C.I.P.

Moorhouse, Geoffrey *1931–*
    Imperial city.
    1. New York. (City). Description and travel
    I. Title. II. Series
    917.47'10443

    ISBN 0-240-49939-7

Printed and bound in Great Britain for Hodder and Stoughton Paperbacks, a division of Hodder and Stoughton Ltd., Mill Road, Dunton Green, Sevenoaks, Kent TN13 2YA. (Editorial Office: 47 Bedford Square, London, WC1B 3DP) by Richard Clay Ltd., Bungay, Suffolk. Typeset by Hewer Text Composition Services, Edinburgh.

To
Matthew and Connie
with love and thanks

ACKNOWLEDGMENTS

This book could never have been written without the help of many New Yorkers, who gave me all manner of assistance and encouragement. If I thank Roger Graef before anyone else, it is because it was he who first suggested that I ought to make the attempt, and then allowed me to tap his knowledge of the city. Others to whom I'm indebted include Connie Fogler and Matthew Stevenson (Mr and Mrs Stevenson), Marian and Tony Wood, Ellen Levine and Ivan Strauss, Nick and Shirley Stevenson, Frank and Delora Hercules, Joseph and Lesley Owen, Michael and Shirley McLoughlin, Lynn Franklin, Alan Sagner, John White, Sheila Porter, Benedict Nightingale, Richard Kieler, Diane Coffey, Tom Hoban, Joan Gudefin, Anya Schiffrin, Susan Franks, Richard G. McGrath, Victor and Tikkie Biswas, Lisa and Sven Lindblad, Tracy Bernstein, Tom Wallace, Evelyn Benjamin, Jackie Flamm, Tom McCormick, T. D. Allmann, Mark Gibson, Captain Thomas McGovern, Richard Amster, John Tishman, Laurie Grove, Patricia Erdman, Peter Wawra, Nanette Stevenson, Julie Stevenson, Shaun Benet, Everton Richardson, Bill Tucker, Richard Aurelio, Joseph Murphy, Dan Wolff, Perry Knowlton, George Mead and Antonio Cabrini. Although a great deal of the text is a result of my own observation and conversations with numerous people, its basis is research that was often undertaken in the library of the New York Historical Society, whose staff were unfailingly helpful, during visits spread across a couple of years.

I have a different reason for thanking some people much nearer home. I had almost finished my researches, but hadn't yet written a word, when I was taken ill and crashed my car in the process. Two ambulancemen, Kevin Fisher and John Wilson, most certainly saved my life that day. It was subsequently preserved by the skills and the care of three doctors, their colleagues and their staffs, working under the National Health Service – Dr Roger J. Wolstenholme, of Wigan Royal Infirmary, Dr Alan F. Mackintosh, of St James's University Hospital, Leeds, and Mr Duncan R. Walker, of Killingbeck Hospital, Leeds. In a very special sense, they are all co-authors of this book. My heartfelt gratitude to every one of them.

G.M.
Gayle, Wensleydale, October 1987

CONTENTS

1   The View from the Bridge   17
2   Upwards and Outwards   37
3   The Boiling Pot   77
4   A New Jerusalem   109
5   Them and Us   135
6   Almighty Dollar   167
7   Making It   195
8   You Gotta Keep Moving   223
9   A Slightly Rotten Apple   253
10 The Overlords   281
11 Imperial, but Potholed   313
12 It's a Helluva Town   335
Bibliography   357
Source Notes   361
Index   383

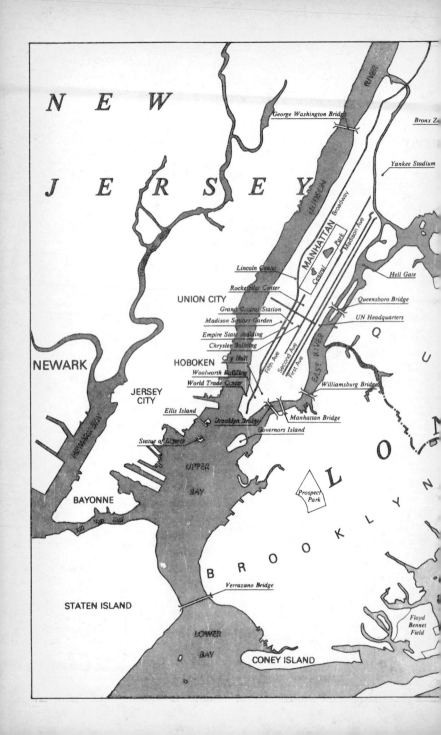

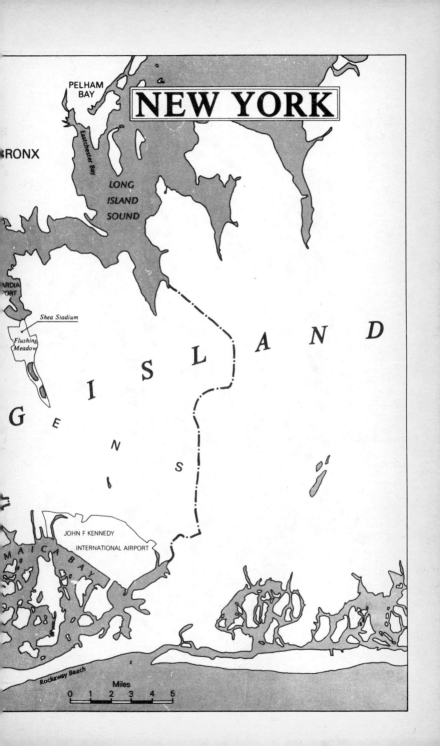

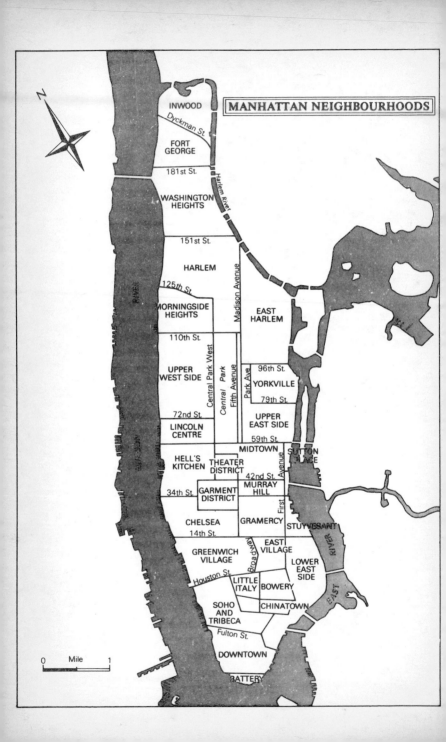

'We will discover and uncover this new Imperial City of Today, celebrating its peak of arrogance.'

– Felix Riesenberg and Alexander Alland,
Portrait of New York (1939)

ONE

THE VIEW FROM THE BRIDGE

The most sensational city walk in the world begins unpromisingly, on a concrete path, surrounded by graffiti, with traffic howling by on either side. There is a speed restriction along Adams Street, as there is elsewhere in New York, but few drivers appear to heed it as they hurtle into Brooklyn here, or accelerate in the opposite direction, going hard for the bridge approach. Half a mile before the Brooklyn Bridge takes off from the land, Manhattan-bound, the street is divided straight down the middle by the concrete path, where pedestrians and cyclists may proceed without hazard from cars and trucks, apart from the racket that assails their ears. Adams is a wide thoroughfare, so that it can easily accommodate the path as well as three lanes of vehicles going each way, flanking them at first with a succession of solid grey buildings, court houses and suchlike, that speak of municipal, state or federal gravity; later with some high brick apartments of a rising worker class, which face a welcome little park, bordered by trees, across the street.

The Family Court building, being a very American institution, carries an uplifting homily graven in stone across its façade: 'Through the guiding hand of Wisdom and Understanding shall the family endure and children grow strong in the security of the home, for they are the hope of the future.' Other texts reveal themselves as the pedestrian makes his way along the concrete path towards the bridge. A low wall on one side of the street carries 'Hands off El Salvador' in white paint; and, a

bit farther on, 'Free Ireland' in green. Adams has deteriorated
somewhat by now into a scruffy no-man's-land, where trash
and weeds and dust mingle beside the endless screech and
hiss of tyres. It is redeemed only a little by the exhortations
which confront all comers to the bridge, across the frontage
of a building which they would crash straight into, were it not
for the sudden bend marking the end of Adams and the start of
the bridge approach. The style, the proportions and the upkeep
of the building suggest some prospering light industry inside,
the manufacture of shoes, perhaps, but its purpose is more
imperative than that, announced across the rooftop with 'Read
The Watchtower and Awake!' – followed, four floors lower down,
by the supplementary suggestion to 'Read God's Word The Holy
Bible Daily'.

This is not advice to be taken instantly by any driver heading
for the bridge, on a sweeping curve and with a great confusion
of merging and dispersing traffic just ahead. At this north-
western edge of Brooklyn, roads swerve in every direction
between factories which are seldom in the neat condition of the
Jehovah's Witnesses' printworks, and sometimes look derelict.
Upon crossovers and by way of underpasses, the trucks and cars
thunder along, in volumes that can bewilder even European Man,
who has for decades been trying to imitate the American Dream
in this as in other respects. So much traffic is wont to pass in
the shadow of the bridge along the waterfront below Brooklyn
Heights, for example, that no fewer than three levels of road
are required to accommodate it, one on top of the other.

Until now, the pedestrian can have no idea of the sensation
that lies in wait for him. He may even be losing his nerve a little,
wondering whether to turn aside; which is impossible, for he is
hemmed in by a roaring madness of vehicles, with nowhere to
go but forward or back.

The first inkling of improvement comes as he walks into
that bend, with a glimpse of the bridge itself ahead, a hint of
skyscrapers some considerable way beyond. This encourages
him to advance rather than retreat, and every step from then on
brings more revelation, new perspectives, an increasing sense
of possibilities, as in a child's kaleidoscope. By the time the

pedestrian's concrete ramp has begun to rise above the spates
of traffic crossing the bridge, has ceased to be concrete and
become a decent boardwalk instead, he knows he is onto a
winner for sure. One of the most familiar views on earth is
shaping up, and neither rumour nor illustration can quite do
justice to the reality seen from the Brooklyn shore.

There, in all its unique drama, is the skyline at Manhattan's
butt-end. It comes into sight gradually, as would some sub-
marine fantasy surfacing from the sea, because the pedestrian
is ascending a gently rising path towards the eastern pier of
the Brooklyn Bridge. First the tops of the tallest buildings
are tantalisingly within view, and the breath catches a little
at the shock of recognition; for recognition there invariably
is. However far the stranger has come to see this view, he
will almost certainly feel that it has been somewhere in his
background for most of his life, courtesy of the cinema or (as
likely) the television screen. As he strides up the boardwalk to
where the bridge levels out, the full density of the phenomenon
becomes apparent across a distance of water.

At this range – the best part of a mile away from that eastern
bridge pier, where the pedestrian is likely to stand spellbound for
a while – the tip of Manhattan appears in outline like a cliff tumbling abruptly into the waves of New York Harbor. Well within
memory, that profile of masonry was not nearly so steep, the
outline being more like that of a headland sloping into the sea: but
a greater congestion of higher buildings arising in the past couple
of decades has somewhat altered the general shape – not for the
better, many local critics say. An outsider, however, is much
more likely to remain impressed by the statuesque grandeur of
it all, by the sense of a powerful fortress, impregnable in the
New World. These obelisks, cubes, cylinders, and uncommon
shapes for which there are no concise geometrical names, stand
so gigantically tall, so massively based, so close together, that
to arrive within sight of them by way of the Brooklyn Bridge,
from almost anywhere on earth, is to be staggered at once by
their collective might. There are many cities in North America
with thickets of skyscraper beckoning the traveller from afar,
offering him the semblance of a refuge; or perhaps a threat.

Boston, reached by the mariner across Massachusetts Bay, is one, and Calgary another, arrived at by road or rail across the Canadian prairie; and there are many more on either side of the 49th Parallel. None, though, can rival in scale or in prospect this vision on the end of Manhattan. None has the same capacity to suggest protection; or possibly to intimidate.

Not even New York's other concentration of skyscrapers in midtown Manhattan – indicated some distance away, across intervening lowlands of brick and ferro-concrete, by the gleam of the Chrysler spire in the shimmering heat haze, and the outline of its old rival, the Empire State Building – not even these have anything like the collective impact of the World Trade Center, the Woolworth Building and their co-habitants at the foot of the island. Part of the magnetism down here is not only a matter of outline, an image of inherent strength, but of implicit and brooding secrecy. Standing there on the Brooklyn Bridge, you really don't know what to expect when you have crossed the East River and arrived at that great bastion, when you will nervously step into any one of the deep fissures that separate each monolith from the next.

In all these ways, this is a skyline to marvel at.

The Brooklyn Bridge, too, is a marvel in its own right. It is hard to think, offhand, of another bridge anywhere which is held in nearly as much affection, or which has been celebrated as often in paint, in verse, in prose and even on the stage. Some of these sallies have been composed nearby in Brooklyn Heights, which has been home for a long succession of writers, before and since the bridge was built. Great Thomas Paine dwelt here, and Walt Whitman, too, and the likes of Thomas Wolfe, W. H. Auden, Carson McCullers, John Dos Passos and Truman Capote. It is where Arthur Miller lived when he wrote *A View from the Bridge* about desperate events on the waterfront, and where Hart Crane was in residence when he worked up a much-quoted and rather overwrought poem entitled *The Bridge*.

What all the celebrations salute is a legendary feat of engineering, and as graceful a structure as craftsmen in stone and metal can possibly contrive, still utterly and elegantly unforgettable after more than 100 years. This was the very first bridge connecting Manhattan with anywhere, and it was the product of New York's bitter winters. The one of 1866 was so awful that the ferryboats which provided the East River crossing were icebound at their wharves for weeks on end, and a lobby developed for the construction of an alternative way over the water. The man chosen to design and oversee the work, John Roebling, had already made his name with bridges at Niagara Falls and over the Ohio River at Cincinnati, but the Brooklyn Bridge, which would be his outstanding legacy, he was never to see. Having almost finished the working plans, he slipped one day by the water's edge and had his foot crushed by a ferryboat, dying shortly afterwards from tetanus.

The beginnings of the bridge were regularly visited by accident. No-one ever kept a tally of deaths among the construction workers, but it is estimated at twenty or so. After Roebling's fatal mishap, his son Washington took over, but became an invalid after an attack of the bends while making the foundations of the bridge's eastern pier, thereafter watching progress through a telescope from an apartment on the Heights. It was his wife, Emily, who completed the Brooklyn Bridge, after teaching herself the elements of the civil engineer's art and craft.

It was opened on May 24, 1883, which was by chance the British Queen Victoria's birthday, thus ensuring that the New York Irish would ostentatiously boycott the ceremony, though almost everyone else seems to have turned up, including Chester A. Arthur, the President of the United States. New Yorkers quickly took to their new amenity in thousands every day (at a toll of one cent per person), and it was this great enthusiasm for the novelty of crossing the river by an aerial route that caused another tragedy six days after the opening. A woman tripped and fell down some steps at the Manhattan end, the crowd panicked, and a dozen people were trampled to death. But that appears to have been the end of the Brooklyn Bridge's spectacularly bad luck. The biggest danger to life and limb these days are the cyclists, cocky young men whizzing down the boardwalks at some speed, who assume that everyone else will get out of their way.

The visiting observer, experiencing all this for the first time, will doubtless have heard that this was the world's longest suspension bridge until 1903, when the Williamsburg Bridge was flung across the East River, some way upstream. He will surely know – for he is among a people obsessed with statistics, who seem to feel uneasy when there is a shortage of measurements, however unimportant – that the main cables of the Brooklyn Bridge are each spun from 5,296 galvanised steel wires, with a total length of 14,357 miles, or more than half the circumference of the earth; which can be a comforting thought 133 feet above the river (at mean high water). Inspected on the bridge itself, those cables are reassuringly thicker than a man's trunk. Seen from a distance, the full complexity of those tautened wires that have enabled this marvel to stand proud for a century and more, appears as delicately beautiful as the radial filaments of a spider's web.

In so far as a suspension bridge stands on anything, the crucial engineering here was that put into the two great piers which counterbalance each other across the river, one on the Brooklyn shoreline, the other at the Manhattan water's edge. When John Roebling began to plan the bridge that caused his death, he first conceived those structures in the style of the massive pylons which form gateways to the temples at Edfu and elsewhere along the River Nile; and although he modified this notion before the drawings were finished, so that the New York piers are much less wedge-shaped than originally planned, a whiff of the old Egypt lingers in them still. In spite of their hugeness, granite block upon ponderous block, the piers are graceful. They, more than anything else, have ensured that the Brooklyn Bridge is wonderfully in scale and in tune with its surroundings, though these have changed out of all recognition since the bridge was built. This is quite a trick, when you think of it.

For in 1883 there wasn't a skyscraper in sight, either here or anywhere else in New York. If you look at photographs of the bridge taken at about that time, when the spire of Trinity Church was the tallest thing on Manhattan (at 280 feet), the Brooklyn Bridge is easily the dominating feature in the entire vista. It looms above the Fulton Ferry terminus at the Manhattan side, as it does above all the waterside buildings on the Brooklyn shore, while the fishing boats and other craft tied to the banks or moving along the East River are reduced to the stature of cockleshells. It looms and it dominates – as though John Roebling had designed it not for his own times, but to harmonise with the Skyscraper Age to come. And now the bridge splendidly holds its own, not smothered (as Trinity Church has been smothered) by the towering range of Progress up ahead. Seen as a foreground to that skyline, it puts the skyscrapers in perspective, as well as giving the composition a touch of ageless class. Whatever they may do to the butt-end of Manhattan in the future, the Brooklyn Bridge will have its place somewhere in the emotional centre of the piece. It fits.

It has been a bridge of many parts. Its Manhattan abutment has doubled as a wine vault, sternly sealed during Prohibition. It assisted a new phrase into the language, defining a simpleton as one who is 'so dumb I could sell him the Brooklyn Bridge'. It was once hitched to a circus act, when Phineas T. Barnum drove a well-advertised herd of his elephants across on the pretext of testing the bridge for safety, as a matter of public concern. There is even a Brooklyn Bridge sound, such as a million swarming bees might make, and it can be heard a mile away downwind for months on end, after which it is extinguished for a year or two before becoming audible again. It is caused by the tarmac on the bridge's roads having worn away to expose metal strips, which produce the high-pitched hum in the endless contact with tyres revolving at high speed; until workmen come to lay fresh tarmac again . . .

Above all, this is the bridge with the view.

There our pedestrian observer stands, on his boardwalk by the eastern pier, which is where the bridge actually leaves the Brooklyn side and commits itself to sheer space above the river. He will be saddened by the mess of rubrics which have been sprayed hereabouts by the graffiti gangs, defacing among other things the bronze tablet which records the genesis of the enterprise; 'erected by the Cities of New York and Brooklyn' some dozen years before they decided to amalgamate. But at least here, as nowhere else in New York, he has everything he could hope for as a diversion from ugly inscriptions. The famous skyline dead ahead is only a part of the sensation now.

Upstream along the East River – which isn't, in fact, a river at all, but a tidal strait separating Manhattan from Long Island – other crossing places are to be seen, the handsome ironwork of the Manhattan Bridge lying companionably close at hand, one end of the superseding Williamsburg Bridge just visible halfway round a bend. The banks of the river up there are not enticing, the humdrum brick tenements of the Lower East Side being cut off from the river by the endless traffic bounding along the Franklin D. Roosevelt Drive, while across the water in Brooklyn there is an untidy sprawl of commercial buildings which look as if they have seen much better days. What used to be the Brooklyn Navy Yard is tucked out of sight down an inlet, since 1966 a defunct relic of the place that turned out warships by the score during the Second World War, including PT boats which made the East River loud with the thunder of their engines, as they churned up and down the channel, testing themselves for serious business along the Atlantic coast.

But the downstream prospect from the bridge; that is another matter.

The Brooklyn shoreline is still unexciting, though the water-front here has been tidied up, and it looks as if there might be an amount of activity at some of the more distant piers. Immediately behind the waterfront close by is the aforementioned stack of three roads, one on top of the other, and above them yet another deck, the Esplanade, where people come to walk hand in hand, to exercise their children, to sit and gape at the view, and to jog with a wide-eyed look that appears not to be seeing very much. This is a short stretch of New York well worth crossing the entire city to enjoy. It is the greatest of the blessings enjoyed by Brooklyn Heights, which has more than its fair share as these things go in the great cities of today, a reason why the Heights continues to be haunted by writers and suchlike. The neighbourhood has seen the one and only Norman Mailer take station in a terrace of brownstones above the Esplanade, in a work room which at one time resembled a trapeze artist's gym more than an author's study, so that one imagined the writer swinging each dawn from window to window of the property upon his climbing ropes and boarding nets, while he imbibed the heady potion of the view, and wondered which windmill to tilt at today.

What Mr Mailer – and the pedestrian observer from the Brooklyn Bridge – can see equally well, in addition to the Manhattan skyline, is a panoramic sweep which takes in the bigger part of New York Harbor, a great expanse of seaway including the Anchorage Channel and the Upper Bay. The way in from the Atlantic, through The Narrows and under the tremendous Verrazano Bridge (a youngster completed only in 1964), is out of sight behind a bulge in the land, yet such is the extent of this Upper Bay, that in wet and windy weather the sloppy little waves that are its norm can quickly work themselves up into an uncomfortable chop. Straight across the harbour from Brooklyn, and separated from Manhattan by the Hudson River, the levels of New Jersey are generally under a haze of smog, for much industry is over there, and the bulk of what remains in these waters of an active port.

There are islands here – quite apart from the island of Manhattan, and Long Island, to which Brooklyn belongs. Blocking much of the view towards the ocean is the considerable shape of Staten Island, one of New York City's five constituent boroughs, home for thousands of its commuters, and allegedly base camp for some of the most off-putting characters in the Mafia. It can also boast the highest ground anywhere along the coastline of the USA between Maine and Florida – Todt Hill, which caps the horizon at a dizzy 409.239 feet.

Closest to the Brooklyn Bridge is Governors Island, so placed across the channel that it makes navigation into the East River from the Upper Bay a tricky matter when the tide is on the turn, with its tumult of currents that may be responsible for the warning of wreckage on the New York Harbor chart, plumb in the middle of the most obvious course to steer. The eponymous governors were those appointed by five English monarchs, starting with William III and finishing with George III, whose tenure was abruptly ended by the Revolutionary War, but not before the gubernatorial incumbents had made various martial dispositions on the island, including a cannon with the royal insignia upon it, which still points menacingly at Wall Street, though Governors Island has been in good republican hands these 200 years, the last twenty of them in the custody of the United States Coastguard.

The most insubstantial islands in the harbour, paradoxically, are the ones which matter most, not only in the history of New York, but in the making of the United States. Were it not for what has been built on them, neither would be noticed much, for they are but low humps barely breaking surface just off the New Jersey shore. But one of them carries the most easily recognised statue on earth, and the other provides the foundations for a building which figures in the genealogy of a large proportion of New Yorkers, and many other Americans.

Monument to American Independence: Liberty Enlightening the World – to give the statue her full style and title – can be seen distantly from the bridge as a diminutive but unmistakable shape, upholding her torch Olympically, while gazing in the general direction of midtown Brooklyn. The decidedly pouting face is said to be that of the sculptor's mother, the generous body beneath the toga that of his mistress, and if the Khedive of Egypt in 1869, Ismail Pasha, had not been so tight-fisted, Frédéric Auguste Bartholdi's monument would have graced the Mediterranean entrance to the Suez Canal, and would have been known as Egypt Carrying Light into Asia. The Frenchman had spent two years making sketches and models with that end in view, before the Egyptian ruler abandoned the idea. It was saved for posterity by what would now be called a Franco-American consortium, with a sharp instinct for marketing its product, which caused it to commission a poem ('Give me your tired, your poor, your huddled masses yearning to breathe free . . .') from Emerson's protégé, the young Emma Lazarus, as part of its fund-raising campaign. And so, with modifications (the torch, for example, being transferred from the left to the right hand, a broken shackle being added to one of the ankles) and under a different name, the statue fetched up beside the Atlantic instead, on what was originally known as Minissais (lesser island), then Great Oyster Island, subsequently Bedloe Island; but which most people today think of as Liberty Island.

When it was found that a century of New York weather had taken its toll of the old girl, that her nose, an eye, a shoulder and sundry other portions of her anatomy needed repair, they tackled her in a full-blooded, very American way, importing craftsmen from France to assist their own, partially dismantling her, and spending dollars as lavishly as if all this came under the defence budget. Having mended her and cleaned her, having coated her inside (to some extent) with Teflon, they then declared a festival, again on an all-American scale, in a uniquely American manner, the purpose of which seemed at least in part to make the rest of the world go 'Wow!'; which it dutifully did, as well as venting several other exclamations. Understandably unbalanced by the often contrived emotion and the always deafening razzmatazz of that Independence Day weekend in 1986, the foreign scoffers generally failed to remember – or chose to ignore – the very genuine importance of the Statue of Liberty in the American scheme of things, which has no need of any contrivance. She is to be saluted and venerated as a simple expression of values tenaciously held, even by some people who betray them regularly; just as the mummified Lenin in his Moscow blockhouse is exalted before and by not-always-faultless Soviet citizens, as a representative of their national ideal. What Liberty represents as much as anything, year in and year out, is an enthusiastic gleam in the eye and a perfectly decent lump in the throat.

She eventually symbolised something other than universal enlightenment; instead, a more parochial American Dream, whose substance was pursued by the generations processed on nearby Ellis Island between 1892 and 1954, when the federal immigration station there was finally closed. In that time some fourteen million migrants – nearly 70 per cent of all those who came to settle in the United States – were unloaded from the trans-Atlantic vessels that had brought them from Hamburg and Genoa, from Liverpool and Gothenburg, from Antwerp and Piraeus and several other European ports. Most of them couldn't understand a word of American when their steamers arrived in New York, which made that first contact with the locals difficult, as they were lined up, systematically examined by Public Health Service doctors, sometimes separated from their families for hours and even days on end, finally awaiting sentence by some petty official, on whose decision the rest of their lives would depend. Surprisingly few (a mere 2 per cent) were sent back from the island, to return whence they had come: fewer still of those allowed to proceed into New York ever retraced their steps voluntarily for more than a sentimental visit to the old home in later years. In the cavernous reception halls of Ellis Island they had been granted salvation, and they knew very well that their luck had changed at last.

The only passenger vessels calling at the island in recent times have been those bringing tourists to wander through the echoing chambers where grandparents once sat, anxiously awaiting their turn. These are the same jaunty craft which take visitors over to Liberty Island, where the compulsive sightseer may ascend the statue as far as the viewing gallery in Liberty's diadem, though no longer up to the vertiginous platform surrounding the flames above the torch, from which a Hitchcock villain once fell, pursued by decent and patriotic Robert Cummings. From his own observation post on Brooklyn Bridge, our vigilant pedestrian can watch these crowded ferries from afar, as they ply steadily throughout the summer months between the two islands and the landing stage by Battery Park at the very end of Manhattan.

The Battery is also the city terminus of the Staten Island ferry, which is justly regarded as America's biggest bargain. For a ridiculous twenty-five cents – which will not even buy you a copy of the *New York Times* – it is still possible to ride to Staten Island and back at no extra charge; to do so, what's more, perpetually if anyone is perverse enough to put value for money above any other consideration, and determined enough not to step ashore. Throughout the day and night at least one mustard-coloured steamer may be seen trudging back and forth along the length of New York Harbor, and at rush hours there are several of them, all loaded to the rails with commuters and vehicles, travelling between Manhattan and home. Double-ended like them, but smaller and white with a distinctive red stripe down their sides, are the ferryboats which take the Coastguards and their families the relatively short trip from the Battery to their little colony on Governors Island, and back.

All this is part of the view from the bridge, as is much other activity around the port. Only a Staten Island passenger will get a grandstand eyeful of the merchantmen which are biding their time in the Anchorage Channel until the New Jersey dockmasters tell them to come in. But our watcher is well placed to see big freighters moving carefully across those treacherous river currents before being manoeuvred to a berth against the Lower East Side. If a speedboat thunders under the bridge these days, it will not be a patrol craft making for the Navy Yard, but a zippy number belonging to some well-heeled civilian, heading for a passage of Long Island Sound. A deeper rumble coming downstream announces the slower progress of a tug, shoving half a dozen barges full of metropolitan garbage towards a landfill on Staten Island. And that thing over there, crowded with people who are being talked at by someone with a loudhailer on the bridge, that's a Circle Line boat taking more tourists on a two-hour trip right round Manhattan, so that they can go back home to Vermont and Idaho, to Minneapolis and Des Moines, to all points of the compass no doubt, and tell those wondering country bumpkins that, yessir, New York City is indeed one helluva town.

Occasionally a cruise liner may be detected slipping into or out of the Hudson with a quiet electrical hum and with the Caribbean in mind, most like; and if it's the *QE2* outward bound on a Saturday afternoon, it will be gallantly escorted down harbour for a while by a fireboat hosing water into the sky. Now and then the grimmer shape of a warship will appear, bent on less publicised business almost anywhere, and an aircraft carrier has even been known to tie up at the pier right in the lee of Brooklyn Bridge, from where our watcher above would be able to wave to the sailors taking a constitutional round her ample deck. The most frequent activity at those nearest wharves is occasioned by the intermittent arrival of large fishing factory boats, often from the communist countries of eastern Europe, which plunder the rich grounds on the edge of the American continental shelf for weeks on end, then replenish their stores in New York before going back for more fish. For some years now (perhaps still, when this is read) the only regulars at Pier 3 have been a pair of huge merchantmen, deserted, tethered fast, sailing with no tide; forfeits to the Port Authority, it's said, because too much was owing on their harbour dues.

When he has had his fill of this maritime sampler, this splendid coming and going of ferries, freighters, speedboats, liners, barges, fishing craft and tugs – and even the occasional seaplane, which sets itself down buoyantly on the water at the bottom of Wall Street – our watcher will decide it's time to move on from his observation post by the eastern pier of Brooklyn Bridge, and will continue his stroll along the boardwalk towards the Manhattan side. As the features of the approaching river bank become more plain, he will be intrigued by three large inflations situated on what appear to be otherwise derelict jetties. They look a bit like dirigibles only half pumped up, but are in fact indoor courts where athletic financiers from Wall Street and surrounding district may play tennis nineteen hours a day for astronomical fees. Close by is another money-spinner fashioned from a waterfront that had become sadly run down.

When the Brooklyn Bridge was built, the Fulton Fish Market was in its heyday, having been started in 1821 'to supply the common people with the necessities of life at a reasonable price'. It was the biggest thing of its kind along the Atlantic coast, kept busy by the scores of boats that trawled the ocean throughout the year on its behalf. Even until a relatively few years ago, this short stretch of the Manhattan riverside was characterised by the keen and tinny smell of fish and by the boisterous ways of fishermen, who would unload their catches at the market, then thread their way through the adjacent sailors' bars, or make for a comforting chowder in Sloppy Louie's quayside eating place. None of these things has yet vanished from the neighbourhood – there is still some activity in the market, where Otto and Son advertise their soft-shell crabs and shad roes, and the Korean Seafood Assn of NY Inc lies alongside Smithy's Fillet House, while Sloppy Louie's still does one of the better chowders in town – but almost everything isn't quite what it used to be, overtaken by much smarter events.

At the foot of Fulton Street, a floating museum of the sea maintains a fair collection of no-longer-working craft, including what was once a Gloucester schooner fishing Georges Bank, and the old Ambrose Lightship, which marked the beginning of the sea lane into New York Harbor. But setting the pace these days in what is known as South Street Seaport, is an extravagant shopping mall, whose most flamboyant accessory is that red three-decked arrangement you can see jutting out from the water's edge; Pier 17, which was opened in 1985 with a multitude of balloons being released, a choir of 1,000 singing 'I Love New York', and various other expressions of civic self-regard. Here is still peddled one necessity of life, in a series of restaurants and other eateries serving unremarkable food at very pretty prices; but here mostly is a collection of boutiques and other catchpenny stores, all determined to cash in on a carefully cultivated appetite for New York chic.

Just behind this so-called seaport, the skyscrapers begin. And it is now possible to appreciate their individual distinguishing marks, which are matters of texture and detail as well as of shape and altitude. There are some hypercritical souls who would say that there are no distinguishing marks worth mentioning on most of the buildings in that skyline today, being the products of a vulgar age that puts profit and bombast before anything that an aesthete might applaud; and such a concatenation of curtain walls certainly lacks something of the charm that informed the view before the real estate boom of the 1960s occurred. There is nothing in contemporary high-rise like the inspiration that – against all the odds – made the neo-Gothic Woolworth Building one of the two most endearing skyscrapers in New York (a neo-Gothic *skyscraper*?!) with its crockets and ogees, its tracery and buttresses, its mullions and pilasters, not to mention its ecclesiastical lobby, where getting into an elevator is suspiciously like entering the confessional. There is a famous photograph, taken from an aircraft well over half a century ago, of the building's topmost pinnacles rising improbably above the New York overcast, a phantom shape that might have belonged to Dracula. Happily the Woolworth – like the Chrysler midtown – is still there, standing bravely representative of an age which perhaps had more taste than ours. So are some companions from way back, though not all have managed to hang onto their original names or even owners. What started off as the Bank of the Manhattan Company in 1929 is known simply as 40 Wall Street, and there's plenty of it, capped by a pyramid that also disappears sometimes into the clouds. What began as the Merchants' Exchange now belongs to Citicorp, but is usually identified as 55 Wall Street, presumably because there's no telling who will be running it this time next year.

Of all the modern buildings at this end of Manhattan, none has caused such a tarradiddle of indignation as the twin towers of the World Trade Center, and it must be supposed that this was at least in part because they brashly rise higher than anything else in New York, condemning the poor old Empire State Building to second place by 100 feet, with 110 floors surpassing the former champ's 102. Yet the World Trade Center seems but the logical conclusion of a progression begun when skyscrapers were conceived; the utterly simple box, elongated and poised on one end – two of them in this case, standing sentinel together over everything else. They are the last things the mariner sees of the great city as he sails into the Atlantic swell, two minute points on the western horizon, when all else has disappeared below the ocean's rim.

If he's coming into port on a fine summer's morning with the sun rising at his back, it's possible that his first awareness of New York will be the faraway glint of reflected light from those two towers. Any sunrise on a clear day produces a dazzling effect along that Manhattan skyline, mostly from a variety of the despised new buildings, whose glass and burnished metals flash and glow as though aflame with molten heat; and, when evening comes, the setting sun produces a second such display, best enjoyed by someone coming up the harbour, or standing on the New Jersey side. With darkness, the skyline becomes entrancing in the manner of an illuminated Christmas tree, twinkling as millions of lights are switched on. And it is a fact that, whatever time it may be between sunset and dawn that you look at those skyscrapers, all are partially lit, on different floors at different hours, each band of illumination signalling the nocturnal progress of the cleaners as they work their ways methodically up or down.

By the time our pedestrian on the Brooklyn Bridge has crossed the East River, and reached the pier on the Manhattan side, the skyscrapers are rearing close by his left hand. He comes alongside them soon after the boardwalk has given way to a concrete path again, a downward slope now, skirting a tall apartment block which is not yet stained with age. On the twentieth floor, someone has made the bravest possible gesture against the artificiality of dwelling so high off the ground, which round here reverberates with unnatural noise as the west-bound traffic pours off the bridge. A tree, a sturdy sapling flourishing in a tub, and a variety of creeper already spreading across the neighbouring brickwork, issue from the balcony of a home where the American Dream may be a little confused by now (what's that about 'huddled masses yearning to breathe free'?).

The traffic is high-tailing it down ramps which swerve in every direction, just as the ones on the Brooklyn side did, making for destinations announced by white words on large green signs – FDR Drive North and South, Civic Center, Manhattan Midtown and Lincoln Tunnel. Our pedestrian is himself heading straight for the Civic Center, where the government of New York City is spread around the edges of a small and busy park. The curving monstrosity in white stone, topped by a confection that would be more appropriate on a wedding cake, is the Municipal Building, where most of the civic clerking goes on, and where the innocent, the eager and the unwary may acquire licences to wed. Across the street is an altogether more attractive building, which has been there since early in the nineteenth century, on a site significant for all Americans. This is City Hall, where His Honor the Mayor of New York, abetted by a numerous supporting cast, gives daily performances of the serial drama this metropolis has long been accustomed – possibly addicted – to.

It stands where, one day in July 1776, a courier arrived post-haste from Philadelphia, the Continental Congress there having just made its Declaration of Independence from King George. The courier brought a copy of the precious document and here, with General Washington standing by, the Declaration was repeated to the populace of what, when the Revolutionary War was won, would be the first capital city of the new United States. Nine years later, the grateful New Yorkers were pleased to give George Washington the freedom of their city and, in accepting the honour, he had this to say:

> I pray that Heaven may bestow its choicest blessings on your City. That the devastations of war, in which you found it, may soon be without a trace. That a well regulated and beneficial Commerce may enrichen your Citizens. And that your State (at present the Seat of the Empire) may set such examples of wisdom and liberality as shall have a tendency to strengthen and give permanency to the Union at home, and credit and respectability to it abroad . . .

In that phrase enclosed by brackets is the origin, so far as we know, of the state of New York's nickname – the Empire State; but it is quite impossible to tell, from the text of Washington's letter, what it was he had in mind when he uttered those seven enigmatic words.*

Our pedestrian, then, has come to earth off the Brooklyn Bridge into a Manhattan which patently represents all that thrusting Progress has aspired to so far. He has arrived at a plot of ground where lofty ideals were once proposed in resounding words which have never lost their power to move and to inspire. He stands, tingling with anticipation no doubt, on the threshold of an experience which, his senses will already have told him, may be unlike anything he has ever known before. Slipping into the city's heart through that great bastion of architecture on the riverbank, he will suspect that some rare new adventure is about to begin.

Strangers entering the walled cities of medieval Europe and Asia must have felt a bit like this, as they passed beneath the

---

* Washington's acceptance of the freedom is undated, but the document is endorsed 'Read in Common Council 2nd May 1785'. Professor Morison has noted that it was another thirty years or so before the words 'Empire State' replaced the old-fashioned 'York State' in local references.

ramparts into the mysterious, protective but slightly forbidding communities within. But neither Europe nor Asia nor anywhere else can now offer anything to compare with the walk across the Brooklyn Bridge. There is nothing to match it in any land: not that marvellous baroque traverse of the Charles Bridge towards the heights of Hradcany in Prague; not a crossing of the Tiber by Castel Sant' Angelo and a long stroll to the monumental embrace of St Peter's Square in Rome; not a walk through the bazaars of Varanasi to the teeming religious devotion along the Ganges ghats; not a descent from the hillside of Galata across the Golden Horn at Istanbul into the dusty but still intoxicating legacy of what was once Byzantium. Not even such lustrous passages as these can quite compete with the sensation of crossing the Brooklyn Bridge towards the island of Manhattan in the city of New York. The others have great visual drama, too, and are brushed even more with stirring memories of the past. But here alone the stranger feels that he has come upon an epic still being made.

TWO

UPWARDS AND OUTWARDS

At the bottom of Wall Street, yet another high building is on its way up. A framework of steel girders has already risen twenty floors off the ground, with maybe as many more still to come. When it is finished the building will – if we're lucky – impress us with its graceful proportions, with the delicate imagination displayed across its surfaces. Just now, though, in its not even half-completed, its stripped-down state, it attracts attention above all because of the tensile strength built into that frame.

The girders are not quite naked at this stage in the construction. Up to the eighteenth storey, crude floors of concrete have already been poured into wooden shuttering; and, above that, temporary platforms have been rigged to support the derrick that swings the huge beams of steel into place up there. But no walls have been put into this building yet, so that its steel framework is still almost wholly exposed, its various levels cluttered with the bric-à-brac of craftsmanship and hard labour, a rudimentary hoist for the workmen clipped to one of its sides, great sheets of translucent plastic strung up here and there to keep the weather out while the work goes on, and a cascade of white-hot sparks tumbling from somewhere up above.

What work is visible depends on the observer's vantage point. From the street he will be most aware of the periodic arrival of steel, concrete and other bulky substances, which are then hauled aloft without delay by a gigantic crane which has been planted in what will eventually become the building's main elevator shaft. These materials have been conveyed by truck from distant stockpiles – more often than not in New Jersey – and are then hurried off the street because, in the congested surroundings of this site, there simply is nowhere to put anything in quantity without creating such an impediment to traffic that the entire Financial District of Manhattan would grind to a frustrated standstill. It requires the organisational skills of a naval beachmaster when the invading army starts coming ashore, to be certain that the hardware of construction arrives where it's wanted, at pretty much the time specified when the building schedules were drawn up months ago. Hence the contractor's men patrolling the kerb, with hard hats shading apprehensive eyes, and with walkie-talkies jammed to their ears.

Someone in an adjacent high-rise building is best placed to see the activity near the sharp end of things, where the newcomer is thrusting towards its highly competitive place on the skyline. On the lower floors, men are doing indistinct things by the buttery light of low-power lamps; probably adding refinements to the floors themselves. But high in the air, where there is nothing much but framework yet, where progress takes place in the open without need of artificial light, the work seems just a shade less casual, and in some cases is downright alarming. Whatever the work may be up there, unless this is in the immediate vicinity of the derrick and its accompanying platform, it is conducted where the foothold is often nothing more than a steel girder, eight inches wide. Half a dozen hard hats, standing on such a beam, are coaxing a new girder into place, while it gently, menacingly, sways on the end of the derrick cable. Some welders, also precariously placed, are causing those small explosions of sparks as they operate upon other billets of steel. And, oh my God, someone is sitting on an upturned box, drilling holes in a girder, with his back to, and a whisker away from, the vertical drop straight down into the street. It makes the palms sweat just to watch these men earning their daily bread.

In the trade, they will tell you that 40 per cent of those iron-workers – the men who perform hair-raisingly on the rising sky-scrapers of New York – are still Indians. They are not descended from the Algonquins who were the original settlers of what they called Manahata (sometimes Manahatin), the fairly passive and rather innocent people who sold their island to the Dutch West India Company's governor, Peter Minuit, in 1626 for knives, cloth and haberdashery worth sixty guilders, or about twenty-four bucks. The ironworking Indians are much more recent arrivals in town, mixed-blood Mohawks whose native stamping ground has long been the Caughnawaga reservation a few miles outside Montreal, on the south bank of the St Lawrence. They seem to have entered the construction industry in the late nineteenth century, when a bridge was being built across the river for the Canadian Pacific Railway, and they allowed the engineers to cross their land in exchange for some employment. It soon became apparent that they were possessed of remarkable agility, and had a fearless head for heights. Within a couple of decades, Caughnawaga Indians were working on bridges all over Canada.

About 1915 one of them came down to New York, a man named John Diabo, who obtained work on the site of Hell Gate Bridge crossing the East River, as did three other people of his tribe who followed him shortly afterwards. But Diabo missed his footing one day when high up on the bridge scaffolding, fell into the river and was drowned. His companions took his body back to the reservation, and nothing more was seen of Caughnawagas in New York until 1926, when they were attracted by the great metropolitan construction boom that was to result in the Chrysler and Empire State buildings, among others. The first gang to arrive is said to have been recruited to work on the Fred F. French Building on Fifth Avenue, and to have signed up with the Brooklyn local branch of the ironworkers' union, the International Association of Bridge, Structural and Ornamental Ironworkers, American Federation of Labour. The Caughnawagas haven't looked back – or maybe down – since. They have roamed across the United States and beyond in the intervening years, taking precarious employment wherever it has been offered, as far away as the Severn Bridge in England. But always they have returned to New York, where a colony of them has gradually taken root in the North Gowanus neighbourhood of Brooklyn; about 700 people, according to a recent estimate.

Some of those early Indian ironworkers appear in the brilliant photographs Lewis Hine took during the construction of the Empire State Building, which he followed with his camera, from the first excavations into bedrock to the installation of the mooring mast for dirigibles a quarter of a mile above the ground. In his folio, Hine catalogued the various skills that go into the making of a skyscraper, identifying the particular craft of each worker appearing in his compositions. There is one of a foundation man, smothered in the dust that will shorten his life with pneumoconiosis after years of drilling into rock. There are shots of derrick crews hauling on ropes hitched round the bull stick, by which means the gantry can be swivelled in the right direction. There are several where burners and welders and riveters are amputating, fusing or merely puncturing steel, each riveter assisted by his bucker-up, who holds the rivet in place while the pneumatic gun blasts away. There's a hoister, who guides each steel girder into place, at a fairly safe distance on the end of a rope, and a plumber-up, who uses his plumb line to make sure that upright beams are precisely vertical and not half a degree this way or that, before it's too late to correct.

Of these, the riveters and their buckers-up together with the plumber-up, are the men who share a spectacular exposure every working day of their lives, with a handful of other specialists. Hine took a picture of a bolter, an elderly man with a walrus moustache, perched astride the girder he is securing to another with the spanner in his hand. Over his shoulder the photographer managed to include a panoramic view of midtown Manhattan and the East River, with the Chrysler Building in the middle distance and the Queensboro Bridge beyond, all of it seen from above. The end of the girder, no more than a few inches behind the bolter's backside, sticks out at some unthinkable height above 34th Street. That old man, preoccupied with his craft, is sitting where no creature but a seagull has any right to be.

There's a bucker-up who has rigged a flimsy contraption of planks so that he can actually be in space to do his job, which involves neither standing nor sitting, but squatting in a posture guaranteed to produce serious cramp within minutes. There's a safety man crawling up the outside of the Empire State's scaffolding to check for loose planks, stray wires, or forgotten tools that might drop to the street and brain some innocent passer-by. There are photographs galore of connectors, who appear to be the most pathologically nerveless ironworkers of all. Their function is to ride the girders as they are swung into position, so that they can slip the bolts into place as a temporary measure before the bolter appears to tighten them up. The connectors, in short, are in the most exposed places when nothing has been even half-secured. Lewis Hine has caught them balancing superbly on those eight-inch beams, nonchalantly handling tools, waving directions to the derrick crews, sometimes flaunting their manhood by careering through space from one level of the steel framework to another, clinging to the dangling hook of the derrick itself. There isn't a safety belt in sight.

The rare brilliance of the photography, of course, consists in the horror which the average viewer is made to feel on looking at pictures of men working up there in the sky, quite obviously in peril of plummeting to earth, should something break, or slide, or if they themselves just slip or have an attack of vertigo. It required considerable nerve by Lewis Hine himself to take some of those shots, two of which are especially calculated to haunt a normal acrophobe whenever he may contemplate a building more than two or three storeys high.

In one, a man is standing on a girder at the very corner of the rising Empire State, and his right foot is clearly jutting out into thin air, only the heel in contact with the steel, the tremendous exposure emphasised by a background of downtown Manhattan a long way below. The man – clad in singlet and trousers, with his cap worn back to front – is distinctly leaning outwards as he signals to someone underneath. One gloved hand is gesturing down, the other is pointing above his head. Only one thing prevents gravity taking its course: his other foot, hooked around the corner of the beam.

But the most dreadfully magnetic photograph of all has the Hudson River and New Jersey in the background, at about the same range an airline passenger might expect to see them from, three or four minutes before coming in to land. The shot appears to have been taken at the topmost level of construction, if the protruding ends of upright girders are anything to go by – except that the focal point of the composition gives the lie to that. A steel hawser is stretched tightly in a diagonal across the picture, from bottom right to top left, and although it is plainly attached to girders somewhere out of sight at the bottom, it is hard to figure out what it has been fixed to above. No matter; there the cable is, twanging in the breeze somewhere between heaven and earth. And halfway up it, at least yards from anything else he might grab in emergency, is this young man in dungarees, doing very little but hang on for his life, it seems, with bare hands clenching the greasy hawser and feet wrapped tightly round it in the manner of a trapeze artist coming down his rope to the circus floor. It is difficult to see what task that youth can be performing up there in such a desperate stance, except to make us sweat and admire the cold-blooded courage that has gone – and still goes – into putting skyscrapers up. Lewis Hine entitled that photograph 'The Sky Boy' and made the lad immortal by picturing him so. He'll be in his late seventies now, if he's still alive.

None of this great daring would be necessary, were it not for a convenient geology of the island underneath. Nowhere in the world is more suitable for a tremendous weight of building than Manhattan, where solid rock is generally not far below the surface and sometimes (as in Central Park) visible in outcrops above the ground. What's more, in a land where the catastrophic earthquake is not unknown, even minor tremors are virtually stranger to New York, a result of the relatively shallow glaciers that once flowed here, which simply weren't heavy enough to produce the rock faults that lead to massive upheavals. The area's geological mixture is seasoned with, among other things, deposits of precious and semi-precious stones, 170 varieties having been uncovered from time to time on Manhattan alone, including a garnet crystal which was once dug from the line of West 35th Street, large enough to serve as a doorstop before finally fetching up in the Museum of Natural History. Of much greater cumulative value than all the gems that might be mined locally, however, has been the abundance of a kind of mudstone which the experts identify as Manhattan schist, and which covers deeper layers of limestone. It glitters attractively because it has a high content of mica, but what matters most about it is its stability, its hardness, its mass. It has been suggested that without Manhattan schist underground, no building in New York would ever have risen above the sixth floor; and while that may be more graphic than strictly accurate, the point is perfectly valid. The place was a standing invitation to build as high and as densely as you could wish. Surrounded by water, and so naturally endowed with a setting for spectacle, Manhattan was waiting to demonstrate one of the greatest turning points in the history of architecture.

The word 'skyscraper' entered the language at the end of the eighteenth century, when it described nothing more than a small triangular sail set above the skysail of a square-rigged ship. A hundred years passed before it carried any other meaning in print. In 1890 a Mr John J. Flinn, in a book about Chicago, wrote that, 'A new system has found much favour here, and is being generally followed now in the construction of mammoth buildings known as "Sky-scrapers", which has given Chicago a new celebrity.' He was referring to structures which climbed no higher than 260 feet off the ground; and when, in 1892, Chicago saw the completion of what was briefly the tallest building in the world, a Masonic temple, its skyscraping was done by the twenty-second floor. That same year in New York, the Pulitzer Building topped out at 309 feet above Park Row. Never before had a secular building been the highest thing in town, and Trinity Church had to give best at last.

It has been well said that there is no neat answer to the question, 'Which was the first skyscraper?' It is not even clear whether Chicago or New York got there first, some experts adamantly awarding the title to New York's Equitable Life Assurance Building (six storeys high, finished in 1871), others to Chicago's Home Insurance Building (ten storeys, finished in 1885), but whichever of the two may have it over the other, both were made to look stubby little things within a few years: pictures of the Home Insurance bear a strong resemblance to a cube. It all comes down, of course, to an agreed definition of the word; and the only general agreement seems to be that skyscrapers were not possible until the invention of two things – the steel frame and the elevator. The introduction of steel meant that at last you could build strong and high without needing impossibly thick walls of stone or brick to bear the huge load above. The arrival of the elevator meant that people could rise to abnormal heights without coronary repercussions. The metal frame had first cropped up in New York in the middle of the nineteenth century, but it had been of cast-iron, which meant a limited potential, and it was the Chicago architect, William LeBaron Jenney, who led the way with steel in his Home Insurance Building. The New York engineer, George P. Post, on the other hand, had installed the first office elevator in the Equitable Building much earlier than that.

For a time both cities appeared to be in some sort of competition to put up outstandingly high buildings on sites which invited their display; for whereas New York had the island of Manhattan heaven-sent for the purpose, the business district of the Chicago Loop was almost as well-placed alongside Lake Michigan. In fact, whatever competition consciously occurred had much more to do with commercial greed than with the pursuit of prestige at first. From the moment the elevator broke through the height barrier which had stood at five storeys or about sixty feet for as long as anyone could remember, land values dramatically increased as the advantages of cramming more and more money-making activity into proportionately smaller and smaller ground areas, became obvious. 'Never before in history,' according to a sage voice from the twentieth century, 'had the demand for profit been so explicitly related to architecture.' By 1900 both cities were transforming their skylines as new buildings edged higher and higher, and so were other places in the country, like Minneapolis, Boston, Buffalo and St Louis. Although Chicago never dropped out of major contention with New York for any prestige that might accrue from skyscraping (at the time of writing, its Sears Tower has for a dozen years been the tallest building in the world), in the long run New York power, New York ambition, above all perhaps New York energy, steadily put Manhattan ahead as a succession of striking new office blocks went up – the Flatiron, the Singer, the Metropolitan Life and several more. The builder, Theodore Starrett, rubbing his hands at the prospect of a 100-floor contract which never got off the ground, ecstatically announced in 1906 that, 'Our civilisation is progressing wonderfully. In New York . . . we must keep building and we must build upwards.'

In 1913, with 792 feet and sixty floors, the title was clinched for New York when President Woodrow Wilson pressed a button in distant Washington and illuminated the new Woolworth Building on Broadway. The inventor of the ten-cent store had required both a headquarters and a symbol of his success when he commissioned the building, and he got rather more than even he might have bargained for. It remains the HQ of Woolworth's to this day, when most of its contemporaries have long been transferred to other hands, been used for other purposes, or simply been pulled down. The success of Frank Woolworth's chain stores was more than symbolised by his paying cash for the new building – $13.5 million of it – and this may well be the only property of such size that has never known a mortgage. But beyond all that was the effect the Woolworth Building had upon local skyscraper designers, with its felicitous combination of American technology and medieval European style. Cass Gilbert's *tour de force* was not just recognised at once as a rare kind of masterpiece; it begat imitators, though none from Europe, where they were at last emerging from their neo-Gothic phase. In 1922 the *Chicago Tribune* ran an international competition for planning its new offices, and architects from several countries entered. No fewer than twenty of the competing Americans submitted neo-Gothic designs, clearly under the influence of Woolworth, and one of them was adjudged the winner with a tower that still stands.

Beyond imitation was the Chrysler Building, which added a different kind of fantasy to the Manhattan skyline before that decade was through. Once again a powerful entrepreneur was wanting a success symbol as much as anything, this time to signify his importance as a maker of automobiles, and Walter Chrysler's architect, William Van Alen, obliged him with a skyscraper which has remained unique for well over half a century. It is reckoned to be the tallest brick building in the world still, but its lasting fame is based wholly on its details inside and out, and especially for what happens at the sixty-first floor and above. There, eight huge gargoyles project into space, shining metal eagle heads which became more familiar than they might otherwise have been at that height above the street, when Margaret Bourke-White (who had a studio on the sixty-first floor) clambered out of a trapdoor in one of the eagles to shoot some panoramas of New York, and was herself famously photographed setting up her camera on that sensational perch. A few floors above the gargoyles, the brickwork gives way to Chrysler's inimitably tapering helmet of stainless steel, which itself is surmounted by the slenderest of spires. That owes its existence to a rivalry between Van Alen and a former partner of his, who was building a tower for the Bank of Manhattan Company at 40 Wall Street when the Chrysler was also going up. When it looked as if the bank was set to become the tallest building in the world, Van Alen had his spire secretly constructed in the Chrysler's helmet. The moment the rival building was irrevocably topped out, Van Alen's spire – seven tons of it, 185 feet long – was shoved up through the apex of the stainless steel and bolted down, for the Chrysler to take the record with something to spare.

And then came the Empire State Building. This was a commercial speculation pure and simple by a consortium of moneymakers who saw a giant skyscraper as a means of making more, an ambition which was gilded by the recruitment of Al Smith – old Tammany boss and four times Governor of New York State – as president of the board. Alas for ambition, the building was started only a few weeks before the crash of the stock market on Wall Street, and by the time it was completed in 1931 the great Depression had commercial New York on its knees. Instead of being in a position to rejoice in the fact that they now owned – at 102 floors, 1,250 feet – the highest structure on earth, the company was nearly bankrupt, possessed of a hulk in which no-one could afford to rent space. Al Smith had been given to understand that $50,000 per annum came his way for the respectability attached to his name and nothing more; but in this crisis he was made to earn his keep by crawling to Washington to beseech his old protégé, now President of the United States, Franklin D. Roosevelt, to arrange for as many government agencies as possible to shift their existing locations into what had become known derisively as the Empty State Building; which was done, with some federal organisations being shunted from as far away as Philadelphia to provide the speculators with sustenance. Notwithstanding this Presidential favour, it has been estimated that the owners only managed to survive those first few years by paying the building's taxes out of the income derived from the observatories on the eighty-sixth and one-hundred-and-second floors, to which New Yorkers began to flock for the novelty of the view fifty miles away.

The Chrysler had won the city's affection – and has increased its share of this over the years – because its daring style struck a sympathetic note, much in harmony with the Jazz Age that saw it arise. There was bravura in that shiny new tower lancing the sky. There was more than a touch of class, there was tasteful opulence in the decoration of its thirty elevators, panelled in exotic wood veneers with no two alike, nowadays recognised as superb examples of Art Deco. The Empire State Building secured its place in the mythology of New York mostly because of its altitude, but perhaps also because it came to symbolise a dogged endurance against heavy odds. In appearance somewhat dull compared with the Chrysler, its architectural virtues are altogether less striking, yet it was a highly respectable essay in building big within the limits of the city zoning laws; which call for brief introduction here, to avoid tripping over them periodically in this book. They regulate a surprising amount of life in New York.

Most cities in the world have long had regulations which specify what can and cannot be built in the various areas of a given community; a form of such regulation has existed in England since Norman times. In New York by the start of the twentieth century, the regulations governed fire and structural procedures, but only in the case of tenements was there a stipulation governing the occupation of space – how much of it and in what way it was to be filled. It was not unknown for a building to occupy its ground area right up to the roofline, and then for a roofline cornice to project as much as fourteen feet beyond the ground area's edge. That all ended with the arrival of the new Equitable Building on Lower Broadway in 1915, still to be seen a few blocks away from the graceful Woolworth, and in every way its antithesis.

It was, and is, a monster which goes up straight as a cliff for forty-one storeys, occupying one whole block, with a total floor area no less than thirty times the area of the site; a commercial advantage to the Equitable's owners which was paid for by the occupants of existing buildings nearby, who at once had much of their natural light cut off. It took a couple of years for objectors to persuade the city that no such thing must be allowed to happen again, but then new zoning laws were drafted, with separate regulations for residential districts, business districts, and those parts of New York left to industry and other purposes. The most crucial advance on the old building code was in the protection of 'air rights' – not a phrase much used then, but nowadays well understood by all New Yorkers, and a matter of contention to many of them. A formula was devised, whose basis was the ground area of a building site. It was then stipulated how high something could be built vertically before it had to be set back if it was to continue upwards; and this meant that anything in the skyscraping class would have to rise in a series of steps, with more and more space separating the structure from any neighbours the higher it went. The Empire State Building's great architectural achievement was in soaring to an unprecedented height within the law, and doing it handsomely by means of one setback after another – ten of them in all.

The Depression and the Second World War ensured that the frenzy of building which had continued non-stop for twenty years would slacken off for some considerable time to come. The war put the American economy well and truly on its feet again, but New York still needed to get its breath back after the two calamities before it could embark on another bout of skyscraping. When this began to get under way in the 1950s, many things had changed since buildings like the Chrysler and the Empire State were designed – different styles were in fashion, different materials, too, methods of construction perhaps most of all. The craftsmanship that had gone into the Chrysler's elevator panelling had all but vanished, and large-scale prefabrication even of a building's outer walls had become an accepted thing. For a while the long obsession with record height appeared to have abated at last. Buildings were instead to be seen as pieces of monumental sculpture, like the United Nations headquarters beside the East River, which combined three different geometrical forms in one – the slab, the parabola and the drum. Or they came in the shape of bland glass boxes standing on end, attractive mostly for their texture, like the Seagram Building, with its bronze curtain wall which has to be oiled once a year to prevent it from tarnishing into an uninviting green. As the big money began to muscle in on building development in New York again, numerous smoky-glassed boxes made their appearance in Manhattan, most conspicuously on Sixth Avenue, where a procession of these totems now proclaims the prosperity of Time & Life, Exxon, McGraw-Hill and Celanese, one after the other, and are as near alike as makes no matter.

The skyscrapers continued to crowd upon each other so densely that, by and by, the architects and their clients were driven to extraordinary lengths to establish the individual identity of their buildings, in which the corporate images are much at stake. Be different at any cost became the watchword now, and it has produced some truly eye-catching shapes, chiefly to impress inspectors of the horizon, it sometimes seems; for it is, after all, difficult to appreciate a skyscraper from the adjacent sidewalk unless you lie flat on your back, and if you move one block away in Manhattan you've very often lost him behind someone else's corporate image which looms just as large. This struggle to advertise the client's identity – for it is, in essence, architecture reduced to advertising – has in recent years produced the Citicorp Center, whose distinction is to be clad in aluminium and to have its roof tilted at forty-five degrees; an effort, it's said, to harness solar energy which didn't come off. Then there is the bizarre American Telephone and Telegraph Building with its incongruously notched roofline, which might be regarded as an infringement of copyright if the architect Robert Adam were still alive (for he employed the same stylistic trick on a bookcase in the eighteenth century). This is nothing more than the broken pediment, conceived by some distant Renaissance Man.

The seventies saw the rise of New York's last claimant to the world altitude title, the twin-towered World Trade Center, although 110 floors and 1,350 feet were only good for a few months of record-holding before the Sears Tower went higher in Chicago. Much disliked by professional critics – 'pretentious and arrogant; it is hard not to be insulted . . .' and 'stolid, banal monoliths' are among the lofty judgements passed on it – the World Trade Center has intimidated the more sensitive New Yorkers by its sheer size as no other skyscraper ever did. But on at least three occasions it has sent the citizens on their way with a spring in their step. An unemployed construction worker once managed to evade security guards and reach the roof of the north tower before parachuting to the ground, where passers-by did not fail to notice a biblical reference emblazoned on his chest – 'Matthew 19:26' (which reads '. . . With men this is impossible; but with God all things are possible'). A couple of years later, after an early breakfast, a young mountaineer spent three and a half hours scaling the vertical face of the south tower, while thousands cheered him on from below, and policemen sent to arrest him secured his autograph first.

Both escapades had been inspired by the sensational entertainment provided by a Frenchman, Phillippe Petit, on August 7, 1974, which was the stuff of which New York legends are made. Petit, who subsequently claimed that he could never resist a challenge ('If I see three oranges I have to juggle. And if I see two towers I have to walk across'), had once crossed a tightrope strung across an end of Sydney Harbour Bridge, another time had walked from one spire to another in mid-air high above Notre Dame Cathedral in Paris. In New York, he and three accomplices had made 200 visits to the Trade Center to plan a new aerial coup, and then over several days, disguised as construction workers, they had taken the necessary tackle to the roof of the north tower, which was not quite finished by the builders. Just after dawn on the chosen day, they used a crossbow to fire a line across to the roof of the south tower, and 131 feet of galvanised steel wire was then hauled over, stretched tight between the two buildings, and anchored at both ends. Whereupon Petit stepped out into space with his balancing pole, and for the best part of an hour proceeded to entertain great crowds of office-bound workers who began to assemble in the plaza far below. After turning himself over to the waiting police, amidst general acclaim, from the constabulary as much as anyone, he was hustled away to be charged with disorderly conduct and criminal trespass.

And then the great genius of New York intervened; this city's sublime talent for sometimes doing the perfectly right thing, deftly and with an imagination rare in the conduct of civic affairs anywhere. Manhattan's District Attorney and the New York Parks Commissioner announced that they had done a deal with M. Petit. They would drop all charges, provided he gave a free show of his high-wire act in Central Park for the benefit of the city's kids. It was the happiest of endings to an invigorating, spectacular day.

Everything about skyscrapers is spectacular, whether or not they aspire to record-breaking height. Consider any statistics associated with these buildings – they are not hard to come by; their promoters gladly chuck them around like confetti – and they are sometimes so overwhelming that they defy credulity, as they are doubtless intended to. Can it be possible that 50,000 people work in the World Trade Center every day? That there are 6,500 windows to clean in the Empire State Building twice a month? That enough steel went into the Chrysler's framework to have manufactured 20,000 automobiles? That anyone installed in an office on the seventieth floor is going to spend the equivalent of a full working week every year just going up and down in the elevator, a distance of 200 miles? And so on.

They are spectacularly dangerous, potentially at least, as the cinema industry has realised with some profit, though long after any towering inferno of the movies has been forgotten, folklore will cherish the memory of King Kong, defying the biplanes of the Army Air Corps from the top of the Empire State Building after creating mayhem on the Third Avenue 'El'. The spectacular accidents in real life have usually been caused by objects falling from skyscrapers, including people.

James Agee is one who contemplated committing suicide this way, in despair at the journalism he was obliged to practise in the Chrysler Building in order to subsidise his verse and his novels, but having got as far as the outside window-ledge of his office on the fiftieth floor, he changed his mind and came back when a colleague entered the room to find him poised over the street. Preventive measures taken in buildings that high, to protect unsuspecting people down below against missiles from above, include space heaters in the Chrysler's steeply sloping roof to stop the formation of mid-winter ice which could slide off into Lexington Avenue with lethal results. But in spite of the safety man whose job is to prevent hardware falling, it sometimes does: like the piece of glass which dropped off the Trump Tower before it was finished and killed a pedestrian on Fifth Avenue; and the crane which collapsed on a building under construction on Madison, killing one passer-by and hurting sixteen.

The most terrible accidents have involved aircraft. One was an awful fluke, which happened when parts of a helicopter tumbled off the Pan Am Building in 1977. The machine had just settled onto the rooftop landing pad, which had been made there so that airline passengers in a hurry could be ferried between midtown Manhattan and Kennedy Airport. Its engines were idling while boarding for the return flight took place, when the undercarriage gave way, sending the helicopter on its side. One of the whirling rotor blades snapped and cut down four people on the spot, then flew off the skyscraper's parapet towards the street fifty-nine floors below. On the way down it hit the building and broke into two; which caused the pieces of the blade and shattered glass to fall over a wide area. Some debris fell onto Vanderbilt Avenue, directly underneath, but skyscrapers often induce swirling vortices of wind even on relatively calm days, and one of these carried other bits of metal and glass clean over the top of the Biltmore Hotel opposite the Pan Am, dumping them onto Madison Avenue beyond, where other people were hit without warning. The total casualty figures were five dead and seven seriously injured; which was less frightful than it might have been, given that the accident happened when the evening rush hour was at its height.

It was always on the cards that the really high skyscraper and the aircraft – which both took off at approximately the same moment of history, during the first decade of the twentieth century – would one day collide in New York; and it is perhaps rather more surprising that this did not happen until 1945. In the middle of a Saturday morning in July, with a great deal of low cloud about, people in midtown Manhattan heard an aircraft overhead. It was a B-25 Mitchell bomber, on the last leg of a flight from South Dakota by way of Massachusetts, scheduled to land just across the Hudson River in New Jersey. In a thickening fog it had flown over La Guardia Field minutes before, and ground control had suggested it should land there, but the pilot said he would continue to Newark as planned. If he had wanted to fly across Manhattan he should have been at least 2,000 feet up, according to regulations, but when someone saw the plane overhead through a gap in the mist, it was a great deal lower than that, weaving about as though its rudders weren't working properly. It was then – banking slightly, according to an appalled office worker, who looked out of a window and saw the plane apparently coming straight towards him – that the bomber flew smack into the Empire State Building.

It struck the skyscraper 913 feet above West 34th Street, driving a hole into both the seventy-eighth and seventy-ninth floors. Most of the wings sheared off at once and dropped into the street, though a propeller remained embedded in the wall. One of the two engines ploughed straight down a corridor on the seventy-eighth, went through the wall at the other end, and crashed onto somebody's roof on 33rd Street. The second engine plunged down one of the Empire State's elevator shafts, taking the elevator with it. Some sections of the fuselage were blown – by the impact and by the explosion of the plane's fuel tanks – up to the observation platform on the eighty-sixth floor. Other parts remained sticking out of the hole in the wall. People on the street said that an orange glow spread eerily up the side of the building behind the mist: inside, flames were everywhere, as blazing aviation fuel began to pour down stair wells and across office floors. The shock of the impact was felt several blocks away. Survivors in the Empire State itself said the building seemed to rock a couple of times before settling very gently down. Then it stood fast.

The three men aboard the bomber were killed at once. So were some office workers, while others died later, ten civilian fatalities in all, mostly charred bodies by the time they were found, though one man saw flames coming towards his desk and was killed after jumping through the window. Twenty-six people were hurt, more or less badly. The civilians were working for a wartime charity run by the National Catholic Welfare Conference, and if it had not been a Saturday morning, many more would have been there. One person had a fabulously lucky escape. She was Betty Lou Oliver, a twenty-year-old elevator attendant, whose cabin fell straight down the shaft from the seventy-ninth floor to the cellar beneath. She survived because its automatic safety device, though broken, still slowed the elevator down.

That is reckoned to have been the last time the brakes failed to stop a runaway; which will be a comforting thought to New Yorkers, with an estimated 32,000 elevators operating in Manhattan alone. Every one of them is checked for safety twice a year by the city's inspectors and once by the owner's maintenance firm, and we may be sure that these scrutineers pay close attention to the appliance which has been working in Gramercy Park East since 1883 – the oldest elevator still functioning in New York, operated as always by hydraulics from water stored on the roof instead of by new-fangled electric motors which can send several dozen people at a time whizzing non-stop through fifty floors or more. It is not, however, express elevation and descent that some queasy souls are referring to when they claim to experience motion sickness in the tallest skyscrapers on Manhattan. What they mean is that the building flexes perceptibly in a stiff breeze.

The likelihood is that the skyscrapers will be getting higher and higher if the big developers have their way: also coming in even odder shapes than we have yet seen. When it was announced in 1985 that the City of New York was going to sell the site of the Coliseum for redevelopment, the effect on speculators was electrifying, the apprehension of citizens with a care for their environment almost deafening. What worried them was not the demolition of a totally undistinguished structure used to house trade exhibitions, but its position on Columbus Circle at the south-west corner of Central Park. In making the announcement, the Mayor of New York, Ed Koch, a man much more notable for his promotional instincts than for his aesthetic sensibilities, suggested that whoever was awarded the redevelopment would get 'a once-in-a-lifetime opportunity to make an indelible mark on the city's skyline'. That was precisely what had the non-speculative citizenry palpitating. The advantage to any corporation whose new skyscraper arose on that site would be, as another voice from City Hall spelt out, that, 'The park's there, so that no-one can build on top of you. You immediately dominate the skyline and you're guaranteed to do it for ever.'

The competing designs indicated the shape of things to come, not only overlooking Central Park, but in other parts of New York that would be built upon in future. Here were plans for skyscrapers rising 121 . . . 135 . . . 137 floors off the ground. Not many of them were much like anything the city had erected before. One was shaped like a ten-sided rocket. Another looked a little like the scaffolding that surrounds NASA's real rockets before they are launched at Cape Canaveral. There was even one with a gigantic terrace spiralling outside from top to bottom, which made the irreverent wonder whether it might have been big brother to a stage prop loaded with lovelies in a Busby Berkeley production.

Abundantly clear, long before the competition finished, was the commercial impact the winner would make across the city's most treasured open space. Here would be a corporate advertisement as stunningly effective as the first neon sign ever switched on above Times Square. Chicago would be put in its place again, to be sure, but that is not what would matter above anything else. It was the rustle of dollars that counted most here. The $331 million . . . $353 million . . . $447.5 million that were being bid for the site: the $40 million that would change hands each year in property taxes alone: the . . . but nobody dared dwell on the profit that might accrue from rents in a spanking space-age skyscraper on a bonanza site like this, when an antique like the Chrysler Building, after several years of neglect, was still netting from tenants a cool $30 million a year.

An architectural expert from the Museum of Modern Art, adapting a celebrated pronouncement by Le Corbusier, gave us a new definition of tall buildings. 'Skyscrapers', he wrote, 'are machines for making money.' That is, perhaps, the most relevant thing of all about the new boom in New York.

But although they are characteristic of this city – 'that bold signature of New York' as someone has put it – they are not at all typical of the way the metropolis is generally built. The stranger visiting New York for the first time cannot do better than to embark on a Circle Line boat for the two-hour excursion round Manhattan, with glimpses of the other boroughs as well. This will at once disabuse him of the notion (common among foreigners) that New York is full of skyscrapers from one end to the other. That is not even true of Manhattan, where almost all the skyscrapers are, the great thicket in the Financial District at the bottom of the island being counterbalanced by another growth for a block or two on either side of midtown Fifth Avenue. Otherwise, Manhattan's structural profile does not often reach the tenth floor, which doesn't count for much as these things go nowadays. As for the four other boroughs of the city, really high buildings are conspicuously missing. There is nothing at all as yet either on Staten Island or in Queens. In the Bronx a few housing blocks have climbed as high as thirty floors, but there is nothing else. In Brooklyn the only genuine skyscraper is the Williamsburgh Savings Bank Tower, which much resembles the innumerable palaces of culture that communism introduced to the cities of Eastern Europe during Stalin's time. It went up in 1929, when talk of redevelopment in that quarter of the city was heard, but which the Depression stopped. The Williamsburgh Tower has stood there unaccompanied ever since, a rather forbidding thing when rain and cloud sweep across Brooklyn, and in brighter weather looking just a bit forlorn.

There are other forms of building just as characteristic of the city as its skyscrapers. Among the surviving old tenements of the Lower East Side and elsewhere, the fire-escape is still to be seen dog-legging its way up the front wall, just as it was when

Henry James remarked that a whole street thus equipped was like 'the most spaciously organised cage for the nimbler class of animals in some great zoological garden . . . it seems to offer, in each district, a little world of bars and perches and swings for human squirrels and monkeys.' Companion piece to every fire-escape is the cast-iron fire hydrant on the sidewalk nearby. Suggesting nothing but a more dignified, less hurried period than the one we're passing through now, are the handsome terraces of brownstone dwellings that embellish Manhattan and other quarters of New York. The masonry was mostly quarried in New Jersey and Connecticut between the middle of the nineteenth century and the Great War, artfully handled by master builders and occupied by the rising well-to-do (the already risen lived in bigger brownstones which stood prosperously well apart from any neighbours). The terraces came with a short flight of steps up from the street and gracefully bowed windows on their two or three floors: but some windows were bowed more plumply than others, the front steps were tricked out with cast iron banisters and even carriage lamps, and the parapets above the top floors might be unobtrusively decorated with classical details – in which case passers-by could be sure that the occupants were rising indeed. We may be grateful now to those quarrymen, those builders and their patrons who wanted to live like that, for in a city which alters its appearance more rapidly than most, they have bequeathed to New York a stability, an unmistakable dignity that can endure if it's given half a chance. The same goes for those whose skills and tastes ran to clapboard, which has also survived against even greater odds. Sometimes sorely in need of a lick of paint, but generally cared for in the acid atmospheres of New York, the clapboard houses are to be found in the most unexpected places – even in the often brutalised and badly beaten up Bronx – to show what real class consists of, and to make any New Englander feel an almost physical pain to be home.

If you go by reputation, there is nothing more unexpected than to discover New York's oldest remaining house – clapboard, once a Quaker meeting place, built in 1661 – in the now utterly suburban Queens. Named dutifully after Catherine of Braganza, the Portuguese consort of King Charles II, Queens is territorially the largest of the five boroughs, and also the one most often dismissed by inhabitants of the other four. Manhattan is . . . well, Manhattan has *every*thing and that says it all, they'll say; while Brooklyn is tough and the Bronx is rough and Staten Island is really a bit like living out in the country, which is quite nice if you like that sort of thing. But Queens . . . ? What's Queens got except a lot of cemeteries, those two big airports (and who wants planes landing and taking off over his head nearly twenty-four hours a day?) and that museum model of New York that's supposed to be added to every time a new building goes up anywhere in the city. To such grouchers the best things about Queens are going out to Shea to see the Mets (but they haven't often enjoyed the winning streaks of '85 and '86), or to the Aqueduct to watch the horses (and lose a lot of money) or to Forest Hills and Flushing Meadows for the tennis (whose biggest championships switched from one stadium to the other about the time the players – of both sexes – began to behave like prima donnas). In one respected judgement, Queens has been seen as 'the clearest demonstration that New York is basically a middle-class city', while another commentator has sniffed at 'the job-holding, churchgoing, television-watching, car-polishing, honest, bitter, loyal, unaware, clean, respectful, hung-up home owners and small-apartment-house renters who make Queens as it was, as it is, and perhaps as it always will be'. Queens, in short, is generally and thoroughly patronised. It just happens to be home for nearly two million New Yorkers, and only Brooklyn is more populous.

The patronising approach is rarely offered the Bronx, where it might produce the most aggressive counter-attack. Ogden Nash ('The Bronx/No Thonx') may be the only person to have got away with it in one piece. The only borough of New York which is situated on the mainland of North America, its greatest reputation in recent times has been that it includes what is probably the country's most dreadful and extensive slum. 'Presidential candidates trudge through here every four years, their mouths agape as they look at the destroyed buildings and mouth the inevitable comparison with Berlin just after the war.' The South Bronx became what it is today for many and complex reasons which we shall come across in detail later on, but a crucial factor was that nearly half the people living there by 1969 were under eighteen years old, in fatherless families; and they began to take the place apart. There was systematic arson throughout the neighbourhood, with teenage gangs in 1975 alone responsible for causing 13,000 fires to break out in twelve square miles. They cost Lloyd's of London $45 million in insurance claims, the biggest pay-out in the company's history. Forty people, including three firemen, died in those blazes, which left block after block as the charred and boarded-up ruins that make such a desperately bleak prospect today. It is into these surroundings that no-one but a fool would venture alone once darkness has come: here, not in Harlem, is where New York's greatest violence is done.

Yet there is another side to the Bronx, which might be light years away from its devastated part. Though it is true that a majority of New Yorkers seem to deposit their dead in the endless burial grounds of Queens, the most hallowed cemetery in town is where the No 4 train has come to the end of its run through some of that blitzed wasteland in the South Bronx. By the time it has reached its terminus at Woodlawn, the slums have been left well behind and all is verdant tranquillity. This, as a brochure proudly points out, is the Resting Place of the Famous, so many of them famous in so many spheres that the brochure, obtainable at the sales office by the front gate, lists them under their avocations, together with a map, so that the curious and the bereft can navigate more confidently where a quarter of a million celebrities lie. Here are Military Men, Musicians, Entertainers, Writers, Business, Women's Rights (just three) and a category called Miscellaneous, which includes New York's most widely-regarded Mayor, LaGuardia, and one of its most admired blacks, Ralph Bunche. Not one of them has managed to avoid resting in some style. Frank Woolworth's mausoleum, perhaps surprisingly not neo-Gothic, features a pair of Egyptian sphinxes. Jay Gould, financier, swindler, and man-about-town, favours a Greek temple. The most unostentatious of these former citizens has treated himself to a posthumous obelisk at the very least.

This is not the ugly Bronx of firebombers and muggers, nor

yet the frenetic but perfectly respectable Bronx of Yankee Stadium when the bottom of the ninth has been reached with the pin-stripes still short of the tieing run. This is the Bronx in whose Botanic Gardens you can imagine yourself deep in upstate rather than metropolitan New York, until you round a spinney and surprise a group of supple youngsters limbering up for their karate class, which is what people do only in cities where some danger lurks. It is the Bronx of a famous zoo, where snow leopards may be admired a long, long way from the Hindu Kush mountains where they belong. It is the Bronx which overlooks the Hudson at Riverdale, where mansions are sited enviably above the majestic waterway amid trees and spacious lawns (perhaps the one Al Jolson had in mind when he sang, 'Mammy dahlin', if I'm a success we move up to the Bronx!'). It is the Bronx which can boast no fewer than eight universities and colleges, which do not proclaim whatever Godforsaken gospel incenses the slums. Old Jonas Bronck, who came to Nieuw Amsterdam in 1639 and bought 500 acres from the Indians for the usual mishmash of goods, might be a little confused by the contrasts in his landholding today. So, even, might Leon Trotsky, who lived in a Bronx apartment with his family for a while in 1917, and marvelled at the gadgets which even then were fitted into the kitchens of the American working class.

New York's Staten Island – there is another one, at the very tip of South America, beyond Tierra del Fuego – has been somewhat transformed since the Verrazano Bridge was completed twenty years ago. Before that the only bridge off the island joined it to New Jersey, which was not the most appealing prospect for New Yorkers, who condescend a little to the state next door, and who anyway prefer to get from point A to point B in a direct line. It did not encourage massive commuting to Manhattan – which long-standing Staten Islanders refer to as 'the city' – though there have always been enough of those to keep the famous ferry going day and night between the Battery and St George. So this for a long time remained a semi-rural enclave, inhabited by those without hectic lifestyles and by those whose lifestyles are perhaps so hectic that prudence dictates the domestic part were better isolated from the hurly burly of business. But Mafia bosses are not the only big shots who have made a haven on Staten Island. It was here where Jenny Lind got her breath back between singing engagements; where Garibaldi spent a couple of years in exile, surviving as a candlemaker, before he returned to lead his Thousand from Sicily to Rome in the name of King Victor Emmanuel. Until the last quarter of the nineteenth century, nothing much but farming and fishing happened on the island, but then a little industry began – a shipyard and a chemical works – and the latest development is a space satellite communications centre. But the biggest change has been in population, which has become half as big again since the Verrazano Bridge was thrown across the mouth of New York Harbor from Brooklyn, to give commuters into Manhattan a soaring ride on another roundabout route. Yet in spite of the growing sprawl of houses there, a country air persists down by the oceanside. When guide books, trembling with excitement, reveal that you can even watch cows grazing in New York City, in addition to its other wonders, they're referring to Staten Island.

Nothing as extraordinary as that is visible just across the bridge in Brooklyn, though it can offer West Indians, imitating their Caribbean heroes at cricket on summer weekends in Prospect Park. Here is New York's most considerable rival to the borough of Manhattan in every respect except numbers, where Brooklyn has overwhelming superiority. Were it still an independent city (which it hasn't been since the 1898 Act of Consolidation amalgamating the various parts of New York) it would have the sixth largest population in the United States – behind Los Angeles, Chicago, Detroit, Boston and Houston. It has civic buildings more substantial than most and at least as handsome as any in the land, and a Grand Army Plaza which, as its name implies, is downright grandiose, dominated by the most bombastic triumphal arch west of Paris or Rome (it commemorates the Union forces in the Civil War). It has a museum that any sizeable community would be proud to possess, luckless enough to lie in the shadow of Manhattan's more thriving crowd-pullers, and an Academy of Music internationally admired. It has the biggest collection of brownstones in the country and Winston Churchill's mother was born in one of them on Cobble

Hill. It has a flavoured soda drink, egg cream, which is found nowhere else but here and in Queens. Here is one of the great racial mixtures of New York, with many more blacks than there are in Harlem now, and the most densely Jewish neighbourhood (at Borough Park) in the whole of America. Here is most of New York's still functioning waterfront, and a great deal of its other industry.

Brooklyn so obviously has so much going for it in its own right, that it is hard to account for a certain lack of fizz about it nowadays, the sort of swagger that on Manhattan has to be taken for granted. What has become of Coney Island is somehow typical of Brooklyn in general. Island in name only, but bordering a six-mile Atlantic beach, its career as New York's popular pleasure place began with a pavilion and bath house being built there in 1844. The original developers apparently saw its future as America's answer to the French Riviera resorts, or the English Brighton, and in the early years New York's wealthy dallied pleasantly in the elegant hotels and restaurants that sprang up there. Before the end of the century, largely because railroads opened it to the populace in general, Coney Island's attractions became less genteel, with peep shows, fairground amusements and even prize fights: it was at Coney Island that Robert Fitzsimmons, James Jeffries, James J. Corbett and Tom Sharkey met in a series of epic heavyweight bouts at the turn of the century. Then Luna Park, a forerunner of Disneyland, was developed and a pattern was set beside the Atlantic that would continue at Coney Island until some time after the Second World War; mass amusements provided by a remarkable array of appliances, including the roller coaster, the Ferris Wheel, and Coney Island's distinctive contribution to this genre, the parachute jump carefully controlled by rigging from the top of a specially built tower. Somehow or other – possibly because more New Yorkers have become more mobile and seek their pleasure farther afield in less old-fashioned ways – in the past generation Coney Island's great animal vitality seems to have burnt itself low, if not yet quite out. The boardwalk is still good for a stroll, and the beach can still be packed on a hot summer's day, and Nathan's still produces the classic hot dog, as it always did; but the sideshows are just a bit tatty now, and the parachute jump no longer works, though the framework still stands there as a broken-down reproach. What seems to typify Coney Island as much as anything now is a series of high-rise apartments overlooking the pleasure beach, populated, it's said, by elderly Jews on incomes so modest that they can't afford condominiums in Florida; and, curving round in front of them, an elevated section of subway track, on which D trains filthy with graffiti arrive almost empty after their long haul down from the Bronx.

Many people take the view that Brooklyn's malaise is purely psychological, the result of a blow to its collective morale, which was dealt on September 24, 1957, when the Brooklyn Dodgers beat Pittsburgh three-nil in a night game, after which the lights went out for ever at Ebbets Field. The Dodgers weren't by any means the most successful side in the history of baseball (they won the World Series only once) but they were high in everyone's affections, just like the Brooklyn Bridge, and they hold the most honoured place for bringing Jackie Robinson up to the major league in 1947, the first black man ever allowed to play at that level with whites. It was some time after this that the club lawyer, Walter O'Malley, became owner of the Dodgers, and although the end was still some years off, the ballclub's fate was sealed. The new owner wanted bigger profits than the relatively small ballpark in Crown Heights could provide. The team netted half a million dollars for O'Malley in its final season, but Californians who had for too long been starved of big baseball were dangling much larger baits he decided he couldn't refuse. Los Angeles offered to build a transplanted Dodgers club a colossal new stadium with immensely greater parking facilities. The city authorities there also mentioned oil rights in the area, and said O'Malley was welcome to them if he came. Brooklyn loyalty, Brooklyn pride, Brooklyn sentiment cut no ice at all beside that. Henceforth it would be the Los Angeles Dodgers, and within two years Ebbets Field was not even a ghost of a ballpark. A high-rise housing development took its place, the floodlights went to illuminate a soccer pitch on Randalls Island in the East River, and Brooklyn has been scarred ever since in a way that is hard to understand by those who have never felt a whole community's powerful affiliation with the group of players representing it in a team sport.

Brooklyn has often been the butt of jokes by other New Yorkers. It is said that in the days of vaudeville, a comic only had to utter the name of the Canarsie neighbourhood to have his audience rolling in the aisles; and there was a movie in which John Wayne played a Manhattan football coach berating a young quarterback with, 'Kid, your passing's from Canarsie!' During the Second World War, the Navy had a couple of warships with local names, the USS *New York* and the USS *Brooklyn*. The first was known quite respectfully by all hands as 'Old Nick', the second with a knowing grin as 'the Teakettle' or 'the Busy B'. There is even an establishment in Manhattan which quite recently was running elocution lessons entitled 'How to lose your Brooklyn accent' – which is not more unintelligible than the speech of the Bronx or Manhattan's Lower East Side. Such reflex thrusts as these are often only made as a form of familiarity for people and places held in some regard. In Brooklyn's case they can be seen as acknowledgments of its rich character; which is what poor unridiculed and unadmired Queens doesn't have too much of.

Though Brooklyn, especially, and the other three outer boroughs to a lesser extent, have employments of their own, the four have more and more become chiefly dormitories for commuters. Manhattan sucks in most of its workforce from other parts of the city and from even farther afield. People come from out of Connecticut and New Jersey to beaver away in those skyscraping offices, some of them willing (if not eager and happy) to spend over one and a half hours each way on a train between New Haven and Grand Central Station. They come rocking down the Hudson Valley for their daily bread all the way from Poughkeepsie, which takes just about as long. The Lower Hudson Valley is where New York City ends and upstate New York begins, beautifully lush beside the great river, though that is dotted with small industrial towns above West Point. Not everyone round here needs to commute in order to stay solvent. Even after the English had supplanted the Dutch authority in 1664, translating Nieuw Amsterdam into New York while they were about it, Dutch *patroons* retained their estates up the Hudson, and established dynasties that were to thrive in wealth and influence; like the Vanderbilts and the Roosevelts, who both settled near the village of Stoutenburgh, which was itself in due course to be restyled Hyde Park. Much more wealth and influence – at the gargantuan level of the Rockefellers and below – abides in that wedge of land which lies between the railroad line following the river, and the other one running into Connecticut: here is Westchester County, local byword for extreme prosperity. More wealth still is to be found in many a green pasture along the length of Long Island.

Long Island took Walt Whitman's fancy because of its shape, which he saw as that of a whale lowering its head under Manhattan, its tail fluking in the general direction of Cape Cod. When Whitman was born there in 1819, just off the Jericho turnpike near Smithtown, the island was almost entirely in the hands of small farmers and fishermen, though the township of Brooklyn was beginning to grow at the western end. As the city across the East River expanded, so, too, did the island's economy, especially when it was realised that its light sandy soil was ideal for growing potatoes. And potato farming was pretty much what a lot of Long Island was noted for until after the Second World War. That and the anchorholds of the rich.

They began to settle not too far from the city, but at a healthy distance from plebeian Brooklyn, along the North Shore, where a series of thickly wooded bays come down to the waters of Long Island Sound; and they reached these by sailing down the Sound from Manhattan, where they had town houses, aboard their own yachts. Others who amassed great wealth – and not too choosy how they did so, so long as it came in quantity – bought themselves holdings in other parts of Long Island. Here, beside the water or somewhere inland, were the likes of J. P. Morgan, who fashioned America's first billion-dollar company, United States Steel, and much else; George F. Baker, whose stockholding in US Steel alone was worth $212.5 million in 1920; Charles Pratt and Stephen C. Harkness, partners of the monstrous J. D. Rockefeller in Standard Oil; and a son of Henry C. Frick, whose magnificent art collection was based on a fortune bled from others in the shape of coal and steel. Scott Fitzgerald perpetuated the lifestyles of such figures as these on Long Island in the most famous of his stories, and Jay Gatsby's property – 'a factual imitation of some Hotel de Ville in Normandy . . . and more than forty acres of lawn and garden' – was a fair representation of the standard North Shore residence between the wars. Though the legendary robber barons have long since departed, the North Shore residents continue to live in spacious style, part of Long Island's varied social patchwork today. Its western end is occupied not only by the city sprawl of Brooklyn, but also by that of Queens, which includes the two great New York airports of J. F. Kennedy and LaGuardia. Where the potato fields were, aircraft and other factories supplying the military arose after the Second World War, bringing with them a suburbia of their own. And right at the tail end of the island, amid sand dunes and fresh Atlantic winds, are still to be found fishermen sprinkled among the properties of the summer people, the prospering and young-ish professional families who light out for their cottages in the Hamptons and elsewhere whenever possible, as a blessed relief from the Manhattan apartment and the working week.

Long Island Sound is still *mare nostrum* for affluent New York, throbbing to the noise of motorboats and dappled with voluptuous spinnakers in the fair weather months. During the Second World War it is said that German U-boats regularly sailed up to its eastern end, before putting spies ashore on the lonely dunes at Montauk Point. Cruising right into it one unwitting day in 1942 came Sub-Lieutenant Alec Guinness, his acting career interrupted by the war, not yet an international star of stage and screen. He was in command of a landing craft which the shipbuilders of Quincy, Mass., had just made for the Royal Navy, and Guinness had been ordered to bring it to New York before sailing it home across the Atlantic. He and his equally inexperienced crew managed the passage of Long Island Sound without mishap, but when they entered the East River at the Manhattan end, a dense fog closed in, just as they spotted a notice on the bank forbidding anchorage in the river under any circumstances. Tides fairly rip through that confluence, and Sub-Lieutenant Guinness thought it prudent to go no further in fog. Improvising, he managed 'to sidle in alongside a rather posh embankment, and make fast to a convenient lamp post and park bench' before settling down for the night, and in this way was catastrophe avoided in the foggy dark. Less happily, next morning it was found that insufficient allowance had been made for the changing level of the tide, and consequent adjustment of the moorings: as a result, 'we had managed to dislodge the park seat, dragging it over the embankment as an anchor, and the lamp post was bent in two, like a hairpin.' Sheepishly, the Royal Navy made its getaway in the early morning light before anyone ashore could see this handiwork, young Guinness praying that he hadn't damaged the alliance irreparably.

Mariners have always recognised that Long Island Sound is a safer way of approaching New York in dirty weather than setting the conventional course past the outside of the island and through The Narrows: all that's necessary is draught shallow enough and nerve strong enough to navigate a vessel through the turbulence of Hell Gate, with its dangerous rocks, where the East River separates Manhattan from Queens. There the stream frequently flows at five knots, rising to more than six knots twice a month at spring tides. At Sandy Hook and in the Upper Bay, the usual passage into New York from the Atlantic, the current never exceeds three knots, whatever the state of the tide. This was the entrance used by the two most celebrated early navigators in these waters, Giovanni da Verrazano, the Italian hired by the French, and Henry Hudson, the Englishman in the pay of the Dutch; the first arriving in 1524, the second in 1609, both of them despatched from Europe to find a north-west passage to the Orient.

What each investigated briefly before sailing away again was the most superbly sheltered and commodious anchorage on the eastern seaboard. It was Hudson's report of this to his patrons in Amsterdam that led to further Dutch expeditions across the Atlantic and eventually to Peter Minuit's permanent settlement. By the time the English overtook the Dutch here, competing settlements had arisen along the eastern coastal lands, and in

spite of its great natural advantage, New York was no more
powerful or prosperous than any other. Not even its five years
as capital of the new republic exalted it more than politically over
its great rivals Boston and Philadelphia. Two things changed all
that. One was the chance which caused the British, after their
Napoleonic Wars with France were done, to decide that New
York rather than Boston was better placed for the disposal of
their exports to the United States. The other was the inspiration
of De Witt Clinton, thrice Mayor of New York and later Governor
of New York State, that a canal should be cut from somewhere
up the Hudson, right through a ridge of the Appalachians as far
as Lake Erie, not only to provide access to the Great Lakes as
a whole, but to assist in the great vision of American settlement
much further west. It was Governor Clinton who turned the
first spade of earth in the digging of the Erie Canal: and eight
years later, in 1825, he was there when a triumphal procession
of craft sailed the 500 miles from Buffalo to New York in ten
days. There were then eight considerable seaports on the east
coast between Norfolk, in Virginia, and Bath, in Maine; but
from that moment New York became outstandingly the most
important. It was from the benefits of its maritime trade, its
consolidated position as a great entrepot, that New York was
to be, by 1850, in one considered judgement, 'the unchallenged
metropolis of America'.

For more than a hundred years, the great port held its lead
over all comers, its business in freight paralleled for decades by
its traffic in human beings, as one shipload after another of immigrants dropped anchor in the Upper Bay. So much have things
changed on the waterfront since its heyday, that it is instructive
to read the superlative Works Progress Administration Guide to
this city, to gauge how things were in the port even half a century
ago. In 1938, it tells us, the Hudson River was scarcely visible
from Manhattan's West Side below 23rd Street, so continuous
was the line of shipping sheds and dock structures serving the
busy piers jutting into the river. Along that West Side waterfront
was concentrated 'the largest aggregate of marine enterprises
in the world', even though it was 'but a small segment of New
York's far-flung port'. In the nineteenth century, the East River

waterfront along South Street had been the busiest stretch, but since 1890 that had been displaced by activity along the Hudson. The great passenger liners that came in and out on the trans-Atlantic run several times a week were to be found berthed between 44th and 57th Streets. Cargo vessels crossing to Europe and beyond, or going down to South America, docked north of 14th Street. Coastal shipping and Long Island Sound Lines occupied berths from 14th Street down to the Battery – except Piers 2, 3, 7 and 9, which were the province of the United Fruit Company, whose Great White Fleet of steamers traded in bananas and passengers with the West Indies. 'Opposite the piers, along the entire length of the highway, nearly every block houses its quota of cheap lunchrooms, tawdry saloons and waterfront haberdasheries catering to the thousands of polyglot seamen who haunt the "front".' The guide book gives the impression of a West Side and a Hudson both jumping with movement. All the way up to 59th Street was 'a surging mass of back-firing, horn-blowing, gear-grinding trucks and taxis. All other waterfront sounds are submerged in the cacophony of the daily avalanche of freight and passengers in transit.' On the water was a continuous coming and going of 'the super-liner . . . the freighter, the river boat, the ferry and the soot-faced tug'. The river was especially something to make you gape when the Navy was in town and 'battleships line the Hudson from the Battery to Spuyten Duyvil. At night the crisscrossing beams of their searchlights fill the sky over the whole city with a strange and shifting brilliance, while sailors on leave and their friends congregate in the park.' All of these descriptions referred to but one small part of the great port. Into New York Harbor as a whole during the year ending in June 1938 had come a total of 3,547 vessels with a net tonnage of 20,291,204 – which encouraged the WPA Guide to claim that, 'By every significant statistical measure, this is the busiest seaport in the world.'

It is possible still to get some idea of that tremendous activity by looking at the classic photographs Andreas Feininger took about the same time. There, at pier after pier, along the length of the Hudson, are vessels stern-on to the camera as they lie at their berths; so many of them that occasionally two steamers are tied up one behind the other at a single pier. In midstream, freighters seem to be awaiting the next available space, old-fashioned-looking tubs to our eyes, with superstructures always amidships, rather thin smokestacks strictly vertical, derricks angled round each stubby mast like the spokes of a half-opened umbrella. There were still a lot of coal-fired boilers, judging by the amount of smoke most of the river traffic made. Smudges of it drift across from the Weehawken docks on the New Jersey side of the river, where they were later to film a movie called *On the Waterfront*. A thick black gusher erupts from the tugboat *Ideal*, mingling with another from the Hoboken ferry *Orange*, which is just about to cross her stern. Here are barges laden with railroad freight cars, being butted across the river by more tugs; and ferryboats – one with three stacks – nosed into piers at 42nd Street, white smoke clouding the air towards the nearest skyscrapers; and here are some of the super-liners – the sight so common, according to a caption, that they were taken for granted by most New Yorkers. Here is the *Queen Mary* being nudged into the Cunard pier by a quartet of tugs, and a reminder that on her maiden voyage in 1936 she was given a right royal welcome in this harbour, with aeroplanes circling overhead and fireboats spouting fountains of water. Here is the *Normandie* at her French Line berth, the first vessel ever to cross the Atlantic in less than four days, which she did from Cherbourg in 1937 with just under a couple of hours to spare. Here is the beautiful, rakish *United States*, which bettered even that time and took the Blue Riband for keeps (because that kind of trans-Atlantic racing isn't on any more) with an average speed of 35.59 knots in 1952. And here is her sister ship, *America*, steaming gracefully past the Financial District, outward bound for God knows where, with her name, and her steamship company's name, and two huge replicas of the Stars and Stripes, all painted on her sides; because, says the caption, 'These were the days before American involvement in World War II, and the letters and flags announced the ship's neutrality to German submarines prowling the North Atlantic.' (But where *was* she going, with all Europe at war, and half the ports there already blitzed or likely at any moment to go up in flames?)

It is all somewhat different nowadays. The Port Authority of New York and New Jersey, which was launched (as the Port of New York Authority) and fitted out in 1921 to supervise the business of the great port, now presides over considerably less maritime activity, though it has expanded in some unexpected directions, running commuter trains into New Jersey and owning a couple of bus stations on Manhattan. It has four bridges in its care, including the George Washington, which spans the Hudson dramatically between one wooded bluff and another. It maintains the Holland and Lincoln tunnels under the same river, a truck terminal, an industrial park and the Teleport, which is that space satellite communications centre on Staten Island. It is the proprietor of four airports, of which Newark (NJ) was the biggest until after the war, when it was overtaken by both LaGuardia and John F. Kennedy. The Port Authority also financed the building of the World Trade Center, where its headquarters are in offices notable for great views of New York, carpets into which people sink almost up to their shins, and wall hangings designed by the likes of Miro, Calder and Le Corbusier. It is a very considerable corporation of steady ambition, always looking for new fields to dabble in.

On the other hand, the 3,547 vessels which entered New York Harbor in 1938 had dropped to 2,790 by 1983; the 20.29 million tons had fallen to 13.29 million tons – and of those ships all but 423 had berthed not in New York, but at terminals on the New Jersey side of the Hudson River. By then there wasn't a single working cargo pier on the West Side of Manhattan, and although West Street was still as choked with surging traffic as in the days of the WPA Guide, little of it had anything to do with maritime commerce. Almost all the passenger vessels coming in and out are cruise ships sailing only between April and October, sometimes bent on nothing more worthy of them than a waterborne long weekend, on which a passenger taking a breather from the endless shipboard jollification, might well be able to spot the glow made by the lights of home just over the horizon, if he remembered in which direction to look. Only the *QE2* maintains a token presence occasionally on the trans-Atlantic run, with sadder times having overtaken others of her kind. Pier 76, where the *United States* used to berth, has become a parking lot, as has Pier 57, formerly used by the Grace Line. Pier 40, base for the old Holland-America Line, is now a parking lot and a TV studio combined. Far from being the busiest port in the world any more, New York has been superseded by many, at home and overseas. The Gulf ports of Texas and Louisiana, which handled only three-quarters of New York's tonnage in 1945, handled more than twice as much by 1980. This past few years, when the Port Authority has referred to its development plans, it has generally been thinking in terms of something other than a shipping forecast. It has planned a car rental centre, a 'resource recovery plant' and, where Piers 1 to 6 now stand mostly idle below Brooklyn Heights, a convention centre, a hotel, a marina for the benefit of yuppie boatmen, and some housing which, with that view of Manhattan across the water, will not even be for the moderately well-to-do.

But it is scarcely to blame for the decline in the port of New York. The great and romantic rivalry between the ocean liners was doomed from 1955 when, for the first time, more passengers crossed the Atlantic by plane than by ship, a change of habit that could never be arrested, let alone reversed. The unprecedented rise in oil prices twenty years later compounded local difficulties by persuading the owners of cruise ships to sail them in the winter months from Florida in order to reduce their fuel bills. As for the awful reduction of Manhattan as a cargo terminal, the longshoremen who used to load and unload vessels at those wharves have much to answer for. Their record of pilfering became so bad that some shipping companies decided to work out of less costly ports on the east coast. Then their union – mindful, no doubt, of the humiliating days when dock labour was chosen from surplus manpower at a morning 'shape-up' involving bribes – negotiated a contract with the employers which guaranteed them a full wage based on 2,080 hours per annum even if there was no work to do; and in 1977 alone, some three thousand of these dock workers picked up $16,640 apiece for doing not a hand's turn from the beginning of the year to the end. This continues to be the most expensive port on the Atlantic coast for a shipowner, purely in terms of the demands made by longshoremen. Manhattan already had a considerable problem in the 1960s as a result of the revolution in cargo handling: the arrival of massive container ships which required special docking facilities that could be more easily provided in the semi-derelict wastelands of Elizabeth and Newark on the New Jersey shore, and to a much lesser extent at Brooklyn's Red Hook. In this, as in many other respects, Manhattan was just too cramped.

Another yardstick of decline is the reduced numbers of the Sandy Hook Pilots, who bring the ships in and out of New York. They take their name from the spit of land which curves round to emphasise the limits of the Lower Bay outside The Narrows, between New Jersey and Staten Island; and although at this point a vessel still has seven full nautical miles to go before passing under the Verrazano Bridge to the Upper Bay, Sandy Hook represents an emotional entrance to the port of New York for any mariner who has just sailed in after days or even weeks on the open sea. Pilots have been conning vessels hereabouts since 1694, and the accumulated knowledge of the shoals, the currents and other hazards, together with the intricacies of ship handling, are such that it takes a full fifteen years of application before a seaman is licensed to pilot any vessel afloat to or from a berth in the port, either by way of The Narrows or the more tortuous passage of the East River and Long Island Sound. In 1962 there were 148 such Sandy Hook Pilots. Today their number is 116. Before the century is out, they reckon they'll be down to 102.

Their base is on Staten Island, but they pick up their incoming charges from the pilot cutter stationed for days on end near the Ambrose Light. Once there was a vividly red light vessel permanently anchored there, eleven miles out into the Atlantic from The Narrows, marking the beginning of the channel into New York, as well as the western start or finish to any trans-Atlantic race. Nowadays the light vessel is an exhibition piece on the East River, its place at sea taken by a black and white construction rising from the seabed on stilts. There is forty-five feet of water about there, and the Corps of Engineers regularly dredge the Ambrose Channel to the same depth all the way in, so that even a laden tanker of 288,000 tons can make it safely to the refineries of Bayonne.

As the ships great and small with the pilot aboard trudge in past the Light, bearing 297 degrees, the twin towers of the Port Authority's World Trade Center prick the landward horizon, which is otherwise a low blur against the blue of the sea. By the time Sandy Hook is on the beam to port, condominiums are clearly visible beyond its dunes. To starboard is Breezy Point, another sandy spit which forms the opposite arm embracing the Lower Bay; or, if you like, the jawbone of Walt Whitman's Long Island whale. At Buoy Number 10, the helm is put over till the bearing is 322 degrees, at Buoy Number 14 to bearing 347 degrees, which lays the new arrival right on course for a safe passage through The Narrows, having avoided the Romer Shoal, where the waves can be seen breaking at low tide on the calmest of days, with no more than five feet of water in places at high. Having avoided, too, the threat of West Bank, where birds stand amid salty puddles, watchful for anything that might serve as a meal. By the time the pilot has his vessel straightened for the run in, Coney Island is a stubble of high-rise dwellings and that lonely parachute tower, and the long approach by road to the Verrazano Bridge is gathering momentum in Brooklyn for its leap across the water. Cleanly is the leap made, an impossible distance it seems from the water below for a roadway so slender and so gently suspended by its cables, and elegantly does the bridge gain the western shore on Staten Island. Passing under the bridge is to marvel at the ambition of men who would span such a breadth at such a height; just as to see it from afar is to be thrilled and very glad that they did it in such style.

Once under the bridge, revelation begins. A line of merchant-men tug at their anchor cables against the tide. Ferries and other craft move buoyantly in all directions beyond. It still wants the best part of six miles to the Battery when that sensational skyline slowly slips into full view from behind a bulge in the Brooklyn shore. There is Manhattan, and there, dear Lord, is Liberty herself, a fragment of green on a plinth at this distance, but very soon to be surely gained. Yet another vessel has made it safely to New York from just about any place on earth, where so many have been before. This was hello again for all those glittering people who used the trans-Atlantic liners the way ordinary folk use the Staten Island ferry – except for the ones who had sailed in the *Titanic*, who weren't so lucky after all. This was welcome home for all those Doughboys and GIs who returned in '19 and '45 after winning other people's world wars. Above all, this was the grail sought by those lost souls who were to become America, an age, a security, and more than 3,000 miles ago. Not a ship has come this way across the ocean without at least someone aboard whose heart has quickened at the sight of journey's end. Or maybe missed a beat.

THREE

THE BOILING POT

The two-hundred-and-twenty-third St Patrick's Day Parade came up Fifth Avenue non-stop for well over three hours, while a multitude of spectators applauded the participants every inch of forty-two blocks: this being, as E. B. White once remarked, 'the only event that hits every New Yorker on the head', which it does year after year on March 17 or thereabouts. The city lends itself generously to this annual celebration of Irishness, providing a green line to guide the marchers right up the middle of the Avenue, green floodlighting to illuminate the Empire State Building after dusk, green fluids to stain the waters round Manhattan, green beer and green foodstuffs which do not look as though they were meant for delicate stomachs; also 4,000 cops to take charge of crowd control. Some of the police, relishing a distant ancestry in County Meath and points west, had dyed their moustaches green for the two-hundred-and-twenty-third occasion, and some women cheering on the parade had bravely greened their hair.

This St Patrick's Day began in usual fashion, with the grandees of Irish New York assembling for breakfasts at O'Lunney's Steak House, Ryan McFadden's or Charley O's, making speeches about the Ould Sod and about British imperialism, which they verily believe to be responsible for the atrocities that daily torment the decent citizens of Northern Ireland, Catholic and Protestant and atheist alike. The Grand Marshal of that year's Parade, Peter King, a lawyer from Long Island, said straight out that, 'The message we are sending is that Irish-Americans are united in solidarity against British misrule in Northern Ireland,' and hundreds of supporters in O'Lunney's cheered him to the echo for that. At a mass in St Patrick's Cathedral that morning, Archbishop John O'Connor was applauded five times during a homily in which he said something of the sort himself, but sidelong, as befitted a man in his equivocal position: 'The time has come and is long overdue for those great nations of the world to raise their voices to demand that the oppression end and the slaughter cease. Which nation should lead the way but our own?' Two years earlier, his predecessor, Cardinal Terence Cooke, had pointedly not emerged from St Patrick's to review the parade until Grand Marshal Michael Flannery – a declared supporter of the Irish Republican Army – had passed by at the head of things. Archbishop O'Connor had no such reservations about Grand Marshal Peter King, greeting him warmly on the cathedral steps, though that very morning King's face had appeared in a full-page newspaper ad, identifying himself with 'those brave Irishmen and Irishwomen who are valiantly struggling against the British army of occupation'.

The parade was an always colourful mixture of sentimentality and nostalgia, unbridled enthusiasm and merriment, controlled belligerence and downright political opportunism. Horsemen and women came tittuping past on a squadron of beautiful thoroughbreds, dressed as if in pursuit of fox across that lovely hunting country they have in Kildare (Katie Mulvey Reddington at their head). One Emerald Society after another marched along – formed by the Transit Police, the Fire Department, the Correction Department, the Port Authority Police, the New York Post Office and others – carrying their banners and waving happily to friends and neighbours they recognised in the crowd. The Cardinal Spellman High School and many more of its kind had sent along marching teams dressed vividly like the chorus line in light opera, or cowboys and cowgirls, or just reg'lar all-American cheerleaders. The Grand Marshal had his traditional escort of mounted police followed by a detachment of the 69th Regiment, and as all these were helmeted and uniformed in the most businesslike way, the parade for a few minutes had an untoward military air. There were dozens of functionaries from the Ancient Order of Hibernians, the expatriate pressure group which used to organise riots protesting against the free-thinking dramas of Yeats and Synge and O'Casey and others, which the Abbey Theatre of Dublin would send to New York; though on this occasion, the order's manpower had turned out, sashed in the green, orange and white of Ireland, merely to help maintain a proper sense of order. There were musicians galore to keep everyone in step (or at least stepping lively), marching in bands which played different tunes and even vastly different instruments, separated by just enough distance to avoid any suggestion of discord in the parade. Many of them were pipe bands, clad – a little tactlessly, perhaps – in Royal Stewart, Hunting Mackenzie and other non-Irish tartans, playing 'Scotland the Brave', 'The Rowan Tree' and other distinctly non-Irish airs, but nonetheless saluted by an uncomprehending audience on the sidewalks with exuberant cries of 'Up the Irish!'

The sidewalks were not allowed to forget the point the Grand Marshal had made to his henchmen at breakfast time. The parade had not been going all that long before – a little astern of the Cardinal Spellman band and just ahead of the St Vincent's Hospital School of Nursing contingent – a banner hove into sight, bearing the legend, 'Sean Oglaigh Na-h-Eireann of New York Inc Irish Republican Army Veterans', flanked by a Stars and Stripes and an Irish tricolour. Behind it came a group of men, some elderly, some much less so, who couldn't have marched more proudly if they had been at Iwo Jima rather than in the Bogside and along the Falls. They were succeeded at once by Michael Flannery and his fellow organisers of the Irish Northern Aid Committee, which is generally thought to provide something much more substantial than moral support to the IRA. And then came the car-bombers and the knee-cappers of today, a dozen or so young people in black berets, wearing black plastic jackets with, stencilled on the back in white, a sub-machine gun upheld by a fist above the letters IRA. A lot of people on the sidewalks clapped and cheered as they went by, but as many simply looked at them curiously and did nothing more. The biggest applause in the parade was saved, up and down Fifth Avenue, for the firefighters taking part; biggest of all by far for the firemen who had come over as usual from Dublin, and who were obviously enjoying the great warmth of the New York Irish no end. Several other groups of real Irishmen and women had crossed the Atlantic for the festival; but none, most conspicuously, was here to represent the Dublin Government, which these days takes a rather different view of events in Northern Ireland from that frequently held in New York. It long ago outlawed the IRA, just as adamantly as the British, and it deplored – later in this year of the two-hundred-and-twenty-third parade – the participation of the New York City Police Department Emerald Society's pipe band in a march of sympathy for the gunmen of County Donegal, near the fishing village where Lord Mountbatten was assassinated in 1979. ('They sound,' said an Irish Government spokesman, referring to the New York cops, 'like a bunch of people with no respect for the dead and very little for the living.') Once upon a time, it would have been unthinkable for the Irish President or An Taoiseach not to send a representative, if they couldn't come themselves to New York for the St Patrick's Day Parade. But not any more.

This clearly cut no ice with the New York politicians at the two-hundred-and-twenty-third parade. Up front there in his re-election year was Mayor Edward Isaac Koch (of Polish extraction), wearing an Aran sweater and a green tam o' shanter, posturing to the crowds like a village half-wit in his eagerness to collect anybody's vote: there were balloons all along the route, courtesy of the Koch campaign committee, exhorting everybody to 'Keep the Mayor MAYOR'. More soberly dressed in tweed and carrying himself with more decorum, was the rangy figure of Senator Daniel P. Moynihan, who once absented himself from the parade in a well-publicised gesture of abhorrence at all the violence across the water and some of its sources over here, but who this year had asked to be re-admitted to its senior ranks. Governor Mario Cuomo was there, working hard on his image, as a man must if he is to become President of the United States one day. So were various rivals of the Mayor for his office, and other people whose future prosperity depends on the ballot box; down to Congressman Mario Biaggi, attorney and ex-cop, who might himself have been Mayor a decade earlier if he had not been caught out publicly in a lie about having taken the Fifth Amendment before a grand jury, and now makes what shift he can by cultivating the IRA vote as assiduously as he does the Italian.

The St Patrick's Day fixture is – one way and another – the most extravagant celebration of its kind, but it is not the only parade up Fifth Avenue, and certainly it is not the only occasion when alien folk memories are self-indulgently flourished in what is easily the most polyglot city on earth. A few weeks after that green line has been whitened again on the departure of the Hibernians each year, the Greeks come marching along it in a lather of excitement about their independence from the Turks, which happened way back in 1832. June sees the Puerto Ricans doing their best to pretend that Fifth is the main thoroughfare of San Juan, with almost as big a turnout as for the Irish, and with decorated floats as well as the bands and the social clubs and the pressure groups and the vote-catchers who march in nearly all the big parades. Come September, and the Germans take the same route for their Steuben Day event – named after the Baron von Steuben who fought with Washington at Valley Forge – in a progress notable for heavily syncopated brass, and the waving of beer steins from every passing float. Between spring and autumn there will be scarcely a weekend when, somewhere in New York, some small army of citizens is not going through motions which imply that they may be much, much less than 100 per cent Americans (which isn't often true at all). If it is not along Fifth Avenue, it may be over in Brooklyn, where there is a Norwegian Day Parade every May. Or up in Harlem where, on African-American Day in September, they become soulful about roots in what always was, and still is, a pretty benighted continent. Or down in Little Italy where, for ten days every fall, the air is smoky with outdoor cooking, the nights loud with sub-operatic music, the streets vibrant with the mannerisms and the conversations of Milano and Firenze (even more with those of Napoli, Potenza and places farther south) as the Festival of St Gennaro is celebrated just as it might be in old Calabria itself; except that the saint's statue here is paraded up and down a Mulberry Street. Thus the citizens of New York make their different ritual gestures towards lands which are, in greater or lesser degree, quite foreign to them; and from which they would, almost without exception, run a mile if they thought there was the slightest risk of having to live in any of these alternatives, instead of in the USA. There is maybe just one group which has exempted itself from this curious pattern of having things emotionally both ways at once amidst the various gratifications of New York. No-one seems ever to have held a St George's Day Parade, or to have celebrated in some other public way their arrival on these shores as White Anglo-Saxon Protestants, though such people were by far the most numerous of the nation's founding fathers, gave this city much of its early impetus, and marked it for ever with their name from another place. The lack of annual demonstration in this case may have something to do with the fact that the WASPs are held in some suspicion by almost everybody else; just as most citizens of the Soviet Union mistrust and even dislike the Russians, who provided the Czars with their power base, compounding this offence by occupying the same favourable ground under communism later on.

One thing all but the black community of New York have in common, apart from their American stake: the eagerness of their forefathers to get here. Though the convention is to refer to them or their forefathers neutrally as early settlers or later immigrants, the far-from-neutral reality is that all of them have been, in one generation or another, refugees, in flight from those variously pernicious foreign lands their emotions now so unstintingly cherish. The blacks were transported here as slaves, with no other option but to come. Everyone else made his own move from some place he didn't like enough to stay in, and for some this hasn't ever amounted to very much more than a chance for even greater prosperity than before. Others, the vast majority, have been refugees in the starkest meaning of the word. These are the ones who, in the nineteenth and early twentieth centuries, came to America from Europe in the largest mass movement of human beings the world has yet known. In the one hundred years which ended in 1924, some thirty-four million Europeans crossed the Atlantic to make a fresh start in the United States. Most of them came through this city, and a lot of them went no further.

A medley of nationalities had dribbled over ever since the earliest settlements, but this great stream of refugees began to flow shortly after the Napoleonic Wars, when the Industrial Revolution gathered momentum and left many without work, as machinery replaced the labour and skills of men. America acquired some 600,000 people in the 1820s and thirties as a result of this, mostly from England and Ireland: the Erie Canal, which contributed much to the ascendancy of New York, was largely dug by Irish labour and cost many Irish lives. Within another twenty years, over three million more people had arrived, from Ireland again and from Germany this time. The great potato famine of 1846, and smaller ones that followed it, propelled the Irish on this occasion, and a further incentive to move was provided by the English landlords of their country, many of whom paid their tenants' passages to New York in order to get them off the land, which might then be 'improved'. The Germans took flight as the first of the strictly political refugees to the United States, when their revolution of 1848 – that year of revolution throughout continental Europe – failed with much bloodshed in Berlin. In ten years a million or more of them had crossed the ocean, and a by-product of their arrival was the introduction of a new political philosophy that was to stick, though not very well in New York. The year of revolution was also the year of the *Communist Manifesto*, and the radical Germans who migrated to the city began to teach some of its principles at the Free Workers' School which they opened on Second Avenue. Within a few years, Horace Greeley's *New York Tribune*, which had the biggest circulation in America, was publishing articles by Karl Marx himself, providing him with his only regular source of income for some time.

European penury and European politics continued to supply the growing republic with new blood, in even greater quantities and wider varieties, once the carnage of the American Civil War had ceased. The prospects of higher rewards for similar effort than might be wrested from the rocky soils and rough seas

of Scandinavia, induced Danes and Norwegians and Swedes
by the hundred thousand to sail for the New World in the
1870s, and though most of these made for the agricultural
lands of the mid-west, enough dropped anchor in New York
to stiffen the small colony that had existed there since 1825,
when the sloop *Restaurationen* (the Scandinavian *Mayflower*)
arrived with pilgrims from Stavanger. It was agrarian poverty
of a more desperate, a savagely grinding sort that brought hordes
of Italians soon afterwards. They were peasants from the south
for the most part, from Sicily and Sardinia, Apulia and Calabria,
illiterates who had known nothing but economic oppression by
one of the most notorious feudal systems in Europe. A pauper
in an English workhouse at the time was allotted fifty-seven
pounds' weight of meat a year, but an Apulian peasant was
expected to subsist – and work hard for his landlord – on ten
pounds of meat. An American would think to spend no more
than 41 per cent of his wages on food, a German perhaps 62
per cent; but the Italian was obliged to part with 85 per cent of
his money in order not to starve. Getting out of the Mezzogiorno
in almost any direction was thus the most logical movement in
the world for such people. At first South America beckoned, and
Buenos Aires was largely built with Italian labour: but then that
door was shut, and the migrant ships from Genoa and Naples
crossed the Atlantic to New York instead. These refugees soon
replaced the Irish at the bottom of the city's social pile, also as a
source of unorganised and therefore easily exploited labour, so
that by the mid-eighties it was mostly Italian muscle that was
constructing the elevated railways which had begun to spread
across the city, later the subways, the bridges, the skyscrapers.
Unlike the Irish, the Italians almost always came without their
womenfolk in those early days of their exodus, counting on a
return to their native land one day. Some of them never did go
home, except in a pious reconciliation before death.

While the Italians were clawing their way out of one form
of misery, vast numbers of other nationalities were fleeing
from political and religious oppressions, which meant economic
hardships, too. Most numerous among these were the Jews of
eastern Europe, victims of a pogrom throughout the Russian

Empire ordered by the Czar Alexander III after the assassination of his father, which led to mobs attacking the Jewish quarter of every town between Kronstadt and Odessa, a violence that before long had spread to the *shtetls* of Galicia, Poland, Romania and elsewhere. There had been Jews on Manhattan from the day in 1654 when Jacob Barsimon arrived from Holland aboard the *Preboom*, and by the eighteenth century they numbered about 4,000; but never had there been an influx to match the torrent of refugees who came on every tide after 1881, which was to give the city a Jewish population of well over one million within thirty years. They were not the only victims of European upheaval who sought refuge in the last decades of the nineteenth century and the pre-war years of the twentieth. The repressions of a corrupt Ottoman Empire caused both Romanians and Slovenes to fly from the Turks, while their neighbours in Serbia and Croatia (eventually to be united with the Slovenes as Yugoslavia) were in similar plight as vassals of the Hapsburgs. The Austro-Hungarian Empire was beginning its own steep decline, which would end in its dismemberment by the Great War. But in the last quarter of the nineteenth century, the imperial edicts of Vienna, enforced by martial law and a secret police, still held much of Central Europe in thrall and provided another powerful incentive to emigrate. One empire collapsed before the First World War even began, when the Russians were defeated by the Japanese in 1905, there was mutiny aboard the battleship *Potemkin*, and the first soviet of workers was formed in St Petersburg. At these first rumblings of the tumult that was to shake the world a dozen years later, another multitude of the fearful – from Russia, from the Ukraine, from Latvia, from Estonia, from Poland – embarked on that harrowing journey which began with the long train ride to Bremen or Hamburg, harassed by frontier guards and all manner of pimps, ending weeks later on Ellis Island, after the harsh conditions of an Atlantic crossing. It was mostly refugees from eastern and southern Europe at about this time who produced the peak for immigration through the Port of New York. In 1907, no fewer than 1,285,349 people were admitted here.

In the following year, a play which spoke to the condition of the European refugee in America opened on Broadway and ran successfully for several months. Its author, Israel Zangwill, put into the mouth of his chief character a phrase which not only served as the title of his drama, but would for ever afterwards be stamped upon mankind's memory of this moment in American history. David Quixano, the Russian Jew who has found refuge in New York from the pogroms of the Czar, makes this declaration in his fervour for the new homeland; 'America is God's Crucible, the great Melting Pot, where all the races of Europe are melting and reforming! . . . God is making the American . . . he will be the fusion of all the races, the coming superman.' It has been pointed out that the author of *The Melting Pot* subsequently became obsessed with Zionism before his death in 1926, which was the kind of commitment guaranteed to prevent the idealised processes of the racial melting pot from ever happening in the world outside the theatre. The point is, though, that in Zangwill/Quixano's peroration can be felt the unbounded optimism, the release from great travail, experienced by every migrant who succeeded in convincing the immigration officials on Ellis Island of his worth.

Whether or not it was heading for a fusion that would ultimately produce supermen, the city's population was certainly expanding at a supernatural rate, assisted by those constant blood transfusions from elsewhere. When the first federal census was taken in 1790, on Manhattan and in the four other areas that were later to amalgamate as New York City, there had been a total of 49,421 people. In 1898, after the amalgamation took place, there were 3,437,202 New Yorkers. By 1913, the population had climbed to 5,620,048. The cheap labour which Europe had so prodigally exported, played its part in the United States becoming the wealthiest nation in the world by 1900, American trade and manufacturing figures outstripping those of Great Britain, France and Germany, the industrial giants of Europe. Cut-price factory fodder was much less welcome to the American labour unions, who claimed that new immigrants from Italy in particular were often used by unscrupulous employers and their agents to break honest-to-goodness American strikes. It was largely pressure from the unions that led to legislation in the 1880s aimed at regulating the mounting flow of refugees.

The most hostile of the new laws passed by Congress was the Chinese Exclusion Act of 1882 (not to be repealed until 1943), which meant not only just what its title implied, but also denied citizenship to Chinese who had been settled in the States since the middle of the nineteenth century; and as these had habitually entered America along its west coast and thought themselves secure there, the disturbing implications of the new legislation persuaded many to move on to the other side of the country, to establish a recognisable Chinatown on the Lower East Side of Manhattan, where only a handful of their compatriots – usually seamen who had sailed in from San Francisco – had dwelt till then. Two other laws, in 1882 and 1891, were aimed at the exclusion of the insane, the criminal, the diseased and the utterly destitute, as well as 'persons who have been convicted of . . . misdemeanours involving moral turpitude, polygamists and . . . contract labourers'. By 1917 it was thought necessary to add to this battery of legislation another bill, which required more thorough medical examinations, and a literacy test in which the migrant was required to read at least forty words in whatever was his native language.

The Great War produced another great yearning to reach the safety, as well as the prosperity, of the United States. It was estimated by the US Government agencies that, from Germany alone, between two and eight million people wished to migrate in the aftermath of Armistice Day, when the Atlantic became safe for shipping again; and in 1920 ten to thirteen thousand refugees a week were being processed on Ellis Island. It would have been surprising if the legislators in Washington had not taken further steps to control this inundation, and what they came up with this time was the quota system. The first Quota Act of 1921, aimed obliquely at migrants from southern and eastern Europe, stipulated that all entries henceforth must be regulated by reference to the United States census of 1910, with admissions of any nationality limited to 3 per cent of its American population in that census year (thus the annual quota from southern and eastern Europe, which had lately been supplying 738,000 people per annum, would be reduced to 155,000). The 1921 Act became effective on June 3, just as three vessels with 3,391 Italians aboard came steaming through The Narrows in an attempt to beat the deadline, which set the Italian quota for that period at 2,500. In the panic which ensued, Congress adjusted its new bill to let these refugees in, together with any who might be upon the high seas that week. But in Europe, masses of people who had gathered at embarkation ports to begin the new adventure, were told that salvation was no longer available because their national quotas had already been filled; in Antwerp alone, 3,000 had their hopes dashed in this way. A much more calculated cruelty, because the quotas were apportioned on a monthly basis, was to last for three full years; and European shippers were at least as responsible as American lawmakers for this.

The night before the new month began, a flotilla of migrant ships would be drifting somewhere off the Ambrose Light, crammed with people who had travelled from the uttermost parts of the northern hemisphere in hope. As eight bells signified midnight they would begin a race for The Narrows, where officials stationed on either side of the opening into the harbour would judge which vessels were to be considered first at immigration control. Passengers aboard the also-rans, if their quotas were filled, were losers indeed. The steamers that had brought them to the New World, simply turned round and took them back to the old one they no longer wished to know. An improvement only came with the National Origins Act of 1924, which actually tightened the quotas even more, allowing into America no more than 2 per cent of any nationality instead of 3 per cent, and changing the basis of calculation from the 1910 census to the more restricting one of 1890. But at least the new Act put an end to the heartbreak of deportation just because a steamship had failed to move fast enough in the final dash for sanctuary; in future, no-one was allowed to embark on a migrant ship in Europe until he had obtained a visa from the nearest American consulate, which issued these only after conducting the customary tests to determine who was eligible to enter the United States, and who was not.

A watershed in this remarkable evolution of New York was reached in 1930, when the city's population had risen to

6,930,446. Of these, no fewer than 2,359,000 people – 34 per cent of the community – had been born in foreign lands, a higher proportion than has been known at any other time, before or since. But in the next twelve months, a mere 97,139 migrants to America passed through the Port of New York, the beginning of a dramatic decline that both the Depression and the Second World War helped to maintain for half a generation: not until 1946 did 100,000 refugees again come to the United States in a given year. Ravaged for a second time in the twentieth century, but much more terribly than before, Europe again began to offer her unfortunates as soon as the war was over, and the United States passed a Displaced Persons Act to help them on their way, with one of those grand American gestures which did much to embellish the restoration of that peace. Another would be made twenty years later when, in the pregnant setting of Liberty Island, President Lyndon Johnson declared that henceforth all generations, of whatever kind, were free to come and dwell in America, provided they had the skills the nation sought. So ended the quota system, which in essence had been directed against selected racial groups.

By then the flow of refugees to the United States, to New York in particular, had altered in shape and texture once more, as it had when the great migration of the Irish gave way to that of the Italians, and again when the Italians were overtaken by eastern European Jews. This time by far the biggest numbers were arriving from Puerto Rico, the American satellite lodged in the Caribbean between the Dominican Republic and the Virgin Islands. Because of the colonial relationship between the two countries (the Americans took possession of Puerto Rico in 1898 – rather as the British took possession of Gibraltar in 1713 – after a war with Spain) the islanders have always been allowed free passage into the United States, being classified as American citizens, instead of as the aliens of traditional migration. But until now they had not shipped themselves over to the mainland in much quantity, in spite of the fact that they dwelt in conditions of 'almost unrelieved misery' after decades of American rule: New York contained no more than 500 of them in 1910, 7,000 in 1920, 45,000 in 1930. From the late 1940s, however, they were to make the transition to the mother country in vast numbers which, by 1960, would put well over half a million of them – 8 per cent of the community – in New York, where they settled most thickly, as they have ever since. If one thing more than another was responsible for this sudden transformation, it appears to have been nothing more momentous than the introduction of a regular air service between San Juan and New York in 1945, which reduced the travelling time from four or five days in a boat, to only a few hours; that and the cheap fares prevailing as twenty-seven airlines, at one point, competed to handle the traffic. It was at about this time, contemplating the swirling human mixture in his adopted city, that Thomas E. Dewey, presidential candidate and for a dozen years Governor of New York State, brought Israel Zangwill's epigram smartly up to date. 'New York City isn't a melting pot,' he said one day. 'It's a boiling pot!'

It has been bubbling away as potently in this last quarter of the twentieth century as it did in the comparable period of the nineteenth. There has again been a steady supply of migrants from the usual European sources, and a continuing expansion of Puerto Ricans of such proportions that it is now perfectly possible to imagine New York becoming a thoroughly bilingual city, an ampler version of Montreal, but with Spanish rather than French as the alternative speech. They have been joined by other Hispanics, as New Yorkers are wont to call them, coming from areas to the south of the USA (like the Dominican Republic which supplied the city with 98,420 Spanish-speakers between 1965 and 1980), so that by the last census there was a total of 1,429,000 such people living in New York. West Indians – who, before the war, preferred to be mistaken in America for Puerto Ricans rather than homegrown blacks, because they felt at less of a disadvantage in the job hunt using that pretence – have lately descended on New York as never before: probably because London, which received thousands of migrants from the Caribbean for three post-war decades, has pulled up the drawbridge on a traditional West Indian refuge. For the first time in any quantity, New York has also become host to a motley of people from Asia, other than the Chinese; many from the Indian sub-continent, a distinctive colony from Korea, and a variety of refugees from recent imperial wars. There are five columns of names beginning with 'Ng' in the Manhattan telephone directory, another four columns in the Brooklyn book, representing the luckier flotsam left over from the American passage of arms in Vietnam. At City College in 1985, the co-athlete of the year was a young Afghan who fled from his country after the Red Army marched in. In the past twenty years or so, something like 80,000 new immigrants have come to settle in the city every year. By 1980, when the last census was taken, and New York's population was tabled at 7,071,639, some 1,675,000 of the citizens were foreign-born – or 23 per cent of them, the highest proportion since that 1930 plateau.*

It is a powerful, an intoxicating mixture when it is encountered in the flesh. New York's progress towards bilingualism is manifest during the shortest journey on the subway, where notices forbidding the traveller from walking between carriages through the connecting doors say, 'No use esta puerta', and advertisements for a brand of cigarettes say, 'Winston lo tiene todo', as well as coming in English versions. If you keep your ears open as you walk the streets, in an average stroll you will have picked up smatterings from half a dozen or more languages, which are no more than a token sample of New York's pentecostal range of tongues. Someone has reckoned that in the borough of Queens alone, well over a hundred nationalities have settled down together, each of them communicating among themselves at least part of the time in the speech of their ancestors. In the Roman Catholic diocese of Brooklyn, services are regularly held in twenty-six different languages, including such exotics as Chichewa (St Mary Gate of Heaven Church, Ozone Park), Creole (at fourteen different churches), Armenian (Our Lady of Mercy, Forest Hills), Old Slavonic (St Mary's Chapel, Brooklyn) and Maltese (in five widespread congregations). There are said to be sixty foreign-language newspapers printed in this city; but as there are also said to be no fewer than eleven different

---

* The figure does not take account of illegal immigrants in New York, estimated at between 450,000 and 550,000.

papers published in Chinese dialects, the first figure may be, if anything, an underestimate. Beyond dispute is New York's pre-eminence as a latter-day Tower of Babel. There cannot possibly be anywhere else with such a linguistic variety as this.

Nor can there be many places, even in a land as dedicated to eating as the United States, where the general awareness of foods originating in other countries is as high as it is in New York. There are junior stenographers here who can steer you deftly through the intricacies of one ethnic menu after another, picking and choosing with unerring taste buds between the various merits of *sushi* from Japan, *cacciucco* from Italy, *ajweh* from Syria, *dien hsin* from China, *palacinky* from Czechoslovakia, *koenigsberger klopse* from Germany, *kokoretsi* from Greece, *fatanyeros* from Hungary and *gravad lax* from Sweden, not to mention *bhelpuri* from Bombay, *bacalaoito* from San Juan, *solyanka* from Moscow, *feijoado* from Rio de Janeiro and *knaidlich*, which issued from every Jewish ghetto between the Urals and the Rhine. The reason why a kid from Brooklyn can have acquired such a sophisticated palate as that, though she may never have been farther afield than Niagara Falls, and probably thinks that New Zealand is as Australian as Tasmania, is perfectly simple in the all-embracing circumstances of this city: her friendships since schooldays have spanned a score of national origins, and they have involved an expanding process of discovery and experiment in each other's favourite eating places, as well as in each other's homes, where parents will have one or two of the old recipes ready and willing to be wheeled out whenever somebody hungry drops by. You can not only eat your way through, conceivably, every dish known to mankind in the restaurants of New York. In its delicatessens, its greengroceries, its other food stores, you can patiently track down every ingredient, every comestible, every delicacy that has sustained, nourished, or merely pleasured the gastric system of every race and creed. As a monument to this aspect of New York's internationalism, there is nothing more breathtaking than Zabar's emporium, where Broadway rises through 80th Street on the West Side. It is one of those establishments that only America seems to produce (L. L. Bean's incomparable store for the Great Outdoorsman up in Maine is another such), which prides itself upon quality, for sure, but even more upon its inexhaustibility: it challenges the customer to ask for something it hasn't got! At Zabar's an upper floor appears to be stocked with every kitchen appliance invented since the pestle and mortar; but it is the ground floor that is designed to make the mouth water most. Here are coffees and breads and sausages and caviars and smoked fishes promoting hunger on the spot, merely with the fragrance they release. And here are cheeses, which have apparently been fetched from every dairy in Europe and even beyond. On a single day there can easily be in that cheese department – as well as truckles from Italy, Holland, Greece, Germany, Finland, Britain, Denmark, Canada, Norway, Sweden, Switzerland, Bulgaria, Belgium, Australia and Argentina – no fewer than 142 different varieties of cheese from France. Imported they may have been, but the taste for them has mostly been acquired right here in New York.

The French, as it happens, form one of the smaller European colonies of New York; unexpectedly, when one considers the strong historic links between their country and the United States. A thin trickle can be traced, like many others in this city's cosmopolitan bloodstream, to the very beginnings here 300 years ago. But the first sizeable transfusion did not occur until after the First World War, when the Michelin Tyre Company imported a workforce from France to run the factory it had just built in New Jersey. At about the same time, a number of self-improvers were working their passage across the Atlantic on the French Line boats, and staying in the city to find what work they could after the liners had docked at the West Side piers. As often as not, the work they found was in the catering business, which has always been well-stocked with French: it is said that there is a small town in Brittany largely populated by ex-restaurant owners from New York. After the Second World War, just as large numbers of young Americans went in search of cultural stimulus in Europe, so quantities of young French followed the well-beaten path to the economic opportunities of New York, again mostly in the hotel and restaurant trade; until that alteration in immigration procedures, which opened new prospects for would-be immigrants who had generally been discouraged because of their race, simultaneously closed many traditionally open doors to Europeans who had nothing much to offer America but their youth, their energy and – if they were French – their charm. The French colony then remained static until a few years ago, when (at about the time Perrier water began to displace all rivals as the smart non-alcoholic tipple in Manhattan) Messieurs Mitterrand and Fabius began to strike terror in the heart of every instinctive capitalist on both sides of the Atlantic, with their vision of a far-from-communist France: 1981 is generally held to be the year in which an increasing number of French entrepreneurs, with their supporting cast of rising young French executives, switched their enterprises to where they would be more leniently taxed, beside the Hudson. What characterises almost all the French in New York, therefore, whether their daily labour consists in waiting on table at La Mirabelle, La Petite Marmite and a score of other fashionable eateries, or in doing deals at the Crédit Lyonnais, at Pechiney World Trade or other enterprises scattered near Wall Street, is that by and large they circulate only where the big money is.

Other small colonies take the city pretty much as it comes at street level, even when their inhabitants have arrived with superior qualifications. By 1977, more than half the interns and resident doctors staffing the municipal hospitals of New York, had come to them after training in India and Korea, though immigrants from those parts of Asia are much more familiar to New Yorkers in more humdrum contexts. It has been an observable fact in recent years that the vast majority of news stands in Manhattan are manned by Indians who, apart from any other such positions they may hold, have obtained the concessions to 80 per cent of the stands in the gift of the Metropolitan Transportation Authority. If you surface from the B, the D or the F train at 42nd Street, it is a bewhiskered Sikh who will readily supply you with anything from the *Times* to a girlie magazine in the lee of the Public Library; while, just a block or two away, a young couple from Gujarat preside over everything that American journalism can contrive to catch the eye of the traveller hurrying through the frenzied concourse of Grand Central Station. As for the Koreans, they have transformed the city's greengrocery trade over the past few years, so successfully that they now run most of the shops in New York (950 out of 1,100 according to the Korean Produce Association). There is scarcely a block in Manhattan nowadays without premises where the rows of tomatoes and icebergs, carrots and green beans, apples and grapes and melons and the rest are presented in rank upon rank so immaculately that it seems a shame to disturb them for the purposes of trade. Almost always, in the centre of the floor are the manifold compartments of an extended salad bowl, the ultimate in convenience foods for single people who drop by on their way to the office, where they will breakfast at their desk, and pop in on their way home from work, too whacked even to make themselves a meal by then, and always too conscious of calories to eat anything heartier than this on – as they will say – a day-to-day basis. Those salad bowls in the greengrocery were an inspiration, given the workaday schedules and the everyday phobias of New York. The Koreans sprinkling water over the produce at frequent intervals to keep it good and fresh, and the Koreans with their shops still open through most hours of the day and night . . . well, these are just Oriental habits of taking pains and diligence, which still estrange them from many people in New York and elsewhere in the western world.

They and the Indians are not the only new New Yorkers who seem to have cornered some aspect of the city's commerce. There is a deposit of Albanians at Bedford Park up in the Bronx, almost all of whom earn their daily bread by managing apartments. In those workshops of the Garment District in Manhattan which specialise in millinery, the chances are that the young women cutting and stitching and deftly shaping the hats came here not so long ago from the Dominican Republic. There is a Greek colony so thoroughly Hellenicised that it is known far beyond Queens as Little Athens, where people pursue every trade and vocation they might do were they still living in the shadow of the Acropolis, as Greeks have since they began to arrive in New York a hundred years ago. Outside their own neighbourhoods they have something of a monopoly in selling hot food on the streets, which is one of the most characteristic forms of enterprise in New York. Up and down and crosstown in Manhattan, on almost every street corner, mobile stalls fume away in a devilishly tempting aroma which says be damned to the waistline and enjoy a fresh bagel or knish, or a bag of roast chestnuts, or a steaming hot frank (and most New Yorkers do).

The likelihood is that the fellow drumming up trade with his sing-song chant, is a second or third generation young Greek from Astoria who, as is the custom among local males, doubtless spends much of his off-duty time at the Lefkos Pirgos *kaffenion* or some such establishment, putting the world to rights with cronies over thick, black, bitter coffee. In due course they will conclude, as generation upon generation of migrants to this city have, that there are many worse places to be than this; many more. It is known for a refugee to find haven here from some benighted place and then to be slowly crushed by the often brutal push and shove, the sometimes overwhelmingly cruel indifference of democratic New York; like Conrado Mones, biology teacher and fugitive from Castro's Cuba, who found himself so at odds with everybody else's Big Apple that, one despairing day in 1982, he climbed over a safety fence at Central Park Zoo, where a polar bear obligingly mauled him to death. But many more people, after they have got through the bewildering, struggling first few years, find themselves in the buoyant position of the Medvedevs. He was an engineer, she a hairdresser, when they came to New York from Leningrad in 1974. For a decade they worked together in small restaurants until they had enough capital to buy an old Italian food shop in Brooklyn; with which prosperity beckoned at last. 'Here,' Dimitri Medvedev told a newspaperman one day, 'they give a man a chance to grow up – like trees put out leaves. Now, after ten years, I'm the boss. Only America can make people like that.'

It was a predictable remark, though such people are not always predictable. On the corner of Brooklyn which contains Coney Island there is also Brighton Beach, which has been colonised in recent years by many migrants from the Soviet Union, so thickly that it is now known throughout the city as Little Odessa-by-the-Sea. Here you will not normally hear

English spoken unless you yourself invite it, and without much effort you could imagine yourself in some resort along the Black Sea coast – though *Pravda* is not among the newspapers printed in Cyrillic script and readily available here. There is a restaurant on an upper floor, as big as a ballroom, which does a roaring trade every Saturday night, when entire families turn up to celebrate another week in the promised land. And so Russian are they still that, although their clothes are new, obviously their party dresses and suits, they are cut old-fashioned to the western eye, maybe twenty-five years behind our stylish times. The place is packed by mid-evening, the customers mostly seated round long tables, as if they were guests at some wedding feast. And there they set to with a will, as one dish after another is served up: *borscht*, of course, and stews steaming with the fragrance of thyme and coriander, and pasta packed with spinach, dripping with sour cream, and curd cheese dumplings to keep raw hunger at bay, and pancakes oozing cherry and apple, honey and more cream, and much, much more of everything if that's not enough. Meanwhile the sweet red wines of Georgia circulate (favourites of the unlamented Stalin though they were), the vodka even more; and this is not in any of the brands we are accustomed to in the west, but *pshenichnaya* which, as any Muscovite will tell you, is the only vodka for the connoisseur.

People break off from their meals from time to time and begin to dance between one course and the next, or even in mid-plateful. A space has been left for dancing beside a small stage on which musicians with balalaikas and accordions play. For an hour or two it is utterly Russian out there in music and dance, wild and mournful by turns, but always unmistakably instinct with and belonging to the Slavonic east. Only later does something happen that defies expectation, that turns an assumption about refugees upside down. They have started in nostalgic mood, remembering and relishing their past. But as the good food and the strong liquor has gone down, as inhibition has been loosed, so the music has changed, the balalaikas on that stage have been cast aside. Come midnight, and all those Russians in Little Odessa-by-the-Sea are hugging to music like Americans of quite some time ago, while the Glenn Miller sound is drugging the room from some immortal tape. Which is the reverse of what one might have supposed.

Among the older New Yorkers, the Germans have become curiously the least distinct, their thumping enthusiasm when the Steuben Day parade comes round being untypical of their general demeanour these days. It has been remarked on before now that there is no German vote, as there most certainly is an Irish vote, an Italian vote, a Jewish vote in New York; that the two Robert Wagners, father and son, are still the only notable politicians with German roots this city has known since Carl Schurz retired here from Washington in 1881 and eventually had a riverside park named after him to signify his illustrious career; that although Germans are to be found in every part of the metropolis, at every level of its life, they hardly ever function as a cohesive group. The argument goes that all this follows from their integration into the WASP conglomerate (together with Britishers and Dutch) since those years in the nineteenth century when they formed one-third of the city's population, and came second only to the Irish as the biggest single community with a recognisable profile. More plausibly, perhaps, they may instinctively have tried to be inconspicuous after the disconcerting experience since then of being associated by their neighbours with the enemy in two world wars, though many a Schmidt and Wolff who fell at Belleau Wood in 1918, as in the Ardennes twenty-six years later, were boys from Yorkville on Manhattan's East Side.

The Irish, by contrast, have never been ones for keeping their heads down. And this is, after all, the most dignified response a people can make when they shake off an alien oppression and hardship by uprooting themselves, but then find that in the Utopia across the ocean they face just as much prejudice as before; which was the case when the first Irish came to New York. A local repercussion of England's Glorious Revolution of 1688 (in which the Protestant Dutchman, Prince William of Orange, took James II's throne by popular request in a bloodless coup) was that Catholics in New York were disfranchised, a disability that would not be fully repaired until some time after the American Revolution had been won. By then the former colonists, brimming with self-confidence and perhaps pardonably smug in their triumph over the English tyranny, were building beside the Hudson the very model of a democratic city – quietly growing, steadily prospering, owing nothing, fearing God and no man. They were achieving a largely Protestant vision of the heart's desire. It was as bigoted as anyone else's, and it was to be sorely disturbed when the Irish they had only just come to terms with were joined by the hordes of refugees in flight from the Industrial Revolution, the potato famine and other ills. In the anti-Catholic, anti-Irish feeling that was galvanised by the arrival of poverty-stricken thousands landing from the trans-Atlantic vessels, there arose some odious organisations dedicated to 'the elimination of all foreigners and Roman Catholics from public office, the establishment of a twenty-one-year naturalisation period for all aliens, the deportation of foreign paupers and criminals, Bible-reading in the public schools, and the preservation of Protestant domination in all areas of public life'. That ambition belonged to the Order of Free and Accepted Americans, otherwise known as the Wide Awakes, who had been spawned in New York by an equally rebarbative outfit founded in 1853 as the Order of the Star-Spangled Banner, whose alias was the Know-Nothings. On such long-since defunct specimens as these is a suspicion of WASPs still partly based today.

The Society of St Tammany, or Columbian Order, was also mostly a creature of the WASPs, and one of growing power. Launched in 1789 in the wake of similar societies in Pennsylvania, Virginia and New Jersey, it took its principal name from a mythical chief of American Indians and was as bizarre as Freemasonry in some of its rituals (ranks of sachems, sagamores and wiskinkies adopted the French Revolutionary bonnet for their more solemn ceremonies). Starting as a straightforwardly nationalist society, it swiftly moved to the narrower interests of the New York Democratic Party, which its members founded. By the 1860s, Tammany had fallen into the hands of William March Tweed ('Boss Tweed . . . the last vulgar white Protestant to win a prominent place in the city's life'), a political manipulator of legendary corruption who defrauded the city of $75 million or even more, but who was finally nailed in 1873 by a jury which found him guilty on 204 out of 220 counts. The indictment which put Tweed behind bars was effectively the proclamation of Catholic Irish ascendancy in Tammany, which meant control of the Democratic Party machine within a few more years. Even before the tidal wave of Irish immigration had rolled ashore in the middle of the century, the vote of Irish New Yorkers had been significant in city elections. Afterwards it became all-important. From being the victimised newcomers, they transformed themselves into political bossmen and obedient political cohorts who were not squeamish about the methods used to achieve political ends. They had given everyone else some taste of their mettle in 1863, when they led and formed the mobs which rioted against the Civil War recruitment draft into the Union Army, a pandemonium which lasted three days, saw much property burned down, and left maybe a thousand people dead or injured.

The Irish control of Tammany was to last until after the Second World War, their heyday in the more general life of New York being a little shorter, spanning the years between Tweed's departure, and the day in 1932 when Mayor Jimmy Walker – another scandalous Tammany figure, but an engaging and well-liked one – resigned his office after an incriminating enquiry into the municipal finances, and went into European exile with his English mistress. During that period, the Irish had managed the remarkable feat of simultaneously running the dominant political party of New York, its police force, part of its underworld, and its Roman Catholic Church. The Irish grip on the police was so unshakeable for decades that Italians, Jews, Protestants, Puerto Ricans and Poles in the force organised societies to protect their various interests, and it was not until 1952 that the Irish cops felt so similarly insecure that they started their Emerald Society with the same purpose as the rest. Yet, a generation before that, while the Lower East Side of Manhattan was the province of Italian and Jewish criminal gangs, the West Side was controlled by Irish mobsters like the Gophers and the Hudson Dusters, who began as teenage thieves working the railroad freight yards and the shipping wharves, before maturing into fully-fledged burglars and armed robbers. Meanwhile, a succession of Irish priests were building the Archdiocese of New York into one of the most powerful political instruments in the United States, as well as a corporation of impressive and mounting wealth: doing so on foundations laid in the 1840s and after by the city's first Archbishop, John Joseph Hughes, a great fund-raiser who has been described as 'an aggressive prelate not too particular about his methods' (he waited until the Draft mobs had almost exhausted themselves, and had lynched many blacks, before 'he gently recommended to the rioters that they might be better off at home').

The Irish still maintain their hold on the Church in New York, in spite of the fact that some time ago they became a minority of the city's Roman Catholic population, and a diminishing one at that. Archbishop O'Connor and his two secretaries in 1985 were Irish, as were seven of the nine priests associated with St Patrick's Cathedral, and five of the seven auxiliary bishops of New York. They were the seniors in an archdiocese which has not noticeably taken a liberal line on any of the issues that have exercised the Catholic world since Pius XII departed this life, the New York hierarchy's support for Senator Joseph McCarthy in the 1950s being fairly typical of its continuing outlook, dutifully imitated by the New York Irish in general.* Far from being the under-privileged labouring class they were when they first came to New York, the Irish are indistinguishable in status from any other long-established group. They are as well represented on the Stock Exchange as anyone, and better than most, and one of the biggest savings banks in America (the Emigrant) is an Irish holding that owes its foundation to the mercenary promptings of Archbishop Hughes. Irishmen are plentifully spread across the entire range of New York law firms (which is power indeed) and although the New York Police Department is no longer an Irish fiefdom, most of the senior officers are said to be as Irish as ever. After the awful hardships of their early years in New York the

---

* The archdiocese continues to accrue wealth at impressive rates. It is reckoned to be the largest owner of real estate in the city; and it has been noted that in 1985, when its stock and holdings were computed at $386 million, its church collections on Sundays and holy days realised another $55,122,058.

Irish, in short, have made it, as completely and respectably and powerfully as any refugee peoples can. Without their presence this past two centuries and more, the city today would be a rather different place. Yet a New York Irishman has said (a little cruelly, perhaps) that the most visible Irish contribution to New York has been the saloon bar.

The leadership at Tammany Hall was lost by the Irish to the Italians, who were insignificant in the organisation until about the time America entered the Second World War, when funds were in short supply from every source except the Italian crime syndicates, who were happy to put their surplus dollars into what might reasonably be regarded as a lucrative investment; the most powerful centre of patronage adjacent to city government, with infinite plunder in prospect for those controlling it. The Irish being without the resources to withstand the takeover, 1949 saw Carmine De Sapio become the first Italian Tammany boss, ready and willing to fulfil the hopes entertained of him; eventually to be imprisoned – not too stiffly – for offering bribes. His punishment would have been much more severe had another Italian, lately retired from high office and dead just before De Sapio was installed, had anything to do with it. That was Fiorello Henry LaGuardia, who was remarkable in many things – a Protestant (not a Catholic) Italian with a Jewish mother, a former Ellis Island interpreter in half a dozen languages, a First World War flyer, a lovable eccentric with a mania for following fire engines about the city – and conceivably the straightest Mayor New York is ever likely to know.

The bugbear of the Irish masses in the nineteenth century had been the WASPs; but much worse was the plight of the Italians arriving just after them, who were exploited by other Italians, very often from their own villages back home. These were the *padroni*, the fellows a bit smarter, more commanding, more ruthless than the rest; the ones who picked up before anyone else enough English to parley with the employer, the semi-literates among dumb illiterates. They were merciless in abusing their compatriots, swindling them of their money, deceiving them about their job prospects, posing all the while as their best friends in the strange land. The mass of Italian immigrants were ripe for this plucking, especially by men whose families had been virtually kin of their own from the beginning of time (they should have remembered better than they did the treacheries that have always disfigured Sicily and other places in the south); they were peasants who had been bred to understand, as well as they understood anything, that the humble worker must always submit to the *prominenti* of his community, those who inherit or assume leadership in any form. This was a reflex mostly unchallenged until LaGuardia – then a Congressman from East Harlem – and one or two like-minded people, themselves became *prominenti* after the First World War. But it is still a powerful instinct in the Italian community, which goes far to explain the hold the Mafia has maintained in the city for well over half a century now. It may also explain why the working class Italians of New York, strong supporters of Franklin Roosevelt during his first Presidential term, became bitterly hostile after his condemnation of Mussolini's attack on France in 1940.

It is possible that one of these days the same power struggle that occurred in Tammany Hall forty years ago will be re-enacted in the hinterland of St Patrick's Cathedral, much more decorously, of course; though, if so, the dominant Irish of today will be challenged not only by their Italian brethren but by the swelling army of Spanish-speaking Catholics as well. Nothing is more puzzling to the stranger – or even to the New Yorker outside the Catholic community – than the information that religious observance among Catholic Italians was weak until the 1940s. It is put down to the poor quality of Italian priests during the early days in New York, to many Italians ignoring the sacraments, to increasing abandonment of the Church altogether by more than one generation of young men who crossed the Atlantic without their families. There was also, before the First World War, a contingent of Italian Protestants vigorously proselytising their fellow citizens here. As an Italian middle class rose out of the sweated labour that fashioned the New York superstructure early in the twentieth century, however, and most especially as America in general after 1945 concluded that religion was a moral weapon in the cold war, as well as a bankable commodity at home, so there was a return to the old faith in the Italian suburbs of New York. The remaining hindrance is in the priesthood, where the continuing dominance of Irishmen and relative shortage of Italians is said to be chiefly the result of a different tradition of masculinity: the Irish male in the old country was conditioned to celibacy often until he was past caring very much, because of peasant attitudes to inheritance and marriage; the southern Italian especially regards his sexual appetite as something to be satisfied at all costs from the moment puberty has struck.

Those Italian suburbs have remained rather more static than most patches of ethnic turf. In a city of phenomenal mobility, where individuals and even groups of people with a common background are for ever packing up in one area and moving away to another, the Italians have seemed reluctant to budge except under what they perceive to be social pressure from blacks. Twenty years ago it was noted that, 'While the Jewish map of New York City in 1920 bears almost no relation to that in 1961, the Italian districts, though weakened in some cases and strengthened in others, are still in large measure where they were.' The situation has changed very little since then. The generations have stuck together, which will have a lot to do with it, so that when a migration to some other part of the city has taken place, it can easily have involved anything up to great-grandparents in the move. Clannishness and its corollary, suspicion of strangers, have remained as high in the brick row streets of Canarsie and Bensonhurst as ever it has been in those intricate stone villages that punctuate the hillsides above Palermo and Termini. It is almost tactile between Broadway and the Bowery, above Canal Street and below Prince, in the oldest Italian quarter of New York.

Here, in Little Italy, a feeling of nostalgia and bravura, domesticity and a sense of doom intermingle quite startlingly at times. Here are fire hydrants vivid with the national colours of red, white and green. Here are families pausing for *cappuccino* and *granita* at Ferrara's, on the way home from visiting relations, no doubt – and so many women are clad in black. Here are the same tenements where, after thrilling the WASP-ish patrons of opera at the Met, Enrico Caruso would join his familiars for

late-night poker and *scopa* in some Neapolitan café-club. Here is
Umberto's Clam House, with dark-windowed limousines drawn
up ominously along Mulberry Street, just as they probably were
the night in 1972 when Joey Gallo dropped by with his wife and
step-daughter to celebrate his forty-third birthday, and was shot
dead at the table as he ate.

Little Italy will be almost as self-contained as any of those
antique villages up in the Sicilian hills, its menfolk between
them able to build anything, fix anything, do anything that can
be done with a craftsman's pair of hands, its women capable of
managing everything else, including each other's childbirths if an
emergency occurs. More widely, the Italians of New York are
said almost to monopolise the removal business in this mobile
place, and to hold the whip hand in the disposal of the city's
garbage – all 22,000 tons of it every day. Yet if there is such a
thing as an Italian stereotype in New York, it is that of the family
running a food shop of some sort, with the man and his daughter
serving up front, the wife busy making pasta or something else
for sale in a kitchen at the back.

All the national quirks and national flavours that make New
York such a magnificent human pastiche – with more Irish than
there are in Dublin, more Italians than in Florence, more Jews
than in Tel Aviv, and all the rest – have stayed as distinctive
as they are because intermarriage has been a strangely slow
process here. The bride and groom in such a union still often
risk the ostracism of one or the other group for the supposed
betrayal of an ideal. The Catholic Church provided the most
fruitful common ground in the middle of the nineteenth century,
when Irish and Germans of that confession began to wed, but
the rivalry between Irish and Italians made their intermarriages
relatively rare until after the Second World War. Within the
Jewish community there is a similar inhibition between peoples of
a common faith but different nationality, an even bigger gap to be
crossed between observant and nonpractising Jews, comparable
to the Christian divide between Catholics and the rest. Biggest
of all, inevitably, has been the primitive restraint on matches
between the different races here, as everywhere else. Some
blacks and whites, some Gentiles and Jews, have risked the

snubs that would undoubtedly follow to greater or lesser degree and have married across the boundaries; but almost always they have been people from sophisticated levels of society, where racial and national distinctions are ignored as much as possible.

So frictions occur from time to time, and occasionally something worse than friction. Where Chinatown is beginning to expand into Little Italy, bringing a distinctly different style and outlook with it, an Italian response has been to mess up the Chinese characters on street signs by scribbling on them with felt-tip pens. More nastily, over in Canarsie, Italian vigilantes have threatened whites who have been prepared to sell their homes to black families. The New York Irish, who violently opposed the abolition of slavery in Abraham Lincoln's time, were observed conspicuously not supporting organisations promoting racial harmony in Jack Kennedy's. In 1968, a strike by most of the city's teachers closed the public schools for weeks, and in spite of the educational issues invoked it was started by mutual hostility between Jewish teachers and the black community in the Ocean Hill-Brownsville parts of Brooklyn. This was a reminder, if anyone needed one, that a boiling pot can be more painful than a useful image or a handy platitude.

The people who have come to stew in New York from all the corners of the earth can be characterised in almost as many different ways. Their sheer variety creates an excitement that no other city can match, and the stranger has to be a stubborn misanthrope to be indifferent to it. They have all manner of physiques and facial patterns, wondrous shades of colour and texture, contrasting kinds of vitality, diverse expressions of pleasure and melancholy, a multitude of emphases in speech and movement, assorted habits of looking at things, and many, many distinctive ways of saying what is on their mind. In their infinite difference, they give New York a lot of its zip. They also tend to have long memories and deep grudges, to sour their emetic sentimentality about both the present and the past. When General Jaruzelski came to the United Nations in 1985, the local Poles took out a half page ad in the *New York Times*, protesting against his visit. Even the mildest leader from the most inoffensive country in the world – the Prime Minister of Iceland, let us say – would be lucky to come here without finding at least a handful of New Yorkers held in check behind a police line, raging to settle some old score.

There is something offensive about lumping people together in groups for the sake of convenient identification, instead of regarding each one of them as an individual different from anybody else. But in New York above all places, so many groups insist on the collective identity. And there they are, any day of the week, sitting opposite the stranger on the Lex, as it buckets its way through the bowels of Manhattan. There's a Greek totting up some figures in that peculiar script, and a Puerto Rican from El Barrio up in the Bronx, and that WASP who just got in, with Harvard Law School written all over him, and an Irishman talking to a priest in the brogue of Bay Ridge, next to the old Jew studying the scripture for today, with two Italian ladies gossiping in the argot of the old south, while the guy reading that paper with yet more funny lettering must be a Russian from Brighton Beach, and there's this big black lady in a T-shirt ('SEX IS A MISDEMEANOUR,' it says. 'De more I miss de meaner I get') which has everybody else smiling or looking embarrassed while she stares straight ahead at the flickering tunnel wall . . .

What strikes you on the subway, with maybe a dozen different sub-species of our race in a row of twenty marvellously individual citizens, is not how badly they sometimes behave towards each other, but how remarkably well they get on with each other, by and large. New York has produced an untidy sort of *esprit de corps* among its people. And that is not a small thing.

FOUR

A NEW JERUSALEM

The people with the longest memories streamed over the bridge
that September day in 1985 in an epic from another age, and the
irrepressible thought was that it could have been something like
this at the crossing of the Red Sea. Here was a host of biblical
proportions, marching shoulder to shoulder, but with every man
and woman sticking to an individual pace, so that this awesome
mass of heads bobbled unevenly as it came curving down off the
bridge towards City Hall. The men were, without exception, clad
in heavy black suitings and wore black homburgs perched on top
of skullcaps, and even very young men scarcely in their teens
were dressed like this, which made them seem unusually grave
for their age. Many of them also wore prayer shawls, whose
tassels sometimes dangled from under their black coats. The
day was hot, so that by the time the multitude had crossed
the East River from Brooklyn, faces were shiny with sweat
and the sidelocks of the men and boys were dripping and
lank. The women in their summer dresses were better off,
but most of them were pushing tiny children in push-chairs,
which couldn't have been easy on such a determined march,
for such a distance, in such sticky weather as this. Scores
of children who were neither infant nor adolescent were the
lucky ones, for they crossed the bridge in a convoy of those
foursquare mustard-coloured buses which in America always
mean school. They had preceded the marchers, and the buses
also came with crates of soft drinks, which were dispensed to

all and sundry as the arriving crowds began to assemble on
Park Row. No detail had been overlooked in the organisation
of this event. Several days before, the leaders of these people
had given notice that they proposed to do this thing, and the
New York Police Department, ever obliging when significant
communities decide to demonstrate, had stopped traffic using
the eastbound carriageways of the Brooklyn Bridge for most
of the morning and part of the afternoon, to allow the epic
to take place as planned. These were the Hasidishe Yiden –
the Hasidic Jews – from Williamsburg and Crown Heights, and
they had an important and contentious matter weighing heavily
on their hearts and minds.

It arose from the city's perennial struggle to dispose of its
garbage, which comes in quantities that (like so many things
about New York) leave everywhere else far behind. In 1977
someone calculated that more trash was generated beside the
Hudson than in London, Paris and Tokyo combined, and matters
are unlikely to have changed much since then. In 1973, the
Commissioner of Sanitation wrote that unless the city spent a
lot of money wisely, that unless there was also 'a high degree
of political sophistication on the part of the public . . . we
are doomed to face an ecological nightmare of New York buried under its own garbage'. The city's traditional method of
refuse disposal has been to dump it in landfills, mostly on
an unattractive bit of Staten Island opposite New Jersey in
recent years; but by the end of the century there will be
no more room for garbage there, and nowhere else to dump
it. The solution the city produced was to build a 'resource
recovery plant' in the old Brooklyn Navy Yard, the first of five
that would eventually be constructed – one in each borough –
throughout New York. Henceforth garbage would be taken to a
mammoth incinerator and there burnt, producing in the process
much steam and electricity for sale to the Consolidated Edison
Company, which supplies New York with its energy. All well
and good, except that some experts claimed the incinerator
would expose neighbouring parts of Brooklyn to toxic fumes;
a worry that was reflected in the closeness of the vote taken
by the Board of Estimate at City Hall on whether or not to

build the Brooklyn plant. By six-five the board decided to go ahead – but only after the Borough President of Manhattan, Andrew J. Stein, had changed sides on the issue at the last moment. This was the matter which had brought forth the Hasidic community to demonstrate on this overheated day. The Brooklyn Navy Yard is just up the road from where they live.

Their organisers had parked a truck in front of the Municipal Building, turning it into a platform for speechmakers, with microphones and amplifiers so that what they had to say would be heard at long range. There was much need of these by the time the last of the marchers had come down off the bridge, the whole area between the Municipal Building and City Hall being packed with aggrieved folk. Old men with long grey beards were seated on the platform, and standing nearby were younger fellows, whose beards were shorter and black. It was a rebbe* who at last got up and began to address the multitude, explaining in tremulous and nasal periods why it was that they had assembled in that place. 'We are here today . . . in sweltering heat . . . crying out in anguish and fear . . . not only on behalf of our own lives . . . and-there's-nothing-wrong-with-that . . . not only for our community . . . and-there's-nothing-wrong-with-that . . . but for the whole city of New York.' A cry did go up then, not of anguish and fear, but heartily approving what the old man had said. 'Ay . . . Ay . . . Ay,' the people roared with one voice.

They did so in response to gestures made by one of the young fellows standing beside the old man. His arms urged them on, as though he was bringing a great orchestra to symphonic climax, his black coat flapping with his movement, his black homburg tilted on the back of his head. The old man sat down and another rebbe took his place, and this one made the first of some brutal thrusts that came from the platform that day. He recounted the chief elements in the plan for an incinerator in the Navy Yard, and then he said the unthinkable thing: 'Is this the Final Solution, Mr Mayor?'

* 'Rebbe' is the Hasidic rendering of rabbi.

That drove the young man into a frenzy of urging, with more roars of approval from the crowd. His other function was to utter a chant, which the crowd would then take up. At his prompting, 'Dump Koch! Dump Koch! Dump Koch!' they bayed, in the middle of the speech which concentrated their Hasidic anguish and fear on the Mayor of New York.

Yet another leader rose, and switched the attack to the man who had changed his mind during the decisive vote. He alleged that the Manhattan Borough President had once changed something else – his name, from the original Finkelstein. 'Andrew Stein has prostituted himself,' he shouted; then quickly put his hand over the microphone while he muttered something to the henchman with the energetic arms. Obediently the slogan was launched from the platform at once. 'Down with Stein! Down with Stein! Down with Stein!' screamed the young fellow hoarsely. The crowd took that one up, too, and roared it back with one imperious voice.

Not long after the speeches began, someone claimed that there were 20,000 of them there, and half an hour later someone else aired the notion that 40,000 were besieging the walls of City Hall. The exact numbers didn't matter, when there was so obviously an indignant multitude, which could not have failed to impress those who came to office windows in order to see what all the noise was about. It was about emotional blackmail, about mass intimidation of a remarkable kind; and the most remarkable thing of all was that it seemed in the end to be directed rather less at the potentially offensive – possibly even dangerous – Brooklyn incinerator, than at the performance of two city officials who also happened to be Jews. They were made the victims of a notoriously tortured cultural history, which was played upon most skilfully that blistering day in New York.

It was an extremity of the Jewish experience in the most Jewish city on earth. New York's claim to that title is founded well enough on head counting in the first place, for nowhere else can match its Jewish population of 1,118,800 – almost 16 per cent of the total – with another million Jews living in the immediate dormitory areas of Long Island, Westchester County and elsewhere.* From the day in 1654 when twenty-three migrants (whose ancestral roots were in Spain and Portugal) arrived from Brazil in the barque *St Charles*, a few months after Jacob Barsimon had stepped ashore from Holland, this city has been an unfailing refuge for the people whose immediate destiny has far too often been refugee. The growth was steady but unspectacular for well over two centuries, so that even in 1880 there were no more than 80,000 Jews in the city, mostly from Germany, Austria, Hungary and Bohemia. The great exodus from the Czar's domains meant that by 1910 this figure had swollen to 1,250,000, a population which by all accounts has not varied much in the twentieth century, though it has periodically been supplemented by fresh waves of immigration, to offset those New Yorkers who have migrated to Israel and elsewhere in the past four decades. Perhaps the most arresting calculation was made a few years ago: 'The Jewish population of metropolitan New York constitutes one out of every five Jews in the entire world.'

Yet New York's intensely Jewish status is much more than a merely statistical one: it is to do with flavour, with outlook, with commitments, with influence, with the deep impression that generations of Jews have left on the community as a whole at almost every level. Nathan Glazer has memorably written that 'never in the Diaspora have Jews wielded such weight and power in a great city', and the *Encyclopaedia Judaica* has amplified this with a view of the relationship from both ends:

It is doubtful indeed if anywhere else in the history of the Diaspora has a large Jewish community existed in so harmonious a symbiosis with a great metropolis without either ghettoising itself from its surroundings or losing its own distinct sense of character and identity. Nor can the relationship

* These figures are unofficial. It has been pointed out that while certain Jewish organisations have resisted attempts to include questions about religion in the US census, others 'have developed techniques for estimating the Jewish population'. In 1979 it was claimed that about one quarter of New York City's population was Jewish. The population of Tel Aviv in the 1980 Israeli census was 1,005,000; that of Jerusalem was 448,200.

be thought of as having been merely one-way. If the Jews gave to New York unstintingly of their experience, energies and talents, they received in return an education in urbanity and a degree of cosmopolitan sophistication unknown to any other Jewish community of similar size in the past. It is little wonder that many Jews developed an attachment to New York that bordered on the devotional. Above all, when the 20th century New York Jews thought of the city they lived in, they did not simply consider it a great capital of civilisation that had generously taken them in; rather, they thought of themselves – and with every justification – as joint builders of this greatness and one of its main continuing supports.

The encyclopaedia's use of the historical past tense is of more than grammatical interest: here is a measured pronouncement intended for inclusion among posterity's lasting judgements.

The symbiosis was not easily achieved, for New York, too, has been stained with mankind's most pernicious disease. Racial discrimination does not appear to have been directed much against local Jews as long as their numbers were relatively small, but by the last quarter of the nineteenth century they had begun to find that various social clubs in the city, much frequented by prospering businessmen, had become unavailable to them. Anti-Semitism at that level took its most grotesque form when Jews were excluded from holding private boxes at the Metropolitan Opera, a ban which applied to the banker, Otto Kahn, as much as to anyone until the Met relented and allowed him a box in 1917, though he had been a director of the opera company for fourteen years by then, responsible for bringing both Mahler and Toscanini to conduct in New York. Discrimination in the city reached its most pervasive heights in the next couple of decades, and played its part in the 1934 contest for Mayor. Hitler's theories had begun to seep across the Atlantic and caused Nathan Straus, a prominent merchant (the family business was Macy's) and former state senator, to decline the mayoral nomination (though it was urged on him by an impressive coalition of Jews and Gentiles, ranging from John Foster Dulles to Jacob Javits, and Ira Gershwin to Alexander

Woollcott) on the grounds that, with Herbert Lehman already seated in the Governor of New York's chair, a second Jew in high political office might offer too much ammunition to the already hostile; so the coalition hoisted Fiorello LaGuardia instead.

Until America was trundled into the war against Hitler by the Japanese attack on Pearl Harbor, it was accepted as an axiom in the Jewish community that employment in engineering or the big corporations would be almost unobtainable. Even in the city's intellectual circles – where Jews have probably met less discrimination than anywhere else over the years – a number felt so insecure that they changed their name for camouflage; like Ivan Greenbaum, who started to call himself Philip Rahv.* A member of Lionel Trilling's class at Columbia University, hoping for a teaching job there after graduation, was told that, 'we have room for only one Jew and we have chosen Mr Trilling'. Trilling himself once said that his post at Columbia 'was pretty openly regarded as an experiment, and for some time my career in the College was complicated by my being Jewish'. A network of state and federal legislation enacted in the past generation has effectively stopped racial discrimination in education and employment since, but anti-Semitism has not exactly vanished as a result: not when the more disreputable Italians are heard to mutter, '*Mazzacristi*!' – Christ-killers – under their breath; and not when some of the posher WASP clubs are still painstakingly without Jewish members – which is what any Jew in the city will tell you, what he believes.

A measurement of Jewish power and influence in this city, however, is that few people would nowadays dare to voice hostility out loud, except in particular instances of friction between Jews and blacks; and this turn of events has a great deal to do with a quite recent Jewish response to their past, and especially to their sufferings in the Nazi death camps. Although the Middle East was the place where the Jew rejected his historic role as everybody's victim, and chose to fight back aggressively at last, New York is where he was armed for that fight; where he has

---

* A rather thin camouflage in this case. A Rav in Hebrew is a religious leader and teacher in the grand tradition.

been spurred on most sharply, where the propaganda has been made most assiduously, where the fighting funds have been raised most substantially, where the most deeply entrenched positions have been dug, including those in Israel itself. This has been the home of every major Jewish organisation in America, worthy and unworthy, like the Jewish Defense League, which originated the slogan 'Never Again!' and which at various times in recent years has bombed Arab shops in Brooklyn, tear-gassed an audience watching ballet in Manhattan, and exported to Israel the appalling Rabbi Meir Kahane, whose personal slogan in his New York period was 'A .22 for every Jew', and whom some Israelis regard as a one-man insurance against peace in their part of the world. It is an age since the American Jewish Committee in 1935 opposed the establishment of a Jewish state in Palestine, because it feared that by giving its support it would be suspected of disloyalty to America.* Things have changed so much in the meantime that it now sometimes seems as if Israel was created in order to be reduced, at some convenient moment for American domestic purposes, to a sixth borough of New York. If you listen to someone like Norman Podhoretz – editor of *Commentary* and ideological scoutmaster to the Reagan administration – you may be forgiven for concluding at times that Israel is being used as a stalking horse in some unimportant acrimony belonging exclusively to the Upper East Side, which is about 5,000 comfortable miles away from the real firing line.

It was convincingly argued a few years ago that there are two Jewish communities in New York, not always or even very often seeing eye to eye any more. One is of those who have become

---

*It is also an age since Jewish writers on *Partisan Review*, like Clement Greenberg and Philip Rahv (who founded the magazine), strongly opposed America's entry into the Second World War. As early as the Munich crisis of 1938, Rahv was writing that radical intellectuals on their side of the Atlantic had no business taking sides in 'this contest of national imperialisms'. Twelve months later he observed that, 'the more the allies are exhausted by this war, the better for the interests of American capitalism.' A recent study of Rahv and his circle has noted that, 'it is remarkable how rarely the pages of *Partisan Review* and the various other writings of the New York Intellectuals contained references in the late 1930s to the persecution of the Jews.'

assimilated into the community at large, prospering in varying degrees, liberal in their political and social attitudes, sometimes treating their own Jewishness casually – until they hear the anti-Semitic remark. The other Jewish population (styled 'ethnic' in this argument) consists of those to whom Jewishness is the overriding factor in life, who see everything in strictly Jewish terms, whose very first question will always be, 'Is it good for the Jews?' when any policy is announced by city, state or republic; who quite deliberately do not integrate themselves into the wider community of New York, seeing it as a sacred duty to keep the faith as in olden times, and to maintain the purity of the race in a desperately polluted world. 'As a generalisation, the ethnic Jews are older, more Orthodox in religion, more conservative in politics, and poorer than the non-ethnics.'*

That sentence was written in 1973, but it might just as well have served to describe the Jewish migrants who started to arrive at Ellis Island a century ago in the great exodus from central and eastern Europe, many of whose descendants now constitute a large proportion of the assimilated Jewish population in New York. If we study photographs taken along Hester Street and adjacent parts of the Lower East Side in the 1890s and 1900s, we are seeing an area so thoroughly Jewish that it was known throughout the city as 'The Ghetto'. The Irish, the Italians and many other nationalities also had their start in New York here, of course; it was close to the landing stages where all new arrivals got off the boats ferrying them from the immigration station, handy with cheap lodgings for the first few nights that often became an extended stay. But the shop signs in Yiddish along those narrow and crowded streets reveal whose patch it mostly was in that generation of hope. The crowds of people shuffling slowly along are buying, or wondering whether to buy, things from other folk whose wares are spread out on push-carts. Sometimes these contain fruit or other food, but as often as not they are piled with bits of clothing, or materials that could be

* In the course of this argument, it was acknowledged that there are 'tens of thousands of Jews who do not fit into this pattern, Jews who exhibit both ethnic and assimilative tendencies'.

made into clothes. This was the way a lot of Jews made their first American living, by pushing carts full of buttons and bows and the like. This was the fresh start that might lead to better things in the New World, as it did for Sender Jarmulowsky, who peddled piece goods on Hester Street so successfully that by 1895 he was able to open his own bank on the corner of Canal Street and Orchard.

Behind the crowds and the pushcarts in the old pictures are the everlasting (many of them are still there, at any rate) brick tenements of the Lower East Side, with their fire escapes clinging to the street fronts like some form of creeper unknown to horticulture anywhere else. They used to be known as 'dumb-bell tenements' because that was the floor plan right through five or six storeys, narrowed at the stairwell in the middle of the building to admit a little light and air. They were crude, dark and foetid places none the less – every expanding city in the western world was throwing up dwellings like them for their working masses at about this time – without hot water and with minimal facilities of any kind. Ten people might very well share one damp room, which meant that tuberculosis and other pulmonary diseases were rife: which is why these streets were disparagingly referred to as 'lung blocks'. They very often housed the sweatshops that Jacob Riis described in *How the Other Half Lives*, which came as a disconcerting revelation to the New York well-to-do:

> Five men and a woman, two young girls, not fifteen, and a boy who says unasked that he is 'fifteen' and lies in saying it, are at the machines sewing knickerbockers, 'knee-pants' in the Ludlow Street dialect. The floor is littered ankle-deep with half-sewn garments. In the alcove, on a couch of many dozens of 'pants' ready for the finisher, a bare-legged baby with pinched face is asleep. A fence of piled-up clothing keeps him from rolling off on the floor. The faces, hands and arms to the elbows of everyone in the room are black with the color of the cloth on which they are working.

Not every Jew was destined to rise above this subsistence with one leap like Sender Jarmulowsky. For many the way ahead was by organising better conditions in the work they thought themselves lucky to have, and nothing came more readily to men and women whose thinking was partly moulded by the same European socialism that Germans were now teaching in Faulhaber's Hall on Second Avenue. The Jewish equivalent of that Free Workers' School was the *Arbiter Ring*, the Work-men's Circle, which not only provided Yiddish schools, but laid on cultural activities and even insurance benefits (it shared a building on East Broadway with the *Jewish Daily Forward*, which was notable for its socialism and for its Yiddish agony column, entitled 'A Bintel Brief' – a bundle of letters). The great New York tradition of Jewish leadership and representation in the labour unions began with the amalgamation of several small groups into the United Hebrew Trades in 1888, and was then reinforced mightily by the formation of the Ladies Garment Workers' Union in 1900, the International Fur Workers' Union in 1904, and the Amalgamated Clothing Workers of America in 1914.

At the same time the Jews of New York were revealing one of the most notable characteristics of their people everywhere; an appetite for education. More specifically, 'Eastern European Jews showed almost from the beginning of their arrival in this country a passion for education that was unique in American history.' The same WASP hostility that excluded them from boxes at the opera and clubs off Fifth Avenue, also kept them for a long time out of the older educational establishments, as Lionel Trilling's friend discovered (and medical schools were particularly hard to get into if you were a Jew). But up on 138th Street, City College had stood since 1849 by the principle of teaching any pupil who could pass its entrance examinations, whatever his parents' creed, whether they had money or not. The aspiring Jewish families on the Lower East Side fell upon it like manna, so that by the turn of the century their youth formed 85 per cent of its roll, a proportion that did not diminish until educational opportunities arose elsewhere.

The drive to obtain education was, of course, chiefly in order to rise in the world, to get a job in one of the professions; but it was more than that, too. The admirable WPA Guide noted drily in 1939 that the students of City College 'have a reputation for an interest in economics and political science that extends beyond the curricula': inevitably, given that so many of them had been reared in the traditions of the *Arbiter Ring* and tough negotiations with the bosses in the garment industry. There was a drive among these people not only to get the best deal going for themselves, but to do so for others as well – the others didn't have to be Jewish to qualify. The conjunction of a college education and a family background in the trade unions turned many young men towards active politics in New York in the years after the Great War, and although the Jewish vote and Jewish candidates could at first waver unpredictably between the two major parties (in 1920 New York sent six Jews to Congress, all but one Republican, but two years later the tally was three Democrats and a Republican) the rising and educated class increasingly put its shoulder behind the radical movements. Sophisticated young Jews have thus been found at various times in the ranks of the Socialist Workers Party, the Labor Party, the Liberal Party, the Fusion Party: it was largely because of the sterling work done by young Jews of the second generation who were active for Fusion, that the Tammany juggernaut was stopped in its tracks the year LaGuardia was first elected Mayor. By and by, the wider Jewish liberal tradition in New York politics became more and more focused on the Democratic Party at both local and national level, failing its Presidential candidate only once in half a century, when the Jews backed Dewey against Truman in 1948 (but, then, Dewey had earned their vote by being LaGuardia's right-hand man in attacking New York crime). And, unlike WASPs and Catholics, who tend to become Republicans when they become rich, the Jews have mostly stayed Democrat even when they have amassed wealth.

By the mid-thirties, Jews were prolifically in small family businesses throughout New York, which has ever been one of their greatest economic strengths. They owned some of the city's department stores, from Macy's in Manhattan and Abraham & Straus's in Brooklyn, down to lesser emporia. They virtually monopolised the manufacture of clothing, and they had a healthy foothold in banking. They were proprietors of the *New York Times* and of the *New York Post*. They had made a tremendous mark on the entertainments industry in New York, through the Gershwins and the Marx Brothers, through Al Jolson and Eddie Cantor and many more, including Isidore Baline, who was better known as Irving Berlin. There was also Reuben Ticker, who had been a choir boy at the Shaare Zedek synagogue in the Brooklyn of the twenties, before crossing the river to become a cantor on the Lower East Side at the First Romanian-American Congregation on Rivington Street, a part of town where he worked during the week as a street peddler. But singing was his life (young Ticker was spoken of by the knowing in the same breath as the great Yoselle Rosenblatt, than whom none greater had ever given voice in the synagogues of New York) and finally he got a job professionally with the Metropolitan Opera, as did his brother-in-law, Jacob Perelmuth, also from the Rivington Street synagogue. By then they were more widely known as Richard Tucker and Jan Peerce; and when Tucker died, they held his funeral in the Metropolitan Opera House, where once they wouldn't even have admitted him to the box seats. In many ways, the life and times of Reuben Ticker were a paradigm of the Jewish experience in New York. In becoming accepted by the establishment here, in providing something of the energy and brilliance that had made the city what it is, Jews had made their own accommodations with what had originally been an alien world.

The Jewishness of New York was very strange to Isaac Bashevis Singer, coming here straight from the ancient traditions of Warsaw in 1935 when he was thirty-one years old. He lived for a start in the Sea Gate cantonment alongside Coney Island, which plunged him instantly into the deep end of New York Jewish history, for once this had been forbidden territory to his people, when it was owned by the Atlantic Yacht Club. It was trauma enough to be exposed there to the full exhilaration of a Long Island winter, with the ocean smashing into the icy shore, when he came from somewhere remote from the sea. But what bewildered him was to do with the head and the heart:

Not only was I cut off from my language, but I also felt my way of thinking, my options and my concepts had been distorted. There was no place for demons in the din and clamor of Manhattan or Coney Island. Synagogues in this city resembled churches, boys played football in front of their yeshivas. Mortuaries were built alongside banks, restaurants or garages, and the coffins were carried in limousines. As to the mourners, they could just as well have been guests at a wedding.

I could no longer recognise my people by their speech patterns, their dress, their gestures and their mannerisms. The women appeared tough to me. They smoked cigarettes and spoke like men. I imagined that something of a mental catastrophe had taken place here, some sort of biological and cultural mutation for which I could find no words in my Yiddish vocabulary.

Singer's own life since has, in its own exalted way, exemplified a continuing pattern for Jews in New York. Having turned his back on a rabbinical career in Poland, where he began to write, he found American employment at *Forward*, for whom he wrote journalism under the pseudonym Warshofsky, later contributing short stories under his own name. Yet for thirty years or so, his stories drew on his old European experiences, not on America, and he was not published in English till 1953, probably the last major figure to compose first in Yiddish for translation later. New York didn't figure in his writing until he had lived there for as long as he had lived in Poland. By then he had adapted to the new ways (though without losing touch with the old; and in his case language has been the unbroken link) and some time ago he had become yet another dignified old Jewish gentleman residing on that well-upholstered stretch of the Upper West Side, which is known to its familiars as the Golden Ghetto.

In the half-century or so since Singer arrived in New York, the city has become even more tinctured with Jewishness than it was in 1935. It has been estimated that approximately half of all the school teachers are Jewish, including a high proportion of school principals; also about 15 per cent of all government employees, which is not a considerable ratio, but one higher than will be found in other American cities. Book publishing and other areas of communication are said to appoint Jews to senior positions as often as anyone nowadays, which was not so before the Second World War.* When Nathan Glazer wrote his celebrated survey of New York Jewishness twenty years ago, he singled out two other areas with strong Jewish connections. One was in real estate and building construction. Manhattan was in the midst of an office-building boom, much of which was in the hands of good Jewish firms – who survived a slump in the seventies to flourish again when the next boom occurred ten years later. Here were the builders Tishman and Uris Brothers and Erwin Wolfson, the developers Kalikow, Goldman and Zeckendorf. Here also were numerous people who simply owned and sometimes transacted property, preferably without public attention, including most of the New York apartment houses; that European invention which became more highly developed here, achieving its apotheosis in the high and mighty Dakota building on Central Park West (in style not so much Scottish Baronial, as some of its inhabitants suppose, but rather Edinburgh Mercantile) where *Rosemary's Baby* was filmed and where John Lennon was shot.

The other stronghold Glazer noted ('in America a peculiarly Jewish product') was psychoanalysis, with large numbers of New York practitioners and their patients being Jewish. This, he suggested, was no more than coincidentally because Freud and other central European pioneers were Jewish.

For the East Europeans who made up the greatest part of New York Jewry, and for the bourgeois German Jews of the nineteenth century and their descendants who made up a small part of the community, nothing could have been on the face

---

* 'The world's most powerful newspaper' – as the *New York Times* has unblushingly described itself – often leans over backwards to be balanced on touchy matters, as when it assigned a reporter of Italian origins to write about life in a Hasidic family. But, knowing well which side its bread is buttered on in New York, it refers to Palestinian hi-jackers as 'terrorists', to IRA gunmen more sympathetically as 'guerrillas'.

of it more foreign than psychoanalysis. The East European Jew was blind to any kind of psychological abnormality: for him there was only one kind of abnormality, the social one, and all his intelligence was applied to changing the abnormal social position of the Jew.

Nor did Glazer even consider the possibility that the phenomenon, as a Jewish peculiarity, was especially related to the stresses associated with a metropolitan existence. He saw an explanation

in the effects of secularism on Jews, who have been so rapidly divorced from traditional religion and who have accepted the possibilities of science and intellect so completely that a movement like psychoanalysis – even had its founder been a German anti-Semite – would have been irresistibly attractive. For here was a scientific form of soul-rebuilding to make them whole and hardy, and it was divorced, at least on the surface, from mysticism, will, religion, and all those other romantic and obscure trends that their rational minds rejected. And then, too, it was also a new field with room for new people, which fact may explain why so many Jews became analysts. But it is primarily the complex secularisation of the second-generation East European Jew in America that explains why so many became patients.*

Here, then, has been the battlefield on which one of New York's two Jewish communities has sustained injuries inseparable from repudiating an ancient culture and embracing a relatively new one; helping, in fact, to create the alternative, though this has not yet achieved its final form, in alliance with people from completely different backgrounds. The price paid by the

* In an effort to give some statistical backing to his thesis, Glazer cited a New York study in which an unspecified number of people were asked where they would seek advice for a child's behaviour problem. Half the Jewish respondents suggested a psychotherapist, but only 31 per cent of the Protestants and 24 per cent of the Catholics.

assimilated Jews of the city has not been confined to whatever psychological strains may have required soothing in expensive consultations around Manhattan. There was a time, within this generation, when they were regarded as the Jewish community to reckon with, as the people who established the Jewish position on any topic that arose, as the ones who spoke for all the Jews of New York and promoted the New York Jewish reputation for principle in all things and altruism whenever possible. It was almost as if there were no other Jews in New York than these. But there were, and they have since asserted themselves as they never did before, while the influence of the assimilated Jews, as Jews, has manifestly ebbed. The political scientist who proposed the idea of two Jewish communities, foresaw the moment when repudiation of the ancient culture might be total. 'Ultimately, more and more assimilated Jews, many of whom are today only Jewish in name, will cease even to be that.'

It is reckoned that the balance between the two communities tipped some little time before 1968, though it was not widely noticed until the teachers' strike of that year. Ostensibly, this was caused by an educational experiment that went badly amiss, an attempt by well-intentioned bodies, including the Ford Foundation, to encourage a poor black population in its various aspirations by giving it a bigger say in the schooling of its children. Ocean Hill, at the centre of the subsequent controversy, lies beside the Brooklyn slum areas of Bedford-Stuyvesant and Brownsville – 'a highly discouraging place in which to live and bring up one's children', according to a Jewish commentator who was himself involved in what happened there. The population at the time was about 70 per cent black and 25 per cent Puerto Rican. Before the experiment began, almost all the teachers in the local schools were white, most of them Jewish, and some had been at odds with the local parents, who tended – as parents everywhere will often do – to blame the teachers for any failure by their children. A black administrator was brought in to supervise the new order under the authority of a school board reflecting the Ocean Hill racial mixture. Before long, nineteen teachers were suspended and not always fully qualified blacks were brought in as substitutes. The administrator said of the sacked whites that 'Not one of these teachers will be allowed to teach anywhere in this city. The black community will see to that.' When the teachers' union objected, intimidation was organised by people who had nothing to do with education. On one occasion, eighty-three frightened teachers were surrounded and abused by fifty men carrying sticks and wearing bandoliers of cartridges. On another, a flood of crudely anti-Semitic literature was released – though the Jewish commentator on these events suggested that the union made far more of this than it perhaps should have done, when 'some of it was simply the ravings of a single fanatic with access to a mimeograph machine'. On the opening day of the school year in September 1968, nearly 54,000 of New York's 57,000 teachers went on strike and stayed there for five full weeks. They were standing pat on a basic union principle: but more to the point in the long run, they were picketing in 'the first significant confrontation between Jews and blacks in New York since the end of the Second World War'.

It polarised Jewish attitudes in the city more obviously than anything had done before. Some of New York's traditionally liberal Jews had applauded the experiment when it was first announced, seeing in it an expression of those values they cherished more than anything else; many of them, after all, had marched with blacks across the south just three years earlier in support of civil rights. They were not the ones who put their Jewishness above all other things. Speaking for those who did when the mess had been cleaned up, was a rabbi from another part of Brooklyn; 'I can tell you that the masses of people in Canarsie saw the Ocean Hill-Brownsville struggle as a black-Jewish struggle. Here we were, Jews marching for civil rights, really gung-ho, marching along in Selma, Alabama, but it came to the public schools and it became "Get out of my community. I want your job". It started a lot of people thinking.' It also produced more recruits to the Jewish Defense League.

It has been said that the East River defines the limits of Jewish liberalism in New York. This is not quite what Norman Podhoretz meant when he wrote, 'One of the longest journeys in the world is the journey from Brooklyn to Manhattan,' to express the gradual estrangement of the talented Jewish boy from his deepest cultural traditions as he ambitiously pursued his individual star. Certainly it would be misleading to imply that the assimilated Jewish community dwells exclusively in Manhattan, while the 'ethnics' reside in Brooklyn and elsewhere. Nothing is much more ethnic than the old Jewish part of the Lower East Side, contracted though it has become this past generation or so. What is left, however, would be perfectly recognisable to the people who came off the ferries from Ellis Island a hundred years ago, with knish bakeries on every block, and other shops selling everything Jewish from kosher wines to bar mitzvah sets. True, as a result of Chinatown's expansion, *Forward* has been obliged to move to premises on East 33rd Street, but the old building still stands proudly under its new ownership on East Broadway, the paper's Yiddish title in majolica letters retaining its original position below the rooftop clock. That street is the boundary between the Chinese and Jewish quarters today, so that just across the way from the Hwa Yuan Szechuan Inn, two or three *shteeblech* are still maintained for constant prayer. In these small rooms, just off the sidewalk, with windows and shutters flung back to catch any air that may be stirring on a warm day, old men may be seen bent over books far into the evening, swaying rhythmically in that hypnotic movement which possesses pilgrims at the Wailing Wall in Jerusalem. No more than a few hundred yards from these timeless devotions is the East Side *mikveh*, the bath-house where Orthodox women ritually cleanse themselves after menstruation, in water which (scripture ordains) must issue directly from a spring or be collected from rain.

Brooklyn has every right to consider itself the heartland of Judaism in this city, however, and not only because half of all the synagogues in New York are to be found there. It holds the title also because it shelters the Satmar Hasidim of Williamsburg, who are the most ultra-Orthodox Jews of all.*

---

* The Satmar are only one of several Hasidic sects in Brooklyn. Others are the Habad Hasidim (more widely known as the Lubavitcher community), the Bobover and the Munkotch Hasidim. The name Satmar is derived from the town of Satu Mare (St Mary) in eastern Hungary, where this sect originated.

They are so utterly surrendered to their faith and its historical impedimenta, so uncaring of anything else, that Reformed Jews might belong to a different religion, and even normally strict observers of the Judaic law, those who scrupulously abide by Torah and Commandments, appear to be lax in comparison. It is not at all uncommon for good observant Brooklyn Jews of other congregations, to emerge from their synagogues and overhear Hasidic children disapproving of them, sometimes even referring to them as *goyim* (non-Jews). They are not often amused by this.

The origins of these Hasidim lie in nineteenth-century Hungary, in a schism over the interpretation of the Shulhan Aruch, the Judaic law, after the Jews had been emancipated by Franz Josef in 1867. There they lived in increasing isolation from the Reform Jews, mostly occupied in rural jobs like shepherding, peddling, or making a variety of religious objects for sale in nearby towns. They appear not to have been troubled overmuch by the periodic upheavals of Europe until the Nazis happened, when they suffered as much as anybody else. It was after the Second World War that their survivors came to the United States and found an already strong Hungarian Orthodox tradition established in Williamsburg. Compatriots of theirs, not quite so obsessive as themselves, but holding the faith more demonstratively than the majority of American Jews, had been settled into the neighbourhood for a quarter of a century or so by then.

The Satmar set about building their new community in a very practical way, after the shatterings of invasion and the concentration camps. Married couples were forbidden to practise birth control, and if more than two years elapsed between the arrival of each child, the parents were gossiped about openly and maliciously, or subjected to other forms of pressure: as a result, some produced as many as fifteen children, and the average has been reckoned at six. This has been the basis of an unyielding hierarchy, in which everyone is in no doubt about his place and its relation to everyone else's – and in the case of the men, wearing something akin to uniform, which varies distinctively at each level, so that they may be recognised for what they are. At the top comes the rebbe, who is not only the religious leader and instructor, the model for everyone else, but probably the latest in a dynasty of rebbes, which may be traced back into the misty distances of Hungary. Aspiring to this eminence is the Shtickel rebbe, a man of some education and religious training, who will busy himself in Hasidic works beyond the norm expected of everyone. Also carrying much weight in the community are the Sheine Yiden, pious men who may teach scripture to the young, or be employed in ritual professions, such as the slaughter of animals or the circumcision of infants. Less exalted are the Talmidei Hachamim, though these are acknowledged scholars, so dedicated in their studies of scripture and exegesis that they are invariably poorer than the two classes below them on the Hasidic scale. Immediately below are the Balebatishe Yiden, who because of their business activities contribute most of the wealth in the community, charitably or in other ways. Some of it is passed directly to the Yiden, who are at the bottom of the hierarchy, often in the employ of those just above. A temptation to commiserate with them as the Hasidic underdogs should be resisted, though. The Yiden 'outdo everyone else outside of the Hasidic community in religious performance. In their own eyes, therefore, they are not the lowest of the low, but the lowest of the exalted.'

In this rigidly patriarchal world, the way a man dresses and the way he cultivates his hair are matters of much more than fashionable importance. The Yiden are advised not to attempt anything more elaborate than dark and double-breasted suits which button from right to left, together with the *yarmulke* and the black homburg on the head, which many other Orthodox Jews wear, too. But the moment the Yid rises just one rank in the hierarchy, he must grow *bord und payes*, which is beard and sidelocks, the characteristic of all but the lowliest of these exalted men. Upward mobility is thereafter signified by various accoutrements, until the fully-fledged rebbe emerges each *Shabbos* clad splendidly in a wide-brimmed hat of sable, a long silk coat with pockets at the back, knee breeches and white hose below the knee, with a distinctive kind of slipper on his feet. Yet while all these carefully groomed males have been self-consciously ascending their sartorial ladder, the women have been required to do nothing but dress modestly, which means showing no flesh below the Adam's apple or above the wrist. They step more strictly into line the moment they marry, though, when they have to cut off most of their hair and wear a covering (usually a wig) over what's left. It is scarcely to be expected that unions between such men and such women are achieved according to the social norms of America, even at its most sweetly chaste. The Hasidic couple are permitted the final say on whether or not they wish to marry, but otherwise matters are out of their hands. The father with a marriageable daughter contacts the *shadchan*, the marriage broker, who arranges everything with the parents of a suitable boy.

Here is a people in thrall to their concept of purity, as perhaps none others are apart from high caste Hindus. At a practical level this means not only that the women must ritually bathe in the *mikveh* after menstruation, but immediately after childbirth, too: also that the corpse must be ritually immersed before anyone's funeral is held. To them, the customary Jewish concept of kosher is woefully inadequate; whatever they eat must be *glat* kosher (the word literally means 'smooth'), slaughtered or packed or canned or cooked, not only by a Jew properly trained in these meticulous arts and crafts, but by a *Hasidic* Jew sponsored by a rebbe well known for his integrity and rigour. Having assured himself that everything he consumes is *glat*, the Hasid must then have no doubt that every garment on his body is without a trace of *shatnes*, which means a combination of linen and wool. An obscure sentence in Deuteronomy is responsible for this worry, which has resulted in a cottage industry unlike any other in the United States.* It can be taken for granted that no clothing manufactured by Hasidim will fail to pass the biblical test, but clothing bought off the peg from other sources might very well be polluted in this tiresome way; and so there is a *shatnes* laboratory in Brooklyn, where such apparel is taken apart at the seams for examination, to be stitched back together again afterwards with any offending material removed or substituted if necessary.

* Deuteronomy 22:11, 'Thou shalt not wear a garment of divers sorts, as of woollen and linen together.' The same injunction is found in Leviticus 19:19.

Such fastidiousness as this was bound to discourage everyday social intercourse with others less pernickety in their habits, and the Williamsburg Hasidim do hold themselves apart almost as much as the Christian Amish of Pennsylvania. They will have no television or radio in their homes, and the only newspaper they will countenance, apart from local sheets they publish themselves, is a weekly called *Der Yid*. It has been known for a man to be ostracised because he sued another member of the community in a civil court after an automobile accident, when it was held that properly he should have had the dispute arbitrated in the *shul*, which is something more than a synagogue; it is where authority and judgement is expressed on community affairs, as well as where worship is held. Most surprising of all the things that characterise these Williamsburg Jews of immiscible belief is their profound antipathy to Zionism. Some Hasidim even in Brooklyn – the Lubavitcher community, for example, which is centred on Crown Heights – take a conventional view of Israel, seeing there not only a national home for all Jews, but a sign that Messiah is indeed to come before too long. But these Satmar Hasidim of Williamsburg, 'reject everything and everyone that is associated with the new state. They conceive that the existence of the state of Israel is a threat to their traditional perception of the Messiah, because "all of it must emerge through holiness".' When the great festival of Succat comes round, for which the pious Jew is adjured to have by him the citrus fruit they call *esrog*, in Williamsburg they pointedly ignore supplies flown in from Israel, where New York Jewry in general obtains its fruit; they get theirs from Greece or Arizona instead.

Not for these people the missionary instincts of the Lubavitcher, who betake themselves to Grand Central Station every Friday aboard a large van, park it by the sidewalk and use it as a mobile HQ while they urge Jewish commuters to attend to their faith more assiduously. The proselytisers also seek out co-religionists who may be having a nice day quietly on a park bench until a posse of Lubavitchen arrive to say prayers over their heads, to the occasional embarrassment of some old gentleman who decided years ago that, although he would not be anything but a Jew, the agnostic approach was the one that seemed to suit him best. Yet the Hasidim of Williamsburg do not seal themselves off from everyone totally, any more than the Amish do, for there is an economy to be maintained and, unlike the Amish, who are country folk, they cannot even be almost self-sufficient in the most complicated metropolis on earth. Many of their Balebatishe Yiden have businesses in Manhattan, including one which retails all manner of high-tech equipment, from Hasselblad cameras to IBM computers, and is reputed to take over $100 million a year in sales from its four shops. Its 200 employees are transported in a small fleet of reconditioned school buses between Brooklyn and Manhattan each day, in one of the more startling adjustments made by the New York commuter.

On leaving work, with its telex keeping track of foreign exchange rates, and with customers wanting expert advice on exposure control, on modems, on the difference between bits and bytes, these Hasidim in no time at all find themselves not just across the East River, but in another world. Its through traffic and its buildings give it away for somewhere in New York, but otherwise it seems wholly out of time and place. People here address each other not only in the language of Exodus and the Prophets, but with the ancient sentiments as well. 'My brothers, the slaughterers, I am begging: Look and see a new thing! "If not now, then when?" Slaughter knives . . . for large cattle, small cattle, poultry, stainless, a bargain buy!' And again, 'I succeeded with God's help in erecting a hand mill of stones; the flour is actually cold and fine in quality. All is from fine selected wheat that can be seen without any chaff – I invite all in to see it. Give your orders right away so that I shall be able to satisfy you in time because I shall have only a limited amount . . .'

Men in strange wide hats of fur stand talking, confidentially, on the streets. Boys pass by wearing prayer shawls, sometimes over their long drab coats. There is no bustle, no confusion, no metropolitan uproar, little of anything that means right here and now. It speaks of the ghetto, of Mittel Europa, of centuries bygone, of dybbuks and strangely forbidding things. It would be no surprise at all if, just round that corner there on

Bedford Avenue, an ox-cart came lumbering, creaking along, an old Slavonic *bydlo* drawn by a swaying tread of beasts, to Mussorgsky's sound of deeply measured brass.

These people are one of New York's astounding, marvellous assets; and for them the long persecution is past.

FIVE

THEM AND US

Three times a week, between spring and fall, the bus takes a load of white voyeurs to scrutinise the blacks. The passengers rendezvous at a dingy office across 42nd Street from the Port Authority Bus Terminal, where Greyhound and Trailways and Leprechaun and all the other long-distance operators convey people from New York to just about anywhere in the United States. The office across the street serves as terminus for no-one but the Penny Sightseeing Company, whose trade is not only very local, but specialised, too. It may be that occasionally some tourist from Liberia, Nigeria or Sierra Leone will take advantage of Penny Sightseeing's facilities to go and find out how the brothers and sisters in Harlem are getting on, but the object of this enterprise is quite otherwise. What follows, thrice weekly for a few hours, is meant to educate ignorant whites more than anyone else, with a few home truths about life on Manhattan above West 110th Street, where Harlem these days is reckoned to begin. 'Harlem tours of Penny Sight-seeing Company,' says the publicity leaflet, 'are operated by Black Americans who feel that there is more to this great community than the sensationalism of the published story.' This after making the point that black American history began with slavery at the hands of whites, and a hint that matters have improved but little since those days. As the passengers gather for a seminal expedition into this area of darkness, a frisson of anxiety quivers through all their anticipation. They are straining with goodwill and amiable curiosity; but is this going to be enough?

The young woman who leads this guided tour goes into her patter soon after the bus begins to thread its way through the mid-morning traffic along the West Side. Standing behind the driver with a microphone in her hand, she points out some landmarks that these out-of-towners may not recognise, though they'll be familiar enough with the names – the Lincoln Center and Columbus Circle, the Dakota building and Central Park itself. She is informative and fluent, though she does not explain why it is that Central Park West quite suddenly changes from opulence to shabbiness on the corner of 96th Street: she is saving that kind of contrast for a few blocks later on. Nor, although she will politely answer questions throughout the tour, does she radiate much warmth or encourage more than a correct civility in return; which is perhaps why the questions, few to begin with, have dwindled to an inhibited silence before the trip is halfway through.

It says something about the human composition of New York generally that the bus is well into Harlem before it strikes the observant passenger that it has been quite a while since he saw any whites out there on the sidewalks: negritude is so normal in this city, distinguishing it from almost anywhere in Europe, that in itself it is not noteworthy until the contrasting pallor has been missing some little time. By then the bus is on its way to the first stop of the tour, which is not an opportunity to get out and meet some inhabitants of Harlem, but to inspect one of New York's historic monuments, the handsome clapboard Morris-Jumel Mansion ('in the Tuscan-columned Georgian-Federal style') which was George Washington's headquarters for a time during the Revolutionary War. For anyone who has come with preconceived notions of Harlem as a sprawling black slum, bearing some manifestations of seething resentment against whites, the trip thus far will have been a surprise. There have been areas of shabbiness, to be sure, but nothing much worse than that; and round the Jumel Mansion everything is really rather smart, including a terrace of clapboard homes which might house a loftiness of Boston Brahmins as probably as a solidarity of Harlem blacks. The avenues running from north to south are unexpectedly wide and often tree-lined, and because up here they aren't pullulating with traffic and people, as they are below Central Park, they give the place a very ample dignity.

They have been marked with a dignified form of racial pride. Eighth Avenue in Harlem has been renamed Frederick Douglass Boulevard, to commemorate the former slave who became an abolitionist and one of America's first token blacks in government. Seventh Avenue is Adam Clayton Powell Boulevard, after the flamboyant playboy preacher who made it to Congress long enough to see a passion for civil rights sweeping the land. The first of these thoroughfares, the Penny Sightseeing guide tells her charges, has a lot of drug trafficking and is not very safe; and then, as if to amplify this warning, she adds, 'Up here they don't take kindly to cameras. They feel their personal space is being invaded.' The passengers look even less likely than before to start aiming their Nikons through the bus windows, at people who are strolling or merely shuffling along and paying not the slightest attention to anybody else's thing. The guide says that unemployment is running at 33 per cent out there, 'among blacks and other minorities', but does not make the most of this statistic by forgetting to add another one; that in New York the overall rate is no more than 7.9 per cent. And, to be sure, there is an air of real seediness on the western side of Frederick Douglass, which hints at every form of social and political failure, including the corrosion of drugs. The guide points out another one as the bus cruises along 125th Street; large metal shutters covering shop frontages, which, she says, are known as 'riot gates', and her passengers need no further explanation. They brighten visibly when two or three of these fortifications come into sight a-splash with colourful cartoons; the work of a Jamaican painter, they're told, who is seizing an opportunity in the best traditions of American free enterprise.

And now comes the second stop of the trip, much more impressive than the first. The whites have not failed to notice how deeply religion has been implanted in Harlem, with practically every block containing at least one place of worship, and

some two or three, in a wondrously cavalier flourish of denomi-
nations. The Abyssinian Baptist Church has been singled out for
attention by the guide, because that was where the two Adam
Clayton Powells, father and son, occupied the pulpit one after
the other. But there is also the African Methodist Metropolitan
Church, the Holy Messiah Baptist Church, the Transfiguration
Lutheran Church, the Temple Church of God in Christ, the First
Caribbean Church, the Salvation and Deliverance Church and the
African Orthodox Church, all flashing past in an exuberant access
of witness and praise, before giving way to just as much variety
all over again. Outside one of these buildings, the bus stops, the
passengers invited to get down and step inside. Instantly, they
are attacked.

Two or three couples have been sitting on the top steps of
their brownstones in this street, watching the arrival of the bus
and its contents with much the same sort of blank curiosity the
whites have been spending on Harlem. The blankness gives way
to something between amusement and shock when a battered-
looking figure lurches across the street, loosing invective as he
goes. He is middle-aged, life has not been easy, his clothes are
bedraggled and stained, and he is plastered with booze, reeling
with an intoxication of liquor and abuse: it is the New York black
man's version of the performance Glasgow drunks put on whenever they think they may have a Sassenach in their bleary sights.
It is no more than abuse, though. The man comes to a standstill
ten yards away and screams unprintably while the shaken whites
descend from their bus and make for the church door, the guide
bringing up the rear after giving him a very dirty look.

A welcome awaits the visitors inside. Four men and a woman,
aided by a young fellow at the piano, have been primed for this
arrival, ready to give these whites a taste of old-fashioned
Harlem gospel singing. One of the men has a deep Paul Robeson
bass, and there is a pair of tenors, as well as a boy whose voice
ranges remarkably all the way from a light baritone to coloratura
soprano. The music exploits it all, and is not meant to soothe
anyone who has just come a little nervously off the street,
wondering what in the world may be about to happen next. These
words, that syncopation and heavy beat, those spiralling upward

voices, are meant to make people *jump* – with gladness and joy for preference, but jump anyway, even if they're feeling a bit sick. 'Hallelujah! We are going to see the *King*!' is the challenge fairly thrown down from the altar rails by that quintet, who are not just putting heart and soul and voice into this production, but a fair bit of beef as well, swinging their bodies in unison to the surge and swell of the sound. In close harmony, of course. No more than one arm's length separates any of the singers. Down in the pews, some twenty-five whites, after the relative confinement of their bus, have rearranged themselves according to their natural inclinations, with great spaces separating them right across the building, only the couples standing side by side. But at least by the time 'We came *this* far, my friend!' has swung into life up front, the white faces are looking a little less strained, and there's a girl from Ohio who is beginning to move just a little in tune with them, before the singalong is done. It is done after the singers reach a fever of excitement such as the white man's Church has never known, not even those self-indulgent corybantic churches that litter the Californian coast, springing up anew every time someone else has an urge to be a bishop leading his flock. 'God is a *holy* God!' is the number now, and has no other words but these, repeated over and over, with the emphasis changing line after accelerating line. 'God is a holy *God*!' they sing, and the boy begins to take off into a realm of his own, head back, eyes shut, coloratura rippling into high cascades of ecstasy, which are inexpressible in words, only in pure sound. But '*God* is a holy God!' the Robeson bass insists along with the other three. 'God *is* a holy God!' beyond peradventure, my friends, which is why we're all here today, why Penny Sightseeing brought your footsteps to this place, why this praise is coming at you in this bounding, vibrating, skirling crescendo. Which suddenly cuts out! To be replaced with a gradual exhalation of post-ecstatic murmurings by the choir.

'Such a holy, holy, *holy* God,' chuckles the Robeson bass, with a beatific expression on his face. 'Oh-ho-ho, yes'm, didn't we just praise him there . . .?'

'My word, my Lord, oh ay*men* to that . . .' the woman croons, shaking her head with her eyes still closed.

The coloratura boy appears still to be lost on that sensational height, as he flicks drops of sweat from his forehead with a delicate hand.

The whites remain awkward, but say their thank-yous most earnestly, and then file outside to board the bus. Couples are sitting on brownstone steps as before, but the belligerent drunk has gone somewhere else.

And the rest of the tour, though it runs for another hour, is something of an anti-climax after the gospelling. The bus cuts eastwards along 116th Street, which ceases to be that the moment Fifth Avenue is crossed, and becomes instead Luis Muñoz Marin Boulevard in memory of Puerto Rico's most famous politician, the man whose government was sometimes described as an island version of Roosevelt's New Deal administration. The whites have just entered East or Spanish Harlem: they have crossed a boundary into a quarter of the city which includes some of the Bronx and is known to its inhabitants as El Barrio. The most obvious difference from what has gone before is the somewhat greater range of human colour on the streets, the different language employed on any notices out there, and the more vivid paints that have been used in the decoration of shop fronts. Where the boulevard arrives at Park Avenue, a large and cheap-looking bazaar is flamboyantly proclaimed with huge and gaudy lettering – La Marquita – on the brickwork of an elevated railroad arch. This may be no more than twenty blocks distant, but is in every other sense a world away from the genteel Park Avenue which terminates at East 96th Street as abruptly as the Harlem Line trains emerge there into daylight for the first time since leaving Grand Central. At that point the Red Apple Supermarket, with its six-packs and its ground meat, stands on one corner facing La Nueva Grocery, with its *frutos tropicales*, on another, like frontier posts separated by a narrow no-man's-land. Park Avenue's cross-streets below 96th are kept trim and tidy on behalf of wealthy inhabitants, and are often striped with that characteristic of Manhattan's upper-class neighbourhoods, the canopy extending from the street door to the gutter, so that no-one shall get rained upon between the apartment and the limousine. Go down 97th Street or anything higher, though, and the pedestrian must negotiate an obstacle course, where men have drawn up their automobiles on the sidewalks, doors wide open, radios blaring, hoods propped up, while the thrifty owners fix engines and clean out the insides. Park Avenue inside El Barrio wears its fire escapes up the front of worn-out buildings, so that it resembles more than anything some dilapidated part of the Lower East Side.

The Penny Sightseeing guide surveys this Latin quarter without enthusiasm, and in the same non-committal tones she has used since the beginning, offers the information that, 'The Puerto Ricans refuse to become part of America's melting pot. Here it is necessary to speak Spanish in order to survive.' This makes it sound even more intimidating to the whites than it looks. By the time their scrutiny of the two Harlems is over, and they have disembarked with polite thanks, scarcely one will have been disabused of a fundamental notion that in the end it all comes down to Them and Us. Potentially dangerous, too, although those people at the church were really great . . .

It has been Them and Us to the blacks as well, ever since eleven of them were brought to Nieuw Amsterdam the year Peter Minuit purchased Manahata from the Indians. They were shipped from Africa as indentured servants, a condition which was not much different from the outright slavery which became the custom when the English supplanted the Dutch as overlords of New York. For almost exactly 200 years, black people dwelt here in legalised subservience, labouring mostly as domestic servants, or doing various jobs that white people preferred not to dirty themselves with – like sweeping chimneys and caulking ships' bottoms. But surprisingly, 'A few, who had obtained freedom from their masters through determination and frugality, owned small businesses' in the city. At various times in that period the Negro – as he was always identified by black and white alike until a very few years ago – rebelled against his bondage in New York.* As early as 1710, a slave

* As recently as 1964, when Glazer and Moynihan published *Beyond the Melting Pot*, they entitled one chapter 'The Negroes', which would not have been thought proper much longer.

took his master to law in a wage dispute, and two years later a group of slaves planned an insurrection, which was swiftly put down. In 1741, when one-fifth of the city's population of 10,000 consisted of black slaves, a rumour spread that they and some poor whites intended to burn down New York. In the subsequent hysteria, thirteen blacks were burned at the stake, eighteen were hanged, and seventy-one were transported to the West Indies; while twenty whites were arrested and three of them were put to death. Thereafter, blacks here found it somewhat easier than before to purchase their freedom, and in the Revolutionary War both sides were happy enough to recruit them into the opposing armies. Black soldiers raised in New York state to fight for America were rewarded with their freedom when the war was won.

The first law of emancipation anywhere in the known world was enacted in 1772, when the English Lord Chief Justice, Lord Mansfield, forbade slavery in the British Isles. Across the Atlantic, Rhode Island was the first of the American colonies to follow suit a couple of years later, while New York State passed a law urging gradual abolition before the end of the eighteenth century, though slavery lingered until 1827. Emancipation was not by any means generally welcomed in New York, as became obvious when the Civil War broke out. Although the Empire State as a whole supplied more troops, materials and money than any other, all to keep Lincoln's Union army fired up, in New York City the prevailing sentiment was in favour of the Confederacy and against the abolition of slavery. Too many local businessmen stood to suffer if the city's share of the cotton trade was disrupted, or if southerners stopped using the city's hotels and patronising the city's stores on their regular visits to the metropolis. At the same time, too many of the city's working-class whites did not relish the extra competition for jobs that widespread emancipation would doubtless bring, and were bitterly against any attempt to make them fight for Abraham Lincoln's beliefs (many of them had fled Europe, among other reasons, in order to avoid enforced military service). Therefore abolitionist meetings in the city were often broken up by mobs. And in one week of July 1863, with the war two years old, massive rioting against the recent Conscription Act was particularly directed against blacks and anyone who tried to protect them. It did not end until 10,000 troops had been mustered to control the situation, by which time there were 1,000 casualties, most of them fatal, with many buildings razed by fire, including the Colored Orphan Asylum on Fifth Avenue.

By then the city's black community, though miserably cramped by racial antagonism, was far from petrified in submission. Although most professions and trades were closed to them still, blacks formed a rising class of innkeeper throughout the area. 'Black Sam' Fraunces, indeed, had been the owner of a tavern made famous under his stewardship in 1783, when George Washington bade an emotional farewell to his victorious army there. Within a hundred years of that event, blacks would be found operating hotels, restaurants and saloons all over Manhattan. The official ending of local slavery had coincided with the first publication of a newspaper produced by and for blacks, *Freedom's Journal*, which was shortly afterwards followed by a number of similar periodicals and pamphlets. Half a dozen years before that, in 1821, New York had witnessed the foundation of America's first black theatre, the African Grove, on Mercer Street, with *Othello* and other plays by Shakespeare among its earliest productions. This may also have provided the first example of blacks repaying whites in their own kind, for whites were segregated in the back stalls of the theatre, a handbill explaining that they 'do not know how to conduct themselves at entertainments for ladies and gentlemen of colour.' The day was still some way off – it would be publicly noted for the first time in 1895 – when 'many Negro men own and occupy brownstone dwellings in fashionable neighbourhoods, employ white servants, and ride in their own carriage behind horses driven by liveried coachmen. Some not only own the houses they live in but also houses tenanted by rich white families, and there are Negro men in New York whose wealth is well along towards the million-dollar mark . . . In selecting servants, Negro people seem to prefer Swedes and Poles, though some hire southerners of their own race.'

The southern blacks were fairly recent arrivals in town, a unique sort of refugee after the terrible emancipation of the Civil War; though, like their European counterparts, they 'had heard of New York as a place vague and far away, a city that, like Heaven, to them had existed by faith alone. All the days of their life they had heard about it, and it seemed to them the centre of all the glory, all the wealth and all the freedom of the world.' The resident blacks, almost all of whom had descended from the earliest New York slaves, referred to them coolly as 'country-bred', though a black minister amplified this one day. The newcomers from the south, he said, 'were once the field or plantation hands, whence they progressed to gangs at sawmills, then to small towns for higher wages, and thence North, herded together, untouched by the civilisation either of the whites or of the educated blacks . . . They bring straight to the evils and temptations of New York the ignorance of the backwoods of the South.' They were not to be the last fugitives from Dixie. Though obliged by the thirteenth Constitutional Amendment to abandon crude slavery after 1865, the southern states never did relinquish their primitive attitude to those who had been slaves. It has been estimated that in the 1920s alone, some 750,000 blacks emigrated from the deep south to the north, fugitives from poverty and prejudice in equal measure. As in the case of those who had uprooted themselves earlier, some – though by no means a majority – made for the sanctuary, real or imagined, of New York. In 1830 there had been 14,000 blacks in the city. By 1900 the figure had risen to 60,000. In 1930 there would be 327,000 – getting on for 10 per cent of the population. But other north-eastern cities were even more attractive to the migrants from the south: New York's equivocation on slavery had made most of them wary enough to steer clear of her.

Disagreeably distinctive, too, was New York's habit of ensuring that virtually all its blacks were concentrated in one part of the city, a ghetto in which they could be kept at arm's length, or perhaps isolated for conflict. 'Almost every contemporary observer remarked upon this fact,' which was not the case in Washington or elsewhere in the north. Until the nineteenth century, almost all the blacks dwelt in lower

Manhattan, no higher up the island than Greenwich Village. By the end of the Civil War they had spread from the west side of Sixth Avenue towards the Hudson, settling into neighbourhoods between the twenties and the fifties, a district which became known as the Tenderloin.* By the last years of the nineteenth century some members of the black élite had broken out of the ghetto and gained a foothold in Brooklyn, but the rest of their people were still packed together along the West Side, the rising well-to-do beside the helots, the old black native New Yorkers together with the incomers from the south. These last may have come to the metropolis in smaller numbers than their fellow migrants had made for Chicago, Boston, Washington, and other cities, but they were nevertheless so ambitiously numerous by 1900 that most of the black professional people in New York – from preachers to entertainers, from lawyers to businessmen – had been born some place else. This produced the sort of reaction from the native blacks that in other circumstances might have come from a stuffy collection of WASPs. They founded the Society of the Sons of New York, a club to which every black man of substance soon aspired, but which steadfastly excluded anyone who was not a New Yorker born and bred. Within a few more years, the list of those blackballed by the Sons incorporated not only their kinsmen from the south, but more recent newcomers from the West Indies. These were thus twice affronted in New York, where they found prejudice against blacks much greater than they had experienced from the white people at home in Jamaica, Barbados and the other islands. That unexpected American antagonism, it has been suggested, accounts for the fact that the majority of black American communists and labour leaders have generally been migrants, or the sons of migrants, from the West Indies.

It was not until the twentieth century that Harlem saw its first blacks. Peter Stuyvesant, the seventh and the outstanding

* This area, celebrated for its dance halls and other revelries, owed its name to a police Captain Williams, newly transferred from a bleaker part of New York. 'I've had nothing but chuck steak for a long time,' he is supposed to have said, 'and now I'm going to get a little of the tenderloin.'

governor of the Dutch West India Company's colony here, had established the village of Nieuw Haarlem on lush agricultural land in 1658. Until the nineteenth century, open country separated it from the major settlement lower down Manhattan, to which it was linked by the old Indian trail known as Broadway, before this went off north into what became upstate New York, and south towards the Delaware. Roosevelts were among the biggest landholders there before selling out about the time the Harlem Railroad was built in the 1830s. This swiftly closed the gap between Harlem and New York City, so that the first was a fashionable suburb of the second by the time Oscar Hammerstein had built the Harlem Opera House on West 125th Street in 1889. Harlem was then populated by Irish and Germans, by Jews and Italians, and the last of these retained their dominance on the East Side between 96th and 125th Streets long after the other whites had moved on, to the extent that until the Second World War the area was still known as Italian Harlem, which was not to be confused with Negro Harlem and Spanish Harlem.

What caused the movement of blacks further up the West Side and into Harlem was, as much as anything, that recurring phenomenon of New York, a speculative building boom. So much new property went up in Harlem at the turn of the century that the landlords could not find enough tenants to fill it, and so blacks were invited to occupy the empty apartments – at higher rents than had been sought from the whites. They came in such quantity that by 1912 a correspondent to the *New York Times* was asking, 'Can nothing be done to put a restriction on the invasion of the Negro into Harlem? At one time it was a comfort and a pleasure to ride on the Sixth and Ninth Avenue elevated, but that is a thing of the past. Now you invariably have a coloured person sitting either beside you or in front of you . . .' By 1930, most of the Harlem whites had decided to avoid these indignities by moving to some other part of the metropolis.* Somewhere in between these two dates, the whites drummed up the blacks to fight in the First World

---

* Not until the Second World War, however, did Harlem become virtually all black.

War, and a regiment recruited entirely in Harlem (apart from its white officers) had covered itself in such glory that when hostilities ceased a great throng of New Yorkers turned out to cheer the troops as they marched for home along Fifth Avenue. This largely white demonstration astonished the black men of the 369th Infantry, now proudly known as the Harlem Hellfighters, because their colour had barred them from soldiering in the front line alongside white Americans; which was why they had been made welcome to share trenches with the French Army instead, as part of its 161st Division. When the Second World War broke out in 1939, the Colonel of the 369th and his son were the only black line officers in the whole of the United States Army, where blacks did not achieve parity with whites until Harry Truman decreed it in 1948.

Harlem after the First World War became 'the greatest single community anywhere of people descended from age-old Africa . . .' wrote James Weldon Johnson, one of its most talented inhabitants, for he was variously a teacher, a songwriter, a poet and novelist, a diplomat, and a secretary of the National Association for the Advancement of Coloured People, which had been founded there by New York blacks in 1909. Johnson proclaimed Harlem as a lodestone for blacks from every corner of the earth, as a deeply religious locality of fraternal decency (though he allowed that it also had 'its underworld, its world of pimps and prostitutes, of gamblers and thieves, of illicit love and illicit liquor, of red sins and dark crimes') as the home of an educated élite who went in for bridge parties and high-powered cars, as well as of masses who struggled to make both ends meet like every other working-class New Yorker, but with the additional handicap of knowing that, as a rule, they would be the last to be hired and the first to be fired. James Baldwin, the first black writer to be reared wholly in Harlem (born there in 1924, son of a southern preacher), subsequently noted another thing about that period: 'this was incontestably a community in which every parent was responsible for every child. Any grown-up, seeing me doing something he thought was wrong, could (and did) beat my behind and then carry me home to my Mama and my Daddy and tell them why he beat my behind. Mama and

Daddy would thank him and then beat my behind again. I learned respect for my elders. And I mean respect. I do not mean fear.'

Weldon Johnson emphasised those characteristics that attracted whites to Harlem again between the two world wars, not as inhabitants (perish the thought), not even as near neighbours, but as onlookers, as scrutineers, as voyeurs. For black Harlem had an infectious gift for enjoying itself, a rare knack of giving pleasure, a unique capacity for entertainment. 'It is farthest known as being exotic, colorful and sensuous; a place of laughing, singing and dancing; a place where life wakes up at night.' The whites had already cottoned on to this before the migration uptown, perhaps in the strutting cakewalk dance that was popularised by the black entertainers Bert Williams and George Walker (billed as 'Two Real Coons') on Broadway; which led to cakewalk contests at Madison Square Garden, with grand pianos and gold watches for the prize-winners. But it was in the settlement of Harlem that the black man came into his own as entertainer supreme, especially as a musician. That was where, in the Savoy Ballroom, some of the greatest jazz improvisers could be heard, Louis Armstrong and Earl Hines, Coleman Hawkins and Joe Smith. It was where, in the Manhattan Casino, James Reese Europe and his band of fifty mandolins, thirty harp guitars, ten banjoes, twenty violins, a saxophone, ten cellos, five clarinets, five flutes, five bass violins, three timpani and drums, two organs and ten pianos – 151 instrumentalists in all – gave a concert in 1913 which attracted rave reviews: 'an epoch in the musical life of the Negro . . . an astonishing sight . . . and when the march neared the end and the whole band burst out singing as well as playing, the novelty of this climax . . . brought a very storm of applause.'

It was where young Fats Waller, son of an assistant preacher at the Abyssinian Baptist Church, used to outdo other pianists dazzlingly at rent-parties – at which the party-goers subscribed to help out someone with his rent – and was otherwise employed as an accompanist for silent movies screened at the Lincoln Theatre on West 135th, while a boy called Bill Basie, later to be ennobled as 'Count', sat beside him day after day, studying the Waller keyboard technique. It was where Paul Robeson, law student at Columbia, was making people sit up when he took 'the low voice part' in close-harmony singings at parties and even on street corners, before he became much more famous as an actor in *The Emperor Jones* revival of 1924. It was also where poor Scott Joplin, driven by an obsession to make something grander than the ragtime of his reputation, one day finally managed to put on his opera *Treemonisha* in an obscure Harlem rehearsal hall, without scenery or lighting or props, just Joplin playing the full score on the piano, before an audience that was not much impressed by either the composer or the large cast of singers. He was broken by that, died a couple of years later, and the opera was lost sight of for six decades.

It was Harlem's entertainment value that pulled in the white people night after night between the wars, and not only American whites. The Cotton Club on Lenox at 142nd Street saw its share of the European upper-crust, the likes of Edwina Mountbatten and Nancy Cunard, causing it to be described by tart Harold Arlen as 'the hangout of the Mink Set, escaping Park Avenue for the earthier realities of Harlem'. This was where Lena Horne first made her name, and one of the club's attractions from 1927 was Duke Ellington and his orchestra, whose leader had been as impressed as any white outsider when he first set eyes on Harlem a few years earlier, likening it to something from the Arabian Nights. If there is to be an epitaph to the celebrated sparkling Harlem of that era, then there is maybe nothing more appropriate than the end of Florence Mills. She was a singer and a dancer, who had first been spotted as the outstanding member of a musical comedy chorus line in 1921. This put her in the big time, and she became a star in a Harlem production of *Blackbirds*, of which the critic George Jean Nathan wrote that, 'Florence Mills is, within the limits of her field of theatrical enterprise, America's foremost feminine player. What Jolson is among the men, she is among the women . . .' The show toured Europe for a year (the Prince of Wales was said to have watched it twenty times in London) and when Florence Mills returned to New York aboard the *Ile de France* she received a welcome that far outdid the one awaiting Mayor Jimmy Walker, who was also on the ship: thousands not only met her at Pier 57, but accompanied her back to Harlem in a motorcade. She had, however, come home fatally ill, and died a few weeks later, at the age of thirty-two. The tributes and the flowers came from all over the western world – $100,000 worth of flowers in one day alone. But that was nothing to the funeral Harlem mounted after Florence had lain in state for a week in the chapel of the Howell Undertaking Parlors at 137th Street and Seventh Avenue. Thousands filed past her open coffin there and even more – reports estimated 150,000 – lined the streets and windows of the district as the cortège went by. There was a band in the procession, and nine automobiles loaded with flowers, including a wreath of red roses shaped into a bleeding heart, which left room for nothing else in the first car. The church was overflowing with mourners, both black and white, though it was a large building with room for 3,000. And after the service, the mourners formed up again, this time accompanying the body of Florence Mills in a slow movement up Seventh to the Woodlawn cemetery, though this was some miles away. Presently an aeroplane flew over the procession on that November day, and released a flock of blackbirds into the setting sun . . .

There were other towering figures in that Harlem, apart from the entertainers. The greatest of them was Dr W. E. B. Du Bois, a New Englander who came to New York after studying at Harvard (where he was the first black to obtain a doctorate of philosophy) and at Berlin, and after occupying the chairs of Greek and Latin at Wilberforce, of Economics and History at Atlanta, as well as a teaching post in sociology in Pennsylvania. In Harlem this polymath became a founder of the NAACP, who argued that racial prejudice was harmful to the moral well-being of the American people as a whole, that Africa and Africans had to be freed from the grip of Europeans. On the side he also wrote the first serious study of the American slave trade. Du Bois, in the jargon of a later age, was a black militant: he would die in Africa, citizen of independent Ghana, after being hounded from the States by communist witch-hunters. But he did not toe anybody's party line. He urged blacks during the First World War to 'forget our special grievances and close our ranks shoulder to shoulder with our own white fellow-citizens and the allied nations who are fighting for democracy'. In this he ran counter to the populist demands coming from the pulpit of Adam Clayton Powell, Sr, who had told his congregation some time before that, 'As a race we should let our government know that if it wants us to fight foreign powers we must be given some assurance first of better treatment at home . . .' Powell, a tall and pale man, who could have passed as a white according to some, made the Abyssinian Baptist Church, which he moved from the West Side into Harlem, the largest and richest black man's church in America. He was an attractive and compelling figure with a gift for rhetoric that a politician might lust after, and with a panache that allowed him to alight at the church door from his shiny new Packard (most clergymen with cars made do with aged and second-hand Model Ts) preach a sermon bemoaning the poverty of others, and milk his rapt and adoring listeners for thousands of dollars at the collection. Before Billy Graham there was Adam Clayton Powell, Sr.

It was on the post-war disillusionment of blacks that Marcus Garvey became a power in the land. A West Indian migrant who reached Harlem in 1916, he lost no time in thrusting himself forward as a messianic figure who would lead his people to glory, launching within twelve months of his arrival the Universal Negro Improvement Association. From its headquarters in Liberty Hall on West 138th Street, and in the columns of its weekly *Negro World*, Garvey spelled out his message of racial pride, racial independence and racial integration with the black man's ancestral home. The nub of the message, delivered by Garvey to the first UNIA convention, was this: 'We are striking homeward toward Africa to make her the big black republic. And in the making of Africa the big black republic, what is the barrier? The barrier is the white man; and we say to the white man who dominates Africa that it is to his interest to clear out now, because we are coming . . .' This was not exactly what a majority of Harlem's black leaders had in mind, and at first most of the UNIA's adherents were poor folk who had lately drifted up from the south, or West Indian new arrivals like Garvey himself. But at the end of the war, blacks of all kinds joined in their thousands, after a series of race riots had broken out across the States. This had been a periodic feature of the landscape in New York – the shift from the West Side to Harlem had been partly prompted in 1900 by the worst racial conflict since the Draft Riots of 1863, and Harlem's first race riot had occurred during a neighbourhood baseball game there in 1911 between blacks and whites – but nothing like this nationwide violence had been known before, with hundreds of blacks beaten to death and lynched, culminating in a massacre at St Louis in the mid-west. Some saw these events related to old grudges which the Civil War had not healed, others laid part of the blame on President Woodrow Wilson, who seemed more intent on an international posture than on justice at home. On these and other black resentments, Marcus Garvey came to the height of his fame.

He was a man of enormous vanity, with a taste for the grandiose. He styled himself Provisional President of Africa, and arranged his supporters at the top of UNIA into a hierarchy of knights and dukes and duchesses, with gaudy decorations for those in whom he was best pleased – Order of the Nile, Distinguished Service Order of Ethiopia, and the like. At the association's annual conventions, there were tremendous parades through Harlem, with Provisional President Garvey taking the salute as cohorts from almost every continent marched past in uniforms of black, red, green and blue. It is said that the parade of 1922, when the UNIA reckoned to have an international membership of between four and six million, was the biggest and most extravagant of any kind that has marched those streets before or since. The extravagance did not endear Garvey to other black leaders, rigorous socialists like Chandler Owen and A. Philip Randolph as well as the cool intellectual Du Bois and the religious demagogue Powell, who generally took the view that Garvey was nothing more than a Caribbean carpetbagger. They wondered, too, about the extent and real purpose of his numerous business enterprises, of which the most ambitious was the Black Star Shipping Line, ostensibly created to prove that blacks could match whites in big business, and to fulfil Garvey's fantasy that they would one day retake Africa in an armada of their own. This was where he overreached himself, being convicted in 1925 of fraudulently using the US Mails to transact shares in the Black Star Line. He did time in the Atlanta Penitentiary for that before being deported to Jamaica, whence he had come just eleven years before. At which the UNIA swiftly dissolved, though not without leaving a message that would be taken up again by Africanists in the next generation.

Not long after Marcus Garvey left Harlem, there appeared on stage another vivid figure in the person of George Baker, alias Father Divine, in whom some saw Garvey's natural heir. He came from somewhere in the south, by way of Baltimore, where he had been a Sunday school teacher and odd-job man, and a part of Long Island (Suffolk County) which was notoriously a centre of the Ku Klux Klan. He was thrown into jail there on some pretext, but had been inside only a day or two when the sentencing judge dropped dead with a heart attack, which was taken by Father Divine's followers as clear evidence of his divinity ('I hated to do it,' Divine said benignly, on hearing of the judge's death). In Harlem after serving time, he enlarged on the reputation he had already begun to build on Long Island, attracting thousands, and accepting their worship of him as God incarnate. He called them all angels and named individuals Glorious Illumination, Heavenly Dove, Pleasing Joy and other fancies. In return they sang hymns with lines like, 'He has the world in a jug and the stopper in his hand'. He preached an upstanding morality which denounced smoking, drinking, crime, racial hatred, bad language, hair-straightening, buying on credit and promiscuity. His headquarters at 152 West 126th Street was called The Kingdom and there no regular prayer meetings were held, just continuous songs of praise and dance music, with an address from Father Divine at eleven o'clock each night. There he also lavished upon his followers colossal banquets, over which this bald fellow presided in a striped shirt, striped tie and grey suit, while the diners gorged themselves on one ample course after another. There were smaller kingdoms scattered around the black community, where lodgings and cheap meals could be had, and there was a variety of businesses – from grocery stores to shoeshine stands, from gasoline stations to dry-cleaning shops – in the hinterland of this enterprise, all in the name of different angels, but all contributing to the conspicuous bounty that Father Divine alone controlled. 'Thus far,' remarked the unimpeachable WPA Guide in 1939, 'all attempts to probe the finances of Father Divine and his sect have been unsuccessful.' They succeeded a few years later, when the sublime man faced due legal processes once more, this time over his dealings in real estate. He was last seen heading for Philadelphia, and in Harlem the evangelical void he left was eagerly filled by the likes of Sweet Daddy Grace, Elder Lightfoot Michaux and old Mother Horn.

Then there was Madame C. J. Walker, who came to Harlem from Indianapolis in 1914 already a millionaire, and left it even richer for a mansion in Westchester County, which became legendary for tremendous entertainments attended by the black parvenus of New York. Her wealth came from her string of beauty parlours, which stretched not only across the United States, but extended to Central America and the West Indies, too. She ran this cosmetic empire with the help of her daughter A'Lelia, who became a hostess in her own right: 'the joy-goddess of Harlem's 1920s', according to Langston Hughes, 'her parties . . . as crowded as the New York subway at the rush-hour', who died young like Florence Mills and was given a send-off almost to match hers, with a night club quartet singing Noël Coward's 'I'll see you again' over A'Lelia's coffin in the funeral parlour on Seventh Avenue. All of this had resulted from the inspired determination of a poor black washerwoman ages before in St Louis; for that was where Madame Walker had been known as Sarah Breedlove, married at fourteen and widowed with a small daughter at twenty. She took in washing to support the pair of them, and over the tub one day had the thought that was to transform their lives. It was based upon the wretched truth that many black women desperately tried to straighten their tight-curled hair, which was an almost impossible defiance of nature. And what led to the fortune derived from the Madame Walker Hair Straightening Process, the Walker College of Hair Culture, and the various ramifications that accompanied them, was the observed fact that crinkled garments could be smoothed by the application of a hot flat iron, from which it might be supposed that if a hot combing iron was used on hair

. . . 'Briefly, the Walker System was a method of laundering hair.'

Harlem would never know another age like those few years leading up to the 1930s, even though the glittering high-life lingered there through the great economic slump, available as ever to the impervious rich. Cab Calloway's band opened at the Savoy just after the Wall Street Crash and, like many other pleasure spots, the place was packed night after night. Yet before long, jobless entertainers were among those who hoped their luck might change if they touched the Tree of Hope which grew near the Lafayette Theatre on Seventh Avenue. Black people in general suffered even more than whites during the Depression in New York, reckoning their unemployment level at 50 or even 60 per cent, whereas the average throughout the city was one-quarter of the working population. And when they did manage to get a job, black men were paid even more miserably than white workmen, their wage packets usually lighter by two-fifths. This was a time when restaurants advertised three-course meals ('As much as you can eat') for forty cents, and when the Harlem churches ran soup kitchens, shelters for down-and-outs, and other charities: at Adam Clayton Powell's Abyssinian Baptist Church in the first three months of 1931, they doled out 28,500 free meals, 525 food baskets, 17,982 garments, and 2,564 pairs of shoes. This was also a time when more than 10,000 people were reduced to living in cellars and basements in Harlem, as tenements became overcrowded with people who tried to keep down the individual cost of rent by spreading the sum demanded by the landlord as widely as possible. Even that didn't always raise the required amount, and evictions were commonplace, from ten to twenty a day in the Harlem of 1931. The blacks of New York emerged from the Depression even more bitter about their exploitation by whites than they had entered it, as bitter as they had been after another dark time: 'Ten years of Depression had been for the Negroes a disaster that almost rivalled slavery.'

Like every other species of New York poor, they were rescued by the Second World War, and when that was over the racial pattern of the city began to change fast. The black population was soon swollen by fresh arrivals from the south, cotton-pickers and the like, of the umpteenth generation, made redundant at last in the land of Jim Crow as a result of agriculture becoming mechanised. It is said that each decade after 1945 saw one million of these people uprooting themselves and heading for a better life in the north. Those who made for New York helped to transform parts of the city which, before the war, had known blacks in not much more than token strength. Only Brooklyn, outside Harlem, had been settled in any quantity, with 110,000 by 1940. Twenty years later there would be more than thrice that number. Over the same period, blacks in the Bronx increased from 25,000 to 164,000, in Queens from 25,000 to 146,000. Just before Harlem entered the war, some 298,000 blacks had been lodged there, and even though some may have felt overcrowded by then, saturation point had not been reached: by 1960 the figure had risen to 397,000.

The racial transformation was accelerated in the post-war years by the great migration from Puerto Rico and other Spanish-speaking parts of the Caribbean – those half million souls who suddenly found New York accessible through cheap air fares, the vanguard of many more who are still coming. They were not so very different from many of the city's English-speaking blacks, some Puerto Ricans also being able to trace a tortuous ancestry to trans-Atlantic slave ships. Another similarity was that large numbers belonged to Spiritualist and Pentecostal sects if they had any religion at all. Although many were nominally Catholic it became apparent in New York that whatever zeal had been shown in the Caribbean paled once the move had been made: one explanation of this was that they regarded the Church as a Spanish colonial relic, therefore to be rejected as soon as possible. Social workers made other discoveries about the newcomers. Although they complained far less than blacks about discrimination at work, the suspicion grew that this was largely because they were less aggressive in fighting for their rights. These Puerto Ricans quickly replaced the blacks at the bottom of the economic and social pile, with lower family incomes and higher rates of unemployment. Their economic plight was increased by their truly phenomenal birthrates, which were anything from twice to five times greater than that of whites, depending on the age group, and one-third higher than that of blacks, achieved as often as not out of wedlock by priapic young men who had not been reared with the discipline of James Baldwin and his peers. These differences passed by the generality of New York whites, though they could not fail to notice the growing incidence of Spanish upon the ear and in public prints, and soon became aware that there was an even greater colour range among the Latins than among the so-called blacks. They paid attention most of all to the news that one-quarter of New York's population by 1964 consisted of this motley collection of distinctly non-whites. Them and Us merely indicated an ampler range of prejudices after the post-war Latins arrived.

Some of the prejudices, as always, were reflected in the jobs that were and were not available to these people. The Brooklyn Dodgers may have broken the major league baseball colour bar by recruiting Jackie Robinson in 1947, but thirteen seasons later the New York Yankees had still admitted no more than one black and one Latin to their playing strength. That was the year when the Rev. Adam Clayton Powell, Jr, dashing son of a magnetic father, told Congress that if New York blacks enjoyed parity with whites they would hold 21 per cent of the jobs in the gift of City Hall, but in fact had only 6 per cent of the plum positions depending on the patronage of Mr Mayor – as judges, Commissioners and other influential folk. This was a better record than in many cities of the north, like Chicago, and New York more often than not came out better than most in such urban comparisons. But this was scant consolation to a community that was increasingly aware, as it had been since the turn of the century, that the hostility of whites was absolutely to be relied on if you tried to go live next door to them – or even if you moved into the same neighbourhood. That was when real nastiness began.

In the old days along the West Side and lower down Manhattan, the blacks had found the Irish the most unpleasantly belliger-ent people around. The mobs which rioted against Civil War conscription had largely consisted of Irishmen, and they were foremost among those who lynched blacks and burned the black orphanage in that desperate week. Now it was the turn of Puerto Ricans to experience Irish animosity, when Spanish Harlem became too small to accommodate the rapidly expanding population of Latins. They began to move into old working-class districts of the Bronx, where one of their Catholic priests was astounded to find that Catholic Irish there met them with outright loathing – 'absolute hatred and disregard'. He tried to see the Irish point of view, comprehending that the Latins might seem to them indolent, feckless, taking everything they could from welfare and producing nothing but too many children: but the fact was that these long-standing pillars of the Irish parishes also hated him, a Catholic priest. They encouraged their young men in the gang warfare which developed, when the Irish bucks would go hunting for 'niggers and spics', armed with chains and baseball bats.*

In this the Irish found ready allies among the Italians, whose hostility to blacks did not go back quite as far as the Hibernian variety, but was just as venomous once it had formed. It was Italian baseball players on the Brooklyn Dodgers' staff – not white players from the deep south – who tried to organise a walkout against Jackie Robinson when he joined the team in 1947. It was Italians in Brooklyn who, in the 1960s, started the Society for the Prevention of Niggers from Getting Everything, its members walking the streets with placards saying, 'Go Back to Africa, Niggers'. They also attacked Mayor John Lindsay with these epithets when he was running for a second term, seeing in him a specimen of the detested white liberalism which was committed to civil rights. Italians throughout the northern United States became prominent adversaries of civil rights, men like Frank Rizzo in Philadelphia and Tony Imperiale in Newark presenting themselves as the great white hopes of immaculate Americans. In New York this role was fulfilled by one Mario Procaccino, a rough-house Democrat who ran Lindsay very close at the polls; of which one Brooklyn voter said, 'I voted for Procaccino because I thought an Italian would knock the blacks out after Pretty Boy Lindsay had let them in.'

* 'Spic' = 'Hispanic'.

That voter was not Italian, but Jewish: and the Jews of New York hold a special place in the disaffections of the blacks. This is in spite of the fact that Jews have supported civil rights as much as any group, and very probably in larger proportions than anyone except the blacks themselves. But there is another side to the relationship, and it tends to figure more prominently in the lore of metropolitan blacks. James Baldwin has remembered 'meeting no Negro in the years of my growing up, in my family or out of it, who would ever really trust a Jew, and few who did not, indeed, exhibit for them the blackest contempt. Jews in Harlem are small tradesmen, rent collectors, real estate agents and pawnbrokers; they operate in accordance with the American business tradition of exploiting Negroes, and they are therefore identified with oppression and are hated for it.' Jews have also often been the landlords of black people; which is not always an endearing relationship, whoever is involved, or where. The two races coincide, too, at the place of work, and sometimes this means that they collide. The Jewish housewife will often employ a black servant woman (though this reality is often camouflaged by the euphemism 'home help') and the Jewish husband may employ a number of black men in his business, or may be part of a union leadership which tells black members what they should and should not do. The black who is in one of the professions – government service, teaching, social work and the like – often finds himself subordinate to Jews, whose chance to climb into the American middle class came a generation or two before his. The opportunities for black resenting Jew are almost unlimited in New York.

They are inherent, as much as anywhere, in the ghetto mentality which still persists to an extraordinary degree in and around the city among observant Jews, of whom Mr Procaccino's supporter was presumably one. When the Jewish builder, William Levitt, purchased a huge tract of empty Long Island just after the war and constructed a new community there, he was not merely offering reasonable housing at bargain prices to returned servicemen and their families, nor even just trying to make a substantial profit for himself. Levittown arose on that site with the intention, among others, of providing a domicile for white

people unpolluted by blacks.* When Mayor Lindsay and his
men tried to introduce a measure of public housing into the
Forest Hills area of Queens, this was instantly seen by that
extensively Jewish community as an intolerable threat to their
safety, for it would almost certainly let blacks in. A rabbi who
tried to convince the Mayor and his staff that it was vital the
plan be dropped, puzzled those decent but parochial gentiles
by referring to Queens as 'our Bar-Lev Line' – a reference,
which any Jew would pick up, to an Israeli fortification in the
Sinai Desert after the Six-Day War, a security against further
Arab attack.

A New York black a few years earlier had savagely expressed
the alternative hostile view. 'Everybody talks about the six million Jews [who went to the gas ovens of the Third Reich],' said
Malcolm X, 'but I was reading a book the other day that showed
that one hundred million of us were kidnapped and brought to
this country – *one hundred million*. Now everybody's wet-eyed
over a handful of Jews who brought it on themselves. What
about our hundred million?' He had been born Malcolm Little
in Nebraska, and had arrived in Harlem early in the war as a
kid selling sandwiches to passengers on the train ride between
Boston and New York. He exchanged that job for one at Small's
Paradise, the black jazz club on Seventh Avenue, but lost it
and drifted into drugs and crime, which put him in prison for
six cataclysmic years. It was there that he was introduced by
another inmate to the Lost-Found Nation in the Wilderness,
the Nation of Islam, the Black Muslims. When he emerged
from the Massachusetts State Penitentiary in 1952, Malcolm
Little was a reformed character and an obsessed one. He had
also become Malcolm X – the X 'a reminder of I don't know
who I am', a gesture to the deepest injury done to the black
man by the whites.

The Nation had been born when Malcolm was only five

* How well Levitt succeeded in his intention may be deduced from a 1980
survey of population in the 4th Congressional District, which includes all of
Levittown and some other parts of Nassau County. Blacks, Latins and Asians
totalled no more than 7 per cent of the whole.

years old, at Detroit in 1930. An indistinct character who went under various names but is now mostly known as Mr Farrad, a door-to-door salesman and possibly an Arab immigrant, presented himself to the local blacks as nothing less than Allah the All-Perfect One. He offered an exotic theology which combined certain familiar propositions with a great deal of mumbo-jumbo, but the burden of it was extremely attractive to exploited and impoverished people who yearned for some historic tables to be turned. They were to get even at last with the devil race, which had taken them out of Africa and into bondage. Mr Farrad quite coolly said that he had come to destroy the white man's world. For four years he lived among those poor people in Detroit, and selected as his chief disciple a man called Poole, who had come north from Georgia after the First World War. Poole was at once translated into Elijah Muhammad, the Last Messenger, and given instructions about the task in hand. Then Mr Farrad apparently vanished, never reliably reported to be seen again.

By the time Malcolm X emerged from prison, Elijah Muhammad was running the Black Muslims from headquarters in Chicago, with his winter retreat at Phoenix, Arizona. The older man took a liking to Malcolm; and many people, both black and white, have testified to his sunny disposition in private, or when his sense of humour was touched on a platform. It was rarely shown in public once Elijah Muhammad sent him back to Harlem to open the mosque there in 1954. He preached steadily and brutally the evil nature of all whites with compelling oratory. The Black Muslims wanted no truck with the democratic approach to change favoured by the civil rights movement, and after Malcolm one night had urged his supporters to show Martin Luther King what they thought of him on the morrow, King was splattered with broken eggs thrown at him by black men on the streets of Harlem. This was as though Marcus Garvey's chief henchman had ordered an assault on Dr Du Bois, which would have been unthinkable back in those days between the wars, which were also passionate. For ten years Malcolm X went on in this vein, a rabble-rousing prince among blacks, and one who more and more took the limelight away from the Last Messenger farther north. It was Malcolm, not Elijah Muhammad, who completed the boxer Cassius Clay's conversion to Islam and presided over his reincarnation as Muhammed Ali the day after he beat Sonny Liston for the heavyweight championship of the world. 'It was Malcolm, not Mr Muhammad, who was second only to Barry Goldwater among the most sought-after campus speakers of the day; Malcolm, not Mr Muhammad, who was approached by Doubleday with a $20,000 advance and a contract for an autobiography.'

It was inevitable that their partnership would break up. A jealous Elijah Muhammad began to isolate Malcolm X from the centre of the Nation, and Malcolm in retaliation had a hand in circulating stories that the supposedly celibate Messenger had made a number of his secretaries pregnant; at which the Messenger made it clear that there was no future for him within the Black Muslim community. So in 1964 Malcolm X set up shop on his own account, in Suite 128 of the Theresa Hotel on Seventh Avenue. The hotel had managed to function without admitting blacks until about 1940, but after that it became Harlem's version of the Waldorf-Astoria; where Joe Louis held parties to celebrate his boxing triumphs, where Adam Clayton Powell, Jr, made many of his political speeches, and where visiting black bandleaders invariably stayed when they came to New York.* It had played host to Fidel Castro when the Cuban leader attended the United Nations in 1960, after he had walked out of an East Side hotel, the Shelburne, complaining that he had been overcharged; and at the Theresa his visitors had included the Russian Mr Khrushchev ('the biggest event on 125th Street since the funeral in 1958 of W. C. Handy, who wrote "St Louis Blues"') and 'a leader of the so-called Muslim movement among United States Negroes, who calls himself Malcolm X'.

Installed in the Theresa himself now, but no longer a leader of the Muslims, Malcolm made a pilgrimage to Mecca and visited Ghana, Black Africa's first ex-colonial independent state, where old Du Bois had died in exile just twelve months before. In these

---

* Until about 1940 the Theresa's position on the corner of West 125th Street was several blocks below Black Harlem's southern boundary. The hotel was named after the wife of a Mr Seidenberg, its first owner in 1913.

travels Malcolm appears to have been innocently excited by the wonder of strange places, and to have revised to some extent his former stance on white devils and its relevance to true Islam: it is conceivable that in Ghana someone had informed him of an historical truth he had not known before; that the most persistent slave trading in Africa was carried out not by evil Christians (and certainly not by wicked Jews) but by devout Muslims from Arabia and adjacent Islamic lands. On his return to the Theresa Hotel, he launched his Organisation of Afro-American Unity, and although he was still deeply hostile to white people in general, a gratuitous viciousness in his homilies seemed to have been toned down. Within the year he would be announcing that, 'I'm waking up America to the great Muslim menace'. That was after his old patron had turned even more uncompromisingly against him. Elijah Muhammad ordered his eviction from the house, a property of the New York mosque, that had been given to Malcolm during the honeymoon period a decade earlier. Before a court ruling on the eviction could be made, firebombs were thrown into the building, with Malcolm, his wife and their four children asleep inside, and they barely got out before the place went up in flames. This happened just one week before he was due to announce his new political programme to the OAAU.

The meeting was to be held in the Audubon Ballroom on 166th Street and, when the day came, Malcolm was roused from his sleep by an ominous telephone call. A voice simply said, 'Wake up, brother,' then rang off. Early that afternoon he set off for the appointment, parking his car twenty blocks from the ballroom as a precaution, and going the rest of the way by bus. Some 400 people were there, waiting for him to speak, and they listened to an introduction – a warm-up speech – from one of his oldest confidants first. Then he himself came on stage and greeted the crowd with, 'As salaam alaikum,' from behind his plywood lectern. That was when two men in the audience began to scuffle with each other, distracting everybody's attention, while a third man slipped forward with a sawn-off shotgun and fired it point-blank at Malcolm X. Elijah Muhammad's Nation had settled its most pressing score.

Twenty-one years later, in 1986, times had changed enough for the New York City Opera Company, no less, to stage a new work based on the life of Malcolm X, whose widow and children attended the première. There were other indications of change that year. The Black Muslims had long modified their position – they were beginning to do so even before Elijah Muhammad died in 1975 – and at Malcolm X's old mosque the rites now resembled the orthodoxies of Mecca much more closely than once was the case. Small's Paradise, where Malcolm got his first job in New York, had but lately closed down; and a lad lounging by the padlocked door that summer reckoned from what he'd heard that it wouldn't be opening no more. The Theresa Hotel had been transformed into the Theresa Towers, an office block, with a motley of shops trailing around its ground floor like a skirt. On Washington Heights, trash and a vandalised car lay outside the shuttered Audubon Ballroom, and there was some talk of it being demolished to make way for a Columbia University redevelopment. Far from trying to straighten their hair in mortification any more, fashionable young black women were ready to pay a couple of hundred bucks or so to have it braided exultantly in complex African styles. And most of the talk just then was not about anything to do with Harlem directly, or even wider New York. It was all to do with a faraway place called Soweto, and the name on everybody's lips was that of South African Winnie Mandela. Menace was not in the air of Harlem that year, except along a few notorious stretches occupied by drug-pushers and the people they had crazed, and just occasionally when a man in liquor stumbled upon a gaggle of pale voyeurs. For the most part Harlem felt a peaceable place, and in Adele's Kitchen on Lenox, over a dish of grits and scrambled eggs, people were warm and made welcome the strange-sounding visitor from Europe who was descended from an old slave-trading breed. They told him that lately a number of white folk, in that New York cycle known as gentrification, had started to move back into Harlem's still elegant brownstones.

It is no longer the black city within a city. Nowhere can make that claim now, for blacks dwell in all the boroughs, though only as a token number on Staten Island. The biggest concentration by far is in Brooklyn nowadays, which West Indians especially have made their own patch, with their games of cricket, and their jerk chicken, and their Rasta dreadlocks arranged sometimes in unlikely bouffants under floppy caps: they have turned Eastern Parkway on Labor Day into a replica of Bridgetown or Port-of-Spain on a Test Match weekend, with steel drummers beatin' pan in calypso time and impromptu limbo dances pulsating along the street. Brooklyn also exhibits the bottom of the barrel as far as the black community is concerned, in poor benighted Brownsville, which was the borough's chief Jewish neighbourhood until thirty years ago, and has since become a shattered slum, as unpleasant in every way as any part of the South Bronx. 'It is the sort of place anybody with an ability to make his own way will get out of, and so it is the province of the helpless and the vicious, the crippled and the criminal.'

For some things have changed not at all in New York since Malcolm X was raging against the fates, and before him all those other black rebels, too, stretching back into a distance before Harlem was black. Discriminations and prejudices still abound. In spite of the Equal Employment Opportunity Commission, the proportion of blacks and Latins obtaining jobs at any level with the big New York law firms is suspiciously low, compared with the record in banking and insurance. In the city's job market as a whole, only one in four blacks, only one in five Latins, appear in the top income group, which is dominated by white men and women; and at the other end of the income scale, 54 per cent of black wage-earners and 64 per cent of the Latins are most prominent, compared to only one-quarter of the whites. Figures such as these can partly be explained by inertia or incapacity among those who come off worst; but not all the time. Therefore other manifestations have remained unaltered across the years: resentments persist. The black community played no part in the official Statue of Liberty celebrations of 1986 – they seemed to have been quite deliberately excluded from the deafening razzmatazz around New York Harbor that weekend – and so in a Harlem museum they mounted a dignified exhibition of their own, to show what they had contributed to this nation of theirs. The Caribbean Cultural Center put on a dancing and musical concert in order to make the same point, advertising this beforehand with posters which were headed 'Sweet Land of Liberty . . . For Whom? Sweet Land of Liberty . . . Will it ever be for us?' And Queen Mother Moore, an old body of eighty-eight who had spent her lifetime working for civil rights, stood up for a reparations committee 'seeking 100 trillion dollars in money damages from the United States Government for the victims of the "middle passage" and those who perished in the traffic of slavery during more than 244 years of enslavement, lynchings, beating, rapings, police brutality, severance of ancestral ties, and *de facto* genocide.'

It is a preposterous claim, of course, and one that hasn't a hope of being met. But what it stands for cannot be dismissed just like that. A balance of power, after all, has changed quite dramatically in New York these past few years. The blacks are no longer the minority they were, and if they make common cause with the Latins they very nearly have the upper hand; may already have it as these words are set down. For in 1980 the city's white population was not more than 52 per cent of the whole. At least one distance separating Them and Us is closing fast – uncomfortably so for some.

SIX

ALMIGHTY DOLLAR

The street frontage suggests drama or ritual inside. There are theatres and churches in Europe which look like this, with a pediment upheld by fluted Corinthian columns, and sculptured figures posing above the cornice. The central character is said to represent integrity, the supporting roles various forms of production, and they are cast in metal nowadays because the original stone carvings disintegrated in the polluted air of New York. This was not a gratifying omen when they were there to embellish the very fulcrum of our economic free-for-all. If there is such a thing as the international headquarters of the capitalist world, then it is right there in the New York Stock Exchange. No wonder George Washington eyes it speculatively from his pedestal on Wall Street, a hundred yards away.* And many's the financial wizard who, emerging from yet another profitable session in the Exchange, will have hailed that virtuous man gratefully (for he, in a sense, began it all) with New York's most buoyant greeting – 'Have a NYSE day!'

Theatrical it is inside, with occasional moments of high drama, on a set which might have been arranged by someone whose first instinct was to produce Greek tragedy, before he had second thoughts and decided to mount a Spielberg fantasy instead. The chamber is vast and all of a piece with that frontage on the street,

---

* Washington's statue stands on the spot where he was sworn in as the first President of the United States on April 30, 1789.

Corinthian capitals again, on the pilasters this time, around tastefully marbled walls, beneath an intricately moulded ceiling. Within this restrained decency, the imagination of the twentieth century has been let loose in what looks suspiciously like a haphazard splat of all the technology we can muster. A network of thick and shiny tubes, straight and bent and curved, occupies most of the space between the ceiling and the floor, coming to ground at crucial points in the Stock Exchange's nervous system. These are great chest-high desks which have been arranged regularly round the floor in twenty or more large horseshoes. Within each horseshoe several men are laagered, together with batteries of telephones, pigeon holes crammed with ledgers and directories, and banks of video screens bolted into frameworks so that they tilt overhead at intimidating angles, bearing green messages that can spell ruin to some. Around the perimeters of the chamber are upright booths less amply equipped, and on the walls above them is what the great communicators of our day call message crawl – more electronic hieroglyphs which roll endlessly by like the Motogram which has been circulating the news across Times Square for the past sixty years. The flashes here keep tally of changes in value; and, not far from each, the orange figures of a digital clock are noted by brokers and clerks in the same knowing glance, for time is money – maybe a fortune – round here.

It is possible for outsiders to watch all this from a viewing gallery, with audio commentaries in several tongues which try to make some sense of the confusion below, on the other side of the sound-proofed glass. This is like looking into a beehive when the lid has been taken off, with insect men crowded round the horseshoe trading posts, others massing round the perimeter booths, even more scurrying from one place to another with anxious, avaricious or merely thoughtful expressions on their faces. And such an untidy hive, with scraps of paper littering the deck everywhere, bushels of them by four in the afternoon and the end of another day. Down on the floor you have to tread carefully if you're not to skid damagingly on someone's discarded bid for riches beyond the dreams of avarice. It can be bedlam, with small pockets of calm where men (and an occasional woman) stand attentively beside a video display, awaiting the signal that will project them, too, into the vortex around. People shout to each other, wave frantically, pass messages, gabble breathless cryptograms into phones jammed under their necks, while scribbling something entirely different on a notepad and thrusting it into a messenger's hand. Someone hails a man passing one of the posts and he dashes – no, he *walks* at speed, for running is forbidden here – to one of the outer booths, snatches a phone from a waiting hand, exchanges half a dozen words down the line, dashes back to the post, taking in the message crawl and the time on his way, grabs a pad and writes, hands the torn-off note across the counter, looks keenly at the fellow who shouted a few minutes before, gets a nod in return – and blows out his cheeks in some relief. He has just completed a transaction worth two million bucks. This is a matter of nerve and judgement and accumulated know-how, and a great deal of mutual trust between people who do business together in here. They also need a taste for making money work, an appetite for wealth above almost anything else. It is, or it is close to, a pathological condition, endemic in New York to a degree few other cities know.

It is not always dignified down there on the floor. That man, who is probably pulling a cool half million for himself each year, senior partner in a brokerage house, used to come to the Exchange in a suit, with a fresh flower in his buttonhole each day. Now he wears a tradesman's linen jacket and sneakers, more comfortably, because the suit was for ever getting messed up with other people's ballpoint marks as they bustled past, and the day someone stole the silver flower-holder from behind his lapel, he decided that was it. When trading goes berserk, which it not uncommonly does, people have had their clothing ripped in the push and shove. Horseplay is not unknown. It is not so long ago since somebody put a canister of tear-gas into the air-conditioning system, which cleared the floor faster than any fire alarm. Water pistols are used from time to time, just to liven up a dull day. A couple of brokers who detested each other and unwarily stood close together in the throng round a post, found themselves handcuffed to each other for several hours, the only people on the New York Stock Exchange who failed to see the joke. And not everyone is deemed fit to participate in, or even be on the receiving end of, that sort of prank. Fewer than 1,500 people are admitted to membership of NYSE, and when a seat becomes vacant it is never cheap to buy; $575,000 was the asking price for one offered in 1986. It is exclusive in another way, too, being almost wholly an axis of Irish, Jews and WASPs, an unlikely combination, but one for whom the American Dream can come spectacularly true any working day of the week. Here the sky is by no means the limit for even the lowliest of the chosen ones, as has been demonstrated more than once. John Coleman was the son of a New York cop with a large family to feed, and he left school at fourteen to become a messenger on the floor of the Exchange, sharp enough and industrious enough and thrifty enough to be a coming man before he achieved his majority. He was already, at nineteen, on Cardinal Spellman's Committee of the Laity soliciting special gifts for the New York diocese, and within months was established enough to become a member of what is nowadays known as the American Stock Exchange, the much smaller beehive just up the road.* Two years later he was back at NYSE, this time with a seat of his own. Thereafter he not only prospered exceedingly, but became a power on the Exchange, finishing as chairman and the man whose word was law there until 1960, when he retired, having also become chief financial adviser to the Cardinal Archbishop of New York, a Papal Knight and a Papal Chamberlain. At which point, worth several millions if he was worth a cent, he comfortably observed that, 'This is the greatest business in the world.'

From its folksy beginning, when brokers signed their agreement under *platanus occidentalis* (the buttonwood tree) in May 1792, this establishment and its hinterland in New York has set the pace in matters financial, first across America, then across the whole world. It isn't quite the oldest institution of its kind: it comes between the London Stock Exchange (1773) and the

---

* When Coleman joined it in 1922, this was still known as the Curb Exchange. In total shares traded in a year it does less than 10 per cent of the business enjoyed by NYSE. A seat there in 1986 cost $145,000.

Paris Bourse (1808). But from the end of the First World War it overtook London in the numbers that count. Since then, this is where both bull and bear markets have originated, a jargon which obscures the truth, as it is sometimes meant to do, that money manipulated in this city, as nowhere else, can settle destinies at home and in far-off lands, determining where poverty and plenty shall be, in what proportions which people shall eat or starve. The hundreds of millions of dollars which change hands in that beehive every day are merely a symptom of NYSE's – of New York's – global influence. What happens in the square mile or two of Manhattan which we refer to as 'Wall Street', affects every one of us in a world which has been reduced by telecommunications and satellites, by fibre optics and the silicone chip, to a manipulator's nirvana. But a full generation before that happened, this place caused a catastrophe which is remembered in one of the most ominous phrases in the vocabulary of the civilised world – the Wall Street Crash.

Wall Street itself would be a nondescript thoroughfare, were it not for Washington's statue outside the handsome old Federal Hall, and for the slender outline of Trinity Church, visible across Broadway at the top end. Nothing else is worth a second glance, in what has been made into a gully – a relatively brief one – by the high buildings on every side. Henry James is not the only person who will have deplored 'the special skyscraper that overhangs poor old Trinity to the north', though 'poor old Trinity' was never a felicitous description, and certainly isn't an accurate one today.* Here is one of the wealthiest parishes in Christendom, which was doing very nicely even before it opened its Center for Ethics and Corporate Policy, to which companies pay $10,000 for short seminars, or up to $100,000 if they wish their executives to be regularly indoctrinated in the meet and right capitalist approach. Nothing at all round Wall Street is worshipped more ardently than the dollar and the flag itself. A building here is incomplete without its

---

* Endowed by Queen Anne in 1705 with a considerable grant of land in lower Manhattan, Trinity Church ever since has been one of New York's most substantial landowners.

pole aslant the sidewalk, billowing the Stars and Stripes. It was in these surroundings that a Rockefeller aide one day characterised the Financial District in one predictably patriotic image: it was, he said, 'the heart pump of the capital blood that sustains the free world'. Someone else has said, sympathetically, that the business of the Chase Manhattan Bank (the Rockefeller holding which spawned American Express) has often been 'indistinguishable from foreign policy itself'. And, to be sure, most students of international affairs will have been struck with the thought that a number of extremely unattractive regimes in Latin America and elsewhere across the globe have been maintained in working order against the contaminations of communism, not so much by the persuasions of diplomats in Washington, as by the more material blandishments of bankers in New York. They may also have noted that this free world of ours is not quite such an assortment of independencies as the phrase is meant to imply. New York is not only the big centre of American banking; it is where the foreigners now need to be most of all. In 1964 there were no more than eleven foreign banks in the whole of the USA. Thirteen years later there were 128 in Manhattan alone. There are more than 300 today.

There was a time when New York was something other than this. In the 1850s it was the most extensive cattle market in America, and within another ten years it had become the chief sugar refinery in the land, converting the crude crystals imported from the West Indies and Brazil. It had considerable heavy industry, with forty firms building steam engines, and one, the Novelty Iron Works on the East River, employing more than a thousand operatives to make marine equipment and other hardware. Here, 30 per cent of all the nation's printing was done, and this was a major provider of American clothing. There was light industry galore in the middle of that nineteenth century, more than 4,300 small factories making everything here from soap to furniture, from telescopes to pianos. By 1860, New York (which still meant no more than Manhattan) was the principal manufacturing centre of the United States, with Brooklyn not far behind in fifth place. Within a single generation, New York 'had transformed itself from a large mercantile city . . . into a world metropolis'. The chief instruments by which it achieved this primacy were, as we have already noted, the expansion of the port to handle its lucrative trans-Atlantic trade, and the enlargement of other communications: on these advantages, industry was able to develop and prosper.

The decline of New York as an industrial city took place over a much longer period, but it accelerated after the Second World War. Between 1950 and 1985 the number of craft and labouring jobs fell from 1,070,000 to 440,000. 'Basic economic factors' were held responsible: jargon again, in this case a decoy for the increasingly high cost of everything in New York – of land, of building, of labour, of all overheads; also for periodic collapses in the stock market, therefore a shortage of money to invest; as much as anything, perhaps, for New York's own altered self-image, its new awareness of the possibilities awaiting it in a world outside America that had not merely been devastated by war, but was utterly and for ever transformed, in some need of confident leadership. There would thus be purely domestic changes, ordained by City Hall, such as new zoning laws to improve the quality of life by pushing dirty, smelly things like factories where they belonged – out of the way. There would be much larger adjustments, policy changes made in the shrewder boardrooms, where they eyed the transformed world with a benevolent gleam and decided it should have the leadership it craved; at a price. What with one thing and another, New York ceased to be a blue-collar city to any significant extent, the garment industry being the only one of its traditional stand-bys which has survived in anything like its old shape.* Within a generation of the war, its biggest employers had become people who did not take kindly to labour unions; banks, insurance companies, corporate offices, large stores, and that organism George Orwell warned us all against, identified with Newspeak in some parts of the world and known as the communications industry over

---

* In recent years, New York factories have employed no more than 14 per cent of the city's workforce: 51 per cent of them need fewer than ten operatives, 80 per cent fewer than fifty. In striking contrast to, say, San Francisco, under one per cent of New York jobs are in high-tech industries.

here. Before anywhere else in the United States, New York decided to specialise in providing services, not goods. It would not make things to produce wealth, it would handle wealth itself, shuffling it about in stocks and shares and bonds and printouts and always, of course, in dollar bills. In its upsy-downsy, cheerfully tough and invariably smart and inimitable way, New York would become 'the international center of capital information exchange, and corporate decision-making'. That, or something like it, was the post-war vision; and it came to pass.

Though this city prefers not to mucky its hands overmuch these days, it still has a healthy appetite for the makings of industry, as the annual *Fortune 500* makes plain. This is a league table of the 500 biggest industrial corporations in the United States, arranged in precedence according to their sales the previous year. In the thirty-odd years the list has been compiled, only two companies have ever occupied the top position; General Motors, of Detroit, and the oil company Exxon, which is headquartered in New York. According to the latest ratings, New York is home base – where the corporate strategy is planned, where the hiring and firing is schemed, where the profits are disbursed – for no fewer than fifty-three industrial giants, the least of which (Phillips-Van Heusen) enjoyed sales in 1986 of $514,387,000. In that year New York had four industrial corporations in the top dozen – Exxon, Mobil, American Telephone & Telegraph, and Philip Morris, which between them sold products amounting to more than $169.5 billion.* The power exerted in New York and the wealth controlled there is even more obvious in the commercial lists. Here were four of the top half-dozen life insurance companies – Metropolitan

* Exxon's profits amounted to $5.3 billion, Mobil's to $1.4 billion, Philip Morris's to $1.5 billion, AT & T's to $139 million. Apart from these corporations, located in New York City itself, three others in the top ten are situated within the city's commuter belt – IBM (at Armonk, NY), General Electric (Fairfield, Conn.) and Texaco (White Plains, NY). In April 1987, two of New York's big four industrial corporations announced plans to move out of Manhattan, on account of high overheads there. Mobil had decided on migration to Fairfax, Virginia. AT & T said it was transferring most of its midtown staff to New Jersey.

Life, Equitable Life Assurance, New York Life and Teachers Insurance & Annuity – with combined assets of more than $187.8 billion. Here were nine of the top thirteen financial companies – American Express (assets $99,476 million), Salomon ($78,164 million), Merrill Lynch (over $53,013 million), First Boston (over $48,618 million), Morgan Stanley Group (over $29,190 million), Bear Sterns (over $26,939 million), E. F. Hutton Group (over $25,921 million), American International Group (over $21,022 million) and Loews (over $19,024 million). And here, most powerfully and profitably by far, were six of the eight mightiest banks in the USA. At No 1 was Citicorp, with assets exceeding $196.124 billion. At No 3 was Chase Manhattan Corp (over $94.765 billion), followed by J. P. Morgan & Co ($76.039 billion), Manufacturers Hanover Corp (over $74.397 billion), Chemical New York Corp (over $60.564 billion) and Bankers Trust New York Corp (over $56.419 billion), the only interlopers at Nos 2 and 7 being BankAmerica and Security Pacific Corp, both on the West Coast.

The biggest business of all with no ramifications outside New York and its environs, is the thriving market in real estate. No-one who has ever staggered under the weight of the *New York Times*'s Sunday edition will be surprised to hear this, when he has just thumbed his way through 100 or more pages of advertisements for property and nothing else, which is that newspaper's regular weekly offering. Here are condominiums rising in midtown Manhattan, with 'a few wonderful apartments' going for $1,525,000 apiece. Here is 'the expanse of SoHo loft space wedded to an uncommonly elegant building, punctuated by the gracious touches of traditional Park Avenue luxury', with a 360-degree view thrown in, yours for $2 million. And a custom-built three-bedroom home out on Long Island, a snip at no more than $1.25 million. And many, many more offerings in the same vein, at always impressive prices, from people who are very eager to sell. One of them used to have printed on his cheques, 'Real estate is the key to wealth'. And no wonder, when he did business in New York.

Inevitably it thrives most on Manhattan, because that is where everyone would ideally like to be for both work and play, at the

centre of things. Housing is traded everywhere in and around
the city; but in Brooklyn, for example, it was stated in 1983
that only four new office buildings had gone up in the previous
quarter of a century. In Manhattan, by contrast, between 1981
and 1984, the developers built as much new office space as either
Boston or San Francisco could muster if they counted all their
commercial buildings, old and new. That was considerably less
than half the amount of new office space built in New York during
the city's earlier development boom, between 1969 and 1972.
Most of these developments have been concentrated along the
midtown stretches of five avenues – Third, Park, Madison, Fifth
and Sixth (Avenue of the Americas); and in these vicinities the
money changing hands can be unequalled anywhere else in the
world. An office site on 56th Street at Fifth in 1985 cost $4,000
per square foot, which was thought outrageous at the time. On
49th Street at Park Avenue in the same year, a deal in air rights
(the owner of a property renouncing his right to build up to the
permissible limit so that the adjacent owner might increase his
own building's size) was struck for $999,999, and the man who
paid thought he'd got a bargain. When the tentacular Donald
Trump was planning his shiny new Tower on Fifth Avenue,
he bought the air rights belonging to the jewellers, Tiffany's,
next door for $5 million, and said this was a major coup of his
entire strategy. Another one would have been the manoeuvre
whereby the adjacent Bonwit Teller fashion house passed into
Trump's hands and became his tenant in Trump Tower, where
the proprietors finished up paying a higher rent than ever before
for a quarter of the space they had previously occupied. A New
Yorker would scoff at anyone who was startled by dealing like
that, for it is the acknowledged currency of this city, where
smartness and toughness and the ability to make dollars are
the most highly esteemed credentials. This is where property
bought for $60 million during the 1976 real estate slump would
now be sold for not less than $300 million. It is where a
developer has bought an old building for conversion into a
housing co-operative, and made a profit of 730 per cent on
the deal. It is where the developer Sol Goldman makes so
much money from his dealings in real estate here, that his

personal tax bill in 1983, according to his lawyers, amounted to $6.7 million.

It has been claimed that Goldman buys and sells more real estate than anyone else in New York, owning about 600 buildings and being worth $500 million. Other nominations for New York's supreme accolade in this field are regularly made in the local press, where such details are picked over in minute and exhausting detail week after week, the surpassing interest of most citizens in real estate being a curiosity in itself. A watchdog of these matters has termed Harry Helmsley 'the king of Manhattan real estate . . . the billionaire who is the richest property magnate of them all'; the man best known to the public at large as the present owner of the Empire State Building, and the husband of Leona M. Helmsley, who occupies the foreground on every publicity photograph (of which there are many) of the Helmsley Palace Hotel on Madison Avenue.

There are dynasties of New York developers, who have been building and trading off this city for generations: the Minskoffs, the Kaufmans, the Tishmans, the Fishers, the Roses, the Dursts, the Milsteins and others. There are the new whizz kids (you can still be regarded as that, almost irrespective of age, in these parts), who have impressed Chase Manhattan or one of the other banks with their potential profitability enough to obtain the loan with which they have taken off: Trump (whose father was in a much smaller league, in Queens) and Kalikow and Solow and Macklowe and Klein and one or two more. There may be nothing bigger in New York property dealing than the Equitable Life Assurance Society ('probably the single largest force in Manhattan real estate today') whose monstrous office block on lower Broadway caused the city to enact its first zoning laws in 1915. Nothing bigger except, perhaps, the Roman Catholic Church, which some people insist is discreetly, self-effacingly, the Daddy of them all. One thing, however, is certain. Most of this activity, by far the biggest portion of this massive wealth, is concentrated in relatively few hands. Of the 12,000 real estate brokers registered in Manhattan, just nine or ten companies between them handle 90 per cent of the business done, estimated at about $3 billion a year. So attractive is this honeypot, so desirable to anyone with a compulsion to become rich, that in the past few years outside developers have come swarming in, not only from elsewhere in the United States, but from much farther afield: the likes of Zuckerman from Boston, Hines from Houston, Portman from Atlanta, Ronson from England, Finkielstain from Argentina, Olympia and York from Canada. And so complaisant is New York with forms of competition in which anything short of homicide goes, that not a voice has been raised telling such foreigners to keep out; only, now and then, complaining that their work isn't up to scratch, by the hypercritical norms of this populace.

In the middle of these wheelings and dealings, as in every aspect of business in New York, will be found, prominently more often than not, but at the very least lurking behind the small print in the contracts, that most potent of American heroes, the man with the law at his fingertips. There is a thesis to be written about how the lawyer has obtained such a stranglehold on the United States, creating at one and the same time the most litigious people on earth, and a society petrified by the financial consequences of making just one mistake; no longer the Home of the Brave so much as the Land of the Free to Sue.* Per head of population there are twice as many lawyers in this country as there are in Britain, three times as many as in Germany, and twenty times more than in Japan. A riffle through the Manhattan Yellow Pages reveals no fewer than thirty-two pages of law firms ready and willing to make money in extortionate amounts for quibblesome clients; and in this climate no more intimidating figure exists than the lawyer who specialises in the commerce of New York. So much is this

* There is a long history of litigation here that would be thrown out of court in most places, or derided so much that some cases would not even be heard. A Mrs Bacon once sued the city, after it had lengthened Park Avenue and consequently threatened an alteration of her house number, which was 1 Park Avenue. The *New Yorker* magazine was sued by an architect whose new building had been described by its critic as having 'the grace of an overgrown grain elevator'. A few years ago, the financier, Saul Steinberg, was sued by a Long Island school for failing to pay part of a gift he had pledged for a new library there; and the court ordered him to pay up.

so that, when Tip O'Neill, sometime Speaker of the House of Representatives, was asked one day to describe the Soviet leader, Mr Gorbachev, he put it like this: 'He's like one of those New York corporate lawyers – strong, glib, talented.'

Gone are the days when gentlemen gathered to practise their law in this city with the measured gravity of theologians, taking their cases one at a time and step by thoughtful step, with considered reference to calf-bound volumes of jurisprudence. Even a traditional and deeply punctilious firm like Milbank, Tweed, Hadley & McCloy – which, *inter alia*, represented the late Nelson Rockefeller, and therefore was obliged to disclose in due course the delicate circumstance in which he suffered his fatal heart attack – even Milbank, Tweed have spent millions these past few years equipping themselves with integrated information processing systems and other computerised office tackle, in order to keep up with the contemporary cut and thrust. The young men and women who pour out of the American law schools in greater numbers each term (500 per cent growth in twenty years), fiercely ambitious and hyperactive with it, too, have their sights on law firms with 1,000 employees or more, which work for their corporate clients twenty-four hours a day in shifts, seven days a week. New York specialises in these as no other city does, one-third of all its lawyers in private practice handling the business of banks, investment houses and big corporations, compared to an American average of one-fifth. This is one of the most notable growth areas in the entire economy of New York, and it has resulted from a consolidation of the city's primacy as a world financial centre. The prosperity of the corporate law firms, moreover, is notable in another way. It has been growing, unwaveringly, in good times and bad. For lawyers just as much as anyone, New York is a compelling honeypot, and this explains the number of big law firms from other cities which have lately established branch offices in the metropolis. The local outfits, though, are still the tops.

This city is home for thirty-two of the 100 biggest law firms in the USA, its nearest competitor being Chicago, with eleven, followed by San Francisco, Philadelphia, Los Angeles, Boston, Washington and Houston, in that order, with seven apiece or fewer. Between them in 1985, the thirty-two employed 6,611 lawyers together with a supporting cast of 20,000 clerical workers; and their customers paid $2.7 billion that year for what they collectively advised, argued, drafted and upheld. The least of these firms, arranged in the usual hierarchy of partners (seventy-three in this case), associates (sixty-five), legal assistants (forty-four) and back-up staff (320) billed its clients for $40 million. The most profitable – Skadden, Arps, Slate, Meagher and Flom – enjoyed billings worth $129 million. The billings are calculated according to the time any member of the firm spends on its client's affairs, on a scale that varies according to the lawyer's position in the hierarchy. On even a small firm by New York standards (like Squadron, Elenoff, Plesent and Lehrer, which has no more than thirty-eight lawyers and five legal assistants, but whose clients include the acquisitive Rupert Murdoch) in 1985 it cost $65 an hour to have a legal assistant working on your behalf, between $75 and $140 for an associate, from $150 to $210 for a partner, depending on his seniority, and $300 an hour to secure the attention of the dominant Mr Squadron himself.

Wall Street and surrounding district is rewarding to the lawyers in so many ways. It is where an investment bank like that of L. F. Rothschild, whose domain extends from New York as far as San Francisco in one direction and Liechtenstein in the other, has found itself regularly sued by shareholders complaining that they weren't told enough about the risks involved in their investments; and Rothschilds will by no means be the only people in their line of business to whom this has happened. It is where the Morgan Guaranty Trust Company, after threatening to shunt its headquarters from New York to Delaware, secured tax concessions from the city and state that were worth $20 million in the first year of staying put; and where Donald Trump was said to have negotiated tax exemption of almost $50 million at the building of Trump Tower. It is where, after financial juggling and fiscal calculations of hideous complexity, the Boston magnate, Mortimer Zuckerman, outflanked Messrs Trump, Lefrak, Kalikow and Zeckendorf of New York to obtain City Hall's assent to his bid of $455.1 million for the Columbus Circle development. The legal man-hours and the corporate billings on any one of these deals probably defy normal imagination, too.

Nowhere at all, however, does the corporate lawyer figure more vitally than in the realm of company mergers and takeovers. These have always and unremarkably been part of the everyday give and take of business throughout the world, as the pedigree of America's biggest bank reminds us. What is now Citicorp, has evolved from Citibank, which was earlier known as First National City Bank, which was a fusion of the National City Bank and the First National Bank of the City of New York; all within the past thirty years, each new style and title signifying an upheaval (or at least a fluctuation) among the bankers themselves. In the past few years, though, the commercial atmosphere has become more tense than before because a new species of entrepreneur, the corporate raider, has appeared on the scene. The most predatory specimen happens not to be a New Yorker, but a Texan rejoicing in the name of T. Boone Pickens, Jr, at whose sound it is said boardrooms throughout the United States tremble with a mixture of anxiety and apoplexy. His activities, and those of other corporate raiders, have inspired an extension of the Wall Street jargon to include such terms as 'junk bonds', which are high-risk, high-yield issues to finance acquisitions and mergers; 'greenmail', which is a buying of shares to panic management fearful of a takeover; 'shark repellent', which can mean changing the company rules to make a takeover more difficult; and 'pac-man defence', a brilliant move which, if successful, means that the raider is raided himself. There are now corporate lawyers in New York who spend their working lives specialising in the tortuous processes of the pac-man defence and other ploys.

Corporate raiding is a classic statement of the fortieth President's belief in the unhindered slop and swill of money, which is known wryly in some quarters as Reaganomics. It involves stealth in acquiring a significant block of stock in the company the raider is stalking, elaborate procedures for moving money around so that nobody can tell what is happening. Dollars are passed through a maze of numbered bank accounts, handled by numerous brokers, and even some senior executives in the raiding party will be kept in the dark until a late stage. That is when the raider declares his interest in the takeover, flourishing by then so much stock that the incumbent board is scared witless, while other potential investors are tremendously impressed. And so the share price mounts, and in the end the raider either gets the company, or he unloads his holding at the propitious moment, scoring whatever happens. When Pickens raided Gulf Oil in 1983, he lost the contest to Chevron after a six-month struggle for control; but from the sale of his Gulf stock he made no less than $760 million in clear profit.

Wall Street well understands the philosophy of corporate raiding, because it is no more than a devious restatement of its own. The idea that big business can always be conducted on the basis of mutual trust and straight dealing would strike most New York practitioners as a fairly comic one in the age of the Quick Buck Economy. In a town which can be outstandingly warm and generous in so many ways, they will tell you without hesitation that *no-one* can afford to be anything but ice-cold and tough where there are dollars at stake. Chase Manhattan and Merrill Lynch are among the New York corporations which commonly use lie-detectors when selecting candidates for jobs or giving employees the push.* That should surprise no-one on whom it has slowly dawned that the word 'aggressive' here is not supposed to make you wince but shake your head, impressed: 'aggressive marketing', 'aggressively expanding', 'an aggressive presentation' are commendations in New York. This is the city of the 'power breakfast' and the 'power lunch', when people on the make continue to flex their muscles over good food, so that they may demonstrate to those serving it up how very tough they can be with underlings.

The nastier habits in the system must obviously be concealed, and there is a profitable business within the business of New York whose purpose is glossification. When the Bank of Boston in 1985 was caught in a financial embarrassment that could have had criminal implications, it summoned a public relations consultant from the great metropolis to do something urgently for its image. He was

---

* There is, as can be imagined, a New York School of Lie Detection.

a top man in the firm of Hill & Knowlton, one of the two biggest PR agencies in the world, and this was a run-of-the-mill operation to someone performing at that level in New York; starting with the first press conference that stuffy old Boston bank had held in thirty-six years. Hill & Knowlton are unusual only in the extent of their overseas activities, with offices in fifty-six places around the world, including Indonesia, their biggest client. Their headquarters on Lexington Avenue is not much different from that of several New York PR firms, with its in-house printing press, its graphics department, its television studio and its satellite link, all helping to bring in $69 million in a recent year. At home they burnish the images of anything from ITT to the Harlem Globetrotters, and when T. Boone Pickens, Jr, was gunning for Gulf Oil it was they who made him as presentable as the man could possibly be. Subsequently he unloaded them like an inconvenient stockholding when an alternative agency took his eye, and in consequence 1984 saw them in the thick of no fewer than twenty-one takeover struggles, but now working for the raided sides. 'We're getting more business working against Pickens,' said the principal from Hill & Knowlton one day, 'than we did working for him. It's the old story of the town with one lawyer who is going broke. When another lawyer arrives, they both start getting rich.'

There are New York agencies specialising in graphics which literally glossify, by producing the shiny-papered annual reports for big corporations, some of whom spend $1 million or more each year on this exercise in image-making. Expensive cameramen are hired to take arty photographs, quality printers are engaged to set type and reproduce illustrations with as much distinction as anything that ever went to press, and the designers themselves take care of layouts so attractive that they can relieve the pain of the financial details which are left until the last few pages, and reveal, alas, that the company has not had one of its better years. When Chase Manhattan was down $24 million on its 1983 banking, the annual report which had to break the news brilliantly minimised it by picturing a series of executive conversations – all blithely imperturbable – which had been shot in front of various pieces from Chase's extensive collection of art. Now and again, by such obfuscations, an annual report has quite plainly set out to limit the damage done in a corporate catastrophe. When seven people died from Tylenol capsules which had been poisonously tampered with after manufacture, Johnson & Johnson, the makers, took the adverse publicity head-on in their next annual report. The message was that the accident had been awful, but only one event in a remarkable corporate year; the master stroke being a double-page illustration of the new tamper-proof Tylenol containers rolling off a conveyor belt. Another industrial giant, Union Carbide, could hardly hope to get away as easily from the numbing fact that 2,500 people had been killed by an escape of fumes from the factory run by its Indian subsidiary at Bhopal in 1984, but it did its best. Not a word was said in the annual report about the deaths, or about what had caused the fatal leak, nor was there a single photograph of Bhopal, taken before or after the disaster: only a couple of pages on multi-national responsibilities in such matters and safety regulations which all should observe – swiftly followed by an elegant, glossy and almost abstract picture spread showing some of the corporation's safer petrochemical products.

There is virtually no end to the stratagems employed in New York to make big business as presentable as possible, to make people feel *good* about even its more disquieting manifestations. Chase Manhattan collecting examples of art to decorate its offices, boardrooms and lobbies wherever in the world it may be making more money, is exceptional only because it has been doing so longer than most corporations (since 1959) and because it has acquired so many – about 11,500 items at the latest count.* But there will not be an executive wall in Manhattan nowadays which does not show off at least a modest collector's piece; and somewhere prominently along the corridor there is likely to be a composition in oils of the chairman or the president, not yet retired but with a weakness for these things, quite possibly commissioned and supplied by a Park Avenue concern named Portraits Inc, which specialises in what may be loosely called executive art. 'Art has become a business tool', according to someone in the inevitable

* But in 1985, the Equitable Life Assurance Society was reported to be 'spending more than $7 million to assemble a collection for its new head-quarters on Seventh Avenue'.

consultancy which has attached itself to this trade. So it seems, with the most improbable conjunctions between the two. The very last sculpture Dubuffet made before he died was destined to fetch up in Westchester County, where it now arises in the grounds of PepsiCo Inc.

Corporate art comes alongside another money-spinner this city operates as no other does. Where lesser people hold their office parties in hotel ballrooms, New Yorkers mount corporate entertainments in some of the liveliest night-spots, taking a place over straight after work; and for a major celebration – a successful takeover, or the launching of a new product on which hopes are riding high – they will borrow for the night some venue as stylish as the New York Botanical Garden, the Public Library or the Metropolitan Museum of Art, which are only too happy to oblige, for the return in dollars which helps to keep them solvent, too. It is all so utterly, so endearingly American, this open-handed lavishness when things are going well and the stock market is up, not at all like those costive little gestures the Europeans make on their more prosperous days. Merrill Lynch may not be everybody's cup of tea with their lie-detector tests, but they don't do things by halves when they're head-hunting some sharp young sprig fresh out of the Harvard Business School, being quite prepared to wine him and dine him on an evening which will leave no change from 1,500 bucks.

But sometimes it all goes terribly wrong, this carefully balanced jiggery-pokery around Wall Street, this absolutely electrifying or stupefyingly banal (according to taste) financial legerdemain. Occasionally the corporate gossip of New York is spiced, or soured (depending on your point of view) with scandal, which does not mean anything that could possibly happen in a satellite as remote as Bhopal, but usually involves some very local fiddling of the books or welching on a deal. Not long ago, six New York executives went to prison after what has been described as the biggest corporate fraud in American history. Their company, OPM Leasing Services (the initials stood, quite brazenly, for Other People's Money), began by buying anything from tractors to computers and leasing them at attractive rates. When this made for cash-flow problems, the president and chairman (brothers-in-law from Brooklyn) concocted a scheme which not only kept them afloat, but made them much more prosperous than they had ever been. They forged documents to secure bank loans for transactions which never actually occurred, some ostensibly made with corporations as large and respectable as the aerospace specialists, Rockwell International. One of these was a fake deal for an IBM computer worth $4 million: and when a bank employee eventually stumbled upon an incriminating discrepancy in the paperwork, it was found that the fraud had been happening for a decade, involving $200 million or more.

If that is one typical case of what can happen in this city, then the disgrace of Richard Whitney is another, still spoken of severely on the Stock Exchange after half a century because of the distance he fell. Whitney was the very paradigm of a successful WASP, Boston-bred and Harvard-educated, who came to New York and rose swiftly both as a broker and as a member of the most exclusive Aryan clubs. He made his reputation with an heroic, though unavailing, effort on the floor of the Stock Exchange to halt the fall in the market during the increasing gloom of 1929, and was rewarded with five straight terms as president of NYSE, becoming known to a wider public as 'The Voice of Wall Street'. What the acclaim failed to recognise was Whitney's lack of real financial acumen: 'he was one of the most disastrous businessmen in modern history', who invested in one fragile company which was optimistically producing peat humus down in Florida for no obvious buyers, and another in New Jersey which was distilling applejack that no-one would drink once Prohibition had been repealed. He lost a great deal in this fashion, with other lunatic investments as well, and to get out of his difficulties began to embezzle monies in his professional care, including securities belonging to the New York Yacht Club, of which he was treasurer. As in the case of the OPM fraud, Whitney got away with his swindle for a surprisingly long time, and it was not until 1938 that he was first suspended from the Stock Exchange and then sent to Sing Sing for grand larceny. Once a millionaire, he came out of jail with $181.01 to his name, and disappeared to a farm on Cape Cod, where he lived for the next thirty years to a ripe old age.

Sometimes things go wrong with the system in general, and

then the misery is widespread. The apparatus of a capital economy appears to be inseparable from a perpetual cycle of ups and downs, of booms and busts, and nowhere at all is this more obvious than in the city of New York. Between 1851 and 1853, so much money came here – largely as a result of gold rushes in both California and Australia – that twenty-seven new banks were launched and the benefit was also felt in local shipbuilding, in the garment industry and by all who had anything to do with trade. Yet by 1857 a slump had set in, which threw 30,000 citizens out of work and caused rioting in the streets. At the turn of the century, New York was riding high again at the start of the Skyscraper Age which also saw the Stock Exchange expand into its new building in 1903. Four years later the Knickerbocker Trust Co failed and started a panic in the stock market, which led to many banks folding, others in New York only being saved by loans amounting to $25 million – a vast sum in those days – made jointly by the US Treasury and J. P. Morgan & Co. Within a decade, the First World War had brought prosperity back to New York, as industrial production reached record levels, the value of stock in General Motors, General Electric and US Steel especially climbing to new heights. This was a preliminary to the boom which preceded the most terrible financial collapse to have happened since the South Sea Bubble burst in London 200 years earlier.

Another sign that the economy was on the up again came with a post-war surge in land values down in Florida, where they enjoyed a more salubrious climate than in the northern United States, causing well-to-do New Yorkers and others to consider winter homes where they might escape their native frosts. Professor Galbraith has remarked that this sudden and huge profit in barren but sunny building plots signified a mood that characterised most of the 1920s, 'the conviction that God intended the American middle class to be rich'. At first the stock market had its occasional small setbacks, but generally it rose as speculations were made more urgently than within memory. Things that ought to have been quite irrelevant to the workings of an economy, like Charles Lindbergh's successful trans-Atlantic flight in 1927, apparently increased the momentum of the cycle, in spite of warnings from some that a headlong rush for easy money would have dire consequences in the end: the Harvard economist, William Z. Ripley, was one who in 1926 fulminated against the 'honeyfugling, hornswoggling and skulduggery' of the financiers, but few paid attention to him or other jeremiahs. The loot was too attractive and too readily available. The day had arrived when the New York banks could borrow money from the Federal Reserve Bank at 5 per cent and instantly lend it themselves at 12 per cent.

What appears to have prompted the fully-fledged boom of 1928 was a decision by big men to push the market ever upwards, for it was a considerable burst of trading in General Motors that began the sequence of events that led to the Wall Street Crash. One of the biggest speculators was Charles E. Mitchell, chairman of the National City Bank and a director of the Federal Reserve Bank in New York, and where someone so prominent confidently led the way, lesser men unquestioningly followed. A Professor Dice from Ohio emphasised this crucial optimism (in God we trust) among speculators when he said at the time that, 'The common folks believe in their leaders. We no longer look upon the captains of industry as magnified crooks. Have we not heard their voices over the radio? Are we not familiar with their thoughts, ambitions and ideals as they have expressed them to us as a man talks to his friend?'

On March 12, nearly four million shares changed hands on the Stock Exchange floor, an all-time high, but by June the record had been broken more than once, trading becoming so furious that the ticker machines could not keep pace with the transactions, sometimes being a couple of hours behind the market itself. When the self-made millionaire, Herbert Hoover, won the Presidential election that October (which meant that the era of the penny-pinching Calvin Coolidge was almost done) this signalled even more stock market euphoria, which Coolidge himself encouraged by observing, just before he left office in the New Year, that things were fine, with stocks 'cheap at current prices'. And so the madness continued, now so pervasive that trans-Atlantic liners did not leave port without taking aboard all the paraphernalia the passengers would need to play the market at any time on the voyage. Ashore, there was rumour of a broker's valet who had made nearly a quarter of a million bucks in his own name, and of a nurse who earned 30,000 by taking the advice of a patient.* But the speculation involved far fewer citizens than the mythology has generally reckoned, as Professor Galbraith has pointed out. Years later, a Senate committee established that at a time when the population of the United States was about 120 million, the member firms of stock exchanges across the nation reported accounts with a mere 1,548,707 customers in 1929. Of these, 1,371,920 were customers of the New York Stock Exchange. 'Then, as now, to the great majority of workers, farmers, white-collar workers, indeed to the great majority of all Americans, the stock market was a remote and vaguely ominous thing.'

The great speculative boom ended on September 3, 1929, when well over four million shares were traded in New York, with the market still strong. That was a couple of days before the financial expert, Roger W. Babson, predicted that, 'Sooner or later a crash is coming, and it may be terrific.' Doubtless he had paid attention, as few others seem to have done, to what was happening that summer away from Wall Street, with industrial production going into decline from June, and the economy generally beginning to stagnate. Yet for several weeks after Babson's warning, nothing seriously untoward happened in New York, and as late as October 15, Charles E. Mitchell, on his way home from Europe, was able to say that, 'The markets generally are now in a healthy condition . . .' But that very week, things began to go wrong, with some of the biggest stocks dropping points. On the weekend of October 19–20, speculators evidently took thought for the morrow; and on that Monday morning the market began to totter. Over six million shares changed hands, the third largest day's trading in history, and once again the ticker fell behind the business itself, but this time in a downward movement which meant that some people did not know they were on the road to ruin until some hours after they were first headed that way. On Thursday – it would be for ever remembered as Black Thursday – nearly

* According to the 1929 tax returns, eleven New Yorkers had incomes that year of over $5 million, seven over $4 million, forty-six between $2 million and $3 million, and 167 over $1 million. Many, many more were millionaires by virtue of their assets. See page 206.

thirteen million shares were sold and the real panic set in. This was when Richard Whitney strode to Post 2 on the Stock Exchange floor, where US Steel was traded, and split the hubbub with his battle cry, 'I bid 205 for 10,000 Steel', when the offering price had long since dropped below 200.* Watching from the visitor's gallery was Mr Winston Churchill, who, some have argued, had some responsibility for the desperate activity going on below: for as Chancellor of the Exchequer in 1925 he returned Great Britain to the gold standard; and this, it has been held, played its part in promoting the insidious American boom.

Whitney had made a gallant attempt to restore confidence around him, but that was draining away on all sides. Five days later, on Tuesday, October 29, came the most appalling few hours any stock market has ever known, when 16,410,030 shares were unloaded in New York, with a crash which echoed round the world. It would be many a day, nearly three years all told, before the market struck rock bottom and people involved in its workings could begin to think in terms of improvement again. In all that time, with occasional pauses, even minute recoveries now and then, things steadily went from bad to worse, as the statistics all too clearly show. Between August 1929 and June 1932 the value of securities listed at NYSE dropped from about $90 billion to $16 billion. A seat on the Exchange which would have cost $625,000 at the peak of 1929, could be obtained for $68,000 in 1932. By then stocks were worth about 12 per cent of their value before the crash. At the high point of 1929, American T & T stock was quoted at 310.25, but by 1932 had gone down to 69.75. Others did even worse; General Electric from 403 to 8.5, Sears, Roebuck from 181 to under 10, US Steel from 261.75 to 21.25.

The human repercussions, of course, were evident straight away. On Black Thursday eleven despairing speculators killed

---

* Another attempt to rally the market that day was made by the American Midas himself, the antique J. D. Rockefeller, whose family prevailed on him to make a public statement, in which he said, 'Believing that the fundamental conditions of the country are sound, my son and I have been purchasing sound common stocks for some days.' At which Eddie Cantor is supposed to have remarked, 'Sure. Who else has any money left?'

themselves, and a day in November was made notable by two men with a joint bank account who jumped hand-in-hand from a high window of the Ritz. But it has been demonstrated that suicides were never as numerous at the time of the crash as the mythology of 1929 has maintained.* What did happen was that the American suicide rate went up as the Depression set in and that in New York it rose in greater proportions than the national average, reaching its peak in 1932 with 21.3 such deaths per 100,000 citizens. A tendency to pin the Depression wholly on the Wall Street Crash should be resisted, when the slump was heralded by industrial events while the speculators were still playing their games months before the market collapsed. Obviously the financial catastrophe affected what happened afterwards, not only by ruining numerous investors, but also by ham-stringing banks and other institutions which might have been expected to support ailing businesses through a recession. By the time the worst was happening in 1932, more than 10,000 of New York's 29,000 manufacturing firms had closed down, with nearly one in three of the city's workforce thrown out of work as a result. A consequence of that was crowds scavenging for food and anything else they might find on garbage tips in Riverside Park, people losing their homes because they could no longer pay the rent, long queues forming at noon outside the Municipal Lodging Houses in the hope of getting a bed for the night, soup kitchens on army trucks in Times Square, more and more malnutrition reported from health clinics, children dropping out of school because parents could no longer provide them with lunch money or decent clothes: it was such things as these, and all the other social horrors of a capital economy which has broken down. One of the searing memories left by that period is of the out-of-work men (6,000 of them, it's said) reduced to selling apples at a nickel apiece from makeshift stalls lining the sidewalks of New York. It has been estimated that 1,600,000 New Yorkers went on public relief. The rest, unless they belonged to the everlastingly rich whom no Wall Street Crash or depression can ever touch, counted themselves

* By J. K. Galbraith, referring to Mortality Statistics 1929 (Bureau of the Census).

lucky to have a job which paid them for only two or three days a week, or kept them working fulltime with their wages cut by more than half. On such short commons, they just might from time to time have been able to take advantage of Mayor Jimmy Walker's inspiration to lighten the traumatic gloom as 1929 shambled hopelessly to another year. Showing all the inappropriate flair of a Marie Antoinette, he asked the cinema owners of New York to 'show pictures which will reinstate courage and hope in the hearts of the people'.

On Wall Street today they will tell you that a recurrence of the Crash is most unlikely now, because various fiscal controls were devised in the wake of 1929 to put a brake on things long before such a disaster could be reached again. Do not be alarmed, they say, by dramatic movements in the Dow Jones index which make its behaviour in the twenties look decidedly placid.* In 1986 that reassurance was important because for the first time since the very worst day of the '29 panic, the index dropped more than thirty-eight points; and did so, what's more, on several occasions between January and September, when it slumped in one day by 86.6 points. After a forty-six-point drop in mid-summer, the *New York Times* did its own bit for market confidence by coming out with a leader (headlined 'Behind the Ow! in the Dow') which demonstrated that the thirty-eight points of 1929 represented a fall of 12.8 per cent, whereas the forty-six points of June 9, 1986 amounted to no more than 2.4 per cent. The market, in short, is so much bigger today than it was sixty years ago that the index points are no longer commensurate. If there is something to worry about much, much more than that, then it will be the fact that the fluctuations on the Stock Exchange are no longer caused by people so much as by computers. The old and time-honoured human sweat upon the floor is gradually yielding pride of place to something they call programme trading. The big operators now have computers with trigger mechanisms which act the moment the market reaches a certain stage, going

* The Dow Jones average prices are of certain representative stocks, followed daily to indicate the market's movement. The system was originated in 1884 by Charles H. Dow, first editor of the *Wall Street Journal*.

either up or down. Instantly, the machine flashes the order to buy or sell; and with large numbers of computers now in competition the combined effect of their orders can be electrifying indeed, the market soaring by twenty points, or plunging thirty in a matter of minutes, which would have meant chaos in the old days. And this is all very well, if you can afford the computer which will enable you to compete in this increasingly impersonal market place, where goodness knows what the future may bring next. A few years ago a man who made a passable income from gambling with other people's money on the New York Stock Exchange floor admitted, in a moment of exhilaration, that 'What we do daily would make some guys' hair stand on end.' The robots are doing it now, which will be even more terrifying to some.*

But not, perhaps, to that many people in this city, where a talent for making money by whatever lawful means is regarded more highly than in many places on earth. This is, after all, where that powerful phrase 'the Almighty dollar' was coined; by Washington Irving, who was born, appropriately enough, just round the corner from Wall Street. This is where, during a historic blizzard in 1888, people stranded on the elevated trains snowbound high above the streets, were helped to safety down ladders, provided they could cough up a dollar on the spot. This is where someone recently hit on a new money-spinner which he called inventory remarketing, buying old and apparently unsaleable goods, repackaging and sometimes finding a different purpose for them, and thus making a $25 million profit in his first trading year. This is where another tidy little business has been built up, by an agency which hires out people to stand in line for other people who cannot bear or won't make the time to queue. Quite lacking the Englishman's humbugging affectation that to

* And was, on Monday, October 19, 1987, when the Dow Jones average fell by 508.32 points, or 22.9 per cent. In a domino effect, stock exchanges in other countries also sustained heavy losses in the wake of panic selling in New York. London was 10.8 per cent down in one day, Paris 4.6 per cent, Frankfurt 7.1 per cent, Hong Kong 11.1 per cent, Tokyo 2.3 per cent, Singapore 12.1 per cent, Sydney 3.8 per cent. Two things were said to have caused the alarming fall in New York prices – the huge budget deficit of the USA, and computer trading in the Stock Exchange.

money shows a lack of breeding, is really not very nice, the New Yorker makes no bones about the fact that if there's money to be made then if possible he'll be there. That is why, in the great concourse of Grand Central Station, Merrill Lynch have a booth where commuters can play the market on their way to and from the trains, in full and inviting view of the passing crowds, which they do in their scores every hour of the day. It is why, when the Black Muslims firebombed Malcolm X's home, one of them, in trying to deflect the suspicion of a newspaperman, chose the most natural argument of all to someone reared in the values of this city; 'We *own* this place, man. We have *money* tied up here.' There will not be a New Yorker who does not feel a very local as well as a patriotic pride, when he reads that one of his city's banks is 'probably the most powerful financial institution on earth', or that this metropolis is 'the financial center of the free world'. Well, yes, he will say, but of course it is. Why, the Clearinghouse Interbank Payments System, which is a mechanism of the international monetary system, this CHIPS clears $300 billion every day, right here in New York. This Big and juicy Apple has three times as large a share of the world's equities market as the runner-up, Tokyo, and eight times as much as poor old London. Just think of that!

And he will chuckle – not gulp, or go cold, or swear, or respond in a number of other permissible ways – at a story told by Walter Wriston, who retired in 1985 from the chairmanship of America's biggest bank, Citicorp. The story will appeal partly because it exemplifies the great American virtue of ingenuity, but mostly because it is proof that the economic system patented here in New York works in the most extraordinary and adverse circumstances. It is about a colonel who, during the American invasion of Grenada in October 1983, decided that he must have reinforcements from Fort Bragg, but was immediately faced with a breakdown in communications. So what did he do, stuck down there on that Caribbean beachhead? He went into a local bar and rang North Carolina on their telephone; and he paid for that long-distance call with his credit card.

SEVEN

MAKING IT

As good a place as any for feeling this city's pulse is in those three blocks of midtown Manhattan which harbour Grand Central Station. The end of the railway line all over the world is often as memorable as anything in its locality, few travellers ever forgetting the unexpected harmony between Rome's stylishly modern Stazione Termini and the nearby antiquities, or the dottily Gothic Victoria Terminus in Bombay, especially when the dabbawallahs arrive from the suburbs, bearing thousands of home-cooked lunches for the office workers each day. Both for its class as a building and for what it can tell you about where it is, Grand Central may be without a peer nowadays. Its great old rival across town, the Pennsylvania Station, was vandalised by its owners a quarter of a century ago, to be replaced by an updated nonentity in which the only residual touch of distinction is the sing-song litany of the station announcer, telling the intermediate stops of the Metroliner to Washington, the Ben Franklin to Boston, and the other big trains, with his final, incantatory cry of, 'All Abooooooooo . . . ard!'*

But Grand Central remains as one of the glories of the city, an ornament as well as a tell-tale of New York. It is nothing less than a township in its own right, abounding in shops where you

_____
* A few relics of the old Penn Station – pieces of sculpture and the like – were salvaged for posterity by the splendid and underrated Brooklyn Museum, in whose grounds they now stand.

can purchase anything from apparel to cutlery, from electrical gadgets to books and toys. It is crammed with premises wherein you can stuff yourself with food, and one of them is among the great fish restaurants of the world, the inadequately named Oyster Bar, where they not only offer a resounding choice of bivalves (Wellfleet and Belon, Bluepoint and Bristol, Chatham and Chilmark and maybe half a dozen more), but also a menu of such exotic alternatives, such compelling marine possibilities, that merely to glance at it is to be transformed from an ascetic to a glutton on the spot. In Grand Central you can not only eat very well and shop comprehensively, but you can also place a bet for any of the metropolitan racetracks, check up on your investments with Merrill Lynch – and hope not to be accosted by the bag ladies and the other indigents, who are for ever rearranging their poor belongings beside the subterranean lockers, where everything smells of stale piss. Or you can simply loiter and admire the place.

There are city halls on half a dozen continents much less ambitiously conceived than this railway station. Even in the relatively small waiting area, where travellers may sit while they pass the time, five huge chandeliers hang opulently from the roof. In the immense main concourse there is a staircase that would not be out of place in a palace, galleries that would go handsomely in any parliament, and a ceiling painted to represent the zodiac, in which electric lights twinkle like the stars themselves. A large and brassbound clock gleams above the information booth in the middle of the marble floor, and beyond it, high on an end wall of the concourse, Kodak display an illuminated example of their less humdrum photography, which is changed from time to time, a panoramic view of some place generally a bit beyond the scope of Amtrak, like the Taj Mahal, the Great Wall of China, or Santa Maria della Salute beside the canal in Venice. That will be one of the most eyecatching places on earth to advertise if it is still true – as someone once calculated – that the number of people going through Grand Central in a year is the same as the population of the entire United States.

They come in hordes across that concourse, surging from the train platforms after commuting from the depths of Westchester

County and even greater distances within the states of New York and Connecticut, erupting from the subway after rattling in from the uttermost parts of Queens, Brooklyn and the Bronx. Here are grey-haired men whose business may be making money, but whose chief satisfaction is to hear others ask 'How far?' whenever they shout 'Jump!': and women, also in their middle years, who have been carefully trained from adolescence to be mistaken for a decade younger by now, which is another reason why some people of both sexes reach the top of the tree: and fellows in trim suits from Barney's with *yarmulkes* hairpinned to their heads, bound for a day's endeavour in some industrious and clannish enterprise: and others swinging snappy cases by Gucci or Louis Vuitton, who can measure to within a balls-aching millimetre the difference between a young urban professional and a young upwardly mobile professional, and are assuredly yuppie or yumpie themselves: and squadrons of even younger people who entertain such dreams, but who must meanwhile take someone else's dictation, or run messages, or in some other subordinate role hopefully work their way from the bottom up: and platoons of folk who will shortly be worn out with a lifetime of trying to make it without even getting close, and are beginning to wonder how much longer they can hold out like this before it all goes down the tubes. They have two things in common, all these people who fill the main concourse of Grand Central at the rush hours every day. They make the best of their appearance, often dressing rather more smartly than they can really afford. And they approach the working day at a tremendous rush, heading home later at a not-much-slacker pace. They make the crowds at the major European commuting stations, like Waterloo and the Gare de l'Est, look distinctly sluggish and just a little dowdy by comparison. These are New Yorkers, which means that they have to keep up, or they are very likely to be trampled underfoot.

Aspirants to this daily ritual also arrive in the city every day, but by alternative routes which finally bring them into the Port Authority bus depot on 42nd Street. At short intervals the buses come lunging in, with a final gust of fumes and a last sneeze of the air-brakes, from every state in the Union, discharging passengers who get down a little stiffly, for they have been on the road for quite a while. Some have ridden down from Seattle for half a week, by way of Butte, Minneapolis, Chicago and Pittsburgh, others have taken the same time to traverse the continent from San Francisco, through Phoenix, Amarillo, St Louis and Indianapolis, and there are those who, for the best part of two days, have come bouncing up from New Orleans, taking in Montgomery, Atlanta and Washington *en route*. They are mostly young people who have crossed their America the punishing but still romantic way, and for all their exhaustion at journey's end, they disembark on 42nd Street with a notable look in their eyes, of wonder and determination, which all immigrants here have worn. For they have come to the city above all others where, with talent and industry and a lot of luck and staying power and a few other things going for them, anything at all is still possible for anyone who wants it badly enough. Or so they believe. There is a song that every kid who rides Greyhound across this continent knows as well as he knows anything,* because it is the promise that if the newcomer succeeds in New York he will, indisputably, be the tops. And that matters to Americans, a people who will go to amazing lengths to avoid a tied game in any of their sports. There must be winners and losers in this country at almost all costs, and there is nothing so perplexing to them as the honourable draw.

It is of supreme importance in this city to be a success, which means public recognition and acclaim and, it goes without saying, substantial emoluments to emphasise that the praise has been well earned. The gifted amateur can never feel properly at home here and will not even be comprehended by the populace at large,

---

* There can surely be no other metropolis which has inspired so many ballads about itself, its different parts, or different aspects of its life; which is maybe what you'd expect of the star-spangled home of the stage musical. Nor can there be another city whose people savour such celebrations of their home town as fondly as New Yorkers do. In the admirable Transit Museum in Brooklyn, on an immaculate carriage which used to work the old Eighth Avenue line in the 1930s, there is a notice which says: 'These cars were the inspiration for Billy Strayhorn's classic swing number "Take the A Train" popularised by Duke Ellington.'

which has been bred to regard the only reliable measurement of skill as the one that can be made in dollar bills. Far from being admired for his disinterested pursuit of excellence, the amateur is merely regarded as someone who didn't quite have what it takes to be a professional. Poor fish, he has been stranded in a society whose primary and most powerful urge is to survive, with a highly developed instinct to go beyond that right to the top, and with little time or inclination to do anything for its own sake. It is this urge and this instinct which has given New York its perhaps enlarged reputation as the rudest and roughest city of all. There exists something called the Association for a Better New York which recently campaigned for more politeness on the streets, in the course of which a spokesperson said, 'It's stunning the first few days you are out of New York. People are so polite and friendly that you are downright suspicious of them. Even in France.' We may take it that that was a bit of good old New York hyperbole, turned on to produce a desired effect. But a reporter working on the story uncovered another New Yorker whose opinion had an uncomfortable ring of truth. He was a former cab-driver selling hot dogs on a midtown street, who said straight out that, 'I have always considered courtesy a sign of weakness.' Weakness you must never show here, for although there is much compassion in this city, there is just as much indifference. And even if you know that you are not nearly first-rate, you must never, never admit it. When the Empire State Building could no longer be represented as the tallest structure on earth, its owners ordered the publicity people to produce a suitably impressive alternative claim, and they came up with a faintly ridiculous one; 'the most famous building ever erected by man'. More famous than the Taj Mahal, the Parthenon, the Pyramids, the Colosseum, St Peter's, Notre Dame, the Houses of Parliament, the White House, the Kremlin . . .?

This is the city which invented that most spectacularly generous applause of success, the ticker-tape parade, a spontaneous gesture of enthusiasm when it first occurred in 1910 to welcome home the only President of the United States so far to have been born in New York City, Theodore Roosevelt. His Presidency had finished the year before and he had gone off to Africa on a hunting trip to fill the awful vacuum after high office. When he stepped ashore from the *Kaiserin Auguste Victoria* on his return, it was to be greeted by Mayor William Jay Gaynor and a detachment of the Rough Riders with whom Roosevelt had ridden (in a manner of speaking, for they had no horses) in the American adventure against the Spanish on Cuba in 1898. He was then escorted from the Battery uptown and 'as the Roosevelt carriage swung along lower Broadway, showers of confetti and colored paper fell on him many times from the office building windows. Rolls of ticker tape also were tossed from the windows.' This form of greeting was to become familiar to New Yorkers at regular intervals after that, and presently the rest of the world, too, became accustomed to the phenomenon on its newsreel screens, as a variety of American heroes – politicians, aviators, soldiers, explorers, sportsmen – were to be seen riding up Broadway or Fifth Avenue amidst multitudes of people, all of whom were partly obscured by the slowly descending blizzard of paper; 1,500 tons of it, someone has inevitably worked out, when New York welcomed home Charles Lindbergh from his record flight. It still happens from time to time; to greet with high and patriotic emotion the return of the American Embassy hostages from Teheran in 1981; to hail with more parochial delirium the New York Mets after winning the World Series against Boston in 1986. The parade has changed in only one barely noticeable respect. Ticker tape no longer being available in the electronic age, and air-conditioning having seen off windows that can be opened, what descends from above now are reams and reams of computer printout, tossed out of bins by workmen standing on the roofs.

People here not only strain perpetually for their own success, are not only generous in their applause of others' success; they are fascinated by its various manifestations, as perhaps no other people are. A very considerable amount of print is spent daily, weekly, monthly, from one year's end to another in New York, in pandering to this fascination and feeding it with up-to-date information. This happens in every big city anywhere, and is supplied by gossip columnists, but nowhere does it happen on the scale of New York, where it is the lifeblood of several publications. In 1985 it was evidently important to know that Barbara Walters (a television interviewer) was buying her dresses from a Park Avenue shop called Martha, where the average customer spent $1,500 per visit, and her linen from a place on Madison, Pratesi, whose best clients spent $20,000 a year. It was of moment to learn that Sanford Weil (a former president of American Express) had bought no fewer than forty executive caviar sets with mother-of-pearl spoons from Balducci's to give as Christmas presents, at $250 apiece. It was necessary to understand that Brian Marlowe (proprietor of a firm that cleans buildings) was allowed into the dining room of the Carlyle before the doors officially opened for breakfast, could regularly command a corner table at Il Menestrello, and lunched frequently at La Grenouille. It was a matter of some consequence that Kathy Keeton (an associate of Bob Guccione in Penthouse International Ltd) kept Rhodesian Ridgeback dogs, one of which was on vitamin therapy to prolong its life, the other with a false tooth made of gold, to replace a broken real one. All four of these titbits came from the monthly *Manhattan Inc*, which keeps a very serious eye on the business world in New York, but is incapable of not presenting it in terms of glamorous success or (once in a while, for contrast) intriguing failure. What the city's business is never allowed to be in those pages, is steady, occasionally exciting, and generally an exhausting slog; it has to be retailed in terms of personalities who must reek of success.

The following year saw the publication of a guide book entitled *The Official New York Map to the Stars' Homes*, which purveyed the names and addresses of 120 people who were not merely successful, but certified celebrities; the likes of Robert Redford, Katharine Hepburn, Henry Kissinger, Jacqueline Onassis, Greta Garbo. The enterprise of two Harvard graduates with a sharp nose for making it, one way or another, it sold 10,000 copies in its first week on the bookstalls, supplying the insatiable demand of many citizens to feel comfortably in the know. Nowhere are there people more knowing than these about the dispositions, the strategies, the tokens of success. That invaluable yardstick, the average New Yorker, can tell you, without even stopping to think, which restaurants are being patronised at present by what stars of stage, screen and real estate. He can pick his way unerringly through the forest of competing clothes designs, watches, leather accessories and the other gewgaws of prosperity, and tell you which indicate continuing success among those wearing them, and which mean that the poor schmuck is no longer quite with it. He can tell you more than you would wish to know about that embodiment of metropolitan success, the stretch limousine, which in New York is becoming annually more ominous as more and more of its users prefer to cruise around the city behind darkened windows through which they alone can see: and he will enjoy a little dig at those ambitious souls who may be seen arriving at theatres and restaurants aboard limousines which they do not own, but only hire for the evening – the ones whose registration number is preceded by the letter 'Z'.

Nomadic tribes in the desert talk of little but food and their animals and the prospects of food over there and their geneal-ogies and the years of famine and plenty in the past, because their horizons are limited to these things; and of these things they will talk endlessly. Much of New York's conversation above the poverty belt is like that, among people whose preferred diet is success and talk of the way success comes and goes. New Yorkers are more uneasy than most of us with the times it goes. Take away success and their ardour cools as rapidly as it came on heat. When the New York Yankees and the Toronto Blue Jays were going neck and neck in the American League East in 1985, as they were until the middle of August, attendances at Yankee Stadium were 50,000 or more at virtually every game. On September 24, when the Yankees had fallen seven games behind Toronto and were out of contention for the pennant, only 16,702 fans turned up to see a match with Detroit. When that charmless prodigy of the tennis courts, John McEnroe, lost his habit of winning in 1986, there came the night in Madison Square Garden when he performed so badly that New Yorkers who had adored him extravagantly for years, turned on him savagely to deride his new incompetence, reducing the champ to a pathetic ex-lout.

There is a fiction that this democracy purified itself at birth of that European blight, the social class system. It scarcely merits serious examination in New York, which has a fine sense of social hierarchy, promoted with European confidence in such matters on Park Avenue South, where the folks behind the Social Register live and move and have their being. This chapbook of inbred American success 'records the full names and addresses of members of prominent families, grouped together, the clubs to which they belong, and the marriage or death of each person as it may occur'. It also suggests how gentlewomen who have lost touch with each other, but who wish to retain their place in the old-girl network, may do this expeditiously: 'If the married name you are seeking has escaped your memory and you can recall the maiden name, reference to the Married Maidens will then indicate the present name.' And there they are, column after obliging column of Married Maidens, starting with Marie E. Abbott (who became Mrs Hill) and ending with Rena M. Zurn (who became Mrs Furweiler). The Register as a whole runs to well over 1,000 pages of gentility, blue blood which was identified in the first place (but has known some tributary dilution since) by Mrs William Waldorf Astor 100 years ago, when she was considering who was socially acceptable. It's said that the criteria were the size of her ballroom and those she would be willing to see in it, together with anybody else who attended the National Horse Show, which signified the start of New York's winter season. Their names alone went into the Register's first edition in 1887.

In it today are all the descendants of those pioneer aristocrats, together with the subsequent arrivistes, in all the panoply of their noble affiliations: Sons and Daughters of the American Revolution, Dames of the Loyal Legion, Descendants of the Signers of the Declaration of Independence, Colonial Lords of the Manor, members of the American Society of the Most, and simply Vassar, Yale and Harvard Graduates. They aren't all New Yorkers by any means, though a high proportion have at least a toehold in the city. The genuine metropolitans among them probably see to it that the betrothals of their children are announced by those quaint headlines in the *New York*

Times ('Nuptials planned by Peter Endicott and Miss Wilder'; 'Mary O'Grady Affianced'). Some of them live in and around Sutton Place, which for some unfathomable reason is the city's most fashionable address, supposedly because Mrs William K. Vanderbilt gave it her blessing around the turn of the century. It is on the Upper East Side, beside the river, and no more than a cock-stride from Bloomingdale's, where tea from London comes at prices out of this world, and where in the scent department the sales pitch can be, 'Win a half-carat diamond worth $1,500 from Sonia Rykiel perfume'. These can be seen as recommendations. But Sutton Place nowadays consists of very ordinary-looking high-rise apartments more than anything else, which is all that most of the inhabitants will be able to see when they gaze from their windows; and the air here is often loud with the racket of machines taking off and landing at the heliport beside the Queensboro Bridge a little upstream. It is in these surroundings that ladies periodically walk their lap dogs with a fastidious care which they maintain even when the creatures defecate; whereupon a gloved hand brings forth a plastic bag and uses it as an extra glove while the unutterable is picked from the sidewalk and deposited in the litter-bin on the nearest lamp post; all in one movement so dexterous, so marvellously lithe, that the observer will probably miss it if he so much as blinks.

The gentlemen of the Social Register, meanwhile, may well be pleasuring themselves in other ways, quite possibly at their clubs. New York has been well endowed with these since a Knickerbocker started the oldest of them, the Union Club, in 1836. Some are almost indistinguishable from European counterparts; like the Yale and the Harvard which, give or take a Yankee twang or two, could well be mistaken for those establishments across the water where they serve anchovy toast for tea. Some New York clubs were started by people who had found admission elsewhere hard to gain, as the financier, J. P. Morgan, started the Metropolitan for himself and for friends in a similar plight, a club which has always maintained this connection with unabashed wealth: it was at the Metropolitan Club in 1983 that the six children of J. Seward Johnson met to start contesting his will, whereby he had left all his money (and there was plenty of it, for it was Johnson & Johnson money) to the woman he had not married until he was seventy-six, and she but the family maid aged thirty-four. But of all the clubs in this city, none is more patrician, more exclusive than the New York Yacht Club, whose frontage, just a little upwind of the Harvard Club, has intrigued many a pedestrian along West 44th; for it looks for all the world as though several old East Indiamen have berthed alongside each other, ornately stern-on to the street, and have there been petrified in grey stone. Inside it is a delight from bridge to keel, most of all in the model room where, under a Tiffany glass skylight, there must be a thousand or more hulls mounted on the walls, models mostly of craft the club members have raced and won in, but with a few more precious pieces, too. Here are half-hulls of the *Kearsarge*, just as she was when she sank the *Alabama* in the Civil War, and of the *Bonhomme Richard*, in which John Paul Jones cocked a snook at the Limeys, sailing her right round their coast. Here is a full model, a work of art, such perfect craftsmanship that it brings tears to the eyes, of great *America* herself in that race off the Isle of Wight in 1851, with her two lifeboats hanging port and starboard from her davits, when she whopped fourteen other vessels and brought the Englishmen's trophy home. And there, pushed into a corner of the model room, where no-one will notice it unless he's looking hard, is a dark round table with a single and heavily carved leg, a curious square bruise on the table top and, plumb centre, a hole clean through all the wood. That's where the America's Cup was bolted down for 132 years, as one challenge after another was beaten off and the New York Yacht Club became more and more arrogant in its success; until the day in September 1983 when an Australian crew won the historic contest, and the New Yorkers had perforce to yield the trophy, which they did most unwillingly, with a sad lack of grace.

As in every other society known to man, New York is topped by people of great means, and here the wealth may have been inherited, or worked for, or it may have descended like manna from above in some fabulously lucky deal. It was here that the word 'millionaire' first entered the American vocabulary, not long before John Jacob Astor, the poor German immigrant who became 'a self-invented money-making machine', died in 1848. There were thought to be ten New Yorkers then who owned property worth $1 million or more (Astor was worth $20 million at his death) but by 1860 there were 115, and after that the species multiplied with biblical obedience. Even at the lowest point of the Depression, 1932, there were reckoned to be 7,000 millionaires in the city, and they are now so commonplace not only here but throughout the United States that the title no longer creates much of an impression among their fellow citizens.* The standard measurement of riches great enough to impress Americans nowadays is inclusion in the annual ratings known as the *Forbes Four Hundred*; the 400 nominees being individuals who could lay their hands on at least $180 million if they had to. And New York in 1986 contained a far bigger number of such people than any other place in the country; no fewer than ninety of them. Its closest challenger was Los Angeles, with no more than twenty-six.†

The wealthiest New Yorkers of all were five men who could each muster a billion dollars (that is, $1,000 million) if need be. Heading the field was Leona Helmsley's husband, Harry, the dry goods salesman's son who started work as an office boy in Manhattan for twelve bucks a week, and at the age of seventy-seven was reckoned to have assets in real estate amounting to well over $5 billion; enough to have given $33 million away in 1986 to New York Hospital. Behind him came the Newhouse brothers, Si and Donald (at least $2.3 billion between them), whose fortune had been made from a newspaper group they inherited and then expanded until they controlled twenty-nine papers, eleven magazines, a cable television company and a publishing house. Then there was David Rockefeller, whose investments in real estate and share of the family inheritance, together with what he'd managed to scrape together from a

* The latest estimate is that there are 574,300 millionaires in the USA.
† After Los Angeles came Dallas/Fort Worth (twenty-five), Chicago (nineteen), Washington (fourteen), San Francisco (thirteen), Wilmington (thirteen), Boston (eleven), Minneapolis (ten), Philadelphia (seven), Houston (seven) and Kansas City (seven).

long career at the Chase Bank, were said to be worth 'over $1 billion'. Lowliest of the metropolitan billionaires was Edgar Miles Bronfman, grandson of a Russian immigrant and son of the man who bought the Canadian liquor firm of Seagram and made a fortune with it during Prohibition. This helped in 1986 to give Bronfman a 'net worth of at least $1 billion', together with his other industrial interest in Du Pont and Cadillac Fairview.

It would be tedious to survey this catalogue of egregious wealth in much more detail, though there were thirteen other people in New York who were worth $500 million or more, and another thirty-two citizens who could put together at least $200 million at a pinch. The wealthiest woman in New York in 1986 appeared to be the cosmetic queen Estée Lauder (née Josephine Esther Mentzer of Queens, daughter of a Hungarian immigrant), who started her business in 1946 with four brands of skin cream, and saw it grow in the next forty years until it was worth over $1 billion, a fortune that she shared with two sons. Much the most fascinating thing about the people in the *Forbes Four Hundred* is how they came by their wealth, and the New York assortment is particularly revealing. The fifty people there worth more than $200 million apiece acquired their portion in ways ranging from inheritance to publishing, from insurance to the oil industry, from running a radio and television empire to juggling money on Wall Street in that nerve-racking activity called arbitrage. There was one man, Michel Fribourg, said to be worth over $800 million by controlling 20 per cent of the world's grain trade. There was another, Leonard Norman Stone (net worth more than $650 million), whose competence was in pet supplies, which was maybe inevitable in the son of a man who arrived from Germany with 2,100 canaries. There was another, Mark Goodson, who had made more than $300 million by producing television game shows on both sides of the Atlantic. But by far the most likely way to make a mint of money in the great metropolis would surprise no-one who had lived there in the previous decade or so, for it was by wheeling and dealing in property. No fewer than twenty-eight of those in the most affluent fifty had got there on the back of New York real estate.

To be a New Yorker is to believe that you have at least

some chance of joining the élite on their pinnacle of wealth and power and recognition; which is not the understanding in, say, London, where very few ordinary citizens will see themselves as potential millionaires, or with their names in lights, to be admired and envied and, above all, *known* by everybody else. The American Dream may in reality be a cruel hoax to some, but for as many more it does deliver at least something of its promise provided they are, as they would say, prepared to accept its challenge. The challenge is there for all to see any day of the week during a ride on the subway. In every car of every train, as conspicuous as any of the repulsive graffiti, is a series of advertisements, each one above a thickness of tear-off cards ('Take One', every card says prominently) offering a variety of services, including, inevitably, that of lawyers. But most common by far are firms and institutions suggesting ways of self-improvement. There is a firm from Yonkers, up the Hudson Valley, which addresses itself to Spanish-speaking New Yorkers, holding out the prospect of acquiring English, and with it wider horizons. There is an institute on the West Side, which also offers English as a second language, as well as courses in computers, electronics technology, air-conditioning, heating and refrigeration, and secretarial skills including word-processing. There is a Brooklyn outfit which guarantees to trundle students through to a high-school diploma ('You will pass first time or we will retrain you free') and another which offers selected courses for Veterans and training in whatever it takes to qualify for Travel & Tour Operations. There are many more come-ons of a similar kind, spattered with exclamation marks and capital letters to emphasise the imperative need to sign up for a glowing future – 'Yes, please rush my FREE TCI CAREER BOOKLET describing how I can get started towards my exciting and rewarding career!' And New Yorkers with nothing to lose, do respond to these invitations, judging by the number of advertisements you see every day with most of their cards torn away.

In a city with a colossal apparatus of scholarship and education, there is nothing more remarkable and nothing more consonant with the New Yorker's perpetual urge for improvement, than

the establishment which everyone knows as the New School,
in downtown Manhattan not far from Greenwich Village. It was
founded in 1919 as the New School for Social Research, when its
declared purpose was the 'discussion, instruction and counselling
of mature men and women' in the fairly new disciplines of the
social sciences; but it soon broadened its scope to include
the arts and other subjects. In the 1920s, Dr W. E. B. Du
Bois there taught America's first university course on black
culture, and before long the New School was offering lectures
and seminars in topics as varied as psychoanalysis and urban
housing. Its reputation was further enlarged in 1934, when
refugees from Nazi Germany settled there and taught in a
celebrated 'University in Exile'. Where it stands nowadays,
was described in a statement of values made in 1984, which
began: 'The New School does not set any limits to its programs in
regard to subject matter. Whatever seriously interests persons
of mature intelligence properly falls within the province of the
school . . .' It is still the only university in the land which
puts a heavy emphasis on adult education, as well as offering
graduate, undergraduate and professional degree courses. Any
mature adult can take a course there, provided he or she can
pay the tuition fees (and *certainly* you may use MasterCard or
Visa if it's more convenient).

The most striking thing about the enormous variety of topics
available for part-time study by people who already are in some
employment or other, is the high proportion of them which
offer a marketable skill to the students. If you enrol at the
New School's culinary arts educational centre and decide to
take the five evening classes in 'Fish and Seafood Cookery',
the object is not so much to become the hostess with the
mostest, or an admirably well-qualified house-husband, but 'to
learn professional cutting and presentation techniques' which
will stand you in good stead should you decide to start a little
catering business. If you sign up for a course in photography,
and take the Saturday morning classes on 'Becoming the Source
of Your Photographs', the intention will be less to impress your
family and friends with the snapshots you pass round in the
album, than to make a living with your camera one day, if the

brochure is anything to go by: 'The course is designed for those who command the basics of photography and want to discover the uniqueness of their own vision . . . Risk-taking is prized and audacious failures are preferred to small, safe successes.' (Yes, that's the authentic go-getting voice of New York.)

There are courses even more bluntly designed to 'assist students develop in their field, help them change their careers, or aid them in entering exciting new professions'. Under that heading they can take a dozen classes on Monday evenings, entitled 'The Business of Art: Making Money in a Tough Field', wherein they will

> Learn how to sell; learn whom to sell to; learn how to conduct your art business professionally; understand the importance of when and how to exhibit art – finding the right galleries and successfully contacting them; explore alternatives to the gallery system for self-promotion; learn about contracts and legal questions, copyrights, taxes, and artists' estates, resources and services available to artists; and get an overview of the current scene from the East Village to 57th Street. In short, be creative but financially successful.

They can enlist for twelve sessions named 'Blueprint for Opening & Running A Gourmet Food Store', which provide

> Guidelines designed for those seeking an opportunity to create their own food emporium. A practical listing of key items relating to the marketing and managing of a food business is discussed. Topics also include: buying and merchandising concepts; the need for inventory control; legal and money matters; visual presentation; cooking and custom-catering opportunities; marketing; and developmental techniques for private label merchandise.

These students can even prime themselves for the Big One by signing on for eight sessions on 'Investing in Real Estate for Use and/or Profit', whose summary comes clean at the outset:

> With its unique combination of tax benefits, cash flow, financing opportunities and equity appreciation, real estate has

proven to be the soundest of investment alternatives. Real estate values have beaten inflation even in these times of spiralling costs. This course is designed to introduce prospective buyers, sellers and investors to the methods and strategies of successful real estate investments. Beginners as well as experienced investors benefit by learning current investment techniques being utilized in today's volatile marketplace. We cover investments in homes, co-ops, condominiums, lofts and commercial properties of all kinds . . .

There are moments when the curriculum of the New School of Social Research in Manhattan reads like the prospectus of a high-pressure college of salesmanship rather than anything a more academic institution would propagate; and it is indeed in part nothing more nor less than the upmarket version of all those improving ads on the subway trains. But, then, part of New York's genius is that it has always taken an intensely practical view of everything, however rarefied the matter might seem to some. Adult education, therefore, is not seen as a purely intellectual enrichment of those already settled into their working lifetime's trade or profession, its primary purpose being to produce the rounded and thoughtful human being. It is chiefly regarded as a means to a remunerated end in this city; and this is no more a heresy here than is the local archdiocese's notoriously comfortable accommodation between God and Mammon.

This outlook has partly been conditioned by a tendency for conspicuous success to be much more accessible here than in most places; partly by bleaker facts of life that have been built into the social fabric of the city through many generations. There is plenty of evidence to support the assertion that, 'Despite its reputation as a melting pot, New York has never been hospitable to newcomers.' Immigrants arriving in the nineteenth century, having already run the gauntlet of crooks and shysters on their way to the embarkation ports of Europe, found just as much heartless exploitation awaiting them when they stepped ashore here. Poor people were easily duped during those first few days in a bewilderingly strange land, and those who were heading for a new life elsewhere in America were often preceded by a coded message from the forthcoming character who had offered them all assistance the moment they got off the boat. It urged accomplices across the country to 'run the OP line strong'; an opaque suggestion which in plain language meant that the migrants were to be robbed of everything they had, their money to be divided up between the thieves. Things became so infamously bad that the state of New York in 1847 set up an investigating committee, which found that the migrants were at risk the moment they reached the metropolis:

> One of the common frauds practised by the emigrant boarding house keepers is that they generally have five or six persons about their establishments who, if they cannot prevail on the emigrant to accompany them to the boarding house they represent, when coming from the Quarantine to the city, on their arrival at the dock seize their baggage by force, and have it carted by cartmen who are privy to their operations, to the boarding houses. With the baggage once in the house, the emigrant, if dissatisfied with the accommodations and wishes his things removed to another place, is met by the landlord with a charge for either storage or one day's board, compelling him to put up with the accommodations offered him, or pay five or six dollars without an equivalent . . .

It was in an attempt to reduce such hazards as much as anything that the authorities in 1855 opened a reception depot for immigrants – forerunner of Ellis Island – at Castle Garden, the old Castle Clinton down at the Battery, which had been built in anticipation of the war with the British that broke out in 1812. For a while the migrants were protected from the worst that New York had to offer them, but by 1887 things had deteriorated again so badly that Joseph Pulitzer's paper *The World* ran several pieces exposing the corruption of the commissioners appointed to safeguard the welfare of all new arrivals to the city. There were stories alleging that the depot was 'a place of unlawful detention, a place for tyranny and whimsical rule, a place for the abuse and insult of helpless women, for the inhuman treatment of mothers and children, for the plunder of the poor, for the lecherous pursuits of shielded employees, for the disgrace of the nation in the eyes of those who desire to become citizens, and for the exercise of the maudlin caprice of two brutal and self-aggrandising old men.' It was said that in the streets outside Castle Garden, migrants who had to travel by train to other destinations did so at inflated ticket prices, that those who were to stay in the city were similarly overcharged for the transport of their baggage, for meals in restaurants, for the rate at which their foreign currency would be exchanged. The paper succeeded in forcing an inquiry by the Treasury Department, and though no report was ever published and no-one was ever charged with so much as a misdemeanour, a result was the transfer of immigration procedures to Ellis Island (at that time a munitions dump), where in theory it would be easier to give the newcomers a more civilised welcome to their adopted country, insulated by the waters of the harbour from the viciousness lurking ashore.

It was a vain hope. Ellis Island had been open for less than a decade before the same stories of intimidation, extortion, bribery, swindling and downright theft were being told all over again. A reason for Theodore Roosevelt's great popularity was that soon after his inauguration as President in 1901, he sacked the New York Port Commissioner for Immigration in an attempt to get matters improved. He appointed in his place William Williams, a millionaire Wall Street lawyer who had been educated at both Yale and Harvard, a man of great integrity who began his new career by putting up notices on the island which said, 'Immigrants must be treated with kindness and consideration.' He himself sacked employees who abused the migrants, but at the same time he interpreted the immigration laws most rigorously (he is said to have had a pathological aversion to the hard-luck story) which itself caused great difficulties for many. Others who succeeded Williams were also men of probity, but the abuses were never more than partly stamped out. In 1921, government investigators found that at least five Ellis Island officers had been trying to extract bribes in exchange for purely notional help.

It would be quite misleading to imply that New York's inhospitality to newcomers in that era was something as simple as

xenophobic American hostility to strangers. The state senators on the 1847 committee, after cataloguing the exploitations
awaiting the migrants here, noted that, 'The keepers of emigrant
boarding houses are invariably foreigners, the native of each
nation preying upon their own countrymen.' Just so did an
Armenian woman, detained on Ellis Island during the 1920s,
complain of the inspectors who held her there that, 'They were
very crude. Many were foreigners, who delighted in the fact that
they could lord it over the new entries, the new immigrants.
They had accents as thick as molasses, every kind of accent,
but they acted the way small people become when they have a
little power. They pushed everybody around, literally pushed.'
It should be remembered that the biggest exploiters of the poor
Italians who began to arrive *en masse* 100 years ago, were the
padroni, other Italians who had just preceded them. Also, that
the odious expression 'kike' may have been used first of all by
German Jews, well-established in New York, to describe the
poor Jews from eastern Europe who arrived in the metropolis
much later on.

These things, none the less, are all part of the city's complicated pedigree now, and they help to explain some of the
behaviour that is most characteristic of New York today; the
intense drive to compete, the strong will to get ahead, that great
daily rush to reach work by commuters into Grand Central. It
is not by chance that the eloquent phrase, 'When push comes
to shove . . .' is heard more frequently in this city than in any
other part of the Union, as the preliminary to a threat, a personal
recommendation, a self-description, or merely a general outlook
on life; and if the phrase wasn't coined in New York by some
thruster who has escaped the vigilance of H. L. Mencken, then
it ought to have been. It is the exordium of a people who have
been born and bred to expect no favours of anyone, who are
inclined to get their retaliation in first, who take it for granted
that you work hard to get to the top and then even harder to stay
there, because so many others are hungry to take your place.
It belongs to the language of citizens whose general speech has
been described as 'the dialect that unifies the fastest town in the
world . . . the hurry-up, short-order accent of America'.

Nowhere on earth do highly qualified professional people sweat their guts out as they do in New York, working much longer hours and taking much shorter vacations than their flaccid counterparts in London or some other places across the Atlantic. The big law firms are notoriously the hardest drivers of all, only the most senior partners allowing themselves to ease off a little, justifying this moderation on the grounds that it is they and their long-established reputations which bring in the most lucrative customers on whom everyone else in the practice may thrive. The habit is for the partners to share the profits, while the associates just below them receive a salary and work the maddest schedules. Fifty hours in a week would be regarded as a barely acceptable minimum at this level, seventy-five hours being much more likely from some ambitious associate in his or her late twenties, hoping that before long this frenzy of work will pay handsome dividends in the offer of a partnership. In this environment, the greatest commendation that can be made of anyone is that, 'Not only does X bill tremendous hours, he also puts in ungodly hours in the administration of the firm.'* That, as it happens, was said of a partner in one of the biggest New York practices (Skadden, Arps) where two senior members regularly take the 6.40 a.m. train from their homes in Westchester County, reach the Manhattan office at 7.20 a.m., and do not often leave again until ten o'clock at night; commonly, in the course of a big merger requiring their attention, being stuck with it till midnight or beyond. Those partners in 1985 were generally billing 350 hours a month, which is eighty-seven and a half hours a week. It was such people a Columbia law professor had in mind when he said; 'The insane-hours issue has been around for a long time, but the takeover practice has really increased it. Anything which involves billions of dollars so that high legal costs are just a fraction of what's involved and time is of the essence . . . creates an élite killing themselves with work. There's a whole class of people who make a lot of money, send their wives to the Hamptons all summer, get divorced a lot, and die.'

* The 'billing', of course, is made to the client, who pays for every last cent of all this hard work.

The rewards are high for those who surrender themselves totally to this treadmill. Of another top law firm it has been said that new partners earn $450,000 a year, and 'from there on, it's a one-way ride on the financial elevator'. It isn't exactly a rough ride on the threshold of such pickings. No-one joining a New York law firm as a prentice associate would expect to be paid less than $40,000 a year in the mid-1980s, and someone in such a company, risen somewhat in the salary scale after only a few years, has confessed that, 'I feel embarrassed when I see my monthly check.' And although the most lucrative New York profession in general is reckoned to be the law, there are several others where enormous salaries are paid. Near the end of 1985 it was reported that the man who gave the weather bulletins on ABC television was earning $700,000 a year. A few months later, some light was shed on the pay structure in the world of advertising. Copywriters with only a few years' experience were said to be getting $75,000–80,000 a year, with the top people in leading agencies collecting as much as $750,000 – 'including perks', according to a man whose profession was to recruit talent for Madison Avenue's most celebrated line of business. The perks range from the statutory car, or an annual trip to some salubrious corner of the globe for r and r on the firm, to something as suggestive as a personal financial adviser supplied by the employer. Such inducements were often what made up someone's mind whether to join this firm or that, rather more than the hard cash offered, 'because after $200,000, salaries themselves aren't the major factor'.

We are, let us not forget, considering highly skilled and expensively trained professional people here. The generality of New Yorkers do not have to weigh up the perks before deciding to take this job or that, and it would be as well to bear in mind that the *per capita* income of these citizens in 1982 (the most recent assessment available) was no more than $12,240; a situation which prompted the following comment three years later: 'The key to economic success in New York is not a good job; it is two jobs.' There can be relatively few able-bodied and employable families in the city which do not contain at least two wage-earners, and this goes for a large number of professional families as well as those of labourers and craftsmen. Often enough a family's solitary breadwinner will be holding down two jobs at once, New York's police and firemen being especially well known as moonlighters who pick up a second wage packet for acting as security guards or watchmen and suchlike, in time left over from their official shifts. And while plural wages are frequently an economic necessity in families with young mouths to feed, in less pressing circumstances they are a calculated choice, a means of acquiring a little capital. For with that to hand, there is no telling what you may achieve in this city, if you get the breaks.

New York has an unrivalled record of providing the breaks whereby people rise from penury to wealth, from obscurity to fame. There was a man named Morris Gest who came to this city from Russia towards the end of the nineteenth century, with nothing at all but clothes to his name. He earned his first money in New York as a theatre ticket scalper, and then enlarged his finances by painting sparrows yellow and selling them as canaries. He ended up as a major producer on Broadway, instrumental in attracting the great Stanislavsky and his Moscow Art Theatre to the city for a season, and jointly responsible for one of the most colossal spectaculars of all time, *The Miracle*, which required the inside of the Century Theatre to be reconstructed into a perfect replica of Chartres Cathedral. Yet in the currency of New York successes, Morris Gest's was not an especially unusual progression or a particularly breathtaking one. Much more recently, another Russian who arrived penniless, Nathan Seril, made his pile in textiles and left his widow more than $100 million in real estate. Yuri Radzievsky emigrated from the Soviet Union in 1973, an electronics engineer who also wrote a newspaper column and television scripts, some of which began to irritate the authorities in Moscow. So he came to New York, taught himself English by watching TV endlessly, and set up a translation company which he sold a few years later for several million dollars, while remaining its president: and *that*, by the lights of New York, was real smart! Smarter still perhaps, was Basia Piasecka, a young Polish woman who came to New York in 1968 with limited English, a degree in philosophy and art history, and $100. Unlike so many of her compatriots earlier in the saga of immigration, she was not given a rotten time by anyone as she made her landfall. Through the New York Polish grapevine, she secured a position as servant on the Johnson family's country estate in New Jersey. Some years later she became J. Seward Johnson's third wife, and it was her inheritance of his $500 million fortune that the children of his earlier marriages decided to contest when they gathered at the Metropolitan Club in 1983.

If there is such a thing as an average New York success story – then it will be along the lines of Zion Yakuel's experience; something that doesn't occur every day of the week, but isn't a rarity, either. In 1972, he was a young Israeli doing his military service, which consisted of running a radio link in the despatch of army vehicles to desert outposts. He was ambitious and, after demobilisation, he migrated to the States, where he got an apartment in Queens and picked up a job as a house-painter. A couple of years later, having brought his fiancée from Israel and married her, he had obtained the precious green card which officially allows an alien to work in America, together with a taxi-driver's licence. Soon afterwards he was in a position to buy the indispensable medallion, without which no-one may operate one of New York's celebrated yellow cabs.* And from that point he started to take off, obtaining American citizenship, renting a garage in Flushing, getting other vehicles, readying himself for the big operation which the Israeli Defence Force had, by coincidence, trained him for. This really got going in 1984, when he was licensed to run up to 250 medallion cabs from a central radio control.

Yakuel had a good business head and he applied it coolly from the start, charging his drivers less than the going rate to join his

* The importance of the medallion is that the yellow cab, unlike any other form of taxi, is allowed to pick up passengers who hail it on the street. The medallion is issued by the city's Taxi and Limousine Commission, which since 1937 has restricted the available number to the mysterious figure of 11,787. The price of the medallion, however, has not remained static. It cost ten bucks to buy one fifty years ago. They now change hands, from one cab owner to another, for $85,000 or so.

radio-controlled squad and putting them through brief training to get the best out of the radios, by keeping in touch with each other and exchanging information about traffic conditions wherever they were. Until his firm – Big Z Two-Way Radio Inc – was properly on its feet, he also undercharged passengers by waiving the three-dollar extra he was entitled to collect as an operator of radio cabs. As a result, he formed a band of loyal drivers who impressed customers with their amiable skills, and a swelling clientele of regular passengers who decided they were getting value for their dollars even when Yakuel concluded that it was safe to impose the radio surcharge. By the end of the first year working out of the Flushing garage, the number of his cabs had risen sevenfold, and instead of just one man controlling the vehicles from a command post with four telephone lines, sixteen people were running the show from there with thirty-two lines. A number of corporations by then had accounts with Big Z, and many people standing on street corners had also come to the conclusion that the cabs in this fleet were a good bet, for cleanliness, civility, promptness and other efficiencies: drivers were penalised for being late or for swearing over the radio. Customers were able to pay cash, open an account or use a credit card to settle with this buoyantly going concern, which eventually had 240 cars on the streets of New York. Zion Yakuel was no longer, in any sense, a struggling immigrant in the United States. Just over a dozen years after landing there, he was another New Yorker who had made it with his energy and talents, and who could see even grander vistas ahead. In the fall of 1985, Big Z was bought by one of the city's biggest cab companies for what would by then have been a very pretty price. After counting the proceeds of the sale, Zion Yakuel and his wife were in a position to decide that the time had come for them to enter the plenteous world of New York real estate.

Well accustomed as they are to stories like that, New Yorkers are also thoroughly familiar with its converse, the tale of the guy who comes down with a bump. They have not yet forgotten the lore of the Wall Street Crash, which may have exaggerated the number of suicides but has never enlarged on that much wider human wreckage, the men standing dejectedly in line at the soup kitchens of the Depression, still clad in the stylish Chesterfield coats and homburgs which were almost a uniform for those who had made whoopee during the boom. At any time at all, this city can bring anybody down on his luck. There was a man named Jimmy Martin who had been a notable dancer with Florenz Ziegfeld's Follies, and had seen his name illuminated (if not exactly in lights) on Broadway for several big musicals between the wars, until a piece of scenery damaged one of his eyes and ended his stage career. For some reason, the Actors' Union would not award him a pension, and he did the best he could as a window cleaner and then as a valet, before ending up as a charity in a scruffy attic of the Dakota building, where he tapped New York's somewhat underrated sense of compassion; for the affluent residents of the Dakota not only had a word in the right ears when *Rosemary's Baby* was being filmed in their apartment house, so that Jimmy Martin was hired as an extra, but they also passed the hat round to provide him with a small annuity, which saw him through extreme old age.

The truly spectacular personal crashes still happen. Within the past few years New York has witnessed the rise and fall, for example, of Charles Agee Atkins, who came to the city in 1978 with some impressive credentials. The son of a mid-western oil mogul, he had carried all before him at the University of North Carolina, at the London School of Economics, and at the Brookings Institute in Washington. With such an education as that he could presumably have chosen almost any career, but what he wanted most of all, and what lured him to New York, was an investment bank of his own, something that would require vast capital to launch. Atkins set about acquiring the capital by first of all starting a company which, while apparently trading in government securities, was actually a tax shelter for wealthy investors. Using family connections to bring himself to the notice of people he needed for his grand design, he impressed them with an expertise they found remarkable in someone so young, however well educated; for on coming to the Big Apple, Charlie Atkins was no more than twenty-four years old. Within a year of his arrival, his investment firm, The Securities Groups, had $5 million in hand, partly subscribed by celebrities like Andy Warhol and Sydney Poitier, Nancy Sinatra and Estée Lauder, partly by a number of extremely experienced Manhattan financiers. It has been estimated that by the time Atkins was twenty-seven, his company was worth something in the order of $21 billion, and that he himself was earning nearly $6 million a year. The investors were doing quite nicely, too, with returns of up to 270 per cent on their outlays. Atkins was living in some style, in a large apartment, with a garden overlooking the East River, at 1 Sutton Place. There he was amassing a rare art collection, from which he sallied forth into New York's most exclusive social gatherings. He was not only a tycoon: he was a man about town. And still nowhere near thirty years old.

But then, quite abruptly, it all began to fall apart. In 1981 Congress changed the tax laws, to prevent people like Atkins's backers making such killings in tax write-offs again. The most experienced of them withdrew their funds from The Securities Groups in quick time. Others sued Atkins when, after juggling elaborately with monies in an effort to maintain solvency, he was unable to meet their demands. By spring 1983, when his company went out of business, it had cash in hand of $6,000 and liabilities of more than $400 million. Far from living luxuriously on New York's Upper East Side any more, Charles Agee Atkins was dwelling as quietly as possible in Florida, while the bitter lawsuits multiplied.

It is not in New York's temperament to dwell on its failures, but to rejoice in its successes and aim to repeat them as soon as possible, though it is deeply in the local character to affect cool indifference to all things except under provocation; just as it is also in the local character not simply to smoulder in envy or resentment of those who are much better off than you are. The New Yorker's instinct is to go out and do something about it, even if that something is occasionally criminal. A slightly crooked man will generally be excused in this town if he can capture the imagination with his wealth, his power, his lifestyle, his large and vivid way of doing things. Time has thus been kind to the memory of John Pierpont Morgan, who crushed smaller men standing in his way without compunction and inexplicably escaped imprisonment after an insurance companies' scandal in

1905. He is remembered in his adopted city only as the Jupiter of Wall Street, as a great patron of the arts who left behind the superb Morgan Library on Madison, as the man who, on returning to New York from Europe aboard a ship which was then delayed in quarantine, simply bought another vessel on the spot, stepped from one to another in mid-harbour, and had himself landed somewhere else.

The glitter which attaches to success is all but irresistible here: few, at any rate, appear to resist it. Supposedly sane people, who have made a name for themselves in various fields, will do much to have their achievements ratified by an appearance on *The Tonight Show*, knowing that they there stand some chance of having a custard pie shoved into their face or shaving cream squirted inside their trousers by the ineffable Johnny Carson; a man who has described the show as 'the intelligent alternative to foreplay' and who, for fronting it in this manner, was said in 1979 to be earning $2.5 million a year plus considerable perks.

And there are thousands of New Yorkers who, knowing that an appearance as one of Johnny Carson's guests is beyond their reach, would give plenty just to be in the audience of *The Tonight Show*, there to shriek with laughter at the antics and dutifully applaud the great man's quips; or, if that was asking too much, they would be happy to supply the studio atmosphere when the next series of *To Tell The Truth* is filmed. At least the neighbours, catching sight of them there on television, would recognise that no longer were they nobodies like other people on the street, but that in this tangible way they had made it at last for everyone in the Big Apple to see.

EIGHT

YOU GOTTA KEEP MOVING

This is a perpetually restless place, a city for ever rearranging itself, a people always on the move. If there is one thing in Manhattan that is even more familiar than the sight of a new building going up, it is the spectacle of an old one coming down.* It is not often possible to walk more than two or three blocks there without coming across the demolition experts at work with their implements of assault, which are strangely primitive for such a sophisticated city as this. The destruction gangs wrench and tear and bash buildings to bits, with claws and rakes and rams and huge blobs of metal, not even leavening this crude battery with the low-technology of a carefully-managed implosion, so that the victim caves in upon itself and subsides wearily to the ground. Dynamite is prohibited where New York might make most use of it because, for all the solid rock on which it is founded, Manhattan is riddled just below the surface of its streets with the tunnels and channels which convey its subway trains, its electricity, its gas, its steam, its telephone lines, its water, its sewage, its cable television and a number of its other services. A good tremor down there would bring the city to a halt. So razing one building to make room for another has to be done the laborious way, usually before a fascinated audience, for whom the contractors sometimes leave

*This is not written for effect. In twelve months recently, forty buildings were constructed in Manhattan, while 185 were demolished.

peepholes in the boarding with which they fence off the job. For there is something perversely more attractive in the sight of the destruction than in the vision of a replacement being raised high, the slow and meticulous advance of the one providing no dramatic competition to the awful violence done the other. The passer-by is impelled to linger and watch the demolition men reducing a builder's pride and joy to a heap of rubble, which will be trucked off to some wasteland in New Jersey. He can spend the best part of a day in a relatively small area of Manhattan, moving from one to another of these devastations, gaping at the brute force employed and half-choking on the clouds of dust, peculiarly thrilled by the finality of each dismemberment and every collapse: until he has had enough of the battering, the noise and the spreading grit, and begins to pine, as Moses Herzog pined, for the seashore and a breath of fresh air.

Other cities, both in America and other countries, are accustomed to the work of the wreckers, too, but nowhere else are they such a regular and persistent feature of the civic landscape: no other place makes such a habit of pulling down old buildings merely to erect on the same spot something a bit more up-to-date (for a great number of the cast-offs are not so very old). Nor is this a recent phenomenon here. New York has been doing this sort of thing for a long time, hence O. Henry's old chestnut to the effect that it'll be a great place if they ever finish it. More seriously, the diarist Philip Hone was complaining in 1839 that, 'The spirit of pulling down and building up is abroad. The whole of New York is rebuilt about once every ten years.' An exaggeration, clearly, though maybe not by very much. Within a few years, contractors digging the foundations for a new building came upon the cornerstone of an old one, already demolished, which Hone had watched rising when he was a young man. 'Overturn, overturn, overturn! is the maxim of New York,' the former Mayor wrote now. 'The very bones of our ancestors are not permitted to lie quiet a quarter of a century, and one generation of men seem studious to remove all relics of those who precede them.' Eleven years later, in 1856, another observer was making the same point just as scathingly. 'New York is notoriously the largest and least loved of any of our great cities,' wrote the editor of *Harper's Monthly*. 'Why should it be loved as a city? It is never the same city for a dozen years together. A man born in New York forty years ago finds nothing, absolutely nothing, of the New York he knew.' Yet the pillaging went on and no building, until quite recently, appeared to be safe from these depredations.

The original Trinity Church having been destroyed in 1776 by one of New York's periodic (and, in those days, usually catastrophic) fires, a second church was pulled down by the parish in 1839 so that an improved version could be built, the one that still stands. The year of the demolition saw the beginning of something just as impressive, to contain drinking water which would come by aqueduct from the Croton River, some distance upstate. This Croton Reservoir took four years to construct, more than half filled the area between Fifth and Sixth Avenues, from 40th to 42nd Streets, and had walls forty-four and a half feet high, along which people were allowed to stroll in order to enjoy the view of Manhattan and its surroundings and, in summer, the coolth coming off the surface of the water. Quite apart from its usefulness, which meant that the citizens no longer had to rely on an increasingly inadequate water supply from private springs and wells, the reservoir was a handsome addition to the midtown streets, its great walls receding slightly towards the top (as the bastions of the Brooklyn Bridge would later on) with an Egyptian elegance. Yet within sixty years, before they could even have been in great need of pointing, they had been pulled down and the New York Public Library was going up on the same ground.

The most famous hotel the city had yet seen, the Waldorf-Astoria, had not long been finished when that transformation occurred. Its fame depended not so much on its design, though that was splendid, in the style of the French Grand Siècle, as on the fact that it crowned a new era in the history of innkeeping. The tradition until late in the nineteenth century was to provide a decent meal and a comfortably clean room for the traveller; nothing more. The Waldorf-Astoria was not quite the first, but it was certainly the most accomplished in changing this formula to one of elegance and luxury that might tempt the long-staying guest, and even the non-resident, with facilities that no-one had thought of before, like shops and a variety of attractive public rooms.* Anyone could drop by the hotel's Turkish Salon, which resembled something from an imaginative translation of the *Arabian Nights*, and there take coffee which was served by a genuine Turk. Until, that is, the day in 1929 when the demolition men arrived and began to smash the old Waldorf-Astoria, which was then but thirty-two years old. A couple of smart fellows with an eye to making a fortune in a new development were responsible for that and for the Empire State Building which took its place.† Cornelius Vanderbilt II's great mansion near the Plaza on Fifth Avenue had just gone the same way, which was another considerable loss, for here had been something akin to a *château* on the Loire, a home so stylishly ample that it accommodated thirty servants as well as the Vanderbilts and any stray house guests. The department store which arose on the same site (which itself gave way to Tiffany's, the jewellers, within little more than a dozen years) was no substitute at all.

Tiffany's took up its position where Vanderbilts had been in 1940, only a few months before the fate of another New York landmark was sealed. Down at the butt-end of Manhattan since the early days of the nineteenth century had stood the structure which began life as Castle Clinton, until it was made a public assembly room in 1824 and renamed Castle Garden. This was where New York welcomed Lafayette on his last visit to America that same year. It was where Louis Kossuth spoke of the terrible things done to Hungary by the Austrian imperialists. Here Samuel Morse demonstrated his new-fangled electric telephone. And here P. T. Barnum put on Jenny Lind's first American concert, before 7,000 people and a floral display whose petals spelt out the message 'Welcome Sweet Warbler'.

---

* It is reckoned that another New York hotel, the Brunswick, pioneered this approach. The hotel has long since vanished from Madison Square.
† One of them was Pierre Du Pont, a member of the American dynasty which has made its money in everything from explosives to nylon stockings. The other was John J. Raskob, a director of General Motors, who is thought to have been as responsible as anyone for the 1929 boom which preceded the Wall Street Crash, by using his influential position to put the market up.

For a few more years Castle Garden fulfilled such purposes as these until it was pressed into service as the immigration station in 1855. That is what it remained for more than forty years, when it underwent yet another transformation, this time becoming the city's Aquarium, probably the finest thing of its kind in the world. Within a generation it figured in every New Yorker's memory of childhood, as near as makes no matter: two and a half million used to visit it each year, to goggle at the sea-lions and the alligators, the turtles and the penguins, the fighting fish and the moray eels, and all the other wealth of marine and seashore life. But then, in 1941, after a political battle which had nothing to do with the building, but with a thwarted scheme for yet another bridge between Brooklyn and Manhattan, the Aquarium was condemned as obsolete in a vindictive response, it has been suggested, to wounded pride. It was later reduced to the empty shell we can wander around today, and its contents were shifted to Coney Island, where they are still worth goggling at, but are not nearly as accessible as they used to be on the Battery site.

The Pennsylvania Station was still a monument to New York's boundless vigour and enterprise then, as deeply embedded in the civic self-awareness as Grand Central Station, with which it vied in every respect. Grand Central was finished in 1913, sumptuously decorated above its Beaux-Arts entrance with sculptures representing Mercury, Minerva and Hercules, its trains running down to the Mississippi in one direction and up to New England in the other. Penn Station was completed in 1910, modelled on the Baths of Caracalla in Rome, its traffic coming from the Canadian border right down to Miami in the south. Of the two, Penn was the rather more impressive inside, as well as being somewhat the more imposing without. It contained a general waiting-room to match the main concourse in its rival, a pair of carriage-ways majestic in design and scale; and, above all, a train shed and passenger concourse of soaring steel filigree empanelled with glass, such as visionaries had erected before only in Crystal Palaces on either side of the Atlantic. It was really rather special, and no-one could possibly have stepped through Penn Station after a long train ride without feeling quite suddenly and unexpectedly refreshed.

Its misfortune was to become involved in the convoluted history of Madison Square Garden, which had not been situated in Madison Square for many a year.* The original arena there had been run by New York's most famous showman when it opened it 1874, as Barnum's Monster Classical and Geological Hippodrome. This was backed by Vanderbilt money until the Vanderbilts decided that there was not enough profit in it and sold out to a consortium led by J. P. Morgan. The existing arena was pulled down and a new one went up on the same site in 1890 – subsequently to be known as 'the old Garden'. It became famous on several counts. It had a statue of a naked Diana with her bow and arrow, poised upon the roof, where all Manhattan could gloat over her. It was during the performance of a musical there that the building's architect, Stanford White, was shot dead by a millionaire whose wife had once had an affair with him. Scheduled events in the arena also gave it a reputation, ranging as they did from political conventions to concerts by Adelina Patti, and championship fights which Jack Dempsey invariably won. The old Garden lasted until 1925, when its landlords, the New York Life Insurance Company, decided that they would prefer to have a new office block alongside Madison Square instead. A new arena, still calling itself Madison Square Garden, soon arose across town, at 49th Street on Eighth Avenue, where it continued to function as a boxing stadium, as a venue for Wild West shows and other circuses, as well as aquatic spectaculars, automobile exhibitions, and rallies by the Christian Endeavour Society. It also became hallowed by the funeral there of Tex Rickards, the former saloon owner who had been the Garden's most successful promoter, both in Madison Square and later on: some 15,000 people filed past his coffin, which was smothered in orchids provided by Dempsey.

Almost anywhere but in America (and in New York especially) a building which had stood for no more than thirty-five years

---

*Those unfamiliar with New York should know that Madison Square lies between East 26th and East 23rd Streets, where Broadway swerves across Fifth Avenue. The present Garden straddles 32nd Street, between Seventh and Eighth Avenues. They are, in short, very nearly a mile apart.

would be thought no age at all; but here, by 1960, the 49th Street Madison Square Garden was thought to have outlived its usefulness, due for replacement on yet another site. Getting wind of this, and scenting money in the air, the Pennsylvania Railroad people lost no time in approaching the Garden's owners with an ingenious plan. Why not, they suggested, bring the Garden sixteen blocks south and relocate it between Seventh and Eighth Avenues – after purchasing the air rights of the railroad's existing property, naturally? All anyone would have to do then would be to wipe out all vestiges of Penn Station above the level of the street and shunt the entire terminus underground, where a number of railroad operations already took place anyway. A deal was struck, for $116 million, and so, on October 28, 1963, the most appalling vandalism in New York's history began, in spite of the fact that distinguished architects and other interested folk mounted pickets at the site, in what they knew was a hopeless but nevertheless necessary demonstration of anger and concern. For this was not just a handsome building disappearing in a city that had already destroyed too many. It was an important piece of New York's heritage, which could have been and should have been handed on to citizens unborn, for many generations still to come. Realising this, in a leading article which it ran a couple of days after the wreckers moved in, the *New York Times* said: 'Until the first blow fell, no-one was convinced that Penn Station really would be demolished or that New York would permit this monumental act of vandalism . . . Any city gets what it admires, will pay for, and ultimately deserves. Even when we had Penn Station we couldn't afford to keep it clean. We want and deserve tin-can architecture in a tin-horn culture. And we will probably be judged not by the monuments we build, but by those we have destroyed.' To which the president of the Pennsylvania Railroad Company coolly replied; 'Does it make any sense to preserve a building merely as a "monument"?'

But at least the station's destruction had a profound effect upon the American outlook in such matters, and most especially upon the official attitude of New York. So great was the outcry on all sides when people could actually see the building being violated, and when the newspapers began to publish pictures of that well-remembered concourse looking as though a bomb had just hit it, that men and women in federal as well as local government took stock of policy, in so far as there was any, on the preservation of fine buildings. Since early in the twentieth century there had been federal legislation authorising the acquisition and protection of national monuments, which meant safeguarding things like the White House, the Statue of Liberty or the Lincoln Memorial, but it had nothing to do with anything of merely aesthetic or local historical importance. In the wake of the Penn Station disaster, however, 1966 saw the passage of the National Historic Preservation Act, which among other things embodied a national register of historic places, where worthwhile buildings and localities throughout the country might be listed, as a guarantee of their authentic importance to the community at large. Federal government also offered various financial inducements to local authorities, in an effort to get them to be more active in preservation, for it was held that the most effective vigilance could be exercised at a local rather than at national level.

New York, in fact, by this time needed no more urging in such matters. Twelve months before Washington passed its bill, the city had voted in its own Landmarks Preservation Act, creating a special commission charged with invigilating anything 'which has a special character of historical or aesthetic interest or value as part of the development, heritage, or cultural characteristics of the city, state or nation . . .' Whatever the commission wished to preserve had only to be thirty years old or more, to qualify for its protection. A building so landmarked had to be kept in good repair by its owner, who couldn't even give it so much as a lick of different paint, or change a sign on it, or install an air-conditioner in it, without obtaining permission first. Not only buildings, but entire districts of the metropolis fell within the terms of the act, like Greenwich Village and Brooklyn Heights. New York was now exercising an authority and showing a concern which had been common in Europe for a decade or so, after they, too, had painfully discovered that property developers are not often sensitive to history or to aesthetic values. Late off the mark it may have been, but New

York suddenly began to tackle the problem more thoroughly than anyone in Europe, and set the pace for every other community in the United States. Twenty years after passing its Landmarks Act, the city had listed forty-four historic districts containing 16,000 buildings, as well as another 690 individual landmarks and forty-five 'interior or scenic landmarks'.

So zealous had it become, that even some of the early advocates of preservation began to think that City Hall was maybe overdoing things a bit, and more than one of them referred to New York's 'landmarking binge'. It was right and proper and absolutely magnificent that a very real threat to Grand Central Station was stymied by this new obsession to preserve but, some sympathisers asked, was it really important to hang onto the useless Parachute Jump at Coney Island, and to cherish a clapped-out section of the old elevated rail track purely on the grounds that it was 'an excellent example of a parabolic braced-arch structure'? If anyone needed reminding that people backing the most excellent causes can sometimes become a little unbalanced when they get worked up over particular details, there was the case of the Mount Neboh Synagogue on West 79th Street to consider. It was abandoned by its congregation, which had moved elsewhere, and had been bought by a developer (also Jewish) who intended to level it and build afresh on the site. But some local enthusiasts opposed his plans solely because of the architectural 'synthesis of Byzantine and other Near-Eastern influences'. In response to this lobby, the preservation commission listed the synagogue as a landmark but later adjusted this ruling and gave the developer the go-ahead to demolish: whereupon the pressure group took to the courts, and the democratic equivalent of siege warfare ensued. It proved costly to all concerned. Years later, when all appeals had been exhausted, the developer had final authority to proceed with his original plans. By then so much of his money had been spent on interest payments and legal fees, that he said he could no longer afford to knock down so much as a wall. The synagogue still stood, but it was now dilapidated and tatty, and likely to become more so as time went on. Even those who had wanted to save it would have preferred to be without such a mess on their doorsteps; but there was nothing that anyone could do about that any more.

Though what is important and valuable may now be unassailable in New York, this is still, as Louis Auchincloss has remarked, 'our cannibal city, which eats itself every generation', with an extraordinary appetite for pulling down and starting all over again. And although the hunger quite obviously follows from an insatiable desire to be making money, this alone cannot be the explanation. It is also as though New Yorkers simply cannot bear to stand still and enjoy what they have accomplished for more than a moment or two, which would indeed be consistent with their other characteristics. They are a truly restless people, and perhaps one of the more significant pieces of absurd research ever conducted in this home of besotted statisticians, is the one which records that New Yorkers walk their town at an *average* speed of 300 feet per minute. That's 3.4 miles an hour, and if it really is the average, including folks sauntering along the Brooklyn Heights Esplanade and round the gardens at the Battery and across the acres of Central Park, as well as those charging down Fifth Avenue and rushing up Wall Street, then these are uncommonly rapid pedestrians. This would, again, be perfectly consistent with a larger and more easily demonstrated pattern of their behaviour; their general mobility, which has always been one of their caste marks. At any moment in New York's history, a high proportion of its citizens has moved from some other place, either abroad or elsewhere in America, to be here: they are not New Yorkers born and bred. At the same time, those rooted here for a generation or more have regularly migrated from one part of their city to another, either in communities or as individuals. A motionless New Yorker is a contradiction in terms.

Until the entire city became densely settled there was a steady movement in all directions to occupy open land for the most natural and obvious of all reasons; a persistently, and often enough dramatically, increasing population. Brooklyn and other places outside the chief settlement expanded in the mid-nineteenth century because Manhattan below Washington Square was far too densely crowded, though it was a different story to the north. In 1854, the two miles of Fifth Avenue between the square and 42nd Street contained no more than 400 families, housed at decent intervals; but a single tenement block downtown was likely to be packed with 700 families. It was estimated in 1861, when there were 116,000 families living in Manhattan, that only 14 per cent of them lived in houses containing one family, only another 12 per cent in dwellings sheltering two. Everyone else was in the noisome tenements. These were reasons enough for people to extricate themselves from the general claustrophobia and move off to something more wholesome. But other factors have produced movement as well, and one of them was sickness. In 1739 there was a smallpox epidemic in the settlement at the foot of Manhattan, and many of those who could afford to pack up and leave did so, not stopping until they had put some uncontaminated ground between themselves and the disease. For more than a century by then, a small community had been growing round a tobacco plantation farther up the island and here the fugitives made new homes for themselves, in what subsequently became known as Greenwich Village. Towards the end of the eighteenth century and early in the nineteenth, the Village again acquired refugees from the bigger settlement of New York lower down Manhattan, this time because of outbreaks of yellow fever; one of which, in 1822, was so frightening that the ferry which had long crossed the East River from Brooklyn, to dock at Peck Slip, changed its sailings to berth more prudently opposite the Village. By then New York was on the edge of its first great explosion of populace, and it had already laid plans for this with remarkable foresight, partly from anxiety about disease, which was befalling the city far too often.

Fifteen years before that worst plague of fever, the Common Council of New York decided that a plan must be made for the city's expansion in the only possible direction, which was north along Manhattan; and that this must be done 'in such a manner as to unite regularity and order with the public convenience and benefit, and in particular to promote the health of the city'. At the time, New York extended from the Battery up to, approximately, the line of today's Houston Street.* What the council wanted, therefore, was a systematic survey of a largely empty island for, other than New York and Greenwich Village, its only settlement was tiny Harlem, and there was nothing else on it apart from some country estates. The council chose a commission of three to direct the work, but the man actually responsible for what emerged was an engineer, John Randall, Jr. It seems to have been a haphazard arrangement, because all manner of obstacles were put in Randall's way, and the council appeared powerless to remove them. He was attacked for trespass more than once, and for allowing his workmen to damage trees with their surveying tools. He was even arrested by the sheriff, and when all was done he had some difficulty in extracting his fee from the council. But what he came up with in 1811 settled much of Manhattan's appearance for good. He gave it the grid plan, and while this was not an original device (thirteenth-century Peking, among others, was a city designed on rectangular principles) it has rarely been executed so thoroughly.

Randall provided for a series of avenues, each a hundred feet wide, to go directly from south to north up Manhattan, with narrower cross streets running through all of them from east to west, leaving substantial blocks of land between each intersection on which building might take place. Numbered from the bottom upwards, these crossings went as far north as 155th Street, which is well on the way to the George Washington Bridge nowadays. Randall's report conceded that, 'it may be a subject of merriment that the commissioners have provided space for a greater population than is collected at any spot on this side of China'. He needn't have worried about derision on that score, for the space would be filled quite soon. More cogent criticisms of the plan – made when it had been partly acted upon, and after other American cities had imitated its principles – were that it paid scant attention to the topography of Manhattan, which is by no means flat, and that it was a scheme for building development unmitigated by anything else. The first weakness

* That is, it occupied only about one-fifth of Manhattan's total length.

meant that there were subsequent problems with drainage and other matters affected by gravity. As for the second, if Randall's blueprint had been followed slavishly and taken to its logical conclusion, there would today have been no relief from a monotony of buildings between the Battery and that topmost point where the Harlem River separates Manhattan from Spuyten Duyvil. For the relief it enjoys, New York can thank Frederick Law Olmsted more than anyone else. He it was, as chief landscape architect to the Department of Parks half a century after Randall produced his plan, who was mainly responsible for the alliance between mankind and Nature on Manhattan; along Riverside Drive, up at Morningside and Inwood, and most of all in Central Park; where, between the rowing-boats and the tennis courts, the statues, the fountains and the joyous Carousel, thickets of Chinese elm, English holly and Korean mountain ash trees flourish, together with Townsend's warbler, the snowy owl and the purple gallinule.*

It is, none the less, Manhattan's grid system that many of today's visitors to New York remember when they have forgotten more important things about this city. Those long, straight avenues, enclosed by high buildings and dipping away to far, blank horizons, offer the illusion of eternal, infinite space beyond their extremities: and this is uplifting, great solace, when viewed from a choking midtown during the rush hours. Some Europeans may affect boredom with the metrical rhythm of numbered streets, all making the shortest distance between two points, but they know very well that they can find their way round here with much more certainty than anywhere on their side of the water. And New Yorkers who complain about the awful congestion of traffic that will be pouring straight down Fifth or heaving up Madison at certain times of the day, should at least once in their lives try riding on a No 25 London bus through those intricately historical streets which must be navigated between

* Central Park's overall design was by Olmsted and the architect, Calvert Vaux. It won a nationwide competition in 1857, but it was Olmsted who supervised the work on the ground. They also collaborated at Prospect Park, Brooklyn, later on.

Piccadilly and the Bank of England: it is interesting, but not to be attempted if you're in a hurry, or neurotic about inhaling polluted air.

Whatever its shortcomings, Randall's plan offered native New Yorkers (and the swelling army of immigrants) the basis for a total occupation of the island, which before the end of the nineteenth century had become the dynamic centre of an expanding and amalgamated city; no longer Little Old New York, but a considerable metropolis. The key to occupying it fully was transport, and no time was lost in arranging that. Within three years of the plan's publication, Robert Fulton had his novel steam ferry *Nassau* chugging across the East River, and the next few decades saw a remarkable increase in waterborne passenger traffic. By the 1850s it was possible to catch a boat across the Hudson to Jersey City every ten or fifteen minutes, so great was the demand by people who earned their living in Manhattan but preferred to live outside New York. There was an even greater service across the East River by then, with half a dozen steamboats taking people back and forth between Williamsburg and Peck Slip, and other craft connecting other districts of Brooklyn and Manhattan. In 1860, over thirty-two million passengers sailed between those two places. By then there were also well-established sailings from Manhattan to somewhere as distant as Croton, thirty-two miles up the Hudson River; and the Staten Island ferry had been trudging the length of New York Harbor to a timetable for a quarter of a century or so.

But much more effective in opening up the city than even the busy ferryboats was the development of public transport upon the land. In the beginning were ox carts, which lumbered around lower Manhattan until they were superseded by horse-drawn omnibuses in 1827. These in their turn gave way in mid-century to carriages drawn along rails by horses, which were still running along lower Broadway as late as 1917. The most potent nineteenth-century development, however, was that of the train running along an elevated railroad track, New York's legendary and still (by some sentimentalists) sorely-missed 'El'. Its inventor, Charles Harvey, demonstrated its possibilities in

1867 when he had girders to support the track erected along a quarter of a mile of Greenwich Street and then, formally dressed, complete with top hat, he boarded a rail-ganger's trolley and pumped the vehicle safely backwards and forwards before an apprehensive but ultimately impressed crowd on the sidewalks below. A company was floated, the line was extended, and the elevated railway had come to stay – for the best part of a century, at any rate. It wasn't a smooth ride, to begin with. Harvey's first idea was for the carriages to be hauled along the rails by a cable which was wound round the drum of a stationary steam engine; essentially the method of traction still used on the San Francisco cable cars. In New York, the cables kept snapping under the strain. He therefore tried a small steam locomotive, its engine enclosed so that it wouldn't frighten the horses in the streets below. That worked, though there were plenty of complaints from people about the soot and cinders showering down. In spite of this, by 1875 elevated lines were being constructed on Manhattan along Second, Third, Sixth and Ninth Avenues. Within a few more years, they were extended to Brooklyn and Queens and the Bronx; and when, in 1902, electrification was introduced, the complaints were only from people whose businesses or homes lay for most of the time in the shadow and within earshot of the 'El'. What it meant to other New Yorkers was conveyed by one of the WPA Guide's authors in 1939:

Despite the prevalent idea that 'the Subway yawns the quickest promise home', the speed of the El is substantially the same as that of the subway. But the El's advantage lies in its rambling trajectory, replete with images of New York which the subway journey (except in brief aerial excursions) lacks. From the vantage point of a window seat, one surveys the slums of Harlem and the East Side; middle class Tudor City, Chinatown and the Bowery; the German and Bohemian quarters of Yorkville; the Wall Street district; the flat suburban reaches of Brooklyn; the hilly jumble of the Bronx; and the quiet tree-shaded streets of Queens. Dingy sweatshops, flophouses, dramatic family groups pass in succession. So, too, do scenes of great beauty: skyscrapers at dusk, glittering rivers, dwindling streets.

The 'El' was doomed from 1938, when City Hall decided that it had disfigured Sixth Avenue too long, and Mayor LaGuardia took an acetylene torch to start the demolition of the line at 53rd Street. In 1955 the last of the lines, the Third Avenue 'El', went out of service, and by the following February its final remains were removed from 42nd Street. Yet it is still possible to get the feel of that wholly American contribution to urban transport, on those 'brief aerial excursions' along today's subway system. Outside Manhattan there are many stretches of track that run down the middle of a street, forty or fifty feet above the ground, and one of them in the Bronx was used by the film-makers for Gene Hackman's car chase of the drug runner riding above him in *The French Connection*. If you take the No 7 train which runs from Times Square to Flushing, by way of Grand Central and Shea Stadium, it is rewarding to ride during daylight in the very last car. For there comes the moment – just before Court House Square station in Queens – when the train climbs out of its tunnel and there, if you look back through the end window, you can enjoy one of the most breathtaking of all New York's views; the midtown Manhattan skyline, seen across the river, just as the WPA writer would have enjoyed it a couple of generations ago.

The nineteenth century saw two attempts to start a subway system, one of which would have had trains blown down and then sucked back along the tunnel by a gigantic fan; but both efforts were opposed by powerful people, including the rail baron, Commodore Vanderbilt, and the landowning John Jacob Astor II; but most of all by 'Boss' Tweed, the Tammany chieftain who took his cut from the city's horse-car and stage companies. As a result, New York was well behind other places in getting this form of transport. The pioneer had been London in 1863, and Glasgow, Budapest, Boston, Paris and Berlin all had railways running underground before Mayor John McLellan drove the first train of the Interborough Rapid Transit Company from the City

Hall station right up to 103rd Street, on October 27, 1904. The delay, however, allowed New York to improve enormously on the original concept across the Atlantic. In London, the underground trains followed one another at short and regular intervals along the same lines, with no possibility of faster trains leap-frogging slower ones anywhere. New York from the outset had two parallel tracks going in each direction, local trains stopping at every station down the line, but express trains covering the same distances much more quickly by overtaking the locals and making only limited stops. It was a system imaginatively adapted for people who were in a hurry more often than not, expecting laggards to get out of their way; also for people who counted their money carefully and did not ask but *demanded* value for everything they spent. This public demand ensured that, as long as it was well maintained, New York unquestionably had the finest subway system in the world; it also meant that the original five-cent fare charged for any ride was continued until 1947, when at last it rose – to ten cents for any distance.

Swiftly the subway lines proliferated after the breakthrough had come. IRT stations could instantly be identified above ground by illuminated blue and white globes beside each entrance, and soon these were visible not only in Manhattan but across the East River, too. From 1915 they were rivalled by the green and white hexagons which signified that down below was a station belonging to the Brooklyn Manhattan Transit system. These were both private companies, whose operations were so profitably successful that within a few years the city of New York decided to go into the business on its own account, the public Independent Subway's distinctive blue street lamps being switched on when the Eighth Avenue line was opened in 1932. The IND stations also differed from those of their predecessors by the use of glazed and differently coloured tiles along the subway walls, so that illiterate passengers, too, could tell where they were when their trains drew into the platforms. Both the IRT and the BMT designers had gone for more elaborately old-fashioned decorations, terracotta and majolica being widely used in mouldings and panels to illustrate New York landmarks or other significant things (at Astor Place, on the Lexington Avenue line, there is still a beaver in bas-relief to commemorate the fact that John Jacob Astor's first fortune came from selling furs). In the end New York finished up with over 700 miles of subway, quite the most extensive anywhere, and operating twenty-four hours a day, which was more than could be said for the London Underground or the Paris Metro.

No citizens anywhere else have ever been offered such cheap mobility as that which was long provided in New York, when for five cents it was possible to ride on the subway from the top of the Bronx to Coney Island, which is the best part of twenty-five miles. As someone has written with feeling, 'It made interborough romance feasible.' It increased the range of available employment. It also played its part in settling patterns of migration, by substantial communities for whom the arrival of a new subway line signalled the moment for them to be moving on. Jews who had made their homes in the dreadful lung blocks – so-called because they bred high rates of lung disease – of the Lower East Side when they first arrived in this city, had levered themselves up to the more salubrious surroundings of East Harlem by the last quarter of the nineteenth century. When the IRT line was flung beyond Manhattan and into the Bronx in the first decade of the twentieth century, building developers anticipated it and made sure that new properties were ready for inspection the moment the subway stations appeared. The properties were appreciably more expensive and just a bit more attractive than dwellings in East Harlem, excellent bait for people determined to make the best of themselves and quite willing to be strained financially for a few years until they got back on their feet again. By the 1920s, there was a considerable Jewish population in the expanding Bronx neighbourhoods of Hunt's Point, West Farms and East Tremont; and Italians had also migrated along the IRT line to settle in Morrisania and Belmont, with Irish doing likewise in Mott Haven, Melrose and Highbridge.

Something of the same sort happened in 1936, when the IND line was extended from Jay Street in Brooklyn to Rockaway Avenue, another four miles farther on, thus establishing the first direct link between Harlem and Bedford-Stuyvesant. Harlem, as we have already noticed, had become desperately overcrowded as a result of the Depression, but economic catastrophe had produced a totally different result in Bedford-Stuyvesant. Since 1870 this had gradually become one of Brooklyn's desirable neighbourhoods for middle-class whites and, in catering to it, the building developers had constructed more property than the market could use after the great bubble of the 1920s burst. So the more prosperous black folk who were beginning to feel cramped over in Harlem, and who could afford to shift, took a trip down to Brooklyn aboard Billy Strayhorn's euphonious A Train, liked the look of Bedford-Stuyvesant and decided to move in. They were, after all, no more than a five-cent ride away from their own people if they needed to drink at the well. Within four years, 38 per cent of the populace in that part of Brooklyn was black.

It has been claimed that what increasingly happened in Bedford-Stuyvesant as black people migrated there – a corresponding withdrawal of whites who preferred to keep themselves to themselves – occurs less in New York than it does in any other American city. It is, all the same, a recurring social reflex in the metropolis and the transformation of Harlem between the world wars is merely the best-known example, with successive waves of Germans and Irish, Italians and Jews (some of whom had lived in the area for no more than twenty years) moving out as soon as the blacks arrived. The working-class Brownsville area of Brooklyn was at that time second only to the Lower East Side of Manhattan as a centre of New York Jewry, with small factories and tenements full of artisans, many of whom had come from eastern Europe in the great Diaspora at the end of the nineteenth century. It changed little until after the Second World War, when some Jews left for improved housing conditions elsewhere in Brooklyn and in Queens. Blacks tended to fill the vacant spaces, and before long more Jews were on their way out, complaining that the old neighbourhood was decaying and becoming lawless (though the blacks who were there at the time, in the early 1960s, apparently recall this as a peaceful time in their lives). From then on the exodus gathered pace until, by 1980, Brownsville was almost wholly black.

Some people have struck camp more than once for the same reason. Just after the First World War, the Charlotte Street

district of the Bronx received numbers of Jews who had fled
from Harlem before the black advance. They were able to start
up afresh here because the new subway line allowed them to
travel on the Seventh Avenue Express down to the Garment
District of Manhattan, where most of the men worked. Just
before the Second World War, their sense of solidarity was
slightly disturbed by the arrival of a Puerto Rican family on
the same patch, but nothing much was made of this until after
the war, when more people from the Caribbean, together with
native American blacks, began to appear round Charlotte Street.
In 1946 it was no secret that many of the Jews were ready to
get out of the East Bronx, held back only because there was
a housing shortage in other areas at the time. There was
occasional violence from some of the newcomers, and, housing
shortage or not, established families began to leave. More Latins
and blacks came in, this time bringing vandals with them, and
more and more property began to suffer from their attacks. By
the 1950s, as far as almost all the Jews of Charlotte Street and
its surroundings were concerned, it was no longer a question
of whether, but one of how soon. The 1960 census showed, as
starkly as sometimes only statistics can, what an upheaval had
taken place by then. Only 11 per cent of the families in that part
of the Bronx had been there before the war; and nearly 60 per
cent had arrived in the previous five years.

The reasons for New Yorkers shifting in communities (or,
at least, in segments of communities) from one part of their
metropolis to another are numerous. Nothing less than American
open-handedness was responsible for one movement of population out of New York to the suburbs just after the Second World
War. President Roosevelt had ratified the GI Bill of Rights which
offered returned servicemen, among other benefits, the finance
to buy their own homes without any down payment and at the
perfunctory interest rate of 4 per cent. More than 160,000
men took advantage of this munificence to set themselves
up in Nassau County on Long Island, with another 76,000
collecting the loan for a fresh start in neighbouring Suffolk
County. An event before the war, the 1939 World's Fair, is
said to have played its part in promoting another migration.

The fair had an unfortunate theme for something that opened the very year in which most of the participating nations began fighting – 'Building the world of tomorrow' – and this unhappy coincidence was responsible for it ending with a deficit so huge that investors could recover only thirty-three cents to the dollar on their outlay. But in its first few months it attracted crowds from all over New York to the site at Flushing Meadow Park in Queens. It has been said with some authority that many of these visitors 'liked what they saw and decided to settle in the borough', which led to 'the creation of instant Jewish communities in Forest Hills, Kew Gardens and Elmshurst'.

Of all the migrations that have occurred in this fidgety place, one stands hauntingly apart from the rest. By the turn of the century, the vicinity of Tompkins Square down the Lower East Side had become settled by Germans, working-class and God-fearing people, almost all of them belonging to St Mark's Lutheran Church on East 6th Street. On a Saturday morning in June 1904, the entire congregation of that church, together with their pastor, the Rev George Haas, set off on their annual outing; a day trip by steamer down Long Island Sound, where they would go ashore for a time before sailing home in the early evening. The steamer chartered for the day was the *General Slocum*, a big twin-funnelled side-wheel paddle boat with a crew of twenty-three. She had been built thirteen years earlier for just this sort of trade, taking New Yorkers for pleasure excursions upon the abundant waters surrounding the city. Well over 1,000 people boarded her at a pier down on East 3rd Street just before nine o'clock that morning; and, with a couple of pilots to see the vessel safely through the turbulence of Hell Gate before the Sound, the *General Slocum* cast off into the East River, her three decks crowded, a band playing in the stern, the cooking of chowder already under way in the galley.

An hour later, she had sailed comfortably past Hell Gate and was coming abreast of 135th Street in the Bronx, when there was an explosion in a galley stove on the lower deck. At once the flames spread furiously, fanned by a breeze off the water, and with them came panic. It was said later that Captain Van Schaik lost his head, so that instead of putting his vessel aground on the nearest land, the Bronx, he drove her towards North Brother Island and beached her on its rocky shore. Before he got there, the *General Slocum* was blazing from stem to stern, and the screams of burning people could be heard in the city. A reporter afterwards described how, 'Women were roasted to death in sight of their husbands, and children and babes by the score perished in the waters of the East River, where they had been thrown by frenzied mothers. With death by fire behind them, hundreds leapt to their death in the river.' Some might have been saved if passing vessels had done all that they could to help, but there was remarkable indifference afloat on the river that day. A ferry crossing from East 134th Street to College Point ignored the disaster. A craft flying the pennant of the New York Yacht Club followed the blazing steamer until she went aground, then went about and made no effort to save anyone struggling in the water. Only the tug *Wade* did its best, and thereby saved the lives of 155 people, including the captain of the *General Slocum*, who jumped onto the smaller boat's deck as soon as his own vessel became fast on the rocks. So did Mr Haas, whose wife and daughter were dead.

No fewer than 1,030 people perished, with several hundred others injured. It was said that not a home in the parish of St Mark escaped bereavement, and some families were wiped out, others nearly so: one man survived only to find that his wife and all six of their children had gone. So searingly painful was the memory of what had happened, that the survivors of the *General Slocum* could not bear to go on living in the old familiar place. After they had buried their dead, these Albrechts and Mullers, Kiessels and Roths, Hoffmans and Weisses and the others, either individually or collectively, decided they must get out of Tompkins Square and pass the rest of their lives some place else that did not contain memories at every turn. Which they did, dispersing throughout New York and leaving behind *in memoriam* a small monument on one side of the square; of a boy and a girl looking sadly at a steamboat.

While most forms of New York mobility have recurred ever since the early settlements, one variant above all others is strikingly of our own times, essentially a product of circumstances which have changed since the Second World War. It has become known in the current mythology as 'gentrification', and it is not by any means peculiar to this city or even to this country. Some urban specialists claim that both the habit and the word describing it originated in and around London, but it is very typical of New York – fascinated as so many of its people are with anything that involves real estate – that a far smaller proportion of the populace will look blank when asked what gentrification means, than would probably be the case across the Atlantic. Some New Yorkers may have an imperfect grasp of all its ramifications, but they will at least have a rough idea of what it amounts to.

At the heart of the phenomenon is a social change that has occurred since the immediate aftermath of the war produced a steep rise in the birthrate. Large numbers of those born to the returned warriors and their wives, obtained a college education in due course as a normal stage in the progression of growing up; which had not often been the case with their parents, who were adolescent or scarcely more than that during the years of the Depression. By the time these children of joyful reunion emerged from college, from the mid-sixties onwards, they were well-educated and potentially prosperous, with a host of lucrative professions awaiting them, many of which had not been in much evidence before the war, but had mushroomed since – consultancies, planning positions, administrative posts in increasingly complex organisms, all on top of those great old standbys in the law and business, which were also thriving as never before. More than this, these well-equipped and ambitious college products had different aspirations from those of the old folks, partly resulting from their education, partly from historical events in their generation that had inevitably changed attitudes. What this meant for the metropolitan society in a broad sense was put like this a few years ago: 'If the typical American urban family – mom, dad and two or three kids – is not exactly extinct, it certainly no longer holds a claim as the overwhelmingly dominant household prototype. A declining cohort of "Father Knows Best" families now stands alongside a growing army of never-married singles, unmarried couples, married couples without children, single parents, empty nesters, and constellations of unrelated individuals.' It was pointed out that whereas in 1950, getting on for half of New York's households consisted of married couples with children under eighteen years old, within twenty years this proportion had dropped to one-third, and was probably going to diminish even more before the end of the century.

This post-war gentry has been characterised in other ways. Its couples who propose to raise families tend to do so later than their parents, often enough because the wife is now in a position to assert her right to a career, too. Nor do they see the city as many of their predecessors did, mostly as a place of work, to be abandoned at the end of each day for home and family in a suburb. Married or not, with parental instincts or without them, today's gentry all prefer to enjoy those things that only the centre of a great metropolis can provide; theatres and concerts, museums and galleries and, as much as any of that, the sophisticated and knowing social life that continues almost round the clock if you know where to look and have the energy to handle it, in cafés and dives and parties in other people's homes. They want to spend time with other young thrusters who, like them, are constantly moving through life, ever upward, ever onward, always achieving and always advancing but never, miraculously, never becoming old. Because they are ambitious, they need to compare professional notes with their peers, and because they are alert to all possibilities that may come their way, they need to keep up with everybody else's gossip which one day may be turned to advantage. It is very important to check things out when you have settled for an existence on this plane; exhausting but absolutely vital if you are even to stay in place, which is not often thought to be nearly good enough here. For such a lifestyle, you must operate virtually full-time close to the centre of things. Your home must not be far from what the yuppie jargon of New York knows cryptically as the CBD, the central business district, which is Manhattan below Central Park, more or less.

Where, then, to live, when this attractive Manhattan was being sold off steadily to the highest bidders, in office blocks and opulent condominiums? It had long been plain – and it has become plainer with every passing year – that to live below the park you must either be excessively rich or exceedingly poor, be prepared to pay through the nose for not enough room to swing a cat round, or be one of those fortunates whose modestly comfortable accommodation is rent-controlled, and therefore not subject to inflation as other domestic accommodation is.* None of these categories has quite coincided with the immediate demand of New York's rising and youngish gentry. But in the 1960s it was perceived that, not so very far away from the CBD, New York contained any number of elegant and very spacious old nineteenth-century town houses, at prices which were within the competence of any well-paid professional person. They were often neglected in some way or other, but structurally they were perfectly sound, and with the expenditure of not too many dollars, they could be restored to the fine condition their builders had left them in a century or more ago. They were nothing less than good old New York brownstones, which always have been one of the great embellishments of this city, and they were mostly to be found within five miles or so of the area that everyone hankered after, a trifling distance as the subway goes. They were houses which had, in fact, been built for just such a people of the affluent middle class as were now about to recover them. They had fallen into neglect in the intervening years, for various reasons which included shifts in population, the refusal of banks to offer mortgages, falls in property values during slumps, and consequent changes in use, which often saw them transformed from the homes of well-to-do families, to rooming houses for people close to the bottom of the pile.

Their rehabilitation was known as the brownstone revival

---

* Rent control (introduced as a wartime measure in 1943) and rent stabilisation (adopted in 1969) add up to an exceedingly contentious and complex issue in New York with no fewer than 1.2 million apartments in the city subject to some regulation. The most significant thing outsiders need to know is that, to qualify, it is necessary to have lived in the property since before the control was applied. This is an advantage no New Yorker lightly surrenders. Mayor Koch has had the benefit of a home in the palatial Gracie Mansion since his first election in 1978; but he has thriftily retained his own rent-controlled apartment in Greenwich Village so as to cushion the shock, one day, of being ejected by the voters from his official residence.

before it became hailed as the start of gentrification in New York. Within a few years so much labour and middle-class money had been spent on such properties that it was being confidently forecast that 'by the end of the century, Brooklyn will be home for the most extensive collection of restored nineteenth-century town houses in the United States, outshining Boston, Philadelphia, Washington and New Orleans.' Two areas of the borough, Park Slope and Cobble Hill, soon began to ascend the social scale again as the prospectors arrived. It was at about this time, when the restoration of brownstones became a regular conversation piece in New York, that the *New Yorker* made its own deft comment on the trend with, typically, a cartoon (by Stevenson). It showed a very suburban street, way out on the fringes of New York, with a sprinkling of one-storey cottages and the occasional car parked at the kerb. Towering over everything else was a town house complete with basement and three upper floors, which looked as if it might have been lifted from a terrace on the Upper East Side or on Cobble Hill. Its proud owners were outside, talking to a couple of the locals, and the caption read: 'We always wanted a brownstone, but prices were sky-high, so we decided to move out of the city and build.' Before too many more years had passed, the gentry of New York were scouring some improbable neighbourhoods, like Astoria and Long Island City, in their search for decent old housing that had seen better days; and they were returning to Harlem, which their grandparents had once abandoned to the blacks.

Meanwhile, back in Manhattan, another discovery had been made by the bargain hunters. One of the most telling changes there after the war was the withdrawal of much manufacturing, which had been there since the Industrial Revolution came to America, a source of New York's economic strength. Weakened in the first place by the Depression, briefly brought to life again during the war effort, it had permanently subsided as a result of those capital market forces which ordained that henceforth New York wealth would be based on business and on services, not on industry any more. As the small mills and forges and workshops one after the other in the post-war years took themselves to more promising places outside the city, or closed down altogether, they left behind a growing number of vacant buildings that no-one could see another purpose for right away. Stripped of their machinery or emptied of whatever had been stored in them, they were something of a dead loss until the early 1960s, when artists began to realise that, with a few adjustments, maybe an extra floor inserted here and there, they would make the most terrific studios-cum-living quarters; and they came as near as anything in New York ever has done, to going for a song. Before long these loft conversions had become as inseparable from the city's Bohemian culture as the café life and the ateliers of Greenwich Village itself. That was the point at which the real estate developers decided to move in and make another killing. Within a decade, the artists had almost all been forced out by rents they could no longer afford, and the lofts of Lower Manhattan were becoming gentrified.* In 1977 it was estimated that loft conversions down there had already produced 10,000 new homes for the well-to-do, with more being added at the rate of 1,000 a year.

These changes are not confined to dwellings alone. Whatever domestic alterations have been made to accommodate the new settlers, larger transformations have invariably followed in each surrounding neighbourhood, so long as the affluent young middle classes have appeared in more than ones or twos. The full meaning of gentrification goes well beyond the smartened-up old brownstone or the revitalised warehouse, with its modishly yuppie occupants. Get a few dozen such households on the block and they swiftly attract a supporting cast of boutiques, restaurants, arty-crafty shops selling ingeniously useless things, galleries offering decent student watercolours at ambitiously professional prices, and plant shops for those who feel lost without *dyzygothica* or *ficus elastica* in the bathroom. The lofted gentry of Lower Manhattan have lately been able to indulge themselves in *la nouvelle cuisine*, and wine coming at ninety-five

---

* A similar process was going on, at almost the same time, but without the advance guard of artists, in the redundant warehouses lining the Thames below Tower Bridge in London.

bucks a bottle, in a classy place on Green Street, all dim lighting, a pianist whose numbers are announced by the maître D, and a sense of expansive well-being: which is not quite what the builders had in mind when they originally made there a garage for the Sanitation Department. Yet transformations of that order are not the only changes that might bewilder some ghosts of old New York if they returned to their gentrified haunts today. They might first of all have difficulty in working out just whereabouts in the metropolis they were, with so many strange-sounding neighbourhoods to identify. No-one had heard of SoHo before this generation, nor yet of TribeCa. These are the brand marks of gentrification, stamped upon that part of Lower Manhattan (So)uth of (Ho)uston Street, and in the (Tri)angle (be)low (Ca)nal Street. Similarly, a stretch of (Lo)wer (Bro)adway between Canal and 8th Street has even more recently been smartified by those with a stake in an easily recalled and snappy title. The most dapper of all these transmogrifications, however, has occurred over on the West Side, at approximately the latitude of Times Square. It was in the nineteenth century that the area between the river and the square first acquired its well-earned title of Hell's Kitchen, which derived from a villainous dive frequented by the hoodlum Dutch Heinrichs and his gang. Until New York's industrial decline, it was still a rough part of town, drawing its vitality from the waterfront, the railroad freight yards and the overcrowded tenements. By the time the sap had all oozed away and Hell's Kitchen was no more, gentrified Clinton had taken its place. And though the Landmark Tavern still flourishes as ever was on Eighth Avenue at 46th, no fisty Irish longshoreman would be really comfortable with what they serve there for today's clientele – upmarket wines racked conspicuously behind the bar, to go with snacks of duck-and-orange paté, and jalapeño dip.

The gentrifying still goes on, as fresh waves of the well-educated and affluent go hunting for the place that they can call theirs, triumphantly discovering in some unsuspected corner a neglected wreck that can be licked into shape again, or the forsaken shell of somebody's failed enterprise that can be given a new and utterly different lease of life. Inexhaustibly they ransack the city for their quarry, with sharp and knowing gaze, unerringly counting the odds on this area coming up in the world if people like them move in, or of that remaining stuck where it is for far longer than they would wish to endure its seediness, its tensions, its slightly menacing air. They are, almost without exception, blessedly colour blind, and there are black yuppies in New York as well as white ones gentrifying the neighbourhoods: it is no less than the truth when any of them say that they care not who their neighbours are so long as there's no hassle and the sidewalk is kept clean. They deceive themselves, perhaps, only when they imagine that they are putting down roots in whatever place they take and revive. Very small and very few roots are the rule in New York: instead there is a peripatetic momentum which is maintained from one generation to another, as if by tacit and general approval. It is so now, just as it was a hundred years ago when Henry James wrote *Washington Square*. Arthur Townsend, contemplating his future with Marian, reassures her that they won't have to stay that long in their small first home. 'It doesn't matter,' he says, 'it's only for three or four years. At the end of three or four years we'll move. That's the way to live in New York – to move every three or four years. Then you always get the last thing. It's because the city's growing so quick – you've got to keep up with it.'

NINE

A SLIGHTLY ROTTEN APPLE

A few days before Christmas 1985, just as the evening rush hour was beginning in midtown Manhattan, an almost new black Lincoln Continental swung quietly into the kerb on East 46th Street. This is a not very wide thoroughfare in a perpetually busy part of the city, and is therefore designated as a no-parking tow-away zone. The driver nevertheless switched off his engine and got out of the car with his passenger, an elderly millionaire with extensive interests in the meat trade, who had just been chauffeured into town from his mansion on Staten Island. The two turned from the Lincoln towards Spark's Steak House, whose title suggests humbler victuals than it actually provides, for it is well patronised for its choice lobster as well as its prime beef, and it has a high reputation for the range of vintage wines it keeps. Neither the millionaire nor his companion even reached the door. As they stepped away from the car three men, dressed alike in fawn trenchcoats and black fur hats, came towards them with automatic pistols in their hands. Twelve shots were fired before the gunmen raced off to a waiting vehicle, which roared away round the corner and was instantly lost in the traffic swirling down Second Avenue: leaving behind two bodies on the sidewalk, their blood running into the gutter. Before long, reporters from the papers, radio and television arrived on the scene and began to ask questions of anyone who might have been in the vicinity when the killings occurred. The man in charge of the steak house told them that he knew well the millionaire, who had been a regular client of theirs. 'He was always welcome,' said the restaurateur. 'We treated him like any other celebrity.' He was indeed famous in the metropolis, and even farther afield, but not for his wealth or for his legitimate business interests. The killers had just rubbed out Paul Castellano, and New York had lost its most powerful Mafia boss.

It was a good story, well covered in the evening bulletins, and worth many columns of newsprint the following day. It was topical, too, because New York had been raptly following the long series of court hearings which would culminate fourteen months later in prison sentences of up to 100 years apiece on a number of Mafia figures. But it was not exactly a novel episode, for Mr Castellano was only following where others of his kind had gone from New York over the years. In 1931, Joe Masseria was gunned down by Lucky Luciano's men while finishing lunch at Scarpato's Restaurant on Coney Island, and Salvatore Maranzano was shot and stabbed to death in his office on Park Avenue. In 1957, Albert Anastasia was riddled with bullets while he was sitting in the barber's chair at the Park-Sheraton Hotel. In 1971, Joseph Colombo was shot at a rally of the Italian-American Civil Rights League, dying seven years later without ever coming out of a coma. In 1972, Joey Gallo was killed while eating a meal on his birthday at Umberto's Clam House in Little Italy. In 1979, Carmine Galante was also feeding when five gunmen murdered him at Joe and Mary's restaurant in Brooklyn. And these were only the leading *mafiosi* who had come to an unpleasant end. Many underlings, too, not to mention hapless citizens who had merely got in the Mafia's way, had also been shot to death or disposed of in some other unspeakable fashion.

The protracted trials leading up to those unprecedented sentences in 1987, revealed a catalogue of viciousness, greed and general rottenness which was scarcely unfamiliar to the populace, except in a few details. It may have been news that a Mafia hit man dipped his bullets in cyanide before loading his gun, so that only one shot would be needed to kill his quarry. But no New Yorker this past half century has been unaware of the fact that Mafia victims often disappear because their bodies have been embalmed in concrete, and dumped in the East River or in the foundations of some new building. Some people were perhaps ignorant of the fact that for many years a member of the Colombo gang had been head of the Cement and Concrete Workers' District Council, and was therefore perfectly placed to organise one of the most infamous rackets the city has known since Prohibition. But it had long been common knowledge that unless building contractors were prepared to pay some sort of levy (2 per cent, in fact) on any construction work they undertook, they could expect endless, ultimately disastrous trouble on the site; and probably some vile assault upon their family life. 'There is no concrete poured in New York that me and my friends don't get a part of,' a Mr Carmine Persico was heard to boast on a tape recording which was produced in court one day. Mr Persico, luminary in an organisation replete with lurid nicknames, was otherwise widely known as The Snake, and among his identifiable accomplishments was the ability to run rackets while still behind bars. Prison poses no insurmountable problems to the Mafia *capo*, provided it is known that he will be released one day. He simply promises terror, when that day comes, to all who have failed him in the meantime: and he unfailingly carries out every threat he makes.

The story of the Mafia is part of the local folklore. Not many may be able to recount the circumstances of its beginning in thirteenth-century Sicily, or even say with certainty when it arrived in the metropolis.* But an educated New Yorker would think someone's local knowledge was defective if he could not promptly name the five Mafia gangs in the city, which the gangsters themselves prefer to think of as 'families': Gambino, Genovese, Colombo, Lucchese and Bonanno.† He

---

*Gay Talese reckons that the word originates in the cry '*Ma fia*', 'My daughter', uttered by the distraught mother of a girl raped on her wedding day in Palermo by a French soldier in 1282; which resulted in a terrible revenge upon the French troops on the island. The Mafia was referred to during a trial in New Orleans in 1890, but the leading gangs in New York then and for several years to come were mostly of Irish and Jews. Not until Prohibition did the Italians begin to dominate.

† The names are liable to change down the years, as the power struggles swing this way and that.

would expect a well-informed citizen to have some acquaintance with the basic structure of the organisation; each gang ruled by its *capo*, supported by his *sottocapo*, his *consigliori* and his *caporegimi*; with the supreme authority over all five gangs, the final arbiter in cases of dissension being vested in the most powerful of the dons, the *capo di tutti capi*. The informed New Yorker would be no more than mildly impressed by someone who could outline the Castellamarese War fought between the gangs in Brooklyn during Prohibition, which led to the murder of Joe Masseria; or the embarrassing occasion in 1957 when no fewer than seventy *mafiosi* were surprised by police in the upstate village of Apalachin, discussing future strategies not only for New York, but for the whole of the United States and the Caribbean.

There was a time when the doings of the Mafia were only a matter for surmise, so completely was *omertà*, the rule of silence, maintained. But in this generation the secrecy has been punctured until it is no greater than that surrounding any other criminal activity. For several years in the 1960s, the Federal Bureau of Investigation gathered an immense amount of information as a result of hidden microphones, and when this was released the *New York Times* published it extensively in a serial which ran for many days. Books have been written authoritatively, sometimes presented as fiction, sometimes not, and these have made further disclosures. Above all, perhaps, two brilliantly disgusting films based on Mario Puzo's *The Godfather* have given everyone within reach of a cinema or a television set some idea of how the Mafia works in New York.

The city's own attitude towards the Mafia is strangely equivocal. When enemy sabotage was suspected along the waterfront during the Second World War, the Bureau of Naval Intelligence sought the co-operation of mobsters, including Lucky Luciano, to protect installations against hostile agents; and Luciano was further enlisted by the Army to arrange assistance from the Sicilian Mafia for the Allies when they invaded the island in 1943. More remarkably, when there was a distinct possibility in 1966 that New York might face race riots such as those that had just broken out in Detroit and Newark, two of Mayor John

Lindsay's aides sought the assistance of the Gallo brothers to pacify Italian teenagers in a potentially riotous part of Brooklyn, and were defended by the Mayor when the news got out that City Hall had been soliciting *mafiosi*, to the dismay of many voters. A few years ago the *Wall Street Journal* published a profile of Salvatore Testa, who had just inherited the vastly profitable rackets controlled by his father, formerly head of the Philadelphia Mafia; and he was perhaps the only businessman so profiled in those respectable columns who was shortly afterwards found tied up in a kneeling position with a bullet hole behind each ear. When the great trials which ended in 1987 were daily attracting galleries full of people at the federal courtrooms in Manhattan and Brooklyn, it was noticed that one of the most attentive spectators was none other that Robert Duvall, who had played the part of a leading *mafioso* when *The Godfather* was filmed; an intelligent man still fascinated by the real thing. When Big Paul Castellano, head of the Gambino gang and *capo di tutti capi* in New York, dined at Spark's Steak House, he was treated by the staff there 'like any other celebrity'.

To a great extent, these are the responses of a community which has become so inured to the violence in its midst that it is not only not as shockable as some places can be, but has decided to come to an accommodation with the sources of violence; which is an expression, as it happens, that the Mafia well understands ('When have I ever refused an accommodation?' asks Don Corleone, the Godfather, when he is bargaining with other mobsters in the middle of a gang war). One way of coming to terms with any form of nastiness in a civilised society is to mock it, diluting its power to alarm with an injection of humour; and the citizens of this metropolis are well practised in this skill. 'Hardly a day goes by, you know,' said flippant Will Rogers, 'that some innocent bystander ain't shot in New York. All you got to be is innocent and stand by and they're gonna shoot you. The other day, there was four innocent people shot in one day – four innocent people – in New York City. It's kind of hard to *find* four innocent people in New York.' Well, yes. And it's not too easy to think of another city where cold-blooded murder would be thought a proper subject for comedy.

It is perfectly possible to argue that this community was conceived in the violence offered in other lands to those who fled from them to the New World; and that, inevitably, many brought across the seas the degree of violence they themselves had needed for survival. This would explain much, but perhaps not everything, when it is evident that New York passed some especially traumatic point two centuries after its foundation, about halfway through the nineteenth century. The New York Prison Association at the time estimated that between 1848 and the end of 1852, theft, burglary and other crimes against property rose by 50 per cent, but crimes of violence against people went up by 129 per cent, murders increasing by 600 per cent. What has been described as 'a decade of disorder' followed the Astor Place Riot in 1849 which, superficially, can be put down to the rivalry between two actors and their interpretation of classical roles. But it went much deeper than that.

One of the actors was Edwin Forrest, from Philadelphia, who would play anything from King Lear to Cardinal Richelieu with more vigour than subtlety, which was much to the taste of the popular theatre audiences before whom he most often appeared throughout the north-east. It was less appealing to the sophisticates of New York, or to the theatre-goers of London, where Forrest toured a couple of times. He was given a rough passage there in 1845 and formed the impression that the hostile audiences in the English capital had somehow been fomented by their own William Macready, an equally striking actor, but in a more mannered tradition. When Macready came to New York, Forrest decided that he should be repaid in kind. By chance, both appeared in town at the same time, playing the same part, Macbeth; but whereas Macready was booked for the Astor Place Opera House, Forrest was at the much smaller Broadway Theatre. And by the time the curtain went up in Astor Place, the battle lines were no longer thespian. Forrest was being represented as the good American democrat, Macready symbolising an alien culture which had been overthrown only with difficulty and must not be allowed to return. A discreditable figure known as Ned Buntline, a gutter journalist and rabble-rouser against all things British, led a mob into the opera house, where the visiting tragedian was pelted so fiercely with rotten eggs and other missiles that he had to retreat to the dressing-room. Unfortunately, he was persuaded by many New York well-wishers, like Washington Irving, to stay in the city longer than he might otherwise have done, and give another performance. More provocatively, these well-to-do supporters published an open letter to their fellow citizens, condemning the organised opposition: which responded with a manifesto of its own, addressed to 'Workingmen! Freemen!'

On the night of May 10, crowds surged around Astor Place, coming in their hundreds from Broadway and the Bowery. Facing them when they got to the theatre were a couple of hundred police, backed up by 300 militiamen. While Shakespeare was being declaimed inside, missiles were being flung at the forces of law and order outside, more furiously than ever when it became apparent that Macready's performance had been unaffected, that he had taken his curtain call. By then several dozen police and militiamen had been damaged, and it is only surprising that the Sheriff delayed until that moment the official order to disperse the crowd. He was catcalled. A volley of shots was fired into the air as a further warning. Still the crowd stood fast. So the militia fired straight into the mob without more ado. That fusillade, and the panic-stricken turmoil which immediately followed it, cost the lives of twenty-two citizens, and events during the next twenty-four hours could easily have cost more. There were mass meetings calling for revenge, intimidation outside the homes of Macready supporters, another mob demonstration outside the opera house, when paving stones and other brickbats were again hurled at the constabulary and the regular infantry which had now been brought up in support. Trouble, for the time being, subsided after a hundred people had been arrested; including Ned Buntline, who was later sent to the penitentiary for having incited the whole affair. Which, of course, had nothing to do with two interpretations of Macbeth. Nor was it fundamentally a manifestation of lingering hostility to the old colonial power.

It was Buntline who gave the game away, after his sentence had been passed. He accused both the judge and jury of having been bribed 'by the millionaires of this city' to send him down. The Astor Place Riot was really an expression of bitter resentment by the have-nots against the haves, inflamed on this occasion into a violent insurrection. That it had been smouldering for some time beforehand is plain from a radical development which had occurred in the city just four years before. New York had at last decided to equip itself with a regular and salaried police force, of 800 men in the first instance, to replace the motley collection of marshals, wardens, street inspectors and nightwatchmen who had up to then been charged with maintaining the law.* The ancestry of today's New York Police Department was established in more ways than one during those first few years. Within twelve months it was reported that some police were corruptly taking favours and orders from politicians: and periodically since, charges of corruption have been made against the police, who perhaps cannot significantly distance themselves from the politicians so long as every new Mayor is allowed to appoint one of his cronies as Police Commissioner, if he wishes. In 1857 there was a full-scale riot by police who were about to be replaced by an alternative force under the control of New York state: and this had its echo in 1976, when four patrolmen demonstrating over pay were arrested by their superior officers, who then had to summon reinforcements when 1,000 angry cops stormed the East Side police station where their colleagues were being held. Eighteen fifty-seven was also the time when the city decided that policemen who had served for twenty years should be granted retirement on half pay; and if there is one thing the citizens of today are united in against the NYPD, it is their general contempt for benefits of that magnitude which come the way of their cops.

But none of these things need have happened in the nineteenth century if the city had not been drifting towards an anarchy which was, effectively, an expression of something a Marxist would recognise at once with a gleam in his eye. In the long debate preceding that decision to create a regular police force, one commentator put the city's situation very cogently indeed.

---

* In London, in 1829, Sir Robert Peel had established the Metropolitan Police in similar circumstances, and for much the same reasons.

'So long as we have one division of people,' he wrote, 'rich and powerful, affluent and ostentatious, and another numerous division wretchedly poor and dependent, as in the case of New York, profligacy, crime and debauchery, immorality and gross corruption will be there, and hence the necessity (as in London) of a civic ARMY, a numerous Municipal Police.' Whatever the relatively well-ordered ground lost after 200 years of settlement, it was never to be recovered again. Riot, if not a regular occurrence, became no stranger to New York; and often enough a basic animosity of the empty-handed poor for the indecently rich was mixed in with whatever was the immediate pretext causing commotion. The Draft Riots of 1863 can be seen as an expression of solidarity with good customers from the south, and as a straightforward act of hostility towards Negro slaves; but they were in rebellion, too, against a clause in the Conscription Act which allowed someone to dodge military service provided he could find a substitute to do his fighting for him, or simply put $300 on the recruiting officer's table.

It was also at about this time that gangsters appeared in New York. Among the earliest were the Dead Rabbits, an Irish band, sworn enemies of the Bowery Boys, whose American pedigrees were generally longer by a century or so. They battled frequently over the same turf on the Lower East Side, most spectacularly on the fourth of July in that momentous year of 1857, when about 1,000 ruffians swarmed through the narrow streets, knifing, slugging and shooting each other and anyone else who got in their way, leaving behind ten dead and many more wounded. As New York steadily expanded up Manhattan, so the gangs increased their territory. By 1868 Dutch Heinrichs had his Hell's Kitchen Gang on the West Side, where there was also a Tenth Avenue Gang which had been bold enough to hold up and rob a Hudson River Railroad express. Instead of fighting each other, the two pooled their resources and dominated that part of the city until the last decade of the century, when they spawned successors. One of these was the Hudson Dusters, which numbered cocaine addicts among its most vicious hoodlums. More frightening still were the Gophers, about 500 thugs who terrorised the West Side until only a few years before the First World War, when they were finally put down by what would now be called a special task force of the New York Central Railroad, which was even more violent than the Gophers, beating into submission those who were not killed in the process of law enforcement. The Lower East Side had by then become a province of the rising Italians, and of Jewish criminals like the Dopey Benny Fein Gang, which was used by both management and the unions in the garment industry to intimidate their opponents; and the Monk Eastman Gang, which specialised in prostitution, gambling and protection rackets, led by a brawler who rarely went anywhere without a pet cat tucked under each arm.

Prohibition was a gift to organised crime throughout the United States; and nowhere was it more welcome to the gangsters than in New York.* From the moment in 1920 when the Eighteenth Amendment, topped up by the Volstead Act, forbade the 'manufacture, sale or transportation' of beverages containing more than one half of one per cent of alcohol, the bootlegging of liquor and beer became big business for the New York underworld, a money-spinner comparable to the drug-dealings of today. In the next thirteen years, until Prohibition was repealed – as much as anything because the Depression had made it imperative to restore employment in a legalised liquor industry – booze flowed almost as freely as ever, but not a drop of it was available without the assistance of, coercion by and rich profit for criminals. The most notorious of them was a product of the Brooklyn slums, Al Capone, who was terrorising Chicago; but his native city had more than its share of gangsters operating in the same fashion. A former West Side longshoreman, Big Bill Dwyer, led a New York syndicate which had police and coastguardsmen in its pay so successfully that he finished up as a millionaire owner of race tracks in Ohio and

---

* It is yet another indication of something going seriously amiss in the social balance halfway through the nineteenth century, that the New York state legislators in Albany had thought it necessary to pass a Prohibitory Act in 1855, specifically aimed at reducing the growing disorders of New York City. This died of natural causes because the temperance lobby was not powerful enough to uphold it in the face of opposition led by the Mayor, Fernando Wood.

Florida. A small-time crook and bully boy, Arthur Flegenheimer, seized the opportunities presented by Prohibition so well that he became the controller of all the beer obtainable in Harlem and the Bronx, and was known henceforth by the more intimidating name of Dutch Schulz. There were many more like them, elevated by this ill-advised legislation into powerful figures who were not to be demoted when the booze flowed legitimately again. For they had developed other interests besides bootlegging during those supposedly arid years. The existing rackets mushroomed throughout the twenties, to be enlarged even more when the takings from liquor were undermined. Frank Costello, somebody else's bootlegger to start with, became king of the slot machines in Manhattan, his thugs forcing storekeepers and others to install these sources of income, whether they liked it or not. Dutch Schulz emerged from Prohibition as undisputed boss of the numbers racket, Lucky Luciano as supreme commander of prostitution, Louis Lepke as the man restaurant owners must pay dues to if their premises were to escape bombing with explosives during the night, or with stinking chemicals during the busiest hours of the day. There was scarcely a corner of business or industrial activity in New York that did not have its violent parasites sucking blood. There was no end to the inventiveness of organised crime, and all of it backed by terrorism. One of its nastiest manifestations was the execution squad headquartered in Brooklyn when a national syndicate of criminals set themselves up (with many other interests as well as homicide) in 1934. But there was something grotesquely appropriate in the name given to the executioners, located where they were: Murder Inc. That had the authentic, the inimitably businesslike New York ring to it.*

Half a century later, organised crime is still an acknowledged part of metropolitan life, in spite of periodic successes in combating it, from the prosecutions by Thomas E. Dewey in the 1930s and the Kefauver Committee's revelations in the 1950s, down to the long trials of leading *mafiosi* in the past few years. When

---

* It is said that Louis Lepke alone ordered more than thirty killings by Murder Inc.

the prosecutors gave themselves a 'de-commissioning party' at the conclusion of their endeavours in January 1987, they were noticeably reluctant to claim that they had put down the New York Mafia once and for all, even though 'Tony Ducks' Corallo, Carmine Persico, 'Fat Tony' Salerno and other *capi* could not expect any other fate than to die in prison. The prosecutors could have made the point that the Mafia had never been subdued for long in the past when leading figures had suddenly been removed from circulation, as often as not by the hands of their rivals. And even if the Mafia were suddenly to collapse, this would not be the end of organised crime in the city, when it is organised by so many different criminals, from every ethnic background. Some believed that any void left by Italians would swiftly be filled by Latins, usually led by Cubans or Colombians; or that dominance would pass to a Chinese network known as the United Bamboo, originating in Taiwan and Hong Kong, well connected with the Japanese underworld, and already running a number of enterprises in New York.

As in the years between the wars, few corners of the city's life are uncontaminated by the various gangs. In addition to its hold on the construction industry, the Mafia has had a powerful interest in the trucking of garbage. Another of its great standbys has been loan sharking, in which the unlamented Mr Salerno was especially effective in collecting his money at interest rates of 156 per cent. The loan shark's quarry is the tradesman and the small businessman, whereas the very poorest citizens are milked just as ruthlessly in the numbers game. This is illegal betting on numerals which may be concocted from sources as diverse as racetrack results, the day's stock market figures, or even random pages from the Bible, the most important thing for any player to know being the odds against winning anything, which are estimated at approximately 1,000 to 1. A survey of the Bedford-Stuyvesant district in 1970 discovered that the Mafia almost monopolised the takings that year of nearly $37 million. But at the same time a Puerto Rican syndicate was ripping off rich profits in the numbers game in Harlem, while two Jewish brothers were doing likewise in the South Bronx.

The Bedford-Stuyvesant survey also reported that for every

increase of one dollar in *per capita* income in that impoverished corner of Brooklyn, at least ten cents went to organised crime; which in one way or another made $214 that year in clear profit from every man, woman and child in the area. Apart from gambling, the most common source of criminal income, as elsewhere in the city, was drugs, which in this generation has done for the mobsters what alcohol did for their predecessors during Prohibition, though even then there was criminal profit from dope, which has been a problem in New York for well over a hundred years. At first, patent medicines containing morphine produced an amount of addiction, which was increased by the number of wounded Civil War soldiers who had been given the same derivative of opium to relieve their pain. The further refinement of morphine into heroin in the penultimate year of the century compounded the addiction further. A Narcotic Act was passed in 1914 to limit the use of morphine and cocaine but, until legislation was enacted in 1924, heroin was astonishingly exempt from restriction, available to anyone who asked for it at the local drugstore. There followed a determined campaign by the US Government to reverse widespread addiction, and by the Second World War it had succeeded to the extent that narcotics were habitually used by no more than an estimated 20,000 throughout the country. Seen from New York now, those days seem impossibly ideal, the statistics a form of make-believe. In 1985, more than 5,000 were arrested on narcotics charges in the metropolis alone. By 1987, it was reckoned that there were 250,000 hard-drug users in New York.

A turning point had come about the beginning of the 1960s, when pushers were working the streets of black and Latin communities, like Bedford-Stuyvesant and the South Bronx, in a way that no-one could remember for a long time. They were purveying heroin, which had arrived by notorious routes from south-east Asia, later to be supplemented from other sources in the mountains of the North-West Frontier between Pakistan and Afghanistan. Cocaine also came in, from Colombia and other South American cultivations. The Bedford-Stuyvesant survey again demonstrated the steady pressure applied to such a community by those who were waxing fat on the gradual

debilitation of their victims. By 1963 there were forty-seven
known drug pushers in the neighbourhood, who had increased
to 321 by 1970. To raise the profit margin in that period, the
product had been diluted – from three grains per packet sold to
only one grain – so that the addict needed to buy more to maintain
the level of his daily fix. On these poisons New York exercised
its great gift for argot, knowing the different products as 'horse'
or 'dogie' or 'smack' or some other vivid invention. By the fall of
1984, it was contemplating the ravages of a new import, 'crack',
a crystallised form of cocaine adulterated with baking soda and
water, which had come to the city from South America by way
of Watts, the black ghetto in Los Angeles. Smoked, rather than
injected or sniffed, this was regarded as potentially the most
devastating drug of all, because it was cheap enough – until the
suppliers decided otherwise – to be obtained even by children;
and it was quite startlingly effective. Someone who watched its
impact on the city over a couple of years, wryly offered the
opinion that, 'Crack gives you more bang for your buck.'

The criminal effect of drug addiction is a melancholy fact of
life almost everywhere which needs no elaboration here: the
relationship is well established in New York, whose newspapers
daily report murders, rapes, muggings and hold-ups, together
with any number of other crimes committed by young men who
were stoned at the time; themselves the dupes, if not the victims,
of organised crime. Here is one reason for New York's unenviable
reputation as the most dangerous metropolitan area in the United
States, the place to be avoided above all others if you wish your
person and your property to remain free from assault.* Its
people are well aware of this from the experience of friends
and acquaintances, even if they themselves have managed to
avoid trouble. When invited by pollsters to nominate their city's
biggest problem, they generally cite crime above anything else
by a considerable margin. One of the first things any foreign
visitor notices is the number of locks that have to be undone
before anyone can enter a New York apartment: two is the

*New York is just ahead of Miami in this league. After them come Los
Angeles, Las Vegas and Atlantic City.

absolute minimum, and four is not at all uncommon. If he has known nothing else about the city before arriving, he will have some inkling that there is a frightful rate of killings here.*

Such things are in the normal currency of life and death, borne by New Yorkers with the same stoical acceptance that other people have shown in time of war when their cities have been under regular bombardment. But just occasionally even New York can be dumbfounded by some concerted criminal act in its midst; and this was so when the inhabitants of the South Bronx began to put their community to the torch in 1969, a stupefying act of self-mutilation that continued for most of a decade. In some cases, slum landlords were known to have arranged for their dilapidated properties to go up in flames, so that they could collect the insurance money on them, but occasionally they did the job themselves, as one man and his son were preparing to when they were caught with five Molotov cocktails in a building of theirs. Some fires were started by adolescents simply for the thrill of it, others because they were paid to do so by landlords, or by hoodlums who wanted tenants terrified into abandoning their homes, so that these might be plundered for their saleable metal and other materials. Two boys, one ten years old, the other fifteen, were caught after starting between forty and fifty fires for three dollars apiece. And then there were the families living in slums on welfare, who burned down their own homes in the hope of getting somewhere better from the municipality; which actually incited this form of arson by placarding the welfare centres with signs in Spanish and English, pointing out that the only way to obtain housing priority was to have lost your existing home through fire.

By the time these signs went up, the burning of the South Bronx was well under way, on such an organised scale that the firefighters simply could not keep up with the calls they received. They would arrive at a blazing tenement to find the families sitting outside, with their pathetic possessions bundled and boxed up, waiting for the authorities to take them into care. Some school

---

* In 1984 there were 1,450 cases of murder and manslaughter in New York, a fall of 14 per cent from the figure ten years earlier; but in 1981 it had been 1,838.

teachers in the area were told by their pupils that they had already packed in anticipation of the blaze that was expected the following week; and, sure enough, a few more days would see the end of the children's education in that school. But many of the calls the firemen received were false alarms: 1,200 of these were made to the company serving Charlotte Street in just one year. By the spring of 1974 the whole of that street and its surroundings were in ruins, and this was when people began to liken the South Bronx to London at the height of the Blitz, or even to Berlin at the end of the war. Yet still the burnings went on, so furiously, so unhampered by anything the authorities could or were prepared to do, that the air over that quarter of the city smelled perpetually of charred wood. In May 1975, Cardinal Cooke, himself a son of the Bronx, was moved to announce a special day of prayer for the area, to be known as Stop Fire Sunday. It made so little impression that 1976 was the most incendiary yet, with well over 33,000 fires of one sort or another – to cars, as well as to buildings – being started in the Bronx. The rate of arson began to tail off after that, and by then, in truth, there wasn't much of the South Bronx left to burn. Some twelve square miles had been devastated, the haunt of gangs like the Turbans and the Royal Javelins, the Savage Nomads and the Black Spades, who wandered the ruins dangerously, ready for pitched battle that could end in death, between each other or with anybody else. A priest who had known the area for years made a sharp distinction between them and the young bloods of the previous generation, like the Jets who were glorified in *West Side Story*. Those gangs were still under family constraints, and ultimately responsive to authority. But these were beyond such sanctions – 'pathological. They engaged in random violence for no reason.'

Twelve months after the great burning had reduced almost everything to smouldering embers, and the Bronx firefighters could expect no more than a normal number of calls in a week, New York was visited, briefly but unforgettably, by something which is best described by a word belonging to medieval history: a fury. It was occasioned by a power failure, which is liable to happen here much more often than might be expected of so wealthy and so technocratic a metropolis. The most celebrated failure occurred in 1965, when New York acquitted itself so magnificently that if there were such a thing as a list of civic battle honours in City Hall, that passage of arms might well head it in letters of gold. The effect of the power failure in July 1977 was rather different. It was the middle of the evening when the whole of New York and Westchester County blacked out, and more than a night and a day were to elapse before all areas had their electricity restored. In that time, proportions of the populace in Brooklyn and the Bronx, East Harlem and the Upper West Side went berserk in pursuit of plunder and general mayhem. As soon as it became clear that the current was not going to come back on, crowds began to pour along the six lanes of the Grand Concourse in the Bronx, heading for the main shopping district and all the loot it contained. A Pontiac dealer had the steel door and windows of his sale-room smashed by the mob, who then drove away fifty of his brand-new cars. Elsewhere in the city, television sets, hi-fi systems, clothing and liquor were hauled out of the stores, and the only shopkeepers whose premises remained undamaged in certain quarters were those who armed themselves and posses of friends with shotguns, and stood guard throughout the night. As the smashing of plate-glass went on far into the small hours, so too did the crackle and shimmer of flames when the vandals set alight whatever they could not steal but were offended by. In that one night of communal madness, over 1,000 blazes were started, while goods valued at more than $1 billion were looted, and nearly 4,000 arrests were made.

It is not far-fetched to see such massive outrages as the contemporary version of the riots that erupted in Astor Place and elsewhere a hundred years and more ago; as the primitive anger of people at the bottom of the pile against whatever fates, and whichever other human beings, appear to keep them there.

The warning uttered in 1844 is as valid today as it was then. For reasons which are entirely its responsibility, New York is still a city containing 'one division of people, rich and powerful, affluent and ostentatious, and another numerous division wretchedly poor and dependent'. No-one need venture into a notoriously poor quarter of this city to suspect that there is truth in that. He finds himself riding the Lexington Express up Manhattan from

Brooklyn, perhaps, and when it stops at Fulton Street a beggar gets in, such a figure as one might hope did not exist outside dread fantasy. The man appears to have been bisected at the crotch, and he could well be part of the wreckage cast aside after the war in Vietnam. He has been settled into a thick leather cup which laces up so that he will not fall out, and this is perched on a miniature trolley, which he propels along the carriage with one hand while holding a tin can for charity in his other. And many people do tip up something, though almost no-one dares to look him straight in the eye, before the train pulls into Union Square and he trundles himself off down the platform to another train. A stroll along the opulent end of Fifth Avenue reveals other beggars, who do not appear to engage as much sympathy as the truncated one. Outside Saks, a middle-aged man wearing a straw hat stands sightlessly with a black Labrador and its waterbowl between his feet. Around his neck is a placard which says, 'I'm blind, please buy a pencil', and he holds some in one hand. Further along, outside Cartier, another man with another dog has a similar notice round his neck, preceded by the line, 'Except for the grace of God, there stand I'. But people intent on selecting expensive clothes and jewellery are not much moved by quotations adapted from John Bradford, or by anything else those indisputably blind men may do to stir pity. You can stand watchfully for half an hour without seeing so much as a penny go into the collecting bowls.

The shocking truth about 'the richest city in the history of the world', is that by the beginning of the 1970s, nearly one-third of its population was in need of some public assistance, and that in the following decade the number of citizens living in poverty increased to 23 per cent. 'Living in poverty' is no haphazard phrase in the United States, which defines it exactly and measures it in dollars. This varies somewhat from year to year, due to inflation and other influences. Back in 1961, a family of four was said to be living in poverty if its income was no more than $3,054. By 1974, the threshold of poverty had been raised to $5,038. In 1985 it had been redefined as $10,178. No fewer than 1.7 million New Yorkers were officially poverty-stricken that year. At the same time, those few score of their fellow citizens who had made the *Forbes Four Hundred* list were said on average to have a net worth of $297 million apiece.

Living in official poverty in New York does not necessarily mean that you do not have a roof over your head. There are, however, many New Yorkers in this most desperate of all plights, though the figures vary from source to source. In 1985, Archbishop O'Connor spoke of 20,000 homeless here every day. Twelve months later, city officials were estimating 15,000 or so. At the start of 1987, a representative of the charity Coalition for the Homeless claimed that 50,000 were more or less consigned to the streets; and this, he suggested, was even worse than in the depths of the Depression. Whatever the accurate head count might be at any given time, a roll-call of New York's most wretched citizens would consist of different sorts and conditions of the down-and-out. About one-third of them are said to be people who were suddenly released from mental institutions a few years ago, in a spasm of liberal policy that was only half thought-out, while others are former prison inmates who were freed before their sentences had been served. The first were restored to society on the assumption that awaiting them would be a number of after-care facilities, which never materialised because of President Reagan's budget cuts: while several hundreds of the second went into circulation again after Judge Morris Lasker in 1981 had ruled that New York's notorious Tombs prison was not only unfit for even criminal habitation, but downright unconstitutional as well. Apart from the unbalanced and the penalised, however, the city's nightly quota of homeless also includes a high proportion of folk who have simply fallen on hard times, having lost their jobs, run out of unemployment and other benefits, and been evicted from their dwellings through inability to pay the rent.

New York knows all of them as the bag people, and generally takes evasive action when it sees one of them coming its way, a shuffling form so bulkily wrapped against the weather that its sex is all but concealed, as it struggles along with its worldly goods stuffed into two or three plastic shopping carriers or sometimes in a supermarket trolley. Some can be seen settling for the night on riverside benches in the little gardens below Sutton Place, after pillaging the nearby litter-bins for blessedly thick editions of the *Times*, which help to keep out the cold. Others seek temporary refuge in the waiting hall of Grand Central Station, where one of the city's numerous charities provides them with some food every night; until 1.30 a.m. when the station closes, and the cops come to hustle everybody out onto the street. And there, in the bitter winters this city invariably endures, every night a few of the older, feebler, sicker ones die, just like their counterparts on the streets of Calcutta. The city knows how to handle them then. It collects their bodies and consigns them to the municipal morgue until such time as it has accumulated enough to make the next stage in their disposal economically worthwhile. In thin pine coffins, the frozen corpses are put aboard a barge and towed up the East River to Hart's Island just off the shoreline of the Bronx. There, in the Potter's Field, they are buried by convicts in mass graves, where New York has dumped all its human refuse since the day in 1869 when the body of Louisa Van Slyke, orphan from the Charity Hospital, was put away.

So appalled were some New Yorkers by the obscene contrast between the city's most exorbitantly rich and its most numbingly poor, that in 1979 they sued on behalf of the homeless and extracted from the courts a judgement that New York had an obligation to provide some shelter for those who had nowhere else to turn; and a couple of years later, the city accepted the obligation. It thereafter created a number of public refuges in Brooklyn and the Bronx, enormous structures built like aircraft hangars, which shelter several hundred people in bunks under the same roof all night, and under blazing lights which are never switched off because the petty crime which flourishes in these places might then turn into something even nastier. The public shelters seem to some only marginally better than the open streets; which is why, by the end of 1986, a shanty-town constructed out of packing cases was illegally beginning to sprawl across some open ground on the Lower East Side, hammered together in the shadow of buildings where apartments were rented for $1,500 a month.

In tandem with the monstrous public shelters were also the seedy welfare hotels. Once they were bargain attractions for tourists, like the Prince George at East 27th Street, just off Fifth Avenue; or they had even more notable pedigrees, like the Grand Concourse in the Bronx, where the New York Yankees used to be quartered throughout their home season. But both tourists and ballplayers began to move out as the city's poor people were installed and the corridors became rowdy with the wild energies of undisciplined kids. By the summer of 1986 there were no fewer than fifty-five such welfare hotels in New York, and the city was spending $72 million on this accommodation for its poor, with one hotel on 42nd Street said to be making more than $3 million a year out of accommodating 250 homeless families at $60 a day in one-bedroom 'apartments', or $100 in 'doubles'. Whole blocks of midtown Manhattan had become socially changed as a result of this influx. Besides the Prince George Hotel, East 27th Street had the Madison and the Latham in the welfare trade, the three places together housing 600 families with 1,500 children; and between there and West 32nd Street there were seven more hotels containing well over 1,000 families, which was about a quarter of all those the city put a roof over. Merchants in these neighbourhoods had begun to close down, because customers were no longer coming to their shops, intimidated by teenagers from the welfare hotels who might – or might not – have mugged them on the way. Residents, tired of the incessant noise and scufflings along their sidewalks, were trying to move out to some other district where the welfare people had not been admitted, but had found this impossible when no-one could be found to buy their properties. Far from solving a problem that had its origins in something that preceded homelessness, the city appeared merely to have created a number of new and unlovely ghettoes. They might yet become something more alarming than that, as their inhabitants increasingly resent their impoverished place in a wealthy city, and resentment turns to anger, and anger to violence. The pattern is already familiar.

New York offers so many occasions for natural resentment, far beyond the bitter anomaly of the homeless and the jobless in a mostly well-heeled and comfortable society. The various corruptions that have infested the city for generations are of an order that in communities even more volatile than this one, sooner or later result in bloody revolution. The height of political criminality was doubtless reached over a century ago, during the most powerful days of Tammany under 'Boss' Tweed, when all municipal building projects yielded commissions of 5 per cent to the Mayor, 20 per cent to the city's Comptroller, and 25 per cent to Tweed himself. But even in the 1930s, Tammany was rigging civic elections by the simple expedient of recruiting mobsters like Dutch Schultz to provide strong-arm support at the polling booths, where they beat up opponents and virtually controlled the voting machines. When Fiorello LaGuardia came to office in 1934, one of the first things he addressed himself to was Tammany's manipulation of the civil service examinations, which effectively excluded all Jews, Italians and blacks from the Police and Fire Departments in particular. Not long after that, largely because of LaGuardia's deep and systematic hostility, Tammany's long supremacy began to dwindle, its reduction symbolised in 1945 by its retreat to modest office accommodation on Madison Avenue after finding the mortgage payments for its Great Wigwam in Union Square too steep to meet any longer.*

The tradition that Tammany represented did not by any means languish with it, however. This was demonstrated in the starkest fashion by the authors of a book which analysed abuses of power in New York in the 1970s, Jack Newfield and Paul Du Brul. They examined the guest list at the annual dinner of the King County Democratic Party, which was given at the Waldorf-Astoria Hotel on Park Avenue in May 1974 – 'the annual dinner of the Brooklyn Democracy'. This is how they began to describe it:

At table 23 is Congressman Frank Brasco, who will go to federal prison for conspiring to accept a bribe from a Mafia trucker. At table 16 is Congressman Bertram Podell, who will

* The former Tammany Hall on Union Square still carries its ancestral device of an Indian head-dress on the pediment above the frontage, however. The offices are now occupied by the International Ladies Garment Workers' Union ('Symbol of Decency, Fair Labor standards & the American Way'): the ground floor facing the square by shops selling, variously, coffee, liquor, cookies and greetings cards.

go to federal prison for taking a $41,350 bribe to influence the Civil Aeronautic Board's decision on an airline route. At table 92 is Eugene Hollander, who will plead guilty to stealing $1.1 million in Medicaid funds from four nursing homes he owns. At table 55 is Queens County leader Matthew Troy, who will plead guilty to income-tax evasion on money taken from the estates of his law clients. And at table 50 is Carmine DeSapio. DeSapio has served almost two years in prison for bribery. Manhattan public administrator Thomas Fitzgerald, who will be indicted with his friend, sits at table 53.

For several pages more, the authors continued with a catalogue of politicians and their hangers-on at the dinner, who had been imprisoned or, at the very least, who were suspected of some considerable impropriety. There were men who had been obliged to resign from public office in messy circumstances, men who were thought to have something more than a nodding acquaintance with organised crime, men who had been caught lying to grand juries, men who had rigged things in order to obtain lucrative contracts from City Hall. At this table was a rogue who had tried to swindle the Stock Exchange, at that table a shark who fed off some of the city's most appalling slums. There was even a judge who had been suspended from the bench for accepting bribes from a lawyer appearing before him: and a couple of party officials who were about to steal the dinner receipts, just as they had already pocketed the takings of the three Brooklyn dinners before it.

That may have been a vintage period for shady dealings in high places, though subsequent infamies seemed to suggest that it perhaps represented some pernicious New York norm. Almost the whole of 1986, for example, was occupied with the sensational disclosures that followed the death of Donald Manes. As borough President of Queens, he was one of the most considerable figures in the city's government after the Mayor, with enormous powers of patronage and opportunities for graft, which he evidently exercised to the full. The unlikely area of car parking offences was his undoing in the end. In a city whose motorists fail to pay some $250 million in fines as promptly as they should each year, agencies are hired to collect the money, and find the task lucrative enough to compete strongly for the contracts. Manes was simply extorting money from the successful bidders, and when he was about to be exposed he committed a messy suicide. At once the investigations intensified and, before the year was out, not only had the city's deputy director of the Parking Violations Bureau pleaded guilty to racketeering and extortion but, in the hope of lenient treatment by the federal authorities, he had incriminated the Democratic Party leader in the Bronx as well.

Meanwhile, New York was also wallowing in the continuing saga of scandals in the New York Police Department. In rapid succession, five officers had been arrested on suspicion of having tortured some young men with electric stun guns; a police sergeant had been charged with shooting a woman in the back and killing her, after they had argued about a minor traffic accident; another sergeant was charged with manslaughter after an old man had been knocked down and killed by a police car which failed to stop; and yet another sergeant was convicted of paying a hit man to either kill or maim the policeman's partner in a health club he ran on the side. Again, this tally was well within a tradition that New Yorkers have long been familiar with. When the Knapp Commission investigated corruption in the NYPD during the 1960s, it discovered police in the Narcotics Division who stole money from drug pushers and then kept the confiscated drugs themselves; and it concluded that 'corruption in narcotics law enforcement goes beyond the Police Department and involves prosecutors, attorneys, bondsmen and allegedly certain judges. While this fact does not excuse the illegal conduct of policemen who accept bribes, it does serve to illustrate the demoralising environment in which police are expected to enforce narcotics laws.' Within weeks of the Knapp report being published, it was discovered that heroin and cocaine worth $73 million had been stolen by policemen from the Police Department's own compound, between March 1969 and late 1972. 'The biggest single supplier of heroin in New York City turned out to be the Police Department itself.'

It is obvious that there would be no such disclosures and no successful prosecution if New York did not contain – as well as the crooks and thugs who soil its politics, its courts and its constabulary – men and women in those same professions whose steadfast dedication and unswerving probity would be outstanding in any company. Nevertheless, aberration in all these areas is a common enough tradition in New York to fuel any resentments that might be directed by its poorer citizens against those better off than themselves; and there are some excrescences on the body politic for which anger is the only appropriate response from anyone. It is not only the poor who can seethe with rage at the amount of swindling, in one form or another, that goes unchecked because bribes or threats have effectively blocked justice.

Resentment and anger easily turn to violence in this city, sometimes in the most improbable circumstances. Literary figures here are quite liable to fight each other with bare fists in order to settle differences which in London would be more deviously ventilated in the spiteful book review or the quiet insinuation during a chat show. A famous brawl once took place in the office of the publishing house Scribner's, between Max Eastman and Ernest Hemingway, four years after the first had insulted the second in an article which was headlined 'Bull in the Afternoon'; and, more recently, Norman Mailer and Gore Vidal scuffled at a Manhattan party, after having previously all but come to blows on the Dick Cavitt show. Other conflicts are not so laden with all the makings of slapstick farce. The blazing altercation between motorists, or between a driver and a pedestrian, is a commonplace on these frenzied streets, sometimes so alarming that passers-by can be seen hurrying away from the scene, lest the worst should occur. For there can be few occasions when a New Yorker would be utterly surprised to see a gun pulled out and fired; and a dismaying number of citizens are legally authorised to bear firearms which they are, presumably, prepared to use if they feel provoked enough. Although the police are said to turn down two out of every three applicants for gun licences, there were still, at a recent count, almost 32,000 New Yorkers certified to carry arms. In the wake of the Bernhard Goetz affair, enrolments at a West Side rifle and

pistol range – one of a hundred in Manhattan alone – rose by
30 per cent.*

Yet it is also within the traditions of this city that New York
can channel even its violent energies into original and compelling
forms, as an acquaintance with the subway system reveals. This
is not, its most ardent enthusiasts will readily admit, the most
attractive underground railway in the world, made disagreeable
by, as much as anything, the chaotic scribblings that deface the
inside of all but the newest carriages; mindless, aggressive
graffiti, applied with deliberate intent to deface as only the
felt-tip pen and sprayed paint will do. Fairly equable people can
be infuriated at having to travel in such surroundings, which are
peculiarly New York in the scale of their disfigurement, and are
found nowhere else on earth. Something of the same mess is
visible on the outside of the trains, too, but there an altogether
different coating began to appear early in the 1970s, almost
obliterating the ugly marks; a new form of pop art which was
inventive, careful, vivid, sometimes inspired. And even though
it may already be a dying fancy, it has been bright enough and
remarkable enough while it lasted to have earned its place in the
enduring mythology of New York.

It originated in the same instincts that produced the ugliness,
adolescents being obsessed with a drive to leave their mark
in public places – and to hell with any damage this might do.
Much was made, in 1971, when the *New York Times* first paid
attention, of a young Greek high school graduate who lived
on 183rd Street and signed an abbreviation of his name and
address all over the city thus: Taki 183. He was not unique,
but the publicity begat imitators, as might be expected, and in
time the competition grew for each to render his sign manual
more conspicuously readable than any rival's. In time, also, the
signwriters concentrated their attention on the subway trains,
which required elaborate preparations, swift handiwork, and a
fair amount of nerve. The trains could only be sprayed with
coloured paints as they lay in sidings, which always had been

---

* Goetz was a white man who, in December 1984, shot and injured four black
youths on the subway after, he alleged, they had tried to mug him.

well patrolled for security's sake, and became even more heavily guarded as the transit authority began to find its rolling stock more lurid in the morning than it had been the night before. In 1975, for the very first time, an entire car, from top to bottom and from end to end, had its exterior covered in these nefarious murals, and after that the ingenuity of the artists was in a league of its own. They developed 'piece books', which were something on the lines of the pattern books belonging to an older artistic tradition. They even created stylised type faces, stranger by far than anything Caslon or Bodoni made, and with more outlandish titles, too; squish luscious, stretch bubble and spiral-gyro-tasmarific, among others.

The No 5 Lexington Avenue Express, tearing across the city all the way from Dyre Avenue in the Bronx to Utica Avenue in Brooklyn, and the No 2 train, rattling from the peaceful surroundings beyond Woodlawn right down to the bedraggled settlements of Flatbush, became the most celebrated bearers of this artistry, flaunting more and more ambitious decorations before the travelling public as the competition hotted up. Cartoons began to appear between the sliding doors, but graphics were still the mainstay, now going far beyond the simple signature of the writer. An express might be glimpsed bidding onlookers 'Merry Christmas' in an elegantly black Gothic script on a grey ground, beneath a rippling frieze of magenta, orange, green and blue. It might bear a moral message – 'Stop the Bomb!' – or a defiant one – 'We are unstoppable, we are uncatchable, we are nasty!' When the Mayor of New York launched a campaign to put an end to all this nonsense in 1982, within a few hours a train was spotted bearing his caricature on its flank, next to the considered advice, 'Dump Koch'.

It was all too insubordinate to last, of course. The authorities were beginning to get angry at the penetration of their security and at the high cost of eradicating this meticulous pop art with special chemicals. Vicious dogs were brought to patrol the sidings at night, but just as effective were the rolls of razor wire which began to festoon all unguarded access points, a peculiarly nasty form of deterrent guaranteed to cut any intruder to ribbons. Within a few years of the Koch campaign, it became apparent that the great days of New York subway art were past, with fewer and fewer fresh decorations to be seen on any line. The system had acquired some gleaming new rolling stock from Kawasaki of Japan, to emphasise how very battered was everything else in sight. With a thorough cleansing of the interior graffiti, the stations and the tracks, with a proper repair of much equipment that repeatedly broke down, this could have been a subway to brag about again. But in spite of periodic efforts by the transit authority, many of the old defects remain, as does the subway's most frightful disfigurement: its dozen or so murders every year.

Those homicides and that art are yet another reminder that this city 'is a place where a laugh and a shudder are not very far apart' – which is one of the most telling observations about New York, and one of the most valid. The day after tens of thousands of New Yorkers obediently made merry to celebrate the Statue of Liberty's centenary, a different kind of uproar occurred on the Staten Island ferry, which was loaded with tourists who had sailed to get a close look at the object of all the razzmatazz. The vessel was halfway down the harbour when one Juan Gonzales, described as a Cuban refugee who had lived in New York for nine years, ran amok with a sword and, before he was overpowered by a retired policeman (who, none the less, was still carrying a gun), killed two people and injured nine others. This was at about the same time that strollers down Fifth Avenue, around 45th Street, were delighted by the sound of music coming wonderfully off the sidewalk one afternoon. Four young men, playing trumpets and trombones, were splitting the day brilliantly with bits and pieces of Purcell, Handel, Mozart, Rossini, Joplin and all, harmonising superbly with a verve to make the heart leap, joy fairly syncopating down the block, compelling all within earshot to laugh and grin and feel happy to be alive that day. All except one man, just across the road. He sat sprawled against a wall, clean but threadbare, inert but utterly sober, with the half-dead eyes of those who have lost all hope and much of their dignity. He made no attempt to accost anyone, but a placard round his neck said it all for him. 'Homeless and hungry. Please help. Thank you.'

TEN

THE OVERLORDS

It has been said that the nearest thing to a New York folk hero is the distant figure of Peter Stuyvesant. This sounds an unlikely proposition at first, when every new fad that seizes this city throws up its prodigy who is elevated to instant stardom, and when many names from the past continue to glow even in the recollection of those not yet born when their reputations were made. People who have never seen the Yankees in the flesh can speak with feeling about the legend of Babe Ruth, just as black folk who loathe violence will take a pride in what Joe Louis did, and citizens who neither know nor care how a skinny boy from the mid-west came to fly historically from a Long Island field in 1927, still believe that Charles Lindbergh was someone special in the epic of New York. In such company Peter Stuyvesant seems strangely at odds, a ghostly shape who was not even popular when he was alive 300 years ago.

He came as the young settlement's seventh governor-general, some twenty years after Manhattan had been purchased from the Indians, finding it 'more a mole hill than a fortress, without gates, the walls and bastions trodden under foot by men and cattle'. His predecessors were not noted for enterprising leadership, and even Peter Minuit, who had made the historic land deal, only did so on explicit instructions from Holland. Stuyvesant was appointed in an effort to put backbone into the colony, arriving in 1647 from another colonial position in the West Indies, where he had lost a leg while storming a French fort on Curaçao. It was possibly this disability that produced the notorious short temper and high-handedness, which did not endear him to the people under his command, and often enough discomfited his own family. He was a religious bigot, who permitted only the Dutch Reformed Church to build places of worship on Manhattan, was hostile to Lutherans, and had Quakers whipped. When Jews arrived from the settlements in Brazil, they were allowed to remain, although Stuyvesant wanted them out. Such dogmatic narrowness extended into many of the matters under his authority, and what had been a relatively easy-going community before he came here, soon found life distinctly more severe. He had the taverns closed throughout Sunday and by nine o'clock every other night. He ordered all hogs running loose to be shot on sight, and forbade the age-old practice of pitching rubbish straight out of a dwelling into the street. But his seventeen-year tenure did see the beginning of municipal government, with the institution of a common council in 1653, forerunner of the New York City Council of today; and by the end of that decade, the first rights of citizenship in the colony had been proposed and legally registered. It was under his governorship – though not always with his blessing – that a number of remarkable social and economic laws were passed. Tobacco planters were obliged to grow a proportion of grain, in order to avoid the risk of famine, and at one period prices were fixed for many articles so that there should be something like fair shares for all. A form of overtime for workmen was introduced and, before he was done, Stuyvesant saw the passage through his council of a measure to relieve the unemployed. His was an uneven presence, offensive and attractive in turn, but it was not one that either his contemporaries or history could ignore. His rule came to an end because the Dutch West India Company's venture was close to bankruptcy, no match at all for the predatory English, who had begun to eye Nieuw Amsterdam with greedy anticipation. It was in Stuyvesant's 'bouwerie' that the terms of the Dutch surrender to the Duke of York's men were signed in 1664. A pear tree that he once planted there was still growing on the corner of Third Avenue and 13th Street until 1867, when two wagons collided beside it, and caused it to die. By then, many generations of Peter Stuyvesant's descendants were with him in the churchyard of St Mark's-in-the-Bowery; and his further memorials today are a number of things named after him, among them a school, a hotel, a housing development, some fifty New York businesses, and a brand of cigarettes.

These are, perhaps, after 300 years, the indisputable accolade of the true folk hero, and it is not hard to see why they will have been bestowed. Peter Stuyvesant represents the first real exercise of power in these parts, and for the powerful New York has always had a healthy respect. It may be a self-evident truth, wonderfully enunciated in 1776, that all men are created equal; but the history of this city at one level has been a constant struggle between the nobility of that sentiment and a more primitive inclination to exalt and submit to those who have achieved a form of majesty, usually based upon crude wealth. ('In Boston,' said Mark Twain, 'they ask How much does he know? In New York, How much is he worth?') Having turned their backs passionately on European notions of sovereignty, the citizens nurtured instead something that has always wobbled between the democracy of their idealism and the overweening rule of plutocrats. Having rejected the vapid aristocracies of the Old World, they encouraged some variable dynasties of their own in the New.

A German immigrant who arrived in 1788 from the small town of Waldorf was responsible for one of them. John Jacob Astor was a poor Manhattan shopkeeper soon after coming off his immigrant ship, but swiftly improved on that by a combination of enterprise and outright chicanery. His enterprise was in becoming a successful fur-trader, operating in places as far apart as Oregon and Minnesota, his chicanery lay in playing a trick on Thomas Jefferson, who had ordered an Embargo Act in 1807 as an act of economic warfare against the British. With a bare-faced deception Astor got a boat to China and back, loaded with a cargo that realised enough to lay the basis of the immense fortune that made him, at the time of this death in 1848, the richest man in America.* He had long since diversified his interests, and his

---

* The trick was that Astor pretended his boat had been chartered by a Chinese mandarin, in reality one of his own clerks. Jefferson was anxious to improve relations with China at the time and lifted the embargo for this one voyage.

most far-sighted stroke was in using his initial wealth to buy up enormous plots of land in parts of Manhattan which were then undeveloped but which, he instinctively knew, would one day become the midtown goldmine. Not long before he died he said that if he could have his time over again, 'knowing what I now know, and had money to invest, I would buy every foot of land on the Island of Manhattan'. It was those landholdings that enabled his descendants to set the social pace in New York for the rest of the nineteenth century and the early years of the twentieth. His grandson's wife, Mrs William Waldorf Astor, became the progenitor of the Social Register, and when she died in 1908 it was said that, 'With her passed not only a social dynasty but also the whole idea of hereditary or otherwise arbitrary social supremacy in America; with her indeed passed "Society" in the old sense.' This will not perhaps be welcome news to today's registrees, but it may partly explain why it was that, about the same time, a branch of the family took root again on the other side of the Atlantic, forming one of those strange Anglo-American alliances that periodically thrive on an infusion of money from one shore and title from the other.

The Vanderbilts came up on the ferryboat business, a Cornelius Vanderbilt having sailed a pirogue occasionally between Manhattan and Staten Island in the seventeenth century. It was another Cornelius, soon to be known more familiarly as the self-styled Commodore Vanderbilt, who established a regular Staten Island ferry in his *Nautilus* in 1817, and on the prosperity that came from it he launched himself energetically into other forms of transportation. Before long he owned a great fleet of steamboats that plied far up the Hudson River, and by the middle of the nineteenth century he was also running the New York Central Railroad; in old age the man who created the Grand Central railhead at 42nd Street in 1871. Not content with the likelihood of a wealth that in time surpassed even that of John Jacob Astor, he expanded into Central America during the Californian Gold Rush, sending his steamers to Nicaragua, where they unloaded freight that reached its destination in the goldfields after being conveyed by mule across the isthmus to other vessels waiting on the

Pacific coast. In Nicaragua, Vanderbilt's ambitions soared to an entirely new dimension: hiring a professional filibuster, the New Orleans lawyer, William Walker, he installed him as the effective ruler of the little country in 1855, and left him with instructions to put down any native insurrections that might threaten the activities of Vanderbilt's Accessory Transit Company there. Within a year, Walker had reintroduced the slave trade with Africa, provoking an invasion from other Central American countries, and before long the lawyer was back in New Orleans, where he was hailed as a hero.* The Commodore thereafter confined himself to enlarging his private empire nearer home, an ill-educated man who founded a university and, more characteristically, operated a trans-Atlantic steamship line. By the time he was gone in 1877, the family was noted for the extravagance of their lifestyles and the opulence of their houses, which extended across all fashionable parts of New York and up the eastern seaboard, a source of some irritation to the other grandees about town. Mrs William Waldorf Astor might have her Four Hundred exclusive acquaintances, with the Social Register in her gift, but Mrs William Kissam Vanderbilt had much more than the patronage of Sutton Place to justify her airs and graces. She was also the chatelaine of a property up at Newport, RI, which, though described by the family as their 'cottage', was in reality a palace, conceived in the same spirit as – and approaching the scale of – Versailles: and it was in those surroundings that her husband presently went potty, imagining himself to be, not a Vanderbilt, but His Royal Highness the Prince of Wales.

Like the Vanderbilts, the Roosevelts could trace their ancestry back to the earliest days of European settlement here, branching out prosperously under Dutch, English and American government alike. One line of the clan stayed in Manhattan and rose steadily in commerce, while another lit out for Duchess County, seventy miles upstate, thriving on their lands in the manner of

* In 1858, both Nicaragua and Costa Rica, fearing annexation by the United States, put themselves temporarily under the joint protection of Great Britain, France, and – of all places – Sardinia.

European squires; and in this fashion each of them, remarkably, produced a President of the United States. The first Roosevelt to make it to the White House, Theodore, was so fragile during his childhood on East 20th Street, that the family doctor prescribed special exercises to develop his muscles. As if in deliberate compensation for such a feeble start, in maturity he became notably muscular in every possible sense, big-game hunting for recreation, aggressively putting down J. P. Morgan's efforts to create a transport monopoly across the country, belligerently thrusting America into an imperial role for which she was not yet emotionally prepared. He visualised something comparable to the British Empire, but holding sway over the Pacific and the Caribbean, and to this end he despatched gunboats to frighten the Colombian rulers of Panama and secure for the United States a canal zone there; emphasising the more general point shortly before the close of his Presidency by sending sixteen battleships on a global cruise to brandish the Stars and Stripes in four South American ports, Sydney, Auckland and Yokohama. He had a vision for his nation which – domestically, at any rate – has not yet been properly accomplished. He couldn't stand those citizens who, after years in New York or anywhere else in the republic, were still unable to make up their minds whether they were Irish, or Poles, or Germans, or something else at heart, rather than straightforward and uncomplicated Americans. 'Hyphenated-Americans', in Teddy Roosevelt's book, were not wanted here.

Twenty-four years after he said goodbye to the White House, his fifth cousin (who also happened to be his niece's husband) arrived for a longer stay than usual; the only man ever to serve for more than two terms in the Presidency. Like Theodore, Franklin Delano Roosevelt had been to Harvard and had been trained in the law at Columbia, had first gone to Washington as Assistant Secretary of the Navy, and had become Governor of New York State. The parallels between their two careers were extraordinary, and there was even a bizarre pattern in their struggles against physical handicap. Theodore overcame his in adolescence, whereas Franklin was healthy enough until he was struck down by polio at the age of thirty-nine, and after that was never able to use his legs properly again.* The courage with which he virtually ignored this disability for the next quarter of a century was also necessary to face the national disaster which coincided with his inauguration in the depths of the Depression. With between twelve and thirteen million unemployed awaiting him, America required drastic, even unconstitutional action, and he gave her just that, closing every bank in the country one minute, demanding emergency powers the next, coming up with imaginatively grandiose schemes like the Works Progress Administration which, among many other achievements, bequeathed to his countrymen the finest series of nationwide guidebooks any people has ever inherited. Not everyone was impressed by Roosevelt's way of handling crises, but a sage estimate of his performance in the thirties is that, 'Not since Lincoln had there been such an artful manipulator of the good, the bad and the bewildered in between. I believe he saved the capitalist system by deliberately forgetting to balance the books, by transferring the gorgeous resources of credit from the bankers to the government, no matter what the national debt might be.' And then, with the same cool bravura, recognising a genocidal maniac when he saw one, Roosevelt almost single-handed propelled America towards a war that most Americans preferred not to know about, while it raged for over two years without their participation. To the likes of Charles Lindbergh it was a foreign war and no business of theirs, and in Madison Square Garden the potential stormtroopers of the German-American Bund rallied in the manner of their Nuremberg models, before floodlit pictures of George Washington, Abraham Lincoln and Adolf Hitler, while Roosevelt admonished Congress that, if it wasn't prepared to fight, then at least let America be 'the great arsenal of democracy'. He lived just long enough to see not only the American honour fully vindicated, on the battlefield as well as in the arsenal, but his cousin Theodore's international ambition at last within reach; dying only months before the peace

* Alistair Cooke has noted that 'throughout the twelve years of his Presidency, the press . . . respected a convention unlikely to be honoured today: they never photographed him in movement.'

that entrusted the world to the last two imperial powers we are likely to know. In doing its bit to secure that peace, New York had by chance given one of its names to the most hideous weapon ever contrived by man. The earliest endeavours which led to the invention of the atomic bomb were codenamed the Manhattan Project, because in New York were the offices of the army general in charge of procurement, security and anything else the scientists led by Dr Robert Oppenheimer needed to get on with their researches in secrecy.*

Among the dynasties of this city, one stands head and shoulders, generation upon generation, above all the rest. The Rockefellers crossed the Atlantic from Germany early in the eighteenth century and in the next hundred years spread themselves in different parts of upstate New York and Pennsylvania before producing a scion who was to be compared (by Bertrand Russell) to Bismarck himself for his impact on the modern world. This was the first John Davison Rockefeller, whose middle name celebrated his Scottish mother's family. His father was a confidence trickster who survived on his wits and managed to maintain a simultaneous and bigamous union for forty years without anyone in the authorised Rockefeller household having a clue about it. John D, as he would eventually be known in the family histories, was as different from this rapscallion parent as could be, an icy young calculator who decided to make money work for him from the moment in boyhood when he lent a neighbouring farmer fifty bucks at 7 per cent and discovered that the return on this investment was more than he would have secured from ten days of hard labour hoeing potatoes. By the time he was fourteen the family had moved to Cleveland and it was there, a dozen years later, in 1865, that he borrowed the money to buy the biggest oil refinery in the city, and was

* The 'Atom General' was Brigadier-General Leslie R. Groves, of the Army Corps of Engineers. The Manhattan Engineering District, which contained his office, was set up in June 1942, only a few months after President Roosevelt had been apprised of the need for experiments to be conducted into the possibility of such a weapon. Not until 1943 did Oppenheimer and his team move to New Mexico's desert, where they remained until the bomb was made.

noticed in a moment of rapture when he thought himself alone, murmuring, 'I'm bound to be rich! Bound to be rich! *Bound to be rich!*' He could scarcely have dreamt how rich. In a few more years he had created Standard Oil, and that became an enterprise the like of which civilisation had never even imagined before. Within a decade of its foundation its tentacles had a hold on forty different corporations, and John Davison Rockefeller was refining 95 per cent of all the oil in America. His was one of the growths that Teddy Roosevelt went after in his campaign against the robber barons, and even though it was dismembered by anti-trust legislation, its wealth remained fundamentally in the same hands. The best measurement of that wealth is perhaps the surpluses that John D always had available for his charities. Even when he was a poorly paid clerk in Cleveland, he had regularly given money to the good causes of the Baptist Church his mother had reared him in. Within a few years of founding Standard Oil, he was giving away $65,000 a year; before the century was finished the figure was $1.5 million; and in 1913 the Rockefeller Foundation was launched with a capital of $100 million, its lofty intent being 'to promote the well-being of mankind throughout the world'. Doubtless this was partly guilt-money; some would have said blood-money. John D knew himself to be one of the most detested men on earth, and not only in malicious envy of his wealth. He was loathed above all for the ruthless way Standard Oil had coldly rubbed out all possible competitors.

The Rockefellers by then were well established in New York, with not only the second but a third generation lined up, ready for the full inheritance whenever the old man might quit. He did not quite manage to be 100 years old, but he lasted until 1937, a caricature of his old self, suffering from an aggressive alopecia which denuded his body of all hair and caused him to wear a series of ill-fitting wigs designed to give the illusion of progressive growth on top. His frail presence was, none the less, a powerful one and probably hampered the full development of John D. Rockefeller II who, almost inevitably in the circumstances, was known as Junior in the family lore, a name which stuck even after his own death at the age of eighty-six. As a boy he had been trained to keep meticulous account of everything he touched – 'Practising the violin at $.05 per hour; drinking hot water at $.05 per glass; killing flies at $.02 per fly.' As a stripling employee in the family business he was expected to pay his father 6 per cent on a loan that was invested so he and his sister might share whatever profits accrued. Everything Junior did was in the image of old John D. He was a big backer of the evangelist, Billy Sunday, before the First World War, and of Billy Graham after the Second. When his three-year-old nephew died, he helped the distraught parents handle the funeral, but later sent his brother-in-law a bill for his expenses. It was he who enlarged the Rockefeller empire vitally in 1930 by acquiring the Chase National Bank, and with it the American Express Company; he who took the decision to shift the corporate headquarters from lower Broadway to a great new complex between Fifth and Sixth Avenues, which would be known as the Rockefeller Center; he who provided New York with one of its most extraordinary museums in The Cloisters, which is essentially a medley of antiquities (not always harmoniously reconstructed here) scavenged in job lots on expeditions through the length and breadth of Europe. Nothing at all that Junior did, however, was to be of greater consequence than fathering the third wave of Rockefellers. There is a photograph of him and his five sons awaiting the funeral train bringing old John D's body for burial in the family plot. They stand like a group of powerful associates more than bereaved siblings, each man expressionless, each with a black homburg, wearing almost uniform suits and neckties. If they had also been wearing topcoats, they would have been indistinguishable from a coven of Mafia.

One of the Brothers was a complete misfit in this company. Bullied by two of the others in childhood, Winthrop became a playboy drunk whose happiest year, he once said, had been spent as an apprentice roughneck on the oil fields, where his refusal to make the most of his family connections had won him the respect of ordinary working men. When he hurriedly married a former beauty queen – ex-Miss Lithuania in a Chicago contest – his parents cut him, and when the marriage bust after a few months and one child, Winthrop retreated to the depths of Arkansas. There, where he could be his own man, he flourished after his own fashion both as a farmer and then as Governor of the state, reforming its barbaric penal system and backing the civil rights campaign. Defeated in his bid for a third term in 1970, he went into another decline, in which cancer was diagnosed. His funeral was the first time the other Rockefellers had been near him in years.

John Davison Rockefeller III was also elbowed aside, and never became more than heir apparent in the hierarchy. Dominated for too long by Junior, as Junior had been by his father, he also had ambitious brothers to contend with, and made no pitch for the family leadership when it became vacant, though it should have been his by right, as the eldest son. It was by dutifully running an errand for his father after leaving Princeton that he became attracted to Japan, and this was to be the basis of a lifelong interest in the Orient which would see him repeatedly enlisted by Washington as an important member of high-powered delegations, not only as an expert but as a Rockefeller as well. In time his expertise would be hallmarked with such as the Order of Sacred Treasure and the Order of Rising Sun from Japan, the Order of Sikatuna from the Philippines, and the Most Noble Order of the Crown of Thailand; exotic decorations for an increasingly thoughtful man who was uncomfortable with much of the family activity. But he threw his energies into the Rockefeller Foundation and the Rockefeller Brothers Fund, which was yet another device by which the family disposed of its surplus and tax-deductible monies in well-publicised donations. JDR3 was the man who, more than anyone else, made sure that New York got its Lincoln Center for the Performing Arts.

Of the three dominant Brothers, Laurence was the most ambivalent. His primary instincts were unmistakably Rocke-feller, and his money-making ambitions first led him to invest in commercial aviation, associating himself with Captain Eddie Rickenbacker's bid for Eastern Airlines in 1938. But he lacked the dynastic ability never to miss a financial trick, selling his shares in the McDonnell company at an $8 million profit when he would have gained much more had he awaited its merger with Douglas Aircraft, which made it one of the three biggest defence contractors for the government. At the same time he was genuinely interested in the great outdoors, and pitched himself advantageously into conservation just as this was becoming a big issue throughout the land. Two Presidents – Johnson and Nixon – had him conspicuously rendering advice in the highest quarters, though people operating at the grass roots of the movement had their doubts about which side he was really on. For while uttering pieties dear to their hearts, Laurence Rockefeller was simultaneously up to his neck in hotel and tourist developments that were doing their bit to change the face of wildernesses as far apart as the Caribbean and Hawaii, Yellowstone and Vermont.

As a brilliant graduate of three universities, the youngest Brother, David, could have made a career in politics and was briefly secretary to Mayor LaGuardia (who didn't take kindly to his habit of answering the telephone with, 'City Hall, Rockefeller speaking'). But during his time at the London School of Economics he had spent hours every week working in the local branch of the Chase National, the bank he was destined to dominate within a few years, after his smooth promotion from one executive position to another, while it expanded into the Chase Manhattan, and became the biggest bank in the world. Its importance at home was signified by its hold over just one sector of the economy, transport; where, by the mid-seventies, it was the leading stockholder of two major railroads and two of the biggest trucking firms, with fourteen principal American airlines deeply in its debt. Overseas, Chase was effectively an instrument of American foreign policy: the financial olive branch held out to Yugoslavia as soon as Tito had broken with Stalin, Franco's obliging creditor the moment he accepted the idea of United States bases in Spain, the first American bank allowed into either Moscow or Peking as soon as the politicians were talking civilly to each other, the American bank that Washington deemed most suitable to set up shop in Saigon in 1966. That last opening was a straight trade for David Rockefeller's public endorsement of Lyndon Johnson's escalation of the Vietnam War; and two years later he was calling for billions of dollars to be cut from the American domestic budget in order to wage the war more effectively. Chase also placed its monies at the disposal of the South African Government in greater quantities than ever after the Sharpeville Massacre of 1960. Its attitude towards another distinctly undemocratic area was best summarised by something David said a year after the Bay of Pigs fiasco in Cuba: 'We have made a firm commitment to Latin America for economic aid and for assistance in containing communist imperialism' – assistance which was to mean, among other purposes, lubricating the machinery used to overthrow President Allende of Chile before long. He was speaking then on behalf of the US Business Advisory Council for the Alliance for Progress (in South America), but what he said represented the position of the Chase Manhattan Bank as well. J. F. Kennedy had set up the council, and he was one of three Presidents who offered David Rockefeller the post of Secretary of the Treasury. The other two were Lyndon Johnson and Richard Nixon, and Nixon also offered him Secretary of Defense and the Moscow embassy. All such offers were resisted, though David clearly got a bang from his increasing occupation of an international stage, where he parleyed with world leaders on equal terms. It has been said that although financial quarters acknowledged his distinction as a friend of kings and presidents, they never thought of him as a first-rate commercial banker; and when Chase gradually lost its eminence to its rival Citibank, much of the blame was attributed to him. Not once, however, did he ever fail the name of Rockefeller. It was he who persuaded Jack Kennedy in the sixties to make a massive tax cut, which apportioned nearly half the total benefit to the richest 20 per cent of Americans.

The effective leader of the Brothers from infancy to the end of his life was the second in line of succession, the coarse and loutish Nelson. The appetite for power which he exercised within the family circle as a boy, would in maturity be fed – but never satisfied – by politics, where he was to get within a heartbeat of the highest position in the land. As a young man he, too, served his apprenticeship in the family bank, then became involved in the oil business, and it was this that shaped the rest of his career. He was touring the Venezuelan fields in 1937 at a time of much unrest, in which the local communists were clearly playing a part; and when, the following year, the Mexicans nationalised their American oil companies, that settled something for Nelson Rockefeller. He would obtain the power he craved and use it to make sure that no such wickedness ever befell his own people. His know-how in Latin America took him to Washington under Roosevelt, and although that patronage lasted only months, after it Nelson never looked back. At the inaugural meeting in San Francisco of the United Nations, he was lobbying to secure membership for unpopular, Peronist Argentina, and cleverly outmanoeuvred the Soviet Union in the process. A little later he threw himself into a campaign to bring the permanent headquarters of the UN to New York, when it might easily have stayed on the West Coast, ended up in Philadelphia, or even gone to some other country: and one of those who succumbed to his forcefulness was his own father, who donated the $8.5 million necessary to purchase the site beside the East River. By the time the headquarters was finished there, Nelson was being spoken of as a possible Mayor of New York, but he had his eyes on bigger fish than that. What he really wanted was the White House, and this was by no means a wild fantasy: Jack Kennedy himself reckoned that if Nelson had secured the Republican nomination in 1961 instead of Nixon, then Rockefeller rather than Kennedy would have won the Presidency.

The best that Nelson would manage was to become Gerald Ford's Vice-President after Nixon had been brought down by the Watergate scandal, and his biggest taste of power was to be as Governor of the state of New York, a position he held for over fifteen years. A measure of his longing for office was the amount of his own money that he spent in trying to achieve it; a total, it has been estimated, of $48 million in one campaign and another. He pulled out all the stops in other ways, in his efforts to achieve success, not hesitating to remind Jewish audiences of the Israel bonds purchased by the Rockefellers, touring Harlem uncharacteristically on the back of a truck, accompanied by Count Basie and his piano, joking with Puerto Ricans in the Bronx in fluent Spanish; being all things to all men until the polling booths were closed. That he never made it to the Oval Office for all his wealth, all his connections, all his political skill and special expertise, is an indication of the deep dislike the name of Rockefeller could still produce; and Nelson Rockefeller had some especially unpleasant habits that were all his own. When his marriage came to an end under the strain of his philandering, he had the official history of the Governor's residence rewritten so that all reference to Tod Rockefeller would be removed. His Governorship was characterised by two other things. Not once, but twice, he vetoed bills which threatened to stop the use of lie-detectors for business purposes in the state, the only one in the north-east where their use was unrestricted. And then, in 1971, there was a mutiny at the state prison in Attica, where 1,300 inmates took thirty-eight officials hostage, one guard dying from injuries sustained in the process. A special negotiating commission, which included a Congressman, a *New York Times* editor, and a black Assemblyman, begged Governor Rockefeller to visit Attica as a sign of good faith which might produce a peaceful ending to the impasse. He refused, and authorised instead an assault by hundreds of state troopers, who shot dead forty-three people, including ten of the hostages.*

After the Rockefeller Brothers came the Rockefeller Cousins: but here, for the first time, the dynastic mould cracked. More numerous than their parents, and much more numerously female (fourteen women and nine men, descended from a solitary sister and five brothers), the Cousins never looked like carrying on the family traditions as before. They were, almost without exception, deeply marked by the burden of being Rockefellers, painfully guilt-ridden for what had already, even before they were born, been done in their name. There was the sheer brutality that so often had been the Rockefeller way with other people. A regular visitor to the Chase Manhattan headquarters was struck by 'the absolute terror of the subordinates where David was concerned'; and when Chase began to be overtaken by Citibank in 1972, David Rockefeller instantly fired one of his longest-serving senior executives, though he himself was held by experts to be mostly responsible for the decline. There was the total inability to see that moral principle must usually take

---

* A commission which investigated the Attica disaster said it was 'with the exception of the Indian massacres in the late 19th century . . . the bloodiest one-day encounter between Americans since the Civil War.'

precedence over money-making in a civilised society. Just after the First World War, a Rockefeller oil company entered into a cartel with the German petro-chemical giant, I. G. Farben, and this was renewed periodically during Hitler's rise to power, with the declared intention of working out some arrangement that would survive a second world war, whether or not the United States was involved. There was the belief that every man had his price and could be bought for Rockefeller purposes. Some very impressive names were in the Rockefeller pay at one time or another, including MacKenzie King, John Foster Dulles, Dean Rusk, Edward Teller and Henry Kissinger; and Winston Churchill was quite willing to delay his history of the English-speaking peoples for a couple of years while he made £50,000 on a biography of John D, but Junior cancelled the deal after deciding it was too much to spend in the middle of the Depression. There was the sometimes spurious philanthropy that gave an undeserved lustre to the Rockefeller name. Often enough the donations were genuine, and Rockefeller money has been magnificently employed for purposes as varied as the restoration of Versailles and the creation of the Institute for Medical Research which later became Rockefeller University. But when Nelson Rockefeller was bent on reaching the White House, he released a list of personal gifts amounting to $24.7 million which he had made over the years, an obvious stratagem to boost his candidacy, which misfired when it became apparent that 'about 70 per cent of Nelson's giving involved what were basically gifts to himself, his family, and their institutional extensions'. There was, above all perhaps, the fact of the dynastic wealth itself; the stifling, inescapable, monstrously hoarded mass of dollars and bonds and stocks and shares and paintings and other priceless objects and properties in quantities which almost defied computation. This wealth must be placed in context if we are to understand clearly what it has meant to be a Rockefeller; and Christmas is just such a serviceable measurement. For this festival each year, the family would gather on the Rockefeller estate at Pocantino Hills up the Hudson valley. That's where it took them – even in the middle of the Second World War, when I. G. Farben was employing slave labour from the concentration camps, and when the loathed communists in Leningrad were reduced to eating earth mixed with sugar, and their pet animals, and finally their own dead – three whole days to open all the Christmas presents.

The appetite for power alone, untrammelled by any apparent desire for great wealth, can also be satisfied in this city, and often enough is, inside and out of politics. There is no more remarkable figure in the annals of New York than that of the formidable Robert Moses who, for the best part of half a century, until he was outmanoeuvred by Nelson Rockefeller, dominated many of the decisions which settled the civic future. He was a public servant who accumulated positions of command the way some people collect small-town committee memberships; being simultaneously the City Parks Commissioner, the City Planning Commissioner, the City Construction Co-ordinator, the chairman of the Slum Clearance Committee, and chairman of the Triborough Bridge and Tunnels Authority, while also sitting on half a dozen boards and commissions of New York state, including the State Power Authority, of which he was chairman. In time, there was very little in the running of the metropolis and its hinterland that could be accomplished without his say-so, and a great deal of its physical arrangement today is a result of his outlook and his exercise of power. Lewis Mumford, who disliked him intensely, and most of the things he stood for, reckoned that he had more influence on the shaping of American cities in the twentieth century than any other person. A citizen who once found himself in the path of some grandiose project of the Commissioner's was not being wholly unfair when he said that, 'Moses thinks he's God, but he's only Moses.' In time he certainly saw himself as a second, but rather more accomplished, Baron Haussmann; and there were obvious similarities between them. One permanently marked the face of Paris, and was acclaimed as the supreme artist with his Universal Exposition in 1867. The other created for New York an environment that can never now be changed, and hoped to crown his life's work with the 1964 New York World's Fair, for which he had campaigned hard and over which he presided. But that, like its predecessor a quarter of a century earlier, was a bit of a flop, which left behind huge debts and – apart from Shea Stadium, which remains a going concern – a rather sad conglomeration of reach-me-downs across the railroad tracks from that ballpark: a wan little museum that in some ways sums up the borough of Queens, a lot of vacant concrete that hasn't weathered too well, and the hollow fretwork of the Unisphere, with its abandoned dedication to 'man's aspiration towards Peace thro' mutual understanding . . .'

Early in life Moses had a sense of vocation, which was demonstrated after he had left Yale and gone to Oxford in 1909. There he was the first American to become President of the Union – a notorious springboard for the indecently ambitious – and there his chosen thesis for PhD was the British Civil Service: there, too, his biographer believes, he acquired the 'supreme contempt' of the educated British ruling élite with whom he was hobnobbing, for those 'considered most incapable of self-rule' and in consequence became an irredeemably arrogant man. After proceeding to Berlin for a quick tutorial in political science, Moses returned home and entered the civil service of New York for which, by then, he was almost excessively well qualified. Not until the 1930s would his larger objectives be openly declared when, in quick succession, he sought nomination as Mayor, and then became Republican candidate for Governor. At the last minute his backers for the first title changed their minds and put up Fiorello LaGuardia instead. In the Governor's election, Moses sustained the biggest defeat in the history of the contest, and a flaw in his own character was mostly responsible for that. He was attempting to unseat the incumbent, Herbert Lehman, who was well known to be one of the most honourable men ever to run the state of New York. Yet Moses went for straightforward character assassinations and little else, so outrageous and so unrelenting that a radio network eventually refused to broadcast his speeches unless the Republican Party took out an insurance policy against action for libel that would cover everything he said.

So he returned to the profession in which he was by then already an acknowledged heavyweight, and proceeded to satisfy his appetite for power piecemeal, by enlarging his empire almost annually, until he was in a position of such commanding influence that no Mayor and no Governor dared to challenge his authority.

His first big break had been in 1923 when, as a coming man, he was taken out of New York City and up to the state capital at Albany to serve as a special assistant to Governor Al Smith. The following year he was given the job from which all else was to follow, improbable though it might have seemed to anyone else at the time: president of the Long Island State Park Commission. What he accomplished there was nothing less than a transformation of the land, which he would later extend throughout the state of New York, and which others would imitate elsewhere across the length and breadth of the United States. When he started work, rural Long Island was to all intents and purposes either farmland or the private estate of the extremely rich, with scarcely a beach or inland open space that might be enjoyed by the citizens from Brooklyn or other parts of the metropolis. The vision Robert Moses entertained was for miles of the seashore available as a metropolitan playground, and with arterial roads sweeping across the countryside, joining this public parkland with others that he would develop elsewhere. He went forth to begin this conversion of Long Island armed with a certain amount of money, together with extraordinary powers of coercion, and an unlimited number of state troopers who would enforce any order made.

Some farmers were willing to sell early on, and this gave Moses the toehold he needed, which was enlarged unexpectedly when a landowning syndicate which was already thinking of getting out also decided to do a deal. The carrot did not immediately appeal to anyone else after that, so Moses employed the big stick. When people refused to sell he threatened them with the appropriation of their land and had lawyers draw up the necessary papers without delay. He didn't hesitate to intimidate in other ways, by sending his survey gangs to the edge of properties he wanted his roads across, and ordering them to begin work with their theodolites and measuring-chains deliberately in full view of the alarmed owners. It was straightforward bullying, and Moses was perfectly ready to apply it to rich and poor alike, except that no struggling farmer ever had the consideration the park boss showed for wealthy Otto Kahn, who offered to donate $10,000 for surveying needs if only a proposed road could run somewhere other than smack down the

middle of his private golf course; and of course it could. By such
varied measures as these, within four years of assuming his post,
Robert Moses had engineered fourteen separate parks amounting
to nearly 10,000 acres. Miles of the seashore had been opened
up, as at Jones Beach, where in 1928 he had an army of men
bent double for days while they hand-planted bundles of marram
grass to prevent the sand dunes from being blown away. Soon
New Yorkers in their thousands were on those beaches, as they
still are every summer, while the Atlantic breakers smash and
suck at the shore and, when the wind is right, the great airliners
come banking in from the sea at the start of the final run in to
their landing at Kennedy.

It was an heroic achievement, even though some of the means
used were questionable; and it was the beginning of a legend
that persisted until quite recently, of Commissioner Moses as
the incorruptible giant who moved mountains to make New York
a better place for all its people. Apart from the brief hiatus of his
failure to become either Mayor or Governor, the stature of Robert
Moses grew with every year that passed, as fresh avenues opened
before him, new opportunities were seized, more and more power
came his way, larger and larger slices of the communal resources
were found to be in his gift. And the gift, ultimately, by the time
he retired in 1968, was that New York had been handed over,
utterly and almost certainly beyond the power of man to retrieve
it, to the automobile. Someone should have thought hard about the
implication of a curious novelty in the construction of those first
major roads he flung across Long Island, which were supposed to
be for the benefit of even the poorest New Yorkers who wanted
to reach the blessed fresh air by the sea. The roads were crossed
from time to time by bridges, elliptical shapes of a new design
which seemed to be unusually low; as they truly were. They
had been deliberately built that way to discourage bus operators
from travelling those roads, to leave the parkways across Long
Island almost exclusively for the benefit of people who owned
cars. There weren't all that many of them in the 1920s.*

*In 1920, New York had only 200,000 motor cars. Today there are 1.9
million in private ownership alone.

It is impossible to get away from the handiwork of Robert Moses today, for all the major roads that gird the city and criss-cross it are his, with the solitary exception of the East River Drive: all those clover-leaves and flyovers and underpasses and expressways, which were built so that New York's madness of traffic shall get from here to there without let or hindrance except when it chokes upon its own congestions, as it frequently does; the Major Deegan Expressway, the Van Wyck Expressway, the Brooklyn-Queens Expressway, the Staten Island Expressway and the others, 627 miles of roadways in all. Moses was also responsible for the seven big bridges that have been thrown across the waters of New York, or other obstacles, since 1931 – the Triborough, the Verrazano, the Throgs Neck, the Marine, the Henry Hudson, the Cross Bay and the Bronx–Whitestone. He often enough encountered opposition at one stage or another of every new scheme of his, and each time he handled it as he had done from the outset, when he was pushing his plans irresistibly across Long Island to refashion it in an image that he alone perceived. Typical was the way he put the Cross-Bronx Expressway through.

When he first announced his plan in 1944, the Bronx was a mostly peaceable borough whose heartland consisted of tree-lined neighbourhoods packed with densely populated tenements. The Moses idea was to drive a seven-mile long, six-lane wide highway straight through this, across 113 streets, where there were thousands of buildings above ground and services galore beneath it, including subway lines and major sewers. It was a monstrous ambition which caused an army general, who had undertaken the building of the Burma Road, to gape in astonishment when he saw what was planned. No fewer than thirty-one local organisations protested when they realised how much damage would be done to their community, but they cut no ice at all with the City Construction Co-Ordinator, whose hat Moses was wearing for this particular campaign. One deputation discovered that 1,530 apartments would have to be demolished in their neighbourhood, though with a slight realignment of the road only nineteen families would be disturbed. Realignment was out of the question, they were told; though this would, in fact, have made the expressway straighter than it turned out in the end. For years thereafter, the line chosen for this particular march of Progress looked like a battlefield, as buildings were flattened, dynamite blasted away rock day and night, and all the gigantically crawling yellow apparatus of civil engineering invaded the Bronx and made a beachhead there. When all was done, something like 60,000 people had been forced to find somewhere else to live, while winos and ruffians were squatting in derelict buildings on the edge of the devastation, that decent people had left in dismay. The Bronx was changed quite fundamentally. This was the start of its great and catastrophic decline. But drivers could get across it now in fifteen minutes flat. Among them are the drivers of trucks laden with spent nuclear fuel from the research reactor at the Brookhaven National Laboratory on Long Island, which cross New York by this route on their way to a reprocessing plant in Idaho.

The massive evictions that Moses ordered in the Bronx for the purposes of his expressway obsession were also enforced elsewhere, when he started to reshape New York in other ways, this time as City Planning Commissioner and chairman of the Slum Clearance Committee. Those blocks of arid public housing that stud the Lower East Side, and many other parts of the metropolis, arose at his behest, after massive clearances of people and property which were made without any attempt to consult those whose lives were to be monstrously changed by the commissioner's paternalistic vision of the future. The property as often as not was in poor shape, though not irredeemably so. Spruced up a bit with municipal encouragement, most of those run-down neighbourhoods would have contributed to the urban ideal memorably described by the writer Jane Jacobs ('A lively city scene is lively largely by virtue of its enormous collection of small elements'). She rallied her neighbourhood to fight an attempt by Moses to demolish the West Village and replace it with tower blocks, and as a result of that campaign, the Village survived, endearingly 'mixed-up, a bit tacky, and full of life'. Other neighbourhoods have not been so fortunate.

Robert Moses had his thoughtful, even his tender side. He looked after his former subordinates well so long as they had remained devoted to him. And he never forgot what he owed to Governor Al Smith, who became a sad and rejected figure in old age, bereft of all influence and power, without even the animals he had doted on in the private zoo he had kept up at Albany. As New York City Parks Commissioner, Robert Moses was overlord of something much bigger and better than that; and he furnished his old patron with a special key, so that he could let himself into the Central Park Zoo at any time of the day or night. Much more often, though, Moses is caught in more unpleasant responses than these. It was he who, when thwarted in his attempt to put a bridge between Brooklyn and the Battery, vindictively ordered the demolition of the Aquarium and the removal of its contents to Coney Island. He once had an East River ferry terminal demolished, in defiance of an order issued by the Mayor, while the ferry itself, loaded with passengers, was halfway across the water. He kept detailed files on all the politicians and anyone else he had ever dealt with, potential ammunition which he would not hesitate to use against any of them, should they get in his way. His ultimate weapon in the post-war years, when his power seemed impregnable, his presence indispensable, his position unassailable, was the threat to resign any one of, or even all, his numerous portfolios. He tried this trick just once too often, on a man who was even tougher, more ruthless and more cunning than him. Governor Nelson Rockefeller said 'Done!', and Robert Moses was at last dispossessed, leaving behind, as Christopher Wren once did in London, a monument which is all around the curious observer, to be read like an epitaph. There is also a photograph which fixes him very well in the mind's eye. He is posed dramatically on a steel beam which projects over water, with the high buildings of midtown Manhattan at some distance in the background. Self-consciously Robert Moses stands there with his legs splayed strongly, his hands defiantly on his hips, a roll of blueprints firmly in his grasp. It is an updated version of the Colossus of Rhodes, perhaps; Hubris beside the East River without any doubt.

The position which he coveted in 1933 has been described as 'the second toughest job in America' – by an incumbent, of course – and it is unlikely that there is a civic functionary anywhere else on earth who shoulders the complex responsibilities or enjoys the power belonging to the Mayor of New York. A fully functioning democracy is headquartered at City Hall, with a City Council and a Board of Estimate, together with a President of the Council, a Comptroller and five Borough Presidents, all deliberating and making decisions in surroundings of municipal good taste and post-Colonial elegance, where the Stars and Stripes for once is upstaged by the orange, white and blue tricolour of the City of New York.* But when all's said and done, the bulk of power in the end resides in the Mayor, without whose assent no bill becomes law round here, or unless any veto he applies is defeated by two-thirds of the City Council. He also has a number of vital posts entirely at his disposal, among them the Police Commissioner, the Fire Commissioner and the Sanitation Commissioner. And although his financial powers are no longer quite what they used to be, he is still the proposer of the city's Expense Budget which, year in and year out, is second in size only to the national budget of the entire United States. His Honor makes policy for this city on a scale that no other mayor ever approaches. He can, in effect, make or break New York with his flair or his ineptitude. That is why he is highly paid and is given Gracie Mansion, one of the most handsome official residences in the land, for the duration of his term. It also explains why the mayoral election every four years is fought with all the vigour, slander, expenditure and public performance that other people tend to save for putting in and out their national governments. A New York civic election is an event in the calendar, and some people with strong stomachs but almost no chance of winning occasionally contest it in order to publicise themselves and some point they have been struggling to make. The columnist, William F. Buckley, Jr, flashed his eyes at the electorate in 1965, when he felt strongly about the fiscal policies of the sitting Mayor, Robert Wagner. Four years later, to the delight of thousands, Norman Mailer stood on a platform that was quickly forgotten, even by those 5 per cent of Democratic voters in the primary stage of

* This can easily be mistaken at first sight for one of several European national buntings and is, in fact, the flag flown by the United Netherlands in 1625.

the contest who weren't nearly enough to put him in the ring for the main bout.*

New York's Mayors have been an exceedingly mixed bunch, right from the beginning in 1662, and even in the past half century or so. There have been nonentities such as Vincent R. Impelliteri, an amiable but dull product of the Tammany system, who was thrust into office almost accidentally in 1950 when his predecessor left City Hall ahead of schedule to become the United States Ambassador to Mexico. That predecessor was the enigmatic William O'Dwyer, whose climb to power was in a classical tradition, for he had got off the boat as a young man with only a few coins in his pocket and had been, in turn, builder's labourer, clerk, plasterer, bartender, policeman, lawyer, magistrate, District Attorney and County Judge before his elevation to Mayor. As District Attorney in Brooklyn he had performed the considerable public service of smashing Murder Inc: but just after beginning his second term at City Hall, it was announced that the Kefauver Committee investigating organised crime was going to conduct hearings in New York and probably going to interrogate politicians; whereupon Mayor O'Dwyer suddenly resigned and reappeared in Mexico City with the obliging assistance of President Truman. Robert Wagner was another Mayor of New York who became an American ambassador, in his case to Spain, and as a hard-earned reward for long service and honest endeavour. He served three full terms, was one of the more highly educated men to occupy the position, and brought to the task a considerable social conscience, pushing through new legislation to stabilise rents, with the fine ambition to create the 'slumless city', which was tempting the fates too much in New York. He was succeeded by dashing John Lindsay, a pure Ivy League figure, whose initial impact was not at all unlike that made by the arrival of Jack Kennedy in the White House: here was not only youthful vigour and much dental charm, but a sense of idealism to top it off. It was Lindsay who, having found that things weren't turning out the way he had planned, consoled himself with

*The most memorable thing that Mailer urged the voters to approve was his proposal that New York City should be declared the fifty-first state!

the thought that he was, after all, doing the second toughest job in
America. His critics, in the stinging manner of so much New York
badinage, put it like this: 'If a letter carrier in Brooklyn awakened
with sore feet, Bob Wagner's arches hurt, and Lindsay wondered
where Brooklyn was.' But at least Lindsay had style, which is
valued in New York. Poor Abraham Beame, who followed him,
had no style at all; a grey little man, who presided over New
York's biggest crisis for many a year so ineptly that Governor
Hugh Carey, up in Albany, seriously thought of dismissing him.

Some of the Mayors have been sheer colour from start to
finish, and such a one was Jimmy Walker. He was the son of a
Tammany Building Commissioner and he was destined for politics
from birth, though his own preferences were for the theatre and
Tin Pan Alley; and as a young man he was a capable song writer,
producing a hit in 1908 ('Will you love me in December as you do in
May?') which still gets played among the golden oldies from time to
time. Two years later he was in the state legislature and presently
became Democratic floor leader, sponsoring the bills that legalised
boxing in New York and allowed baseball to be played there on
Sundays. At the same time he began to build his reputation
as a debonair man-about-town, the always smartly dressed and
usually wisecracking guy who seemed to be at the centre of all
the fun, whether that was on Broadway for an opening night, at
Madison Square Garden for a big fight, or merely spinning away
the small hours in the Central Park Casino with a girl on his arm.
With Tammany behind him it was almost inevitable that he would
become Mayor if he chose to, and he picked his moment with
perfect timing in 1926; for Beau James, as Walter Winchell once
remarked, 'was the living spirit of the terrific 1920s . . . when we
saps believed a rising stock market was taking us nearer to heaven
on earth; when everybody thought the lottery had more prizes
than tickets; when flaming youth and the lights of Broadway were
the vogue – and the torch on the Statue of Liberty was a forgotten,
burned-out electric bulb – Jimmy Walker led the parade.' There
was a touch of predestination, too, about his fall, which came after
the Wall Street Crash, when the Depression was in its depths.
Judge Samuel Seabury had been appointed by Governor Franklin
D. Roosevelt to investigate the civic corruption of New York in

1930, and in the next couple of years uncovered malfeasance on a prodigious scale, involving officials from almost every department of local government, as well as police and magistrates. When the Mayor himself was called to take the stand for a couple of days, he put on the same show of joking insolence that had always pulled in the votes; but now his time was running out. There were nearly $1 million in bank and brokerage accounts that he couldn't convincingly explain. Abruptly he resigned and, within days, sailed away to exile in Europe, leaving many New Yorkers to wonder bleakly what had gone so terribly wrong with their world yet again.

The way was open for Fiorello LaGuardia to make his entrance, though a couple of stopgaps briefly delayed his arrival in 1934 at City Hall, where he would perform, centre stage, for the next eleven years. During that decade and more he built a legend which still glows, and not only in the recollection of people who paid taxes in LaGuardia's time. He was, for a start, a palpably decent man who had the genuinely common touch to an uncommon degree. He was born that way, as a mongrel Protestant-Jewish-Italian, and he had cultivated accessibility both as a young interpreter among the immigrants on Ellis Island and as a lawyer representing operatives in the garment workers' strikes of 1912 and 1913. When he became Mayor, his Sunday radio chats radiated his sentimental warmth as much as his shrewdness in knowing just how to attract the votes. ('Ladies, I want to ask you a little favour. I want you please to wear your rubbers when you go out in this weather. If you don't wear your rubbers you may slip and hurt yourself . . . Now another word about fish.') There are grandparents in New York today who have never forgotten how, when they were kids themselves and there was a lengthy strike of the newspaper delivery people, 'Hizzonor' used his radio time to read them extracts from the comics they were missing. He was the Mayor who would go into the depths of a burning building to comfort a couple of firemen who were pinned under a collapsed wall; the Mayor who once conducted the Sanitation Department band in Carnegie Hall after telling the manager to, 'Just treat me like Toscanini'; the Mayor who, when he could not avoid playing host to some Nazis officially visiting New York, made sure that they were provided with an escort of Jewish cops; the Mayor who, in 1943, when he was sure that he would be asked to forsake civilian life temporarily to govern Italy under the Allied occupation, went so far as to order a brigadier-general's uniform (but the call never came). He was the Mayor whose doings were daily reported in the papers, as often as not illustrated by a photograph taken when he was wearing gear that men in his position are generally unaccustomed to; fireman's helmet and oilskins, subway motorman's overalls and cap; air-raid warden's hardhat and armband; or he might be smashing seized slot machines with a sledgehammer, or cutting down a doomed section of the 'El' with an acetylene torch.

He was not, by any means, a saint. He was quite capable of voting against a bonus for teachers because their national association had criticised him some time earlier. He didn't take kindly to criticism from any quarter, and so his relations with the press went up and down, the Mayor on one occasion snatching a reporter's notebook from his hand, flinging it to the floor and jumping on it. He could throw the most childish tantrums and often did so in City Hall, not always behind closed doors, when an official, or even a secretary, had done something to upset him. There was a high turnover of people there during his administration of New York, and much of it was put down to LaGuardia's petty tyrannies. He once sacked a very experienced and capable secretary when, for the first time, she had one drink too many during her lunch hour. There was a niggling prude inside the genial 'Little Flower', and this caused him to run the burlesque shows out of New York.

Nor was he a master of administration in a purely technical sense, for he found it hard to delegate his considerable powers, and wasted much time and energy attacking trivial matters that might have been left to subordinates. But, to an extent that was (and still is) rare in American politicians, he picked people above all for their merits and not for their politics, nonplussing many of his supporters by his tolerance of several avowed communists in the Department of Welfare. He also had a great and good vision for the city of his birth, which encompassed dancing in Central Park and an end to corruption in civic life; which included a metropolis whose music and other creative arts would stand comparison with those of anywhere in the world, and whose people could walk their streets safely by day or night; which embodied things for all

New Yorkers that most of them had never been able to take for granted, like an assurance of their daily bread, decent housing, and municipal compassion if they fell on hard times.

No administration before or since has undertaken as many public projects and seen them through. LaGuardia was fortunate to be running New York just after Roosevelt had gone to Washington and announced his New Deal, with appropriate funding, to set many untoward matters straight; and a lot of the ensuing activity in and around the metropolis can be attributed to the drive and ambitions of Robert Moses, with whom LaGuardia had an often stormy and always wary relationship.* But it has generally been held that without LaGuardia's own vivid leadership, without his energy and dedication to the task in hand, without his genuine vision of what might be accomplished for the civic good, the federal money would never have come New York's way as readily as it did, or in such quantity. And while public works were in full swing, the Mayor had Thomas Dewey and others hell-bent on cleaning up the New York underworld, with other commissioners at the same time instituting widespread reforms of the civil service, which meant that the day of the placemen was over and that qualifications rather than connections were to be the criteria for municipal employment under this regime. For all these reasons Fiorello LaGuardia is remembered fondly the best part of half a century after he left City Hall. Most of all, people remember his remarkable rectitude. It is an unusual politician who doesn't increase his wealth appreciably during his term of office, and too many in New York have been downright crooks. But after LaGuardia died in 1946, it was found that his total investments were stacked away in a bundle of war bonds – amounting to just 8,000 bucks.

There is a bronze figurine of him on the desk of New York's one-hundred-and-fifth Mayor, and a large oil of him on the wall opposite, which Edward Isaac Koch can eye for inspiration every time he looks up from his work. Not that he has ever shown much of a weakness for supplication, even his election campaigns

---

* LaGuardia was the Mayor defied by Moses in the matter of the ferry terminal.

brimming with a confidence which suggested, after his third term was secured in 1985, that he might easily become the longest-serving Mayor the city has known.* Like LaGuardia, Koch came to office soon after the city had been in a desperate plight; in this case as close to bankruptcy as makes no matter. It was wholly to the credit of the former Democratic Congressman that, building on the emergency measures taken by others, he made the city well and truly solvent again by drastic economies and by a steadfast refusal to take the most convenient but ultimately more expensive way out of negotiation with belligerent unions. So impressed was Washington by the way Koch had begun to tackle the real problems of New York, that he managed to extract federal aid that had once been memorably refused his predecessor, Abe Beame. Ed Koch is illuminating on how he achieved this concession: 'To bolster the City's case, I appeared as a witness before the various committees, most notably Senator Proxmire's. I was friendly; I was easy; but I counterpunched; I bubbled with facts; I cajoled; I disarmed the Senators with my candor; and then I left them laughing. I knew what I was doing. And the editorial writers recognised what I was doing and let the word out.'

On that first success he steadily expanded, representing himself not only as a saviour in the city's hour of need, but as, quite possibly, the most ardent advocate New York has ever had. By his third term the image of Koch was quite indistinguishable from the slogan 'I Love New York', which he had assiduously cultivated from his first days in City Hall, though it had been extant from the year before he arrived, when the state of New York launched it as a commercial jingle – Albany's helping hand for the ailing metropolis.† The image otherwise was one of a highly capable and deeply self-satisfied civic administrator. It was of a man who

---

* If he were still in Gracie Mansion in 1991, the record would be his. The longest run so far is that of the forty-fifth Mayor, Richard Varick, who was in office from 1789 to 1801.
† Since it was commissioned in 1977 by the state's Department of Commerce, 'I Love New York' (music and lyric by Steve Karmen) has been adopted as the official song of New York state.

liked to be seen as a tough-minded liberal in the grandest traditions of New York, but who looked forward to the general restoration of the death penalty and was contemptuous of those who didn't. It was one of unimpeachable rectitude, though the citizens were beginning to murmur about the number of officials close to His Honor who had been caught in compromising positions, one of them fatally. It was of someone so keen on retaining office that during his third campaign in 1985 he was prepared to spend $5 for every vote that came his way in the primary alone. It was of a Mayor who did not hesitate to abuse a political opponent or critic most fluently, but who was transparently thin-skinned if anything of the sort was dished out to him in return. It was of a civic leader who did not bother to hide his disgust at most things happening in the United Nations, just up the river from his office, and who was quite prepared to lecture national leaders there in a way they were not often spoken to abroad, and most certainly not at home; that is, as man to man. The citizenry, on the whole, liked and applauded Ed Koch for this. Just as, on the whole, it admired his ability to produce a book about his life and times, which became a national bestseller and made him $300,000, and was then transformed into a musical off Broadway, in which he stood to gain a percentage of the box-office takings. Having developed a taste for this sort of thing, he found time to produce a second book with the assistance of the same ghost writer who worked on the first. 'What I had going for me,' he revealed in this further memoir, 'was my personal integrity.'

He also had a sharp and very New York wit. When *Penthouse* magazine published a cartoon depicting him as King Kong, it came as manna from above. 'Haven't looked so good since I was twenty-four,' he told a press conference. Always the one-hundred-and-fifth Mayor was to be seen at his best in repartee. There was a day in 1985 when he went on the stump in Harlem, inspecting brownstones that the city had renovated to provide housing for the homeless. Coming down West 120th Street, at the head of his entourage and the accompanying press, he was intercepted by a woman standing by her gate. She was complaining about the taxes she had to pay on her home, pointing out that right next door were a bunch of religious folks who paid no taxes she'd heard of, on account of them running some sort of shelter for the poor. It was apparently no less than the truth, the Mayor established after a consultation with one of his aides. He pointed this out to the woman. He commiserated with her. He said it was tough. He tried to make her see the neighbour's point of view. And the city's. Then he came out with the clincher. 'What it boils down to is this. You cannot tax God!' He liked the sound, the shape, the taste of that. 'You cannot *tax* God!' Yes, that really was quite neat; so let's have it once more, and it might find its way into print. 'You *cannot tax God!*' And he was on his way again, gurgling and happy as a sandboy.

Later that day he was back in his room at City Hall, with its heavily swagged velvet curtains and its dark wine carpet and its sparkling chandelier, with one of Childe Hassam's dappled cityscapes to offset the portrait of LaGuardia, and with another bronze to complement the figurine on the desk; this one of Romulus and Remus being suckled by the Roman wolf. His Honor was there to receive a courtesy call from the Secretary of Labor in the government of Puerto Rico, a small man who smiled nervously as he stepped across the threshold towards the distinguished personage awaiting him. He had come to offer his respects and was received graciously, though without more warmth than was required by the custom establishing relations between the Mayor of New York and an envoy from the little colony. The one-hundred-and-fifth Mayor is quite a tall man, and he used every inch of it now. No-one who had brought a sense of history into that room, observing the Stars and Stripes beside the mantelpiece, and the lupine bronze on a shelf, and the humble attitude of the visitor, and the lofty demeanour of the host, could have failed to recognise where just such an encounter happened distantly before. It would have been something like this in Britannia or Gallia, when one of the subject chiefs came to negotiate tribute with the Proconsul in the age of Imperial Rome.

ELEVEN

IMPERIAL, BUT POTHOLED

We know nothing of W. Parker Chase except that he lived at one time on East 21st Street and that he had been 'the owner of several companies in which a large number of show girls were employed. In one company alone there were thirty-two chorus girls.' Also, that he compiled and wrote a book celebrating New York in the year 1932. That was a remarkable thing to be even attempting, for there surely couldn't have been much to celebrate in that most awful of all the Depression years. W. Parker Chase would probably have replied that if you believed that, you'd believe anything; and what he published may properly be regarded as one of the most memorable books ever to be published anywhere (his superlative approach can be dangerously infectious). It was a cross between a copiously illustrated directory and a panegyric, concocted by someone infatuated with his subject; and its title, *New York: the Wonder City*, is one of the most restrained statements in its 288 pages.

The author did a lot of his thinking in headlines, so that effusions of capital letters spring up throughout the text, as on one of the first pages:

NEW YORK – synonym for big, great, astonishing, miraculous! NEW YORK – mecca which lures the brightest minds, the most brilliant writers, the most masterful artisans to its gates! NEW YORK – home of the world's greatest captains of industry, the world's most stupendous structures, the world's richest business institutions – veritable center of our country's wealth, culture and achievement! NEW YORK – !!! What visions of magnitude, variety and power the name of New York conjures up for human comprehension. MILLIONS and BILLIONS instead of hundreds and thousands are the figures constituting the basis for calculation nowadays in this wonder city! . . .

He particularised. He tabulated 100 SENSATIONAL TOTALS, including the information that, 'New York's area comprises 202,508 acres – 316 square miles'; that, 'There are over 8,000 licensed "push cart peddlers" in New York'; that, 'New York supports thirty different museums – several of which are the largest and most complete in the entire world.' He assured his readers that 'Not elsewhere will be found such wealth. In fact, the wealth of the world is *centered* in New York. And those who *seek* wealth *come* to New York – they find that the best place to *get* wealth is where wealth *is*.' Moreover, 'Taken all in all, New York is one of the very best governed cities in all the world. It is the most prosperous, and there is no city on the map in which it is *safer to live*, or in which citizens have *better protection* . . . There are countless reasons why living in New York is desirable. A careful perusal of this book is corroborative evidence of this fact.' That came on a page decorated with a photograph of a grim-looking cop brandishing a Tommy gun, above the caption, 'The police have orders to SHOOT TO KILL'.

He reviewed 100 OUTSTANDING FIGURES IN NEW YORK'S GROWTH AND FAME. 'Never in the history of any nation has there ever been shown in one publication a more interesting galaxy of red-blooded *he-men* than will be found in the following pages . . . of the 100 outstanding figures who have so largely contributed in making New York what it is today – *truly*, the wonder city of the world! Nothing *could* prevent New York from attaining its present undisputed supremacy, with 100 such men living within its confines and directing their talents and tremendous activities for the common weal.' He extolled the skyscrapers and other prominent buildings, occasionally coming close to orgasm, as in his description of the Waldorf-Astoria,

TALLEST AND MOST BEAUTIFUL HOTEL IN ALL THE WORLD. 'Nothing has ever approached the magnitude, daring, ingenuity and achievement in hotel construction that is exemplified in the new Waldorf-Astoria just completed. Words convey but a faint impression of the stupendity, the grandeur, and the magnificence of this wonder hotel.'

There was virtually nothing that this effervescent man overlooked in his desire to convey the unparalleled marvels of his native city; certainly not the young ladies who had been in his employ, and who were now gallantly noticed in the following terms; 'New York's chorus girls are a very superior type of young womanhood.' That particular sentiment expresses something which, it has been suggested, is the ultimate attraction of the book as a whole – its innocence. Perhaps only a sublimely innocent person could be so obviously unaware how bizarre such a catalogue of excess would seem to anyone retaining some sense of proportion about the world he inhabits. Another proposition is that the book was a patriotic citizen's sturdy effort to do what he could to restore faith in the metropolis in its most desperate hour. The lately completed Empire State Building, after all, was badly in need of tenants and could well have used the generous publicity it received here. (TRULY – THE WONDER BUILDING OF THE WORLD, 'The greatest office structure ever built by man. Words cannot describe this huge building – it must be *seen*.') But New York, and all that therein is, does seem to attract overblown expressions of affection and approval, in good times and bad. At the height of the boom before the big economic crash, even someone as level-headed as H. L. Mencken was moved to claim that, 'It is the icing on the pie called Christian Civilisation.' It was back on its feet again in 1947 when John Gunther hailed it as 'the incomparable, the brilliant star city of cities, the forty-ninth state, a law unto itself, the Cyclopean paradox, the inferno with no out-of-bounds, the supreme expression of both the miseries and the splendors of contemporary civilisation, the Macedonia of the United States.' The general tone and ambition of *New York: the Wonder City* is perfectly consistent with that most familiar reflex of our own time, undiscriminating hype. The spirit of W. Parker Chase lives on and flourishes exceedingly in New York more than half a century after his book was published.

There is the straightforward commercial variety, as in a leaflet given all visitors to the World Trade Center ('The closest some of us will ever get to heaven') which assures all comers that, 'From over a quarter of a mile up in the sky, New York looks like paradise.' There is the understandable exuberance of Mayor Koch, who also has a vested interest in selling New York as hard as he can, describing it not only as 'unique in the history of human kindness', but plainly and simply as 'a stroke of genius'. That sort of emotion is liable to crop up anywhere, so long as there is a civic leader who is not easily embarrassed by anything he has said. What's extraordinary here is that so many other loyalists refer to New York as if this tremendous city were still horribly insecure, for ever in need of the fulsome compliment and the blatant flattery; when it is, in truth, bursting with self-assurance, one of the cockiest and most truculent places on earth. Norman Mailer has dubbed it 'the greatest city in the world; the most magnificent, most creative, most extraordinary, most just, dazzling, bewildering, and balanced of cities'. William H. Whyte has notified his readers that a decade ago this had become 'the dominant world capital' and that New Yorkers are now 'at the center of the universe'. In the course of one book about the city it is possible to read that, 'New York, like a great novel, transcends geographical boundaries or time. It is a world city, the ultimate marketplace' before one learns that, 'it is the eighth wonder of the world' and later that, 'No other city in the world is as much a national treasure or resource. New York is not only the home of the United Nations, but also the world's center of commerce, communications, finance, fashion, ideas.' In another book the applause is first for the 'Titan of cities', which later becomes 'the permanent capital of the world', and a bit further on 'the greatest city in the Western World', which is modified to 'the greatest city in the New World' before the author settles for 'the greatest city in history's richest and most technologically advanced civilisation'. Someone else writes of 'the cultural capital of the richest and most important nation in the world'; and yet another refers to 'that rich diversity found in only one place; New York City'.

These are all respected voices, and that is quite a billing; one that is accepted, more often than not, by people abroad who have not had the opportunity to check up on the validity of this determined salesmanship. Alas, it doesn't always coincide with the reality of New York. As in the case of the Empire State Building's recent publicity ('the most famous building ever erected by man') some of the claims are a little overdone.

There wasn't too much genius apparent in the centre of the universe when the world's financial capital nearly went bust in 1975. Nor had there been for years before it was clear that disaster was not far away. There were many reasons for the crisis that Mayor Beame was landed with, and one of them was that the city's own work force had risen from 266,000 to 338,000 in a decade. Labour costs had doubled in only five years, largely as a result of increased benefits and pensions on top of the swelling municipal payroll. Bus drivers were being paid for an eleven-hour day in which they worked only eight, having secured a three-hour break to do their own thing in the middle of the shift. Social welfare programmes, launched with all the decency that New York can exhibit more often than any other city in the United States, were becoming wildly expensive: like Aid to Families with Dependent Children, which enlarged by 370 per cent in fifteen years. The budget, in fact, had been allowed to get out of control under Beame's two predecessors. Robert Wagner actually said on one occasion that, 'I do not propose to permit our fiscal problems to set the limits of our commitments to meet the essential needs of the people of the city.' Almost as soon as John Lindsay arrived in City Hall in 1966, New York was hit by the first transit strike in its history, more damaging than any other industrial action it had ever known, when 34,400 workers demanded more money than the city was prepared to offer. Anxious to show his muscles at the outset of his administration, Lindsay walked six miles to work every day, instead of going through the laborious processes of negotiation in smoke-filled rooms that were customary every alternate year. This was a costly piece of bravado, because after twelve days of footslogging wearily in the wake of its virile new Mayor, the populace had had enough and His Honor had to capitulate for a far bigger settlement than might have been the case. In one assessment 'Apart from the $70 million or so price tag, the strike's costs were steep. The city's economy lost millions of dollars in sales and other taxes, and employees sacrificed an estimated 6 million work days. The transit fare rose from 15 cents to 20 cents; future deficits were guaranteed when the transit system lost 2.1 per cent of its riders.' Worse, his defeat was the signal to other unions – most notably the teachers and the policemen – to seek exorbitant deals when their turn came to sit round the table.

Before Lindsay left office in 1973, all manner of stratagems were being employed to balance the books, and few of them were in accordance with conventional accountancy. The figure for the 1970 education bill, for example, was reduced artificially by $25 million on paper by the simple ruse of sending the teachers their last pay cheque of the school year on the first day of the next fiscal year; but the money was still borrowed, the problem being solved again twelve months later in exactly the same fashion, by rolling over debts which, of course, the interest rates inflated more and more each time the trick was performed. Such manipulations continued unabated, as one Mayor succeeded the other. The billing of water charges and sewer rates was juggled so that in one twelve-month period the city was collecting for eighteen months; and by some act of legerdemain visible at the time only to Abraham Beame and his closest officials, the municipal payroll was met on the basis of a year containing 364 days! The city even pretended, in order to give an impression of solvency, that it was collecting real-estate taxes $408.3 million greater than was actually the case, by including in its budget properties that never had been and never would be taxed. New York was becoming as uncontrolled in its indebtedness as the junkie who needs a bigger and bigger fix.

By the fall of 1974, the bankers gave warning that unless something drastic was done, municipal bonds would be regarded as worthless and all trading in them would cease. One banker put it to another like this in a memorandum: 'The market for New York City obligations is no longer viable. Concern about the city's affairs has paralysed the market and dealers have heavy inventories of New York City's securities which cannot be sold except at severe losses.' So Mayor Beame laid off municipal workers, the first time such an action has been taken since the Depression. He ordered that all libraries and night-schools should drastically reduce their services. Eight firehouses were closed down. The authorities started planning to issue their workers with scrip instead of pay cheques. They also drew up a list of jobs that might be abolished altogether if the worse came to the worst; and it was decided that the first people to be sacked *en masse* would be the reservoir workers. By this time even the unions had the wind up, and were co-operating to the extent of agreeing to wage freezes and other concessions; which was something else that hadn't happened in New York for many a day. None of this was deemed sufficient by the men holding the purse strings, the bankers and other creditors of the City of New York. The fact was that, when 1975 dawned, New York was spending $12.8 billion with an income of only $10.9 billion, and that it was in debt to the tune of $2 billion. It was as simple, as bleak, as Micawberish as that.

By this time, New York state was deeply involved in the metropolitan fiscal crisis and, to save the city from bankruptcy, Governor Hugh Carey ladled $400 million from the coffers in Albany to those in Manhattan. He also interceded on the city's behalf with President Ford in Washington, in the hope that a federal loan of $1 billion could be extracted to tide New York over the next three months, after which some genuine real-estate taxes would fall due. The word came from the White House that there was nothing doing. So in June the Governor established a Municipal Assistance Corporation to act as watchdog over the big spenders in City Hall, and to give any potential investor out there some small surge of confidence in the management. MAC advertised three bond sales, each amounting to $1 billion: it just about made the figure with the first one, was left with egg on its face in the second, and cancelled the third in humiliation. Albany lent more money, and began to think that the only way of really restoring confidence, might be to get rid of Abe Beame, but held its fire for the moment.* For his part, the Mayor laid off yet more workers, 19,000 of them one day in July. It was apparently having little effect on the outcome now looming dead ahead: which eventually boiled down to this. If, by three o'clock on the afternoon of October 17, 1975, New York had not mustered $449 million in order (a) to pay off bondholders (b) to repay a state loan and (c) to meet an imminent payroll, it would effectively be declared bankrupt. No-one was quite sure what would then occur in the metropolis, because no city had been in such a predicament before. The Chairman of MAC, the investment banker, Felix Rohatyn, said he thought the civic bankruptcy would be like 'stepping into a tepid bath and slashing your wrists. You might not feel yourself dying, but that's what would happen.' The razor was poised to make the first incision: a State Supreme Court order had already been obtained in readiness, and this would allow New York to default on the payment of notes that were due. Meanwhile, an extraordinary lobby was being conducted in Washington to save the city from its own incompetence, and among those who were now speaking up on its behalf were President Giscard d'Estaing of France and Chancellor Helmut Schmidt of West Germany. Still President Ford refused to be moved; except to come down to New York and say so to its face. On October 29 he addressed the National Press Club there and said his piece loud and clear: 'I can tell you, and tell you now, that I am prepared to veto any bill that has as its purpose a federal bailout of New York City to prevent a default.' It was a gift to the headline writer composing the front page of next morning's tabloid *Daily News*, and he received it with open arms. FORD TO CITY: DROP DEAD thus entered the folklore of journalism, and effectively scuppered Gerald Ford's chances of retaining the Presidency in the election of 1976; or so, in the light of subsequent hostility to him throughout the state of New York, he himself always afterwards believed.

Deliverance, in fact, had come secretly the night before the

* The sacrificial lamb would eventually be Deputy Mayor James A. Cavanagh.

deadline for preventing bankruptcy. MAC had been trying to persuade the United Federation of Teachers to invest $149 million of pension-fund money in the corporation's bonds, but the union's president was unenthusiastic. So the Mayor called the head of the Uniformed Sanitationmen's Association, reminded him that they were old friends, and obtained a promise that if the teachers wouldn't oblige, the garbage workers would pull the city out of the mire. Abraham Beame was more or less sidetracked after that, as the Governor and the MAC chairman between them prepared a complicated fiscal programme involving new taxes, a moratorium on the repayment of short-term debt principal, large pension fund commitments to purchase MAC securities, and other expedients. Thus encouraged, Washington at last came up with a short-term loan of $2.3 billion, after being warned by Rohatyn that if New York didn't get out of this scrape, the economy of the entire western world might well collapse, and after being told by George Ball (with all the authority that a former Under-Secretary of State could summon) that if New York wasn't given the necessary assistance, it could be chalked up as a big win to Moscow. The men of money needed no greater spur than that. In the spring of 1976, at a convention of bankers in Palm Springs, Florida, David Rockefeller of Chase Manhattan, and Walter Wriston of Citibank, backed up by the president of the First National City Bank and the chairman of the Manufacturers' Hanover Trust, succeeded in convincing their colleagues that the future of capitalism itself was on the line. In one evening $600 million in New York state bonds were sold, and light at last began to glimmer at the end of the tunnel for the apprehensive people in City Hall. The metropolis would lurch from one deficit to another for some time to come, but at least a sense of reality had been restored.*

Not that this was to be of much comfort to those citizens in the

---

*As late as November 1977, Felix Rohatyn, in a speech at the Union League Club, was still pessimistic enough to say that, 'A Republican president told this city to drop dead. A Democratic president, unless he acts promptly, will be at the funeral.'

wreckage of the salvage operation. The great fiscal crisis had some curious side effects, including the loss of the New York Jets football team, which left town for New Jersey because the changing rooms at Shea Stadium were no longer maintained in a manner to which the footballers thought they should be accustomed. Firefighters on Staten Island had to get themselves to outbreaks by calling dial-a-cabs, because their own vehicles were often unavailable in the new economies. Even more seriously, the days of free tuition at the City University, one of this community's greatest glories, were over and in consequence the enrolments dropped by 70,000 within three years. In the municipal hospitals there were 40,000 fewer beds, and in the city's schools the average size of a class rose from twenty to twenty-five. There was considerable damage to people's livelihoods. Between 1975 and 1978 more than 85,000 municipal jobs were lost, among them 8,000 police, 2,500 firemen, 14,500 people in the schools. But the ones who suffered most of all were the poorest citizens of New York, whose basic welfare allowance was to be frozen for seven full inflationary years, and who were joined by increasing numbers every year. In 1975, some 15 per cent of New Yorkers dwelt below that officially-determined poverty level. By 1985, they had become 23.4 per cent.

A notorious casualty of the crisis was the subway, once the finest system in the world. It had been in decline for some years, but the process accelerated after 1975 until it became, quite possibly, the most ramshackle system of all. Older subways than New York's were being systematically improved. The French modernised and automated four lines of the Paris Metro and installed a new twenty-five mile express line between 1963 and 1981, and the British over approximately the same period put in two new lines and refurbished a third on the London Underground. In 1951 New York had decided to spend $500 million on a new line along Second Avenue, and in the next twenty years a lot of the necessary trenching was dug all the way from the Lower East Side up to East Harlem. In the middle of the fiscal crisis it was decided that the Second Avenue line must be abandoned, and the trenches were ignominiously filled in again. Several cities in North America, meanwhile, had acquired much better systems than New York, including Atlanta,

Montreal, Toronto, San Francisco and Washington – the last two even running trains with carpets on the floor. In New York they had now become accustomed to trains which broke down between stations, trains in which the heating or the air-conditioning didn't work so that they froze in winter and all but melted in summer, trains which stopped interminably at stations because the doors wouldn't open or because they wouldn't shut, trains which felt as if they might fall to bits, and in some cases did, trains which sounded, smelt and looked disgusting, traversing stations which were in much the same state. By 1984 it was solemnly noted that 3,264 trains on the New York subway were being cancelled every month, because they were too clapped out to be let loose, and the resources were not available to repair them. Where other people's subways as a matter of course were becoming fully automated, for speed, efficiency, comfort and safety, New York's was still running on primitive technology, the driver having to do something to stop his train and open its doors, sometimes even having to guess the speed he was making as he approached a potentially dangerous curve in the line. Between 1955 and 1961, New York had spent each year an average of $42 per head of population on the subway, but by 1980 the figure had fallen to $28. In Paris they were spending the equivalent of $70, and even provincial Lille was managing $40. New Yorkers, at the same time, were not doing all that they might have done to help out. It was estimated that they were costing the Transit Authority between $30 million and $50 million a year in unpaid fares.*

An attempt had been made to improve the service by buying new subway carriages which were more comfortable to ride in, better illuminated and equipped with a warning 'ding-dong' sound as the doors were about to close. But they had to be abandoned after a thousand had been purchased, when it was discovered that their electrical systems were liable to short-circuit and start fires even when a train was in the sidings overnight, while at the same time dangerous cracks began to appear in the wheel assemblies. This was not the only occasion New York was badly let down

* While the city could find no more than $28 per person for the subway system, the citizens themselves were spending $225 per head of population on their cars – and $380 in the immediate hinterland of New York.

by a manufacturer from some other part of the United States. In 1979 the city bought 837 buses – the Grumman Flxible – from a company in Ohio, and these were delivered the following year. Almost at once they began to disintegrate, with cracks in their frames, 'and when one bus with a full passenger load screeched to a halt in Queens when the frame split open and the body came to rest on the gas tank, all the Grumman buses were pulled out of service.'

Not that New York can afford to be too critical of failures elsewhere, when its own record of craftsmanship has often left something to be desired. This is the city, after all, which managed to sink the world's largest passenger liner at a pier on the Hudson River by sheer incompetence. In 1943, the French Line's crack trans-Atlantic vessel *Normandie* was being refitted for service as a troopship, when a welder's torch accidentally started a blaze. The Fire Department soon had its men all over her, but unfortunately they decided to use hosepipes on the flames instead of cutting off the oxygen supply, with the result that the great liner rolled over under the weight of water and went onto the scrapheap in Brooklyn instead of on her next voyage. Another fiasco on the same stretch of river followed another fire four years later, which destroyed the Grace Line's Pier 57. By 1947 it was becoming apparent that the steamship's supremacy in conveying people across the Atlantic might not be maintained much longer in the face of mounting competition from airlines. Nevertheless, the city of New York, which leased the pier to the shipping company, decided to construct a replacement of pre-stressed concrete, and this involved much expertise, much effort, and a lot of money. It was a splendid thing when finished, but by then the shipping company had decided that the trans-Atlantic trade was no longer big enough to warrant a renewal of the old lease; and an embarrassed city has had to make the best of its expensive pier ever since as a not-very-convenient parking lot. It may take some comfort from the number of gaffes that occur in purely private enterprises here. The past few years in New York have not only seen a bank unable to remember what on earth it had done with municipal bonds worth $397 million, but a celebrated firm of publishers having to destroy quantities of books in its warehouse simply to gain access to other books that had been stored there.

No visitor, attracted to this city in the first place by the superlative self-image New York generally projects far and wide, can ever fail to be startled by the crumbling condition of the average metropolitan street. Even stretches of Fifth Avenue and other parts of midtown Manhattan will often be so dilapidated that they would disgrace many a city in the Third World. Sidewalk paving is so uneven that not to look where you are stepping is to trip up and go full length before long. Bits of metal, ominously jagged, project several inches above the ground, where signposts have been amputated and ankles can now be dangerously slashed. The roads are usually in such bad repair that to be driven through Manhattan in the small hours, when you get an uninterrupted run over a long distance, is to know what a bad sailor must feel like in a small boat on a choppy day down New York Harbor. Often enough, it seems, repairs have been needed on such an unacceptable scale that nothing has been done but to place enormous and thick metal plates across the cavity or subsidence, and these are often there months or even years after they were first laid down. So notorious are the cavities of this city that there is a Big Apple Pothole and Sidewalk Protection Corporation, an enterprising outfit which pursues claims for damages which aggrieved citizens may make against the relevant authorities. Never having come across anything quite like the normal New York pothole before, the Jaguar motor car company once took plaster casts of some of them, so that these could be reproduced on its test-track in Britain, in order to give the famous suspensions the most gruelling ride they were likely to encounter either at home or abroad. This is not the worst hazard a driver may face round here. More than once in recent years, a road has simply given way under the weight of a heavy truck, which has crashed through the decking of an overpass or other elevated stretch. When a Mercedes fell through the East River Drive at 39th Street, Mayor Koch was asked what he made of it, and got in one of his more appealing quips. 'Typical New York pothole,' he said.

Another phenomenon which quickly impresses every visitor is the steam rising from the surface of the road at intervals, from one end of Manhattan to the other. Sometimes it drifts up gently but persistently in mysterious wisps which suggest some alchemy in the city's depths, but at other times boiling geysers of vapour gust out of the ground, as if this volcanic metropolis were at last about to blow its top. Like every other large city, New York is riddled with a variety of subterranean services, and Manhattan is especially penetrated with tunnels and runnels and channels and pipes – including a network of pneumatic tubes, no longer used, through which the mail was once blown, from one post office to another. Nothing that works down there these days is much more important than the pipes (fifty miles of them) that carry the steam for the central heating of many Manhattan buildings. Because much of this ironmongery is now some distance past its best, it permanently leaks, and the steam comes up through any fissure in the road. More dangerously, manhole covers are liable to be blown into the air here, as gases build up explosively. And it is wholly in the wayward character of this city that, although this is something that happens at least a couple of times every month, and has been happening for many years, New York has not yet made up its mind about the precise reason for these bombardments, and certainly no-one is accepting responsibility. Some see a culprit in the utility company responsible for many of the manholes, and the mishmash of electrical wiring they conceal; but from the company the buck is passed to the city's Sanitation Department, which spreads rock salt on the streets every winter; and this, it's said by the electricians, drips through to the ducts below and corrodes the plastic coating on our wires, producing the gas that finally ignites spectacularly. Meanwhile, hot-dog vendors are occasionally burned on the streets of New York as the ground erupts beside their stalls, and several parked cars have been left the worse for wear – though no-one has yet been decapitated by a flying manhole cover weighing all of 300 pounds.

It is dilapidations of this order, and other failings unacknowledged in the ballyhoo of the publicists, that lead New York's *aficionados* to take a gloomy view of what may lie ahead. When they contemplate the crumbling structures above ground and the rattletrap systems below it, when there is yet another back-up of traffic on the highways in and out of Manhattan, when they remember that raw sewage from the whole of the West Side flows straight into the Hudson River in the penultimate decade of the twentieth century, when they hear of yet more colossal misman- agement in the place which often comes close to bursting with pride in its own smartness and expertise, when the city has escaped by the narrowest margin a major disaster: when the friends of New York recollect these things, they wonder what might be in store for the citizens if New York continues to conduct itself like that. A very thoughtful European well over half a century ago suggested a progression in the development of all great cities if they weren't careful. The metropolis, in his view, became megalopolis, puffed up with its own importance (he was doubtless thinking of London at the height of its imperial vanity) before degenerating into parasito- polis, whose citizens thieved and sponged off each other. Ultimate- ly, thought Sir Patrick Geddes, there was pathopolis, 'the city that ceases effectively to function'. Is this what lies at the end of the road for New York, a condition that might have been reached already if there hadn't been that breathtaking survival on the very edge of bankruptcy? Is the adored metropolis destined to evolve into pathopolis? Another voice has spoken recently of a vivid model 10,000 miles to the east. 'I am fascinated by Calcutta,' said Paul Theroux in 1985. 'It is one of the cities of the world that I associate with the future. This is how New York City could look, I think, after a terrible disaster – or simply in the fullness of time.'

As it happens, New York had a short but very sharp taste of the ultimate urban breakdown a decade before its fiscal crisis, when it was riding high and confidently during a period of expansion and prosperity. It suffered a power failure, which was subsequently blamed by a federal investigating commission on 'a combination of freak technical failures and bad judgement'. The culprit in this instance had no-one else to pass the buck to. It was the Consolidated Edison Company, which supplies most of the city with its electricity and gas, and is therefore responsible for about 60,000 of those occasionally airborne manhole covers in New York. This massive private utility is the result of many mergers over the years, especially in the wake of the Depression, but it traces its most notable pedigree back to the remarkable Thomas Alva Edison, 'The Man of a Thousand Ideas', who either

invented or significantly improved someone else's invention of the
kinetoscope (moving pictures), the phonograph (sound recording), the telephone, the stock market ticker, the voting machine,
the electric light and the electric chair. He took out more than a
thousand patents in his working lifetime, hence his cognomen.
It was he who set up the city's first power station, just off
Wall Street, in 1882 and, by the time he died in 1931, a great
conglomerate was beginning to take shape which, to an extent
no-one then realised, would before long hold the city in thrall.
Con Ed is not much liked by New Yorkers, principally because it
charges so much more for its energy than any other company in
the United States.* It also supplies too many power failures and
power reductions to please people who believe in getting value
for their hard-earned dollars. These interruptions to the normal
service come at intervals, though there has been nothing since
to match the Great Blackout of November 9, 1965.

This was caused, in the first place, by the failure of a relay device
in Queenston, Ontario, and in the next few minutes darkness
spread from Canada down through most of New England into
New York state, across 80,000 square miles with some thirty
million people involved. When the Federal Power Commission
studied what had happened that day, it concluded that a total
blackout could have been avoided if Con Ed had been equipped
with automatic load-shedding devices that would selectively cut off
any area in its network, if it had possessed auxiliary generators for
reserve power, or even if the engineer at the company's control
centre on the West Side had been given any instructions about
cutting off systems that had already blacked out; but the New
York conglomerate lacked automatic gear that was standard in
other companies, its reserve power could only be cranked up
slowly on steam turbines, and the poor engineer, with only ten

---

* A recent survey found that the average annual electricity bill throughout
the United States, was $665 for 750 kilowatt-hours per month. Con Ed of
New York charged $1,318, followed by San Diego Gas and Electric ($1,117)
and Long Island Lighting ($984). Some cities wouldn't expect to pay as much
as New Yorkers in five years or more. The comparable rate for Seattle was
$221, for Portland (Oregon) $324, for Sacramento $335.

minutes in which to avert catastrophe, had no clear idea how best to employ them.

It couldn't have happened at a worse time in New York. Darkness had fallen that Tuesday night and it was 5.27 p.m. when the power went. Office workers throughout Manhattan were clearing their desks before ending work for the day, or they were already on their way out of the skyscrapers, or down in the streets, heading for the buses, the subways and the commuter trains. The traffic was beginning to surge up and down the avenues, nose to tail, impatient to get home, making its way through the familiarly brilliant illumination. Quite suddenly, blackness in every building, and only headlights in the streets. A Vanguard of Air Canada, flying into Kennedy from Toronto, banked just south of Coney Island, where its captain, completing his turn for the run in, expected to see the usual pattern of landing lights ahead, three minutes from touchdown: but they had vanished. A TWA flight from Cleveland was right behind him, and next in line was one of Lufthansa's big Boeings at the end of its seven-hour drag from Frankfurt. Many others were in the stack, circling the city until air traffic control called them in. Luckily, November 9 was perfect for flying, with excellent visibility. The planes overshot Kennedy and flew on either to Newark or even farther, as far as Philadelphia. A persistent mockery of New York this night would be that, throughout the metropolitan darkness, the lights could be seen glittering across the Hudson, along the Palisades, where power was supplied not by Con Ed, but by the better equipped Public Service Corporation of New Jersey. Staten Island, too, was not beholden to Con Ed, and twinkled brightly without a break. But for most of New York, the ordeal was to continue until the dawn.

People at first were irritated when the power cut off, thinking it just another cock-up that would soon be rectified. When the lights didn't go back on, they were bewildered, and some began to think they were the victims of communist sabotage, though Sol Berkowitz, who was caught in his men's neckwear shop on Madison Avenue, later confided opaquely that, 'I thought there must be some trouble out in the Pacific, but I didn't breathe a word. I didn't want to stir up panic.' He was one of those who eventually made their way to one of the National Guard armouries that Governor Rockefeller ordered to be thrown open as refuges, when eight o'clock came and it was apparent that New York had a major emergency on its hands. The luckiest people were those actually on the streets when the electricity failed. It was a chilly but fine and starry night, in which a full moon glowed. Some who lived in Manhattan and decided to walk home, discovered for the first time in their lives how very beautiful a clear sky can be when it isn't outfaced by a great city's customary nocturnal glow. Others, who lived in the distant boroughs or even farther afield, started the evening in long queues at every phone booth, waiting half an hour or more to call home and tell them what was happening in the city; only to hear that it was much the same out there. After a while, housewives from Queens and elsewhere began to drive over the bridges in their thousands, in order to pick up stranded husbands and ferry them back.

Many took refuge where they could. Hundreds were to spend the night in the public rooms of the Sheraton-Atlantic Hotel, and a lot of non-residents sat on rugs in the candlelit lobby of the Waldorf-Astoria. St Patrick's Cathedral threw open its doors to all comers, broached every case of votive candles it possessed, and when its refugees needed the lavatory, directed them to the New Weston Hotel, which had been helping incontinent worshippers for eighty years or more. Hordes made for Grand Central Station, where the police rigged arc lights to produce the only properly illuminated building in midtown after the plug was pulled. In the armouries the National Guard also had emergency gear working, and as the numbers began to mount in one of these shelters, the soldiery were sent out to scour the district's restaurants and cafés for food, but these had given up and closed. Captain Edward McGrath, of the 42nd (Rainbow) Regiment, told a reporter who dropped by that his refugees were getting cross: 'They keep snapping at the men. They keep asking when they are going to be fed.' Well, it was rising midnight, and it had been a long time since lunch. Eventually the Red Cross turned up trumps, with hot coffee and sandwiches. Best off were those New Yorkers who had been clever enough to be stuck in some of the big stores when the blackout began. All the shoppers in Macy's were given an impromptu dinner in the staff canteen. At Altman's, 500 were invited to take refreshments in the delicatessen. Any of Bloomingdale's customers who were still on the premises next morning were given breakfast on the house. One of them had passed a comfortable night on a sofa with a $800 price tag.

For some it was a very frightening time. It was estimated later that about 800,000 citizens were trapped in trains above and below ground when these suddenly came to a standstill in the pitch black silence. Some people on the Flushing line of the subway between Grand Central and the Fifth Avenue stop, seriously thought that New York was under enemy attack. Seventeen hundred commuters aboard four trains which were stuck on the Williamsburg Bridge decided after a while that no help was coming, so they climbed out of the carriages and edged their way slowly along the catwalks high above the East River till they reached solid ground; and it was five hours after the breakdown before all of them were there. In fact, as soon as it was realised how bad the breakdown was, help was organised by the Transit Authority, the police and the National Guard. Between them they despatched hundreds of men into the tunnels networking New York, looking for stranded trains. They found passengers in varying states of anxiety, but almost all of them bearing up remarkably well, largely because at least somebody in every carriage was able to lift morale if only by telling endless stories in the dark. A tenor on an IRT train under Lexington Avenue gave an impromptu recital, as did a man with a harmonica on the BMT beneath Brooklyn. Commuters who found themselves in an IND train jammed below Eighth Avenue, were given a treat by a Scotsman who happened to be passing through New York with his bagpipes under his arm.

The only people whose plight was even worse than that of those caught between stations in the subway, were those office workers who were in elevators between floors when the juice ran out. In the first hour of the catastrophe, 219 such emergencies were reported. Almost all the big skyscrapers had at least one load of people who needed rescuing, and the worst hit was the Empire State Building, where thirteen elevators with ninety-six people aboard got stuck. In some cases it proved possible, with the assistance of a ladder, to escape through the hatch in the elevator's ceiling, when a floor landing was quite near. Mostly, though, the tightly packed passengers had to stay put until a hole could be smashed in the wall of the lift shaft. One load got caught between the twenty-fourth and twenty-fifth floors, and were not released until ten forty-five that night, while another car in an adjacent shaft was stuck for another hour after that. In the Pan Am Building, where six of the elevators were left dangling between floors, the last passengers were not rescued until half past midnight – seven hours after the system had gone dead. As on the subway, these people managed to pass that claustrophobic time without cracking up. They told stories and played word games, and one group, scrunched up together in the Empire State Building, organised a Blackout Club with the most time-consuming first agenda that could possibly be devised. Tempers remained steady, once people began to get the hang of the thing: though one tense fellow was told quite sharply that, no, he could *not* smoke that goddam cigar in there.

Some restaurants managed to function that night, with storm lanterns and kerosene stoves, and with instantly inflated prices in some cases. Other entertainments were obviously off. At Madison Square Garden, the scheduled game of basketball between the Knickerbockers and the St Louis Hawks was cancelled. Not one theatre opened, and some solved the problem of the missing performance by playing the following Sunday instead. But people who had bought tickets at the Imperial Theatre for *Fiddler on the Roof* found that they wouldn't be seeing the musical until sometime in March at the earliest. One man who could have wished that his own particular show hadn't gone on in spite of everything was Michael Meyerson, an oil stock promoter, who was being tried that day at the Court House in Foley Square for income tax evasions of $248,000. Just eighteen minutes before the electricity cut out, the twelve jurymen had started to consider the evidence laid before them, and they decided to go on by candlelight and torch. At five o'clock the next morning – a little tetchily, perhaps – they reached their verdict, which was to convict.

By then, Coney Island, Brooklyn and Queens were illuminated again, partly as a result of naval help; for the destroyer *Bristol*, with only one-third of its crew aboard, had sailed out of Brooklyn Navy

Yard in the darkness to moor off Con Ed's substation in Astoria and feed power into the plant there from its own generators. The current didn't come back to Manhattan, the Bronx and Westchester County until breakfast time, and around Times Square and the adjacent length of Broadway, the theatres and other big users of electricity for advertising displays didn't have it restored until the middle of the afternoon. That was when most New Yorkers who had bothered to turn up for work the morning after the hectic night before, were told to get off home and catch up on their sleep. Some had done that anyway, wherever they had found themselves at the height of the blackout, like the lady who spent a congenial night in the furniture department of Bloomingdale's. As a precaution therefore, the Transit Authority sent inspectors through every inch of the subway system before the current was switched on again, to make sure that no-one was slumbering down there – or even trying to find a way out of it still.

Apart from discovering how completely and in some ways how shockingly their city could be disrupted by a relatively simple breakdown of machinery, New Yorkers were left to contemplate a certain material cost of the Great Blackout. Someone reckoned that in hard cash the loss and damage to businesses amounted to $100 million – and before any claims could be submitted, an insurance spokesman quickly explained that 'only a minuscule amount' of such a sum would be covered by existing policies. The city's newspapers failed to appear that Wednesday morning and neither they nor the television companies recovered their lost advertising and other revenues. Another loss was in food which was spoilt when freezers and refrigerators failed, one restaurant chain claiming that $200,000 worth of its ice cream had melted that Tuesday night. But some people profited in those twelve hours and more of darkness, besides the restaurants and bars that kept going. On 42nd Street, flashlights were being sold for $3 apiece, candles for $1, many times more than could normally be charged for either. Cab drivers were demanding whatever they thought they could extract, and to hell with what the meter said. It cost fifty bucks if you had to get from Manhattan to Port Washington on Long Island that night.

Astonishingly, only two people died because of what happened.

A retired detective in the Bronx fell down three flights of stairs and cracked his head fatally against a radiator; and a resident of the Sheraton-Atlantic Hotel had a heart attack after climbing ten floors up to his room. Even before midnight there had been 300 collisions on the streets of the city, because the traffic lights weren't working any more; but none had produced serious injury. In other ways, too, New York had fared much better than it might have expected to. Though there were more fires than usual, and more false alarms, and though the engines sometimes couldn't obtain water because pumps had stopped, no disaster befell as a result. Most gratifying was the reduced criminality of the city that night. A dozen stores were looted, and sixty-five people were arrested for burglary, larceny and kindred crimes, but normally the police would have reckoned on 380 citizens getting on the windy side of the law in the same period as that of the emergency. It would be much, much worse than this when the next huge breakdown in Con Ed's services occurred, in 1977. Then, the city's nastier instincts would be uppermost.

But New York came out of its 1965 crisis handsomely and well. It was, in its way, a passage of arms for a people who had never been bombed like so many others, never known an enemy's armour pounding at the city gates. They demonstrated to themselves, and to anyone else who might be paying attention, that they, too, could take it when the going was tough, just like the Londoners, the Parisians, the Berliners, the Muscovites. They handled themselves coolly and with aplomb: there was no panic in the streets that night. There was, instead, some great good humour in this short but not trifling adversity. The best of it may have been heard high above the ground, where those people were left suspended in elevators at the Empire State Building. One carload had been there for several hours before the rescuers smashed a hole in the wall of the shaft, which enabled them to reach the passengers. A firefighter, mindful of priorities, called out to them then, 'First of all, are there any pregnant women in this car?'

Smack on cue, a voice replied from the darkness inside, 'Don't be silly, we've hardly even met!'

TWELVE

IT'S A HELLUVA TOWN

There are times when New York, for all its preening arrogance, can feel quite ill at ease with what it has made of itself. It glories in its achievements and in its primacy, and it intends to stay right where it is, on top of the pile; but it does not much care to be reminded of what that amounts to when all the special pleading and all the obfuscation is done. This is no more than the metropolitan version of a national embarrassment when it is true, as a contributor to the *New York Times* has pointed out, that, 'there are two things America is supposed not to have: an empire and a ruling class'. The United States gladly accepts its role as a superpower and would not be anything else, but it is loath to acknowledge that a superpower (of whichever brand) is merely a deodorised imperialist – and that sometimes it smells as powerfully as anything of the kind that went before. The ruling class in this polity, like most others in history anywhere, is that small segment of society which controls the bulk of the wealth and thus manipulates power; and while the wealth is here spread the length and breadth of the republic, most of the control is exercised in New York.

Nor is this a recent phenomenon. Half a century ago, one of those eloquently shrewd people who were banded together by the Roosevelt administration into the Federal Writers Project, noted that because the money and the power had long been here, because national policies were created by that money and power, New York had for years been virtually the capital

of the United States. In one of the most crushing comments
that can ever have been made about the anointed capital of any
nation, or about the politicians who legislate there, he dismissed
Washington as 'merely the loudspeaker through which New York
announced itself'. That is not something that could possibly have
been said at the same time of some comparable pairings that
spring to mind – London and Manchester, Paris and Marseilles,
Rome and Naples, Berlin and Frankfurt, Moscow and Leningrad,
for example. In our own time, with the exceptions of Australia,
Brazil, Canada, Switzerland and Turkey, there may not be
another country in which the capital city is consistently upstaged
by some place which technically belongs in the provinces. As the
FWP writer also remarked, there have been moments when
New York has turned humbly and gratefully to Washington for
whatever succour the White House and Congress might afford
(he mentioned 1932, and 1975 was just such another occasion).
But by and large, year in and year out, New York is where the
pace is set and where the memorable tunes are played, where
the imperial grandeur is most consciously on show, where the
citizens can be most patronising, and where the rest of the
world makes for first, to do homage and to be impressed. A
visiting Englishman, strolling amid the mighty throng on Fifth
Avenue, may reflect that it must have been quite like this for
an Indian, in London from Calcutta or Bombay, when he found
himself ambling along Piccadilly just before the First World War.

   Washington, possibly fortified by the knowledge that it can,
after all, make life quite difficult for New York if it really sets
its mind to it, keeps its own counsel about the insult implicit in
the relationship. Not so other Americans, who have been stung
too often by New York's high opinion of itself, whether this has
been expressed in the flatulent boasts of a Mayor Koch, by
way of a large oil painting entitled *Capital City of the World*,
or through yet another wisecrack by a Groucho Marx ('When
it's 9.30 in New York, it's 1937 in Los Angeles'). Modesty is
not among the virtues New York has ever seen much point in
cultivating, and when some achiever here tries it in public, the
result can sound excruciatingly false. The programme for one of
the great musicals contained a studied portrait of the impresario,

which appeared above the simple caption: '*42nd Street* is David Merrick's 84th Broadway production. He has enjoyed a degree of success in the theater.'

From time to time the authentic provincials hit back. 'The tradition of hating New York started long before it began asking the rest of us to pay its bills, while condescendingly viewing us as amusing rustics.' That was a disgruntled columnist in Chicago, not long after the great fiscal crisis had passed its peak. New York's more sensitive inhabitants are perpetually braced for sallies like that, well knowing, as their finest writer on baseball has observed, that, 'there is nothing that unites America more swiftly or happily than bad news in Gotham or a losing New York team'.* They accept this as the way of their world, *noblesse oblige*, and they have their own way of dealing with it, of putting the whingers in their place. There is, for example, the metropolitan response to a new taste for evaluating the cities of the United States and listing them in a league table, as if they were in a popularity contest: as, indeed, they are, for the *Places Rated Almanac* in which this information seems destined to appear every four years, claims that it has been devised to help Americans decide whereabouts in the country they might get the most out of life, given that each has a distinctly individual set of needs and preferences. Various criteria are applied in making the assessments – crime rates and health care, housing conditions and transportation, economics and education, the arts and recreation, what the weather is like, even the natural hazards if there are any. It is a very American approach to a business known as living, converting even what some may think intangible into facts and figures, which can be added and subtracted and adduced into a measurable final score that admits no possibility of dispute, provided the basic premise is accepted by everyone. When the 1985 assessment was made and the winner was announced, the *New York Times*,

* It was Washington Irving who first referred to New York as Gotham, in a flippant allusion to a village of that name in Nottinghamshire, England. The proverbial Three Wise Men of Gotham in the Middle Ages were not wise at all, but distinctly foolish.

torn between its desire to maintain a reputation for balanced journalism, and its manifestly parochial pride, allotted a full column to the story, but sank this at the bottom of an inside page, under the headline, 'Pittsburgh Bemused at No 1 Ranking'.

It must not be supposed that New Yorkers are uncritical of their city. No people can be more savagely vocal when things, in their view, go seriously amiss, as Mayor Lindsay discovered when white mobs demonstrated against his wholly benign attempt to introduce a public-housing programme for Forest Hills. Just like the inhabitants of any great city, New Yorkers will put up with a great deal of what others might think intolerable – such as the preposterous struggle to get from A to B, which no provincials anywhere would countenance for a moment – but they will bellyache loudly if their metropolitan expectations are not met; and do, whenever the garbage isn't collected regularly in the steaming summers the city experiences. Ask any New Yorker how he or she thinks things might be improved in the Big Apple, and there won't be much pause for reflection; for it is quite possible that these citizens think more often and more keenly than most about what they perceive to be the civic failings, and are therefore primed with their answers the moment the question is put. During the 1985 mayoral campaign, a number were asked to state publicly their grievances, to give the candidates a clearer idea of what the voters really wanted of them. A magazine editor was so dismayed by everything in sight that he appeared to be advocating nothing less than a spiritual revolution on all sides. A lawyer more specifically called for a more effective way of preventing the drug traffic, and a television commentator wanted the prohibition of trucks along Fifth Avenue to be enforced. A civil rights worker's request was simply for more public toilets, especially in the subway, and a law professor wanted the road signs around New York made more intelligible. A magazine writer was impatient for more reasonable housing and fewer office blocks, and an educationist would have been satisfied if New York's streets were kept cleaner. A professional baseball pitcher wanted the roads made safer by raising the drinking age to twenty-one, traffic congestion eliminated, and a new stadium built so that two football teams situated in New Jersey might play in New York, whose name they bear. An engineer with the Transit Authority urged the city to consult its own employees more before making big decisions, instead of hiring consultants to offer expensive advice.

London and Paris, Rome and Tokyo, might very well have produced a similar mixture of serious and petty complaints; just as any of these cities can be accused of overweening pride by their provincials, with varying degrees of justification. Like New York, too, they are complicated organisms full of ambiguities and inconsistencies, with their darknesses and their inspirations, their failures and incomprehensions, as well as those priceless moments when they surpass themselves to the astonishment of their own people – and everybody else's. It is possible to say of other cities besides New York, that here is a place 'highly diverse, incredibly complex, maddeningly contradictory': but none in the Western world, at any rate, really matches it in any of those respects.

The contradictions are probably more difficult than anything else for the nodding acquaintance to understand and explain to his own satisfaction. It is still, for example, true for many citizens, as it was when Fiorello LaGuardia noted it, that, 'Too often life in New York is merely a squalid succession of days': but it is also true that, with money jingling in your purse, New York is incomparably seductive, for it will lavishly satisfy your every whim, however demanding, however singular. New York was where James Joyce's *Ulysses* first saw the light of day, when everywhere else there was a failure of nerve, perception or generosity, possibly all three;* but it was also where the critics were lukewarm about *Moby Dick* and where Theodore Dreiser's publisher tried to cancel his contract for *Sister Carrie*, which the New York booksellers refused to handle. Other contradictions were detected in the very structure and integument of the city by Le Corbusier, who came to the conclusion that, 'A hundred times I have thought New York is a catastrophe, and fifty times,

---

* *Ulysses* appeared here in instalments, between 1918 and 1920, in the *Little Review*, which had moved to the city from Chicago the year before.

it is a beautiful catastrophe.' They were seen in starkly human terms by E. B. White, who was only confirming what millions have discovered down the years, when he wrote that, 'It can destroy an individual or it can fulfil him, depending a good deal on luck.' That great purveyor of stylish commonsense was himself ambivalent towards the city he cared for, and in which his reputation had been made. One of New York's most quoted enthusiasts, he lived off it for most of his professional life, but got out and extolled it from the wholesome distance of a refuge in Maine as soon as he could afford to.

It is common for people to speak of New York in superlatives, both high and low, for there is little here to leave anyone feeling only so-so. It is generally strong stuff, one way or another, and even its blander manifestations – invariably when someone is trying to sell something, quite possibly himself – do not often conceal, beneath the emollient coating, an inexorable toughness and a steadfast determination to succeed. When New York is at its most unpleasant it can be as nasty as anywhere on earth, and there is no need to dwell on its organised crime to substantiate that. The corruptions in its politics periodically bubble to the surface to betray the always lurking presence of what Lincoln Steffens, doggedly muckraking from his base on Newspaper Row around the turn of the century, immortalised as 'government of the people, by the rascals, for the rich.'* A similar stench offends the decent citizens when they contemplate the morality on which much of the wealth accumulated hereabouts is based; until, as one of them has declared, 'One is glad to slip away for a few hours from an environment in which anything less than unadulterated greed has come to be regarded by many as naïveté.' New York has other and even stealthier vices. This is a city with far too many imitation Irishmen, whose blood sport is to incite and finance real Irishmen to kill and mutilate each other 3,000 miles

---

*It was Theodore Roosevelt, adapting Bunyan, who conceived the word 'muckraker' and applied it to writers like Steffens, Ida Tarbell and Upton Sinclair, who were exposing various shortcomings in American politics, unions and business.

away across the Atlantic.* For such failings as these, New York must not expect the extravagant applause it constantly craves.

And yet the marvellous aspirations of 1776 have not been obscured in this city, and nothing nobler than them was ever enunciated by man. Not even the sentiments embodied in the United Nations Charter transcend the fundamental American belief 'that all men are created equal, that they are endowed by their Creator with certain inalienable rights, that among these are life, liberty and the pursuit of happiness'. Nothing at all could be more appropriate than that the United Nations almost from its inception decided to make its home and establish its parliament, the nearest thing to a world government we shall ever know, in the city that had been the first *de facto* capital of these free and independent United States.

This was not by any means an automatic choice. San Francisco was where the United Nations was founded, where its Charter was signed in 1945; and London was where its General Assembly first met at the beginning of the following year. For nearly twelve months after that there was much lobbying about the site of the permanent HQ, and at first the United States Government maintained a discreet reticence about its own preferences. It wasn't absolutely certain that America would wish to associate itself with the successor to the League of Nations it had rejected a generation earlier, and it was to be almost six months after the Charter was signed before the Senate agreed that the USA could participate permanently in the new organisation. The Russians, interestingly, were in favour of an American base for the UN, but most Europeans inclined towards Geneva; and when Washington finally committed itself, President Truman let it be known that he

* According to an unofficial assessment, 2,464 people were killed in the political violence of Northern Ireland between the beginning of January 1969 and the end of December 1985. Of these, 382 were soldiers of the British Army, and 290 were people killed by 'the security forces', which is a term referring collectively to the Army, the Royal Ulster Constabulary, and the Ulster Defence Regiment. The RUC and the UDR are entirely manned by Irishmen. Injuries in the same period numbered 27,876 and included 1,053 cases of knee-capping. There was a total of 8,143 explosions.

would be happy to see Boston or Philadelphia get the vote – or possibly some place like home in the mid-west. The UN came to New York because enough powerful New Yorkers decided that they would like it right here, and began to campaign assiduously to make the thing happen. Robert Moses, almost inevitably, had a hand in it. It was he who worked first of all on the newly elected Mayor O'Dwyer, in order to make the bid official, convincing him that, 'this was the one great thing that would make New York the center of the world'. As a result of his persuasion, Moses was appointed by the Mayor to chair the committee which was to conduct the lobby, and he assembled an array of worthies who would represent various forms of local power, including the publisher of the *New York Times*, the head of IBM, and the up-and-coming Nelson Rockefeller.

This combination was compelling enough to attract the United Nations officials to New York first on a temporary basis, while the officials themselves were sifting the competing claims. Housed at the start in a room at the Waldorf-Astoria, they moved to different premises around the metropolis in the course of several months, migrating from the hotel to the Rockefeller Center, then the Hunter College in the Bronx, before moving on to the Henry Hudson Hotel on the West Side of Manhattan, then uprooting again in favour of a disused factory belonging to the Sperry Gyroscope company in the middle of Long Island, and, penultimately, settling for some time at Flushing Meadow Park in Queens, in a refurbished skating rink left over from the 1939 World's Fair. While these international nomads were wandering from one encampment to another, visiting delegations were trying to entice them elsewhere permanently. San Francisco's mayor hadn't yet given up, and offered the United Nations a site beside the Golden Gate. Boston sent its mayor, the Governor and Lieutenant Governor of Massachusetts, the editor of the *Christian Science Monitor*, and an assurance that the city would build anything required of it at its own expense. The burghers of Philadelphia despatched couriers conveying what was tantamount to a blank cheque: only come to the city of brotherly love, they said, and your wish shall be our command. So eager were so many people to play host to the great new enterprise that, in retrospect, it is strange to think that cold water was instantly poured over an American preference that the United Nations itself expressed at one stage. It rather fancied the idea of setting up shop in Connecticut, perhaps in Greenwich or Stamford, but the good people of those parts, having got wind of the notion, protested so vigorously (on the ground that they would be exposed to unwanted European influence) that the idea was dropped forthwith.

Philadelphia's blank cheque almost pulled it off. Towards the back end of 1946, in spite of the fact that the UN's Secretary-General, the Norwegian Trygve Lie, was known to favour New York, the special Headquarters Committee of the organisation had received instructions from the General Assembly to look elsewhere and, by December 6, Philadelphia was so certain of getting the nod that it set in motion the legal procedures necessary to make land available for the building that would have to be done before the UN moved in. It was at this point that a real-estate baron and a couple of Rockefellers saved the day for New York, with less than a week to go before the decision would be made. The developer, William Zeckendorf, for months had been secretly buying plots of land on the East Side, which was as cheap as anything then available in midtown Manhattan. Known as Turtle Bay because of its original shape along that stretch of the East River, it was an untidy area which had long been used for penning cattle before they were slaughtered in abattoirs there. Zeckendorf now had seventeen acres of it between 42nd and 49th Streets, and although he planned to build great new blocks of apartments and offices there, nothing had yet been finalised. All that was changed when he was induced to sell at a reasonable return, by Moses and the Mayor, and when Nelson Rockefeller persuaded his father to come up with the necessary donation. At the last minute, the Headquarters Committee of the United Nations changed its mind and accepted New York's kind offer of the Turtle Bay site, for which John D. Rockefeller II wrote out his cheque for $8.5 million, and on which William Zeckendorf made a profit of two million bucks.

Until 1952 the United Nations continued to function on the old skating rink, while the unusual new addition to the Manhattan skyline went up just downstream of Welfare Island, which was also to be transformed before long.* With a fine sense of tact, someone decided that Headquarters should be created by a panel of architects from thirteen countries under the chairmanship of Wallace K. Harrison, who has been described as the designer laureate to the Rockefeller family (he was their overseer at the building of the Rockefeller Center) and who could therefore be relied upon to see that Junior's money was not squandered by the foreigners. One of these was Le Corbusier himself, and he it was who decided that there should be three buildings in the composition, but thereafter matters took a course that was to be increasingly familiar in all deliberations of the UN. The thirteen architects could not agree on how this concept should be developed, and in the end the great Frenchman absolved himself of all responsibility for the finished product, whose details became Harrison's more than anyone else's. Meanwhile, the generality of New Yorkers were still trying to make up their minds whether they really wanted this international circus, wished upon them by their overlords, right on their doorstep, especially when it was on a prime site in desirably expensive Manhattan. The city had committed itself to an initial expenditure of $2.5 million on top of the Rockefeller money, and some people, even in City Hall, complained that they ought not to be disbursing funds like that, *and* giving tax exemptions to the hordes of diplomats now flocking there, when the natives of New York needed every spare dollar spending on them for many different civic purposes. There was, too, a whiff of the old American isolationism in the air from time to time, though this was not confined to New York, or even to Connecticut. Senator Joseph McCarthy of Wisconsin, seeking an issue that might restore his fortunes after his anti-communist witch-hunt had been discredited, declared in 1956 that he would

* Welfare Island was where New York for almost a century isolated criminals and the chronically poor. From 1934 it was a refuge for the geriatric and the sick. In 1971 it was given a splendid new lease of life as Roosevelt Island, one of the nicest places to live in New York, and certainly the most soothing for commuters, who come and go with the greatest of ease across the East River in the sort of cable car the Swiss instal upon their mountainsides.

fight 'to get the United States out of the UN and the UN out of the United States'. Much later than that, Ronald Reagan, both before and after reaching the White House, never tried to conceal his indifference to whether the UN stayed or went.

Many New Yorkers continued to grumble about the cost of putting up with the United Nations in their city until, in 1977, a study came up with the information that although the metropolis spent something like $20 million each year in various subsidies of the organisation, the diplomatic community spent in return about $450 million in New York. There were then some 22,000 diplomats working in the city, and their numbers were increasing rapidly. By the time the fortieth birthday came round in 1985, there were nearly twice as many diplomats in New York, together with 5,000 UN employees, and it was estimated that between them they were annually putting some $800 million into the economy, in exchange for the $22 million the city lost in waived real-estate taxes, unpaid parking fines, and the services of the New York Police Department. In that year, the citizens had a further eyeopener when details were published of some notable extravagances by the foreign delegates, who had come to town to celebrate forty years of safeguarding the fundamental rights and dignities of mankind. A South American country ran up a hotel bill of $90,000 in four nights, and another delegation thought nothing of placing 130 room-service orders at midnight. At the same hour a visiting head of state demanded a facial; which, of course, this being New York, he obtained without difficulty for $300. One mission spent $12,000 on flowers alone, while a visitor to the Fifth Avenue emporium of F.A.O. Schwartz came away with $4,000 worth of toys. And then there was the day trip to Washington ordered by President Mobutu of Zaire, an unhappy land where the income per head of population was lately the equivalent of $128 each year. Amtrak laid on two special carriages, attached to the normal Metroliner service between the two cities, and in these the President and his entourage of fifty ate caviar and sipped champagne; the bill for nearly $10,000 being paid on the spot in cash.

New Yorkers have had grouses beyond the pecuniary, like that of the truck driver who knocked down and kicked the chief Spanish delegate one day because the diplomat wouldn't remove his car from a parking space reserved for UN officials. Some landlords have refused to rent accommodation to diplomats because too many in the past have broken contracts and have then successfully claimed diplomatic immunity when the landlord has tried to sue. When the Foreign Minister of Saudi Arabia, who also happened to be a prince of the royal family in Riyadh, tried to buy an apartment on Park Avenue for his private use whenever he had to visit the UN, the building's co-operative board turned him down; but in that case it is likely that the reason was political more than anything else. This is, after all, the biggest Jewish city in the world, and it has been said that what reconciled New Yorkers to having the United Nations beside their East River more than any other single thing, was the UN vote which recognised the state of Israel early on in both their lives. No debate in the General Assembly is reported in New York more meticulously than debates concerning the Middle East, and most especially debates which directly involve the security of Israel. No issue is more likely to provoke demonstration in Dag Hammarskjöld Plaza than one which is seen in New York to threaten Jews wherever in the world they may be. When the Arab nations in the seventies got the General Assembly to pass a resolution that, 'Zionism is a form of racism and racial discrimination', Mayor Abraham Beame described it as 'a sickening act' and some city councillors called for the closing of the New York City Commission for the United Nations, which is the liaison office between the world's talking shop and its American host.

Mayor Koch has called the organisation 'a cesspit' for some of its voting on Israel, and has loudly maintained a tradition which caused the President of Egypt some years ago to remark that New York had a foreign policy of its own, whatever the view might be from Washington. Koch has rarely employed civil language when he has spoken of the United Nations behind its back, and often enough he has gone out of his way to be offensive to its face. During the primaries which led to his re-election for a third term, he seized the chance of speaking in the UN before a Panel of Eminent Persons from eleven different countries, who wanted his views on doing business with South Africa. He had already got much mileage out of his opposition to apartheid during his campaign, and for every citizen who believed that his hostility was genuine there were two who reckoned he was gesturing in the hope of picking up the black vote in New York, the area of the poll in which he had always received tepid support. He repeated his views to the United Nations delegates straightforwardly until the Soviet member of the panel asked him a question about the official New York stance. 'First,' replied the Mayor, 'I assume that you want me to speak totally candidly and not to engage in diplomatic niceties. I happen to think that the Soviet Union is comparable to the Republic of South Africa, in terms of what it does *vis-à-vis* so many of the people in its own country. Having said that, I will now address your question.' A little later, the Bulgarian representative on the panel got the bum's rush, too. 'You'll forgive me if I once again make a comment that is not exactly a diplomatic nicety,' said Mr Koch. 'Bulgaria is not free from criticism. What Bulgaria has done to the Turkish minority in Bulgaria is a sin.' And when it was over, he gathered together the phalanx of journalists who always trail after their Mayor, and headed back towards City Hall, uttering as he went one of his most frequently repeated lines, which are always delivered without a trace of uncertainty: 'How'd I do? Did I do all right? Was that OK?'

Opportunist politicians and vociferous pressure groups apart, New Yorkers long ago came to the conclusion that the United Nations in their midst was something between an honour, a ratification of their city's pre-eminence, and a natural penalty for always saying airily, 'Let 'em all come.' They found in time that not only was the UN not as expensive as they had feared it might be, but that in some ways it actually gave them a buzz. From the beginning of the fifties, that side of town saw a rapid increase in the number of restaurants specialising in good foreign cooking. As more and more sophisticated people from the world's *corps diplomatiques* came to settle here for years at a time, New Yorkers realised that here was a new and permanent clientele for their fine arts and other civilised pursuits, and one that would assist New York's ambition to be second to none in that field, so that not even the most fastidiously cultivated

European would be able to patronise them any more. Here, too, from time to time, was a terrific sideshow that satisfied every New Yorker's fascination with whatever's around that's *new*. One or two United Nations occurrences are already embedded deeply in the local folklore, like the occasion in 1960 when Nikita Khrushchev took off his shoe and banged it on his desk in the middle of a speech to the General Assembly, and the day four years later when Ché Guevara was addressing the Assembly just as an anti-Castro group on the other side of the East River fired a bazooka in his direction (it fell harmlessly into the water, but the cops have patrolled that stretch of the river in launches ever since, during big UN meetings, just to make sure that no such thing happens again). And where else might you see, in the course of just one week, no fewer than ninety-five heads of state or government, as happened in New York during the birthday jamboree in 1985? To be sure, it tied up Manhattan's traffic for hours every day, but there were all these potentates and statesmen, driving to and fro – Juan Carlos of Spain, Hassan of Morocco, Zia ul-Haq of Pakistan, Rajiv Gandhi of India, Nakasone of Japan, Mubarak of Egypt, Kohl of West Germany, Mitterrand of France, Thatcher of Britain, Papandreou of Greece, Zhao Ziyang of China, Nyerere of Tanzania, Mugabe of Zimbabwe and all the others, not forgetting Old Sourpuss himself – the almost eternal Andrei Andreyevitch Gromyko, who had been a Soviet delegate at the Charter-making in San Francisco all those years before, and was now resurfacing in the Big Apple, on the stage he had played so often, but never before as President of the USSR.

That week meant much hard work for the good people of the city who, officially-appointed or not, spend themselves throughout the year in making the thousands of diplomats and their families welcome to New York and as much at home as possible in a place which intimidates some of the foreigners and is to even more of them just very, very strange. Only a handful of the dozens on the City Commission for the UN and the Mayor's own Commission for Protocol are paid workers, and the twenty-five ladies of the Hospitality Committee for UN Delegations take not a cent. The two commissions between them supply the city's greeters, who struggle out to Kennedy every time a new diplomat flies in, to pin a small gold apple on lapel or dress, to issue the official welcome, and to offer any help that may be needed in settling down.* This can mean anything from sorting out domestic problems with landlords and utility companies, to arranging all manner of extra-curricular events, like being given a tour of the World Trade Center, or taken to inspect some aspect of civic life that the public rarely sees. Domestic problems come within the province of the Hospitality Committee, too, whose volunteers also busy themselves cheerfully with wangling free tickets for entertainments in the metropolis, fixing trips throughout the United States, and offering courses in English at a school specially set up for the purpose. Diplomats everywhere are a pampered community, but nowhere is their slightest requirement and whim so considerately taken care of as it is in New York. Almost certainly nowhere else are so many doors opened for them with a warm invitation to come in, and many's the diplomatic wife from some distant corner of the earth whose homesickness has been somewhat relieved by good-hearted people here. Her husband and his colleagues may at the same time be prospering their careers beside the East River in knee-jerk vilifications of their hosts, and it is quite likely that they come from some supplicant nation whose corruptions make the corruptions of New York seem little more than disingenuous peccadilloes, almost venial. The British, just occasionally, put up with something of the sort still when it is London's turn to stage a Commonwealth conference, but no-one else knows anything like it, least of all Moscow. It is an irritation the New Yorkers have learned to live with, without allowing it to affect their hospitality.

Again, the student of New York has encountered one of its many contradictions: for while this city can be heartlessly

---

* It would be nice to think that the greeters offer these visitors an authentic explanation of New York's favourite sobriquet, but the origins of 'The Big Apple' are elusive. The most common interpretation is that it was associated with the Jazz Age, when bands toured lesser venues always hoping for a bigger bite than they were already getting; that is, a bite at the Big Apple ultimately.

cruel in so many ways, it also contains a powerful streak of generosity. The hospitality in many forms which is offered the United Nations diplomats, is no more than an organised version of the simple good nature shown by many individuals all the time: it is Helene Hanff sending food parcels from Manhattan to 84 Charing Cross Road years after London was at peace again, but not yet finished with rationing, and it is countless young New Yorkers setting off for uncomfortable places in their country's Peace Corps because of a deeply-rooted belief in the decencies of 1776 and an instinctive habit of neighbourliness. There is, too, a civic record of care and compassion which is unequalled elsewhere in the United States. One of the reasons for the fiscal crisis of 1975 was that too often someone had tried to do the open-handed thing without thinking clearly enough whether or not it could be afforded. Sanitation men had been allowed to retire on half-pay after only twenty years of work, in 1967, and if anyone complained about that it was pointed out that New York's police and firemen had enjoyed these emoluments since the nineteenth century (and no sooner had the garbage men caught up with the other two than they were put ahead again, now enjoying retirement on full pay after thirty-five years at work). Misguided these arrangements may have been in the circumstances, but they were nothing if not generous. They belonged to a long local tradition which Fiorello LaGuardia was merely upholding in 1944 when he announced a Health Insurance Plan for employed citizens, unparalleled then in any other state of the Union, whereby the worker and his family would receive complete medical care for only half its cost, the employer taking care of the other half. The plan would never develop to the extent its first sponsor intended, but it remains one of the largest pre-paid health care systems in the country. From the same sense of compassion came the inspiration for a vehicle that may be unique to New York, which has had much experience of unorthodox public conveyances, from the purportedly Flxible to the unintentionally collapsible. This one is known as the Kneeling Bus, so-called because at the touch of a control by the driver, it subsides gently towards the ground nearest its door, so that the old and the infirm may climb aboard or disembark with the minimum of effort, before the vehicle is restored to its former level and goes on its way to the next stop.

Although, typically, some New Yorkers regard the Kneeling Bus as yet another lamentable example of good dollars squandered in a soft-hearted gimmick, many more will be pleased that in this way their consciences are being taken care of by somebody responsible for the city's management. More still, probably, are tickled by its novelty, gratified that it maintains the Big Apple's reputation for setting the pace, and for coming up with the new idea that others will surely imitate. This matters in a city where the ambition to get on and improve is both an individual and a communal creed, with a considerable pedigree. It was back in 1853 that the Astor House Hotel on Broadway was attempting to produce whatever climate their customers wanted, the precursor of air-conditioning, first tried out in a chamber of glass and iron which had been erected in the hotel's courtyard. 'The immense space,' wrote an observer of this experiment, 'is heated in winter by warm air from below; and in the summer, jets of cold air will be blown into the room, moistened by the perpetual play of Croton fountains; and at all the seasons the ventilation from the roof will keep the atmosphere fresh and pure.' It is possible that this city invented the cocktail, a word which first appeared in 1809 in the *History of New York* by Diedrich Knickerbocker (alias Washington Irving), of doubtful etymology (we have H. L. Mencken's word for that) but most certainly of local popularity and development. One claimant to the creation of the Martini is Pieter Laurenzen Kock's tavern at No 1 Broadway. But even if it is true that, according to an alternative account, the first such drink was mixed circa 1781 in Betsy Flanagan's tavern between Tarrytown and White Plains – some miles beyond the city boundary even today, and a considerable distance away then – with General Washington's Americans providing the gin and General Rochambeau's Frenchmen supplying the vermouth, it is beyond dispute that the metropolis itself was where the cocktail achieved its apotheosis in umpteen variations which have enriched the tippler's vocabulary with, among others, the Manhattan and the Bronx.

Another New York innovation came early in the twentieth century, when the dancer Irene Castle, finding orthodox corsets too constricting for the athletic numbers she and her partner Vernon performed, discarded whalebone in favour of elastic foundation garments and pointed the way to a new kind of women's underclothes. A more flamboyant social dissent occurred half a century later in an apartment on 115th Street over on the West Side. There it was, according to Allen Ginsberg, that he and Jack Kerouac, students both at Columbia University, together with others, first saw the light that was to mesmerise an entire generation of young Americans. Before Sal Paradise lit out for the West ('Somewhere along the line I knew there'd be girls, visions, everything; somewhere along the line the pearl would be handed to me'), before the transfiguration of Haight-Ashbury, the Beat Generation was conceived and born on Morningside Heights and nurtured down the Lower East Side. Yet of all the things that New York may justly celebrate as its very own, none has remained as supremely and unassailably characteristic as the skyscraper. Though it has become a distinctive feature of the big city throughout the world, not only the originals but the most interesting are still to be found here. As the architectural critic of the *New York Times* has said with a maddening swagger and sickening accuracy, 'Most non-American skyscrapers . . . are merely mediocre imitations of American post-war structures.'

It is a city of great enthusiasms, which it can exhibit in the most unlikely contexts. The New York subway may be a dilapidated apology for its former self, but it is cherished by no fewer than ten different fan clubs, whose members spend a large proportion of their lives in obsessively collecting, photographing and compiling arcana from below the streets (one woman in 1973 even travelled on the entire system – more than 700 miles – in twenty-six hours and thirty-six minutes of continuous riding on sixty-seven trains, just to show it could be done). The Transit Authority itself demonstrated something of the same spirit in 1985 when it announced a programme of 'Music Under New York', which turned out to mean a brass quintet playing Mozart, and other instrumentalists performing the classics at certain specified stations to soothe and entertain the commuters in surroundings which may be grubby, but which happen to have terrific acoustics. New York has never been short of inspired touches like that. In the Port Authority's Bus Terminal on the West Side, there is a contraption of wondrous gigglesomeness encased in a glass box, a thing such as Rube Goldberg or Heath Robinson might have devised, an entertainment of pure genius, self-propelled by a dozen pool balls which run along channels, drop through holes, and are carried up escalators to start all over again, to the continuous sound of whirring and clanking and boinking metal parts. In Central Park there is another of New York's perfect toys, and one which says a great deal about this city's heart as well as its gift for striking ingenuity. A bronze statue of Hans Christian Andersen sits on a bench with a bronze Ugly Duckling standing by his feet. The storyteller has a book open on one knee, and this makes a perfect perch for small children, who climb up and snuggle there in a world of make-believe.

It is a city whose native wit can make a visitor's day, especially if he has just flown in from Europe, where it is unlikely that he will have heard anything quite so unaffectedly, so breezily self-confident before. Early on his first morning he will, perhaps, ring to clinch an appointment made before he left home. A secretary says that the boss isn't in yet, but maybe the call can be returned when he arrives. 'Where are you now?' she continues, bright as the day itself. 'Er, hang on,' says the visitor, still fuddled with jet lag and trying to read the number on an unfamiliar telephone, 'I'm not quite sure . . .' Back comes the girl, before he can say another word. 'My goodness, *you* must lead an interesting life, waking up in the morning and not knowing where you are!' There is one of the genuine voices of New York, to whom it has never occurred for one moment to doubt that she is as good as the next person and probably a lot smarter than most. It is audible to high and low alike, without fear or favour. It has been recounted that when Nancy Reagan rang an upmarket shop in Manhattan about a handbag she'd ordered, wanting to speak to the proprietress, the girl on the switchboard asked who was calling. 'This is Mrs Ronald Reagan calling Mrs Lieber,' the voice from the White House replied. 'What company are you with?' said the girl, to whom one salesperson sounded much like another. Although locally that will be admired as classic *chutzpa*, in which all citizens here take pride, it also comes in the same line of descent as New York's celebrated one-liners, which reached their full height at the hands of James Thurber. Some examples from his drawing board at the *New Yorker* are so memorable that merely to repeat the captions without the cartoons is to stir laughter anew ('Y'know, I keep thinking it's Thursday' or 'You can tell me if I bend my knees, Sugar' or 'This gentleman was kind enough to see me home, darling'). But the one-liner is liable to crop up anywhere. The observant traveller through this city will sooner or later come across the street sign which says, 'Don't Even *Think* of Parking Here.'

It is impossible to do New York justice, for this is a city of infinite variety whose lifelong citizens, even, are quite likely to be unaware of all its parts in their bewildering complexity. It is Ed Murrow going out into the world and telling his people the truth about it in a clear and incorruptible voice. It is Roy Cohn, who may not have had the slightest understanding of truth, either in his lickspittle days with Joe McCarthy, or in his law practice later on, when he had become a rather crooked man-about-town. It is Fiorello LaGuardia refusing to disembark from a plane at Newark, the only local airfield for scheduled flights, because he had bought a ticket to New York – and using the consequent publicity to convince his fellow citizens that they needed an airport of their own, which now bears his name. It is people playing chess at the tables specially provided for them on 42nd Street, studiously unaware of the junkies loafing in Bryant Park on one side of them, and the tumult of traffic pouring along the other. It is the cylindrical wooden watertowers on stilts that stand on so many Manhattan rooftops, just like they stand beside desert railroad tracks in Western movies, and it is the biplane anchored to the roof of 177 Water Street, whose owner used to fly it early in the Second World War. It is the *New York Times* grumbling that 'Anti-Americanism Grows New Roots' in the same week that *Pravda* is probably growling about anti-Soviet propaganda from a similar but obverse point of view. It is the lady in the Dakota building, who had a man come specially from Tiffany's once a week to wind her clocks. It is another lady who was cleared out of Grand Central Station by the cops one bitter winter's night, and was found next morning, perished in the street. It is the sense of elation that suffuses the entire house during a Broadway musical, however many performances it has run, however bored with it the umpteenth change of cast may be, because in that chorus line, in those high-kicking, metronomically precise figures in toppers and tights, the audience sees its fantasies come perfectly true as they do nowhere else on earth. It is the choir of St Thomas's Church on Fifth Avenue singing Tomkins and Orlando Gibbons and Charles Villiers Stanford in C with a tonic brilliance that few cathedrals across the water can match and none can exceed. It is Dwight Gooden, sweeping all before him in the National League during season 1985 and unable even to start in 1987 because success had put him in a drug rehabilitation unit instead of on the pitcher's mound. It is Mel Brooks, inexhaustibly, inventively, tastelessly, glibly, incomparably entertaining us until he has reduced himself to hoarseness and his tuxedo to a limp rag. It is Murray Kempton understanding with rare clarity the depths and the heights of human nature; and telling these verities generously, with uncommon elegance, four times a week in a newspaper column. New York is all these things and many, uncountably many, more.

It is a city of such powerful urges, such frantic endeavours, such enormous determination, such insatiable appetites, that it dominates any natural rivalry more than is perhaps healthy for anyone; but that has always been the way of the world, as an Englishman should know as well as anyone and better than most. London, the old imperial capital, appears to be suffering from a pernicious anaemia now, to anyone who commutes between the two. All human life is here these days, not there or anywhere else in the western world; which means that New York can be disgusting, frightening, maddening, crude. It also means that New York is uplifting, exciting, enchanting, warm.

It is most noticeably, perhaps, a city of boundless energy, and in this, too, it is without any rivals in the west. New Yorkers can be as indolent as anyone when working for someone else unless he cracks the whip. But whatever they are doing on their own account, they give it everything they've got. It is as though they understand a great and universal truth more clearly than the rest of us, and have conditioned themselves to abide by it. The truth can be expressed in many ways, but the neatest, the most New Yorkish way of putting it has lately been visible in a shop window along Fifth Avenue, corner of 42nd Street. The shop specialises in T-shirts bearing slogans across the chest, which are meant to catch the eye and give people a laugh, more often than not. One, however, is nothing less than a serious reminder of mortality, and a call to renewed vigour while the opportunity is still here.

'Life is not a dress rehearsal.'

BIBLIOGRAPHY

Abbreviations

NYT	*New York Times*
NYA	*New York Affairs* (Urban Research Center, New York University)
MI	*Manhattan Inc*
AIA	American Institute of Architects (NY Chapter) *Guide to New York City* by Norval White and Elliot Willensky (rev ed, NY, 1978)
GB	*The Green Book: Official Directory of the City of New York 1984–5*
WPAG	*The WPA Guide to New York City* (Federal Writers' Project 1939, with introduction by William H. Whyte, New York, 1982)
WPAP	*New York Panorama* (Federal Writers' Project of Works Progress Administration, New York, 1939)
WPAS	*New York: a Guide to the Empire State* (WPA, NY, 1940)

Abbott, Berenice, *New York in the Thirties* (photographs, Dover, 1973)

Albion, Robert Greenhalgh, *The Rise of New York Port* (North Eastern UP, 1939/84)

Anderson, Jervis, *Harlem: the Great Black Way 1900–1950* (Orbis, 1982)

Auletta, Ken, *The Streets were Paved with Gold* (Random House, 1979)

Auletta, Ken, *Greed and Glory on Wall Street* (Penguin, 1986)

Baldwin, James, *The Price of the Ticket* (Michael Joseph, 1985)

Birmingham, Stephen, *Life at the Dakota* (Random House, 1979)

Birmingham, Stephen, *'Our Crowd'; the great Jewish families of New York* (Harper & Row, 1984)

Bloom, Alexander, *Prodigal Sons: the New York Intellectuals and their World* (OUP, 1986)

Boorstin, Daniel J., *The Americans* (3 vols, Vintage, 1958/65/73)

Boyer, Richard, and Savageau, David, *Places Rated Almanac* (Rand McNally, 1985)

Brook, Stephen, *New York Days, New York Nights* (Hamish Hamilton, 1984)

Brecher, Charles, and Horton, Raymond D., *Setting Municipal Priorities 1986* (NY UP, 1985)

Burgess, Anthony, *New York* (Time-Life 1976)

Caro, Robert, *The Power Broker: Robert Moses and the Fall of New York* (Vintage, 1975)

Castleman, Craig, *Getting Up: subway graffiti in New York* (MIT Press, 1982)

Chase, W. Parker, *New York: the Wonder City* (New York Bound, 1932; and 1983 with introduction by Paul Goldberger)

Chwast, Seymour, and Heller, Steven (eds), *The art of New York* (Abrams, 1983)

Coleman, Terry, *Passage to America* (Penguin, 1974)

Collier, Peter, and Horowitz, David, *The Rockefellers* (Holt, Rinehart, 1976)

Conrad, Peter, *The Art of the City* (OUP, 1984)

Cook, Leland, *St Patrick's Cathedral; a centennial history* (Quick Fox, 1979)

Cooke, Alistair, *America* (BBC, 1973)

Cooper, Martha, and Chalfant, Henry, *Subway Art* (Holt Rinehart, 1984)

Edmiston, Susan, and Cirino, Linda D., *Literary New York: a History and a Guide* (Houghton Mifflin, 1976)

Feininger, Andreas, and Von Hartz, John, *New York in the Forties* (Dover, 1978)

Fischler, Stan, *Uptown, Downtown; a trip through time on New York's Subways* (NY, 1976)

Fishlock, Trevor, *The State of America* (John Murray, 1986)

Fried, William, and Watson, Edward B., *New York in Aerial Views* (Dover, 1980)

Galbraith, John Kenneth, *The Great Crash* (Penguin, 1975)

Garrett, Charles, *The LaGuardia Years* (Rutgers UP, 1961)

Gill, Brendan, *Here at the New Yorker* (Berkeley, 1975)

Glazer, Nathan, and Moynihan, Daniel P., *Beyond The Melting Pot* (MIT and Harvard UP, 1964)

Goldberger, Paul, *The City Observed; a Guide to the architecture of Manhattan* (Penguin, 1982)

Goldberger, Paul, *The Skyscraper* (Knopf, 1981)

Goldman, Peter, *The Death and Life of Malcolm X* (Illinois UP, 1979)

Goldman, William, *The Season; a candid look at Broadway* (Limelight, 1984)

Hacker, Andrew, *The New Yorkers* (Mason/Charter, 1975)

Hershkowitz, Leo, *Tweed's New York* (Doubleday, 1977)

Hine, Lewis W., (photographs) *Men at Work* (Dover, 1977)

Huggins, Nathan Irving, *Harlem Renaissance* (OUP, 1973)

Israelowitz, Oscar, *Guide to Jewish New York* (NY, 1984)

Jacobs, Jane, *The Death and Life of Great American Cities* (Vintage, 1961)

Johnson, Harry, and Lightfoot, Frederick S., *Maritime New York in the 19th century* (photographs, Dover, 1980)

Jonnes, Jill, *We're Still Here; the rise, fall and resurrection of the South Bronx* (Atlantic, 1986)

Koch, Edward I., and Rauch, William, *Mayor* (Warner, 1985)

Koch, Edward I., and Rauch, William, *Politics* (Warner, 1986)

Leapman, Michael *The Companion Guide to New York* (Collins, 1981)

Lehnartz, Klaus, and Talbot, Allan R., *New York in the Sixties* (photographs, Dover, 1978)

Lightfoot, Frederick S. (ed), *Nineteenth-century New York* (photographs, Dover, 1981)

Little, Jeffrey B., and Rhodes, Lucien, *Understanding Wall Street* (Liberty, 1984)

McCullough, David W., *Brooklyn; and how it got that way* (Dial Press, 1983)

Mandell, Jonathan, *Trump Tower* (Lyle Stuart, 1984)

Marqusee, Mike, and Harris, Bill (eds), *New York; an Anthology* (Cadogan, 1985)

Matz, Mary Jane, *The Many Lives of Otto Kahn* (Macmillan, 1963)

Mayer, Martin, *The Teachers' Strike, New York 1968* (Harper & Row, 1969)

Mayer, Martin, *Madison Avenue USA* (Penguin, 1961)

Mitgang, Herbert, *The Man Who Rode the Tiger* (Norton, 1979)

Morison, Samuel Eliot, *The Oxford History of the American People* (3 vols, OUP, 1972)

Morris, Charles R., *The Cost of Good Intentions; New York City and the liberal experiment* (Norton, 1980)

Morris, James, *The Great Port* (Faber, 1970)

Morris, Jan, *Manhattan '45* (Faber, 1987)

Moscow, Henry, *The Book of New York Firsts* (Collier Macmillan, 1982)

Moss, Howard (ed), *New York Poems* (Avon, 1980)

Newfield, Jack, and Du Brul, Paul, *The Abuse of Power* (Penguin, 1977)

Norton, Thomas E., and Patterson, Jerry E., *Living It Up; a Guide to the named apartment houses of New York* (Atheneum, 1984)

Ottley, Roi, and Weatherby, William J., *The Negro in New York* (Oceana Publications, 1967)

Patterson, Jerry E., *The City of New York; a history illustrated from the collection of the Museum of the City of New York* (Abrams, 1978)

Persico, Joseph, *The Imperial Rockefeller* (Simon and Schuster, 1982)

Poll, Solomon, *The Hasidic Community of Williamsburg* (Schocken Books, 1969)

Reid, Ed, *The Shame of New York* (Random House, 1953)

Rieder, Jonathan, *Canarsie; the Jews and Italians of Brooklyn against liberalism* (Harvard UP, 1985)

Riis, Jacob, *How the Other Half Lives; studies among the tenements of New York* (Dover, 1978 ed)

Sanders, Ronald, and Gillon, Edmund V., *The Lower East Side; a Guide to its Jewish past* (Dover, 1979)

Shapiro, Mary J., *Gateway to Liberty* (Vintage, 1986)

Silver, Nathan, *Lost New York* (Houghton Mifflin, 1967)

Sloane, Leonard, *The Anatomy of the Floor* (Doubleday, 1980)

Spann, Edward K., *The New Metropolis; New York 1840–1857* (Columbia UP, 1981)

Starr, Roger, *The Rise and Fall of New York City* (Basic Books, 1985)

Stern, Zelda, *The Complete Guide to Ethnic New York* (St Martin's Press, 1980)

Talese, Gay, *The Kingdom and the Power* (Dell, 1981)

Talese, Gay, *The Bridge* (Harper & Row, 1964)

Talese, Gay, *Honor Thy Father* (Dell, 1981)

Thomas, Bill and Phyllis, *Natural New York* (Holt, Rinehart, 1983)

Turner, Florence, *At the Chelsea* (Hamish Hamilton, 1986)

Wagenvoord, James, *City Lives* (Holt, Rinehart, 1976)

Whiffen, Marcus, and Koeper, Frederick, *American Architecture 1607–1976* (MIT Press, 1981)

White, E. B., *Essays* (Harper & Row, 1977)

— *Almanack of American Politics, 1985* (National Journal)

— *Chicago and New York; architectural interactions* (Chicago, 1984)

SOURCE NOTES

Page
15 'We will discover and uncover . . .': *Portrait of New York* by
Felix Riesenberg and Alexander Alland (NY, 1939), 2

CHAPTER ONE   THE VIEW FROM THE BRIDGE

20 Great Thomas Paine, etc: Edmiston, 339–40
Winter of 1866: McCullough, 2
22 Bridge statistics: WPAG, 314
Original piers on Egyptian lines: McCullough, 6
Photographs of Manhattan: e.g. Beal's Photographic View of
New York 1876, the original of which is in the Museum of the
City of New York.
Trinity spire: WPAP, 310
23 Bridge wine vaults: WPAG, 314–15
Barnum's elephants: McCullough, 57
24 Mailer's work room: Edmiston, 358
What used to be Brooklyn Navy Yard: McCullough, 89
25 Todt Hill: WPAG, 597
Statue of Liberty's origins: NYT magazine May 18, 1986; also
Shapiro, 19–63
26 Emma Lazarus: Shapiro, 6
27 14 million people: Shapiro, 6
28 two per cent turned back: Shapiro, 6
The Hitchcock film was *Saboteur*, released in 1942.
30 Fulton Fish Market: WPAG, 83
31 The Woolworth photograph was taken by Robert A Smith of
Fairchild Aerial Surveys Inc: see Chase, 188
33 Declaration of Independence: WPAG, 96
34 Washington's acceptance of the freedom: *Quarterly Bulletin of
the New York Historical Society*, Vol 1, July 1917, No 2, p 38.
See also Morison Vol 2, 234

CHAPTER TWO   UPWARDS AND OUTWARDS

39   Manahatin: Patterson, 13
     Peter Minuit: WPAP, 35
     Ironworking Indians: *Mohawks in High Steel* by Joseph Mitchell
     from the *New Yorker* 1949, contained in Marqusee, 37; see also
     Talese/*Bridge*, 24 and 110
42   170 varieties of stones: WPAP, 28
43   No building above sixth floor: MI June 1986, 107
     Skyscraper: first used 1794 according to Oxford English Dic-
     tionary. Its nautical use defined in *Oxford Companion to Ships
     and the Sea*, edited by Peter Kemp (London, 1976)
     Flinn quotation: Whiffen, 439
     No neat answer: Goldberger/*Skyscraper*, 23
     Championing Equitable Life building as first skyscraper: Carl
     W. Condit, emeritus professor of architecture, North Western
     University in *Chicago and New York; architectural interactions*,
     78
     Championing the Home Insurance Building: Whiffen, 238
44   'Never before in history . . .': Whiffen, 238
45   'Our civilisation is progressing . . .': quoted Goldberger/*Sky-
     scraper*, 8
46   Chrysler spire: MI June 1986, 114
     Al Smith as supplicant: Caro, 380
47   Zoning laws 1916: NYA, No 4, 1985, 48
50   'pretentious and arrogant . . .': Goldberger/*Observed*, 10
     'stolid, banal monoliths . . .': AIA, 25
     Phillippe Petit: NYT, August 8, 1974
51   50,000 workers: World Trade Center, leaflet
     6,500 windows: Empire State Building, leaflet
     Steel for 20,000 automobiles: MI, June 1986, 117
     One week in elevator: MI, June 1985, 50
52   James Agee: MI, June 1986, 120
     Glass falling from Trump Tower: Mandell, 174
     Helicopter crash: NYT, May 17, 1977
53   Bomber hits Empire State Building: NYT, June 29 and 30, 1945
54   32,000 elevators: MI, June 1985, 45
55   Ed Koch: London, *Sunday Times*, April 28, 1985
     Other voice from City Hall was Abraham Biderman: quoted MI,
     January 1986, 82

56 Chrysler rents: MI, June 86, 106
'Skyscrapers are machines . . .': quoted Mandell, 27
'That bold signature . . .': WPAP, 409
57 Henry James: quoted Marqusee, 182
The oldest house is the Bowne House on 37th Avenue, Flushing,
Queens: WPAG, 569
58 'New York basically a middle class city . . .': WPAG, xxx
'the job-holding . . .': Jimmy Breslin, quoted Hacker, 76
'Presidential candidates . . .': *Almanack of American Politics*, 826
1975 arson: Newfield, 5
59 Lloyd's insurance claims: Jonnes, 232/364
61 Sixth largest population: Boyer, 85
Biggest collection of brownstones: *New York: a city of neighborhoods* (NY, Chamber of Commerce and Industry, undated), 35
Churchill's mother: McCullough, 259
62 Most densely settled Jewish: Israelowitz, 100
Coney Island and French Riviera: Fischler, 49
63 populated by elderly Jews: *Almanack of American Politics*, 813
O'Malley offered oil rights: NYA, No 4, 1983, 140
64 The John Wayne movie was *Trouble Along the Way*: see Rieder,
14
Ships' nicknames: *The American Language: Supplement Two*, by
H. L. Mencken, 588
66 'a factual imitation . . .': *The Great Gatsby* by Scott Fitzgerald, 11
The Alec Guinness mishap: see *Blessings in Disguise* (Hamish
Hamilton, 1985) by Sir Alec Guinness, 118
67 Tides at Hell Gate: Albion, 22
68 Erie Canal: Albion, 84
'unchallenged metropolis': Spann, 15
'largest aggregate . . .': WPAG, 68
69 'opposite the piers . . .': WPAG, 69
'battleships line the Hudson': WPAG, 285
number of vessels entering port: WPAG, 53
'by every statistical measure . . .': WPAG, 410
70 the record Blue Riband time: Kemp, op cit
71 Tonnage etc in 1983: Port Authority's annual report, 1983,
14
72 Gulf ports overtaking New York: NYA, No 4, 1983, 23
Port Authority plans: annual report, op cit, 7. See also *The
Brooklyn Paper*, October 19–25, 1985
Doomed from 1955: Morris (James), 84
The longshoremen: Starr, 55 and Auletta/*Streets*, 163

72   Continuing to be the most expensive port: *Journal of Commerce*,
     September 16, 1985
73   Sandy Hook Pilots numbers: communicated to the author by the
     pilots' office, August 14, 1985

          CHAPTER THREE   THE BOILING POT

77   'The only event that knocks every New Yorker . . .': White, 120
78   'The message we are sending . . .': *Irish Echo*, March 23, 1985
     'The time has come . . .': ibid
     The full-page advertisement: *Irish Echo*, March 16, 1985
79   Ancient Order of Hibernian riots: Glazer, 248
80   'They sound like a bunch . . .' NYT, September 2, 1985
     Moynihan asks to be readmitted: *Irish Echo*, March 16, 1985
     Biaggi lied: *Almanack of American Politics*, 1985, 830
82   34 million refugees: Shapiro, 69
83   Irish labour and deaths on the Erie Canal: *The Damnable Question*
     by George Dangerfield (Boston, 1976), 14
     Free Workers' School: WPAP, 98–9
     Marx and the *New York Tribune*: *Marx* by David McLellan
     (London, 1975), 19
84   Sloop *Restaurationen*: Morison, Vol 3, 228
     Italian subsistence figures: WPAP, 91
     Jacob Barsimon: WPAP, 126
85   1907 the busiest year: Patterson, 157
86   Israel Zangwill: Glazer, 290
     Census figures: all from Patterson – first census, 87; 1898,
     198; 1913, 213
     The wealthiest nation: Shapiro, 72
87   'persons who have been convicted . . .': Shapiro, 119
     Literacy test: Shapiro, 7
     Germans wanting to come: Shapiro, 244
     10–13,000 a week on Ellis Island: Shapiro, 238
88   Italians beating deadline: Shapiro, 245–6
89   'Almost unrelieved misery': Glazer, 86
90   twenty-seven competing airlines; Jonnes, 99
     'New York isn't a melting pot . . .': Quoted by John Gunther,
     Inside USA (NY, 1947), 524
     Dominican figures: NYT Magazine, November 3, 1985
     West Indians liking to be mistaken for Puerto Ricans: Glazer,
     92

91 Afghan refugee at City College: NYT Magazine, November 3, 1985
    80,000 new immigrants a year: NYA, No 3, 1984, 14
    New York's population: GB (the figures are disputed by the city)
    Number of foreign-born: NYT Magazine, November 3, 1985
    Footnote on illegal immigrants: NYT Magazine, November 3, 1985
    Over 100 nationalities in Queens: NYT Magazine, November 3, 1983
    Brooklyn diocese: 1985 Catholic Telephone Guide.
    60 foreign newspapers: NYT Magazine, November 3, 1985
    11 Chinese newspapers: NYT, September 15, 1985
93 French in New York: NYT, November 3, 1985
94 Indian and Korean doctors: NYA, 1979, No 4, 62
    80 per cent of MTA news stands: NYT, November 3, 1985
95 Korean Produce Assn figures: NYT, September 21, 1985
96 Conrado Mones: NYT Magazine, November 3, 1985
    Medvedevs: NYT, September 25, 1985
98 No German vote: Glazer, 311–12
99 'the elimination of all foreigners . . .': Spann, 338
    'the last vulgar white Protestant . . .': Glazer, 217
    Tweed trial: Hershkowitz, 256
100 Emerald Society started: Glazer, 261
    The gangs: Garrett, 153
101 Archbishop Hughes: Patterson, 111 and 136
    Clergy figures: 1985 Catholic Telephone Guide and Directory
    Hierarchy's support for McCarthy: Glazer, 269
    Catholic finances: MI, December 1985, 156
    Senior police Irish: Starr, 133
102 The most visible contribution: Moynihan in Glazer, 252
    Italian crime money in Tammany: Garrett, 308
103 Roosevelt attack on Mussolini: Glazer, 214
    Italian Catholicism weak till 1940s: Glazer, 202
104 'While the Jewish map . . .': Glazer, 187
    Caruso in Mulberry Street: Matz, 80
105 Joey Gallo killing: NYT, April 8, 1972
    City garbage: Brecher, 154
    Intermarriages: Starr, 133
106 Defacing Chinese characters: NYA, No 4, 1983, 150
    Canarsie vigilantes: Rieder, 87
    Irish against racial harmony: Glazer, 71
    1968 Teachers' strike: Mayer/*Teachers*, 16 passim

CHAPTER FOUR   A NEW JERUSALEM

109   The author was present during the demonstration on September
      5, 1985
110   New York's garbage: Auletta/*Streets*, 35
      Sanitation Commissioner quoted: NYA, 1973, No 2, 67
      Misgivings about incinerators: NYA, 1985, No 2, 19
113   Jewish population: Israelowitz, 7
      1979 estimate: Auletta/*Streets*, 215
      footnote 'have developed techniques': Glazer, 137
      23 migrants from Brazil: Birmingham/*Crowd*, 31
      1880 and 1910 estimates: Glazer, 138–9
      'one out of every five Jews': NYA, No 2, 1973, 113
      'never in the Diaspora': Glazer, 177
      Encyclopaedia Judaica, Vol 12, 1124
114   Otto Kahn's box: Matz, 66
      Nathan Straus: Mitgang, 316
115   Name-changing by Greenbaum: Bloom, 26
      'We have room for only one Jew': ibid 30
      Trilling quotation: *Commentary*, May 1966
      'Mazzacristi': Rieder, 16
116   'a .22 for every Jew': Rieder, 196
      AJC opposition to Palestine: NYA, No 2, 1973, 107
      'contest of national imperialisms': *Partisan Review*, April 1938
      'the more the allies are exhausted': *PR*, Fall 1939 (both quota-
      tions appear in Bloom, 125–7)
      'it is remarkable': Bloom, 138
      It was convincingly argued by Marvin Schick: NYA, No 2, 1973,
      106–20
117   'as a generalisation': ibid, 111
      Footnote: ibid
      The photographs taken on Hester Street; see Sanders and Gillon
119   A Bintel Brief; Israelowitz, 28
      'Eastern European Jews': Glazer, 155
      City College: Glazer, 155
120   wealthy Jews staying Democrat: Glazer, 166
121   Reuben Ticker: Israelowitz, 35, 63, 123
      Singer at Sea Gate: ibid, 115
122   'not only was I cut off . . .': NYT, November 3, 1985
      Golden Ghetto: Caro, 851

122   school teacher estimate: Glazer, 146
123   'World's most powerful newspaper': this appears as the fragment
      of a NYT book review on the paperback jacket of Talese/*Kingdom*
      NYT piece on Hasidic family: by Joseph Giovannini, NYT, June
      19, 1986
      Palestinian terrorists and IRA guerrillas: e.g. NYT, September
      2, 1985
      'For the East Europeans . . .': Glazer, 175
124   Footnote; the study cited was *Mental Health in the Metropolis*
      by Leo Scole and others (NY, 1962), 317
125   'Ultimately, more and more . . .': NYA, No 2, 1973, 113
      'a highly discouraging': Mayer/*Teachers*, 18
126   'not one of these teachers . . .': Rieder, 277
      83 teachers surrounded: ibid, 70
      the anti-semitic literature: ibid, 76
      'the first significant confrontation': Starr, 173
      'I can tell you': Rieder, 124
      East River defines the limits: ibid, 123
      'One of the longest journeys . . .'; Podhoretz in *Making it* (NY,
      1967) 3,
      quoted by Bloom, 25
127   synagogues in Brooklyn: Israelowitz, 91
128   Jews mocked by children: Poll, 27
      malicious gossip: Poll, 30
130   *shatnes*: ibid, 105
131   'reject everything and everyone': Poll, ix
      esrog: ibid, 164
132   High-tech shop: MI, December 1985, 116
      'My brothers the slaughterers . . .': Poll, 155
      'I succeeded with God's help . . .': ibid, 205 (both quotations
      translated from the Yiddish which appeared in *Der Yid*)

CHAPTER FIVE   THEM AND US

136   'in the Tuscan-columned . . .': AIA, 293
137   NYC unemployment rate 7.9 per cent: 1984 figure from Bureau
      of Labor, quote Brecher, 31
138   Sassenach; a word used disparagingly by some Scots referring
      to Englishmen. In fact, the word is Gaelic for Lowlander, and
      therefore a Glaswegian, drunk or sober, is as Sassenach as they
      come.

140   Marin's government likened to Roosevelt's: by, for example,
      John Gunther, op cit, 343
141   Eleven slaves arriving: Anderson, 4
      owning small businesses; WPAP, 133
142   New York state supplied most troops: Patterson, 131
143   Draft Riots: WPAP 136 and 386. But see also a caption in
      Patterson 160 for a qualification to casualty figures.
      'Black Sam' Fraunces: WPAP, 134
      African Grove theatre: ibid
      Handbill quotation: Edmiston, 49
      white servants: quoted Anderson, 27, from NYT, July 19, 1895
144   Southern blacks 'had heard of New York . . .': quoted Anderson,
      10
      750,000 black migrants: Jonnes, 96
      population figures: 1830 Anderson, 5; 1900 Caro, 491; 1930
      Caro, 491
      'Almost every contemporary observer remarked . . .': Anderson,
      7
145   Tenderloin: WPAG, 164
      Sons of New York: Anderson, 26
      West Indians and New York prejudice: Glazer, 35
146   Harlem Opera House: WPAG, 256
      'Can nothing be done . . .': quoted Anderson, 56
147   369th Infantry: Anderson, 107,118
      only black line officers: WPAG, 265
      Truman decree: ibid, 292
      James Weldon Johnson: quoted Marqusee, 143
      'this was incontestably . . .': Baldwin, 659
148   Cakewalk: Anderson, 40
      James Reese Europe's band: ibid, 77
      Robeson; ibid, 116
149   Scott Joplin: ibid, 80
      Arlen quotation: ibid, 174
      Ellington's Arabian Nights: ibid, 142
      Florence Mills: ibid, 181–4
150   Du Bois quotation: ibid, 106 (from *Crisis*, July 1918)
151   Clayton Powell quotation: ibid, 105 (from *Age*, March 29, 1917)
      Garvey quotation: ibid, 123
153   Suffolk County KKK: Caro, 148
      Home-made hymn: WPAG, 260
154   Langston Hughes: quoted Marqusee, 151 (from autobiography
      The Big Sea)

155 'Briefly, the Walker System . . .': Ottley, 238
Jobless entertainers: Anderson, 242
Unemployed figures: ibid, 242; see also Glazer, 28 and Patterson, 222
'ten years of Depression . . .': Glazer, 28
156 Population figures: ibid, 58; see also Caro, 491
Puerto Ricans: Glazer, 116, 117, 104, 207
157 Yankees in 1960: NYA, No 2, 1983, 129
Adam Clayton Powell's 21 per cent: Glazer, 69
Irish belligerence: Glazer, 233
158 'absolute hatred': quoted Jonnes, 114
Italian ballplayers: *Illustrated History of Baseball* by Robert Smith (NY 1973), 180
SPONGE: Rieder, 23
Procaccino voter: Rieder, 129
159 Jews and civil rights: Glazer, 74
'meeting no Negro . . .': Baldwin, 8
Levittown: Glazer, 153
160 Footnote figures: *American Political Almanac*, 795
'Our Bar-Lev line': NYA, No 2, 1973, 115
'a reminder of I don't know . . .': Goldman, Peter, 135
162 'It was Malcolm . . .': ibid, 111
'the biggest event': NYT, September 21, 1960
'a leader of the so-called . . .': NYT, September 20, 1960
163 'I'm waking up America': quoted Goldman, 265
death of Malcolm: ibid, 262
164 New York City Opera: *Guardian* (London), October 2, 1986
165 'It is the sort of place . . .': *American Political Almanac*, 811
law firms and black staff: NYA, No 2, 1985, 48
figures for job market as whole: Brecher, 5
166 Queen Mother Moore: *Amsterdam News*, June 14, 1986
52 per cent of population white: Brecher, 57

CHAPTER SIX   ALMIGHTY DOLLAR

168 Motogram: AIA, 139. It was first used for the election returns of 1928
170 1,500 members: Sloane, 4
American Stock Exchange seat: MI, June 1985, 77
Shares traded: Little, 41
'This is the greatest . . .': quoted Sloane, 137

171   'The hundreds of millions . . .': Sloane, 3
      'the special skyscraper . . .': Henry James, *The American Scene*,
      83
      Center for Ethics: MI, November 1985, 17
      Trinity's grant from Queen Anne: AIA, 18
172   'the heart pump . . .': Warren Lindquist, quoted Collier, 315
      300 banks now: Economic base analysis for 1985, prepared by
      Landauer Associates of New York. See also Auletta/*Streets*, 7
      most extensive cattle market: Spann, 122
      industry in New York: Spann, 406
173   top manufacturing city: Spann, 403
174   'the international center . . .': NYA, No 2, 1985, 85
      New York factory statistics: NYA, No 4, 1983, 66 and 81
      industrial corporations: *Fortune* magazine, April 27, 1987
175   service industries: ibid, June 8, 1987
      real estate the biggest business: Glazer, 153
      real estate advertisements: NYT, March 3, 1985
      'Real estate is the key . . .': MI, May 1985, 30
176   Brooklyn offices: NYA, 1983, No 4, 143
      contrast with Boston and San Francisco: NYA, 1985, No 4, 30
      $4,000 per sq ft: MI, May 1985, 30
      Trump's deals: Mandell, 22 and 23
      rise in property value: MI, March 1985, 29
      730 per cent profit: NYA, No 4, 1983, 122
      Goldman's taxes: MI, June 1985, 11
177   His overall record: MI, April 1985, 56
      Harry Helmsley: MI, June 1986, 29
      Dynasties of developers: NYA, No 4, 1985, 22
      'probably the single largest . . .': MI, March 1985, 22
      12,000 brokers: MI, July 1985, 76
178   Mrs Bacon suing: WPAG, 213
      architect suing: WPAG, 219
      Steinberg sued: MI, October 1985, 104
179   'He's like one of those New York . . .': NYT, September 12, 1985
      number of lawyers: NYA, No 2, 1985, 34
      500 per cent growth in law schools: ibid
180   Squadron billings: MI, June 1985, 110
      Rothschilds sued: MI, October 1985, 117
      Morgan Guaranty: NYT, September 10, 1985
      Trump tax exemption: MI, May 1985, 114
      Zuckerman's bid: MI, January 1986, 85
181   Citicorp pedigree: Collier, 420, 430

182 Pickens's Gulf profit: *Sunday Times*, December 1, 1985
  lie detectors: MI, September 1985, 82
183 'We're getting more business . . .': MI, April 1985, 72
  Chase Manhattan, Union Carbide and Johnson & Johnson reports:
  MI, July 1985, 131
184 Chase art collection: *Forbes Four Hundred*, October 27, 1986,
  3
  corporate art: NYT, September 15, 1985
185 Merrill Lynch recruiting: MI, July 1985, 10
  the OPM fraud: MI, June 1985, 136
186 'one of the most disastrous businessmen': Galbraith, 178
  Whitney's $181.05: Sloane, 70
187 1851–3 boom: Spann, 283
  1857 slump: Spann, 394
  1907 Treasury loans: Patterson, 202
  World War One records: Sloane, 38
  'the conviction that God intended . . .': Galbraith, 35
188 'honeyfugling, hornswoggling . . .': Morison, Vol 3, 285
  Professor Dice: quoted Galbraith, 187
  'cheap at current prices': quoted Galbraith, 53
  broker's valet and speculating nurse: *Only Yesterday* by Frederick
189 Lewis Allen (NY, 1931), 315
  'then as now . . .': Galbraith, 102
  'Sooner or later . . .': quoted Galbraith, 108
  'the markets now are generally . . .': ibid, 116
  footnote on incomes: Chase, 31
190 'I bid 205 . . .': Sloane, 62
  Cantor on Rockefeller: Collier, 172
  Churchill at Stock Exchange: Galbraith, 122
  Drop in securities: Sloane, 46–7 and Morison, Vol 3, 286
191 New York in Depression: Caro, 323
  Apple sellers: Jonnes, 66
192 'show pictures which reinstate courage . . .': quoted Galbraith,
  137
  'Behind the Ow! in the Dow': NYT, June 11, 1986
193 'What we do daily . . .': Sloane, 133
  Washington Irving: WPAG, 93
  blizzard of 1888: Birmingham/*Dakota*, 8
  inventory remarketing: MI, January 1985, 14
  renting people to stand in line: Fishlock, 122
194 'we *own* this place . . .': quoted Goldman, Peter, 263
  'probably the most powerful . . .': Caro, 1067

194   'financial center of the world . . .': Little, 23
      colonel in Grenada: MI, May 1985, 76

                CHAPTER SEVEN   MAKING IT

196   Numbers going through Grand Central: WPAG, 222
199   'it's stunning . . . I have always considered . . .': NYT, September
      18, 1985
      'the most famous building': leaflet given to Empire State Building
      visitors
200   horseless Rough Riders: Morison, Vol 3, 120
      first ticker tape parade: *Famous First Facts* compiled by Joseph
      Nathan Kane (NY, 1981)
      'as the Roosevelt carriage . . .': NYT, June 19, 1910
      1,500 tons of ticker: *New York Access Guide*, 67
201   Barbara Walters and Martha: MI, October 1985, 107
      Barbara Walters and Pratesi: MI, May 1985, 121
      Sanford Weil's caviar sets: MI, September 1985, 68
      Brian Marlowe: MI, January 1985, 54
      Kathy Keeton: MI, July 1985, 24
202   Yankee Stadium crowds: NYT, September 25, 1985
      McEnroe: NYT, January 16, 1986
203   *Social Register*, November 1985 edition preface
      Mrs Astor's list: Birmingham/*Dakota*, 64
204   Mrs Vanderbilt and Sutton Place: Chase, 213
      Union Club: Chase, 63
      J. P. Morgan and the Metropolitan: Leapman, 199
      Johnson family meeting: MI, May 1985, 80
206   'self-invented money-making machine': *New York Herald* quoted
      Spann, 205
      7,000 millionaires: Chase, 31
      Forbes Four Hundred from *Forbes* magazine October 27, 1986
      574,300 millionaires: Boyer, 406
209   New School classes: *New School Bulletin*, 1985
211   'despite its reputation': Jonnes, 34
212   'run the OP line': quoted Shapiro, 106 (based on New York State
      Legislature's Committee of Investigation, 1847)
      'a place of unlawful . . .': quoted Shapiro, 112 from *The World*,
      August 23, 1887
213   'Immigrants must be treated': quoted Shapiro, 147
214   'The keepers of emigrant . . .': ibid, 106

214 'They were very crude . . .': ibid, 247
'Kike': see Birmingham/*Crowd*, 332 and Caro 31. Also *The Joys of Yiddish*, 182, by Leo Rosten, who disputes this theory.
'the dialect that unifies': Richard F. Shepard, quoted Marqusee, 23
215 'not only does X bill . . .': MI, April 1985, 90
'the insane-hours issue . . .': MI, April 1985, 93
216 'a one-way ride . . .': ibid, 91
'I feel embarrassed . . .': Brook, 64
TV weatherman's pay: MI, September 1985, 13
advertising salaries: MI, January 1986, 42
per capita income and 'the key to economic success': Brecher, 5 and Table 1.6
217 Morris Gest: Matz, 120
Nathan Seril: MI, January 1985, 58
Yuri Radzievsky: MI, April 1985, 11
Basia Piasecka: MI, May 1985, 82
218 Zion Yakuel: MI, November 1985, 152
taxi medallions: NYA, 1984, No 4, 36
220 Jimmy Martin: Birmingham/*Dakota*, 112, 120
Charles Atkins: MI, November 1985, 93
222 J. P. Morgan buying a boat: Morris/*Port*, 109
'the intelligent alternative . . .': Tonight Show, October 1962
earning $2.5 million in 1979: Auletta/*Streets*, 162

CHAPTER EIGHT   YOU GOTTA KEEP MOVING

223 footnote on buildings up and down: MI, July 1985, 39
224 O Henry: quoted Patterson, 10
'the spirit of pulling down . . .': ibid, 111
'Overturn, overturn . . .': quoted Spann, 96
'New York is notoriously . . .': ibid, 158
225 Trinity Church: Spann, 3
Croton reservoir: Silver, 88
Waldorf-Astoria: ibid, 65
226 Vanderbilt mansion: Silver, 110 and AIA, 168
Raskob and 1929 boom: Galbraith, 41
'Welcome Sweet Warbler': Leapman, 35
227 Castle Garden-Aquarium: Silver, 96 and WPAG, 307
a vindictive response: Caro, 678
Penn Station: Silver, 32 and WPAG, 165

228 Madison Square Garden: WPAG, 330
     Dempsey's orchids and Penn Station deal: MI, April 1986, 55
229 'Until the first blow fell . . .': NYT, October 30, 1963
     'Does it make any sense': NYT, November 1, 1963
223 National and New York preservation: NYA, 1985, No 4, 145
232 'Our cannibal city': Patterson, 7
     New Yorkers' walking pace: William H. Whyte's introduction to
     1982 edition of WPAG, xxx
233 Density of population 1854 and 1861: Spann, 150
     smallpox and yellow fever: WPAG, 125
     'in such a manner': WPAP, 402
234 'it may be a subject': WPAP, 404
235 Townsend's warbler: Thomas, 154
236 Fulton's Nassau: WPAG, 441
     ferries generally: Spann, 186
     ox carts and horsecars: Fischler, 6–7
     Harvey and the El: Fischler, 8 passim
237 'Despite the prevalent idea . . .': WPAG, 404
238 LaGuardia demolishing: Patterson, 246
     End of El: Fischler, 260
     Powerful opposition: ibid, 10 and 26
     First train: ibid, 41
239 globes above stations: ibid, 48 and WPAG, 402
     coloured IND tiles: ibid, 137
240 'It made interborough romance feasible': Starr, 61
     Jews to Bronx along IRT: Glazer, 92
     Italians and Irish to Bronx: Jonnes, 4
241 Blacks to Bedford-Stuyvesant: NYA, 1973, No 2, 36
     withdrawal of whites in NY: Glazer, 56
     Brownsville: NYA, 1985, No 2, 3
242 Charlotte Street Jews from Harlem: Jonnes, 208
     GI Bill of Rights: Auletta/*Streets*, 39
243 World Fair deficit: Caro, 1085
     'liked what they saw': Israelowitz, 146
     the *General Slocum* disaster: NYT, June 16, 1904
244 Germans from Tompkins Square after the disaster: WPAG, 123
245 'If the typical American urban family': NYA, 1979, No 4, 4
247 Koch and rent control: Auletta/*Streets*, 41
     1.2 million apartments: NYA, 1986, No 4, 72
248 'by the end of the century': NYA, 1983, No 4, 13
     Stevenson *New Yorker* cartoon, 1979: reproduced NYA, 1979,
     No 4, 7

249 10,000 loft homes in 1977, NYA, 1979, No 4, 22
250 LoBro: NYT, September 20, 1985
     original Hell's Kitchen: WPAG, 155
251 'It doesn't matter . . .': *Washington Square*, 24

CHAPTER NINE   A SLIGHTLY ROTTEN APPLE

253 Castellano shooting: NYT, December 17, 1985
254 The Mafia background information comes from various news-
     paper reports of the great trials which ended in 1987; also from
     Talese/ *Father*.
     details of the trials: *Sunday Times*, November 23, 1986 and
     January 18, 1987 NYT, June 14, 1986 and February 27, 1985
256 Luciano helps Navy and Army: Talese, op cit, 219
257 Lindsay enlists Mafia: Morris, Charles R., 75
     Testa profile: Fishlock, 144
     Duvall at trial: *Guardian*, October 11, 1986
     'When have I ever refused an accommodation': Mario Puzo, *The
     Godfather*, 289
     'Hardly a day goes by': Marqusee, 206
258 New York Prison Association figures: Spann, 253
     Astor Place Riot: Spann, 233
259 'by the millionaires': Spann, 239
260 beginning of police: ibid, 316
     police corruption and politics: ibid, 319
     police riots 1857: ibid, 382
     police riots 1976: NYT, October 7, 1976
     police benefits: Auletta/*Streets*, 50
261 'so long as we have one division . . .': quoted Spann, 317 from
     New York Tribune, March 13, 1844
     Conscription clause: Patterson, 135
     Dead Rabbits 1857 riot: Spann, 393
     Dutch Heinrichs: WPAG, 141, 155
262 Dopey Benny Fein: Garrett, 152
     Monk Eastman: Jonnes, 138
     1855 Prohibitory Act: Spann, 373
     Prohibition: Boorstin, Vol 3, 77–87
263 Murder Inc: Garrett, 157
264 United Bamboo: *Guardian*, January 5, 1987
     Salerno's 156 per cent: Newfield, 254
     numbers games: NYA, 1973, No 2, 37 and Anderson, 149

264 Puerto Ricans and Jewish brothers involved: Talese/*Father*, 158
Bedford-Stuyvesant survey: NYA, 1973, No 2, 34
265 narcotics legislation: Jonnes, 140
1985 and 1987 figures: *Sunday Times*, February 1, 1987
266 'Crack gives you more bang': ibid
The most dangerous place: Boyer, 166
New York polls: e.g. NYT January 10, 1985, when 41 per cent
said that crime was the biggest problem
267 rate of killings: quoted by Brecher, 354
burning of the Bronx: Jonnes, 7, 232 passim
268 the gangs: Jonnes, 237, 245
269 1977 power failure: NYT, July 14, 15, 16, 1977
270 'the richest city in the history of the world': Daniel P. Moynihan
in Jonnes, xv
one third needing public assistance: Auletta/*Streets*, 12
citizens in poverty increase: Brecher, 4
poverty lines of 1961 and 1974: ibid, 67
in 1985, with numbers: MI, April 1985, 124. Also millionaires.
271 Archbishop's figure: CBS News, March 10, 1985
City's figure: MI, April 1986, 18
Coalition for Homeless figure: given in Yorkshire Television
documentary on New York homeless, *First Tuesday*, January
6, 1987
homeless mental patients: Starr, 155 and *Guardian*, December
4, 1984
released prisoners: Starr, 124
272 Use of Potter's Field today: Yorkshire TV, op cit
History of: WPAC, 551
city sued in 1979: *Guardian*, op cit
273 fifty-five welfare hotels: NYT, June 13, 1986 and *Guardian*,
July 24, 1986
274 Tammany building commission: Caro, 713
rigged elections: Garrett, 112
civil service exams rigged: Garrett, 133
Tammany leaves Union Square: Caro, 711
'At table 23 . . .': Newfield and Du Brul, 199–203
275 Donald Manes: *Sunday Times*, March 16, 1986 and *Guardian*,
November 27, 1986
276 Police scandals: *Sunday Times*, May 4, 1985
'corruption in narcotics law enforcement': Knapp Commission
Report, 97, quoted Jonnes, 142
'The biggest single supplier': Newfield, 161

277 Eastman-Hemingway brawl: Edmiston, 227
Mailer-Vidal fracas: Vidal's version is given in *The Moronic Inferno* by Martin Amis, 98–9
Gun licences: MI, June 1985, 9
278 Taki 183: Cooper, 14
279 type faces: Castleman, 56
280 'a laugh and a shudder': MI, January 1986, 59
Staten Island ferry swordsman: NYT, July 8, 1986

CHAPTER TEN   THE OVERLORDS

281 It has been said that: Patterson, 20
'more a mole hill': WPAP, 39
For Stuyvesant see also Morison, Vol 1, 120 and WPAG, 124 passim
282 the pear tree: Patterson, 28
283 'In Boston they ask': Mark Twain in *What Paul Bourget Thinks of Us* (NY, 1897), 23
Astor: Morison, Vol 2, 101 passim
284 'knowing what I now know': *John Jacob Astor* by K. W. Porter (Boston, 1931), Vol 2, 940, quoted Spann, 208
'with her passed': quoted Birmingham/*Crowd*, 345
Vanderbilt: see WPAG, 146 passim; also Morison, Vol 2, 237, 348
285 William Walker: Hugh Thomas *Cuba* (London, 1971), 227–8
Vanderbilt's madness: Cooke, 267
286 Theodore Roosevelt: Morison, Vol 3, 147–50 and Cooke, 297–99
287 'Not since Lincoln': Cooke, 331
German-American Bund: Cooke, 340
'the great arsenal of democracy': quote by Mark Arnold Forster, *The World At War* (London, 1973), 96
288 Russell on Rockefeller: quoted by Collier (on title page)
289 'I'm bound to be rich': Collier, 19
'to promote the well-being': Collier, 65
290 'Practising the violin': Collier, 81
Photograph of the Rockefellers: Collier, facing page 123
292 'City Hall, Rockefeller speaking': Collier, 225
major airlines in debt: Collier, 408
instrument of US foreign policy: Collier, 318
293 'We have made a firm commitment': Collier, 415

294 Nelson lobbies for Peron: Collier, 236
     JFK's assessment: Collier, 343
     $48 million spent on career: Collier, 454
295 official history rewritten: Collier, 348
     the vetoed bills: MI, September 1985, 82
     Attica mutiny: Collier, 463
     'the bloodiest encounter': quoted Collier, 465
     'the absolute terror': Richard Reeves, quoted by Collier, 409
296 cartel with I. G. Farben: Collier, 225
     Churchill as biographer: Collier, 629
     'about 70 per cent of Nelson's giving': Collier, 490
     Christmas at Pocantino: Collier, 511
     Farben slave labour: Collier, 226
297 Leningrad hardships: Harrison Salisbury, *The 900 Days* (London, 1971), 563
     Mumford's view: Caro, 12
     'Moses thinks he's God': quoted Jonnes, 119
298 'supreme contempt': Caro, 51
     radio network's ban: Caro, 416
299 Otto Kahn's offer: Caro, 278
300 Fourteen separate parks: Caro, 237
     Low bridges: Caro, 951
     200,000 cars in 1920: NYA, 1981, No 4, 57
301 31 organisations protest: Jonnes, 121
     1,530 apartments demolished: Caro, 878
302 60,000 people displaced: Jonnes, 121
     nuclear fuels across New York: NYT, September 10, 1985
     'A lively city scene': Jacobs, 148
303 Al Smith's zoo key: Caro, 382
     demolition of Aquarium: Caro, 678
     ferry terminal: Caro, 449
     detailed files of politicians: Caro, 728
     Moses photograph: by Arnold Newman, published Caro, 978
     'the second toughest job': John Lindsay quoted Auletta/*Streets*, 242
304 Mailer's election: Hacker, 62
305 Mailer's proposal: Auletta/*Streets*, 262
     O'Dwyer's rise: Garrett, 271
     O'Dwyer's fall: Caro, 787
306 'If a letter carrier in Brooklyn': Starr, 23
     Carey contemplates dismissing Beame: Auletta/*Streets*, 84
     Winchell's view of Walker: quoted Marqusee, 228

307   Walker's unaccounted money: Mitgang, 264
      'Ladies, I want to ask': quoted Morris/*Manhattan*, 62
      LaGuardia with fireman and band: Caro, 444
      LaGuardia providing Jewish cops: Burgess, 135
308   LaGuardia ordering uniform: Garrett, 282
      votes against teachers: Garrett, 120
      relations with press: Garrett, 124
      high turnover of staff: Caro, 445
      secretary sacked: Caro, 446
      Banning burlesque: Garrett, 122
      communists in Dept of Welfare: Garrett, 194
309   federal money for New York: Garrett, 179
      $8,000 in war bonds: Garrett, 121
310   'To bolster the city's case': Koch/*Mayor*, 106
      'I Love New York': MI October 1985, 16. See also programme
      notes by John McGlinn to record album *Songs of New York*
      (Book-of-the-Month Records, 1984)
      Richard Varick: GB
311   Koch on death penalty: see his article in *The New Republic*,
      April 15, 1985
      $5 for every vote: NYT, September 15, 1985
      $300,000 for autobiography: Fishlock, 121
      'What I had going for me': Koch/*Politics*, 9
      'Haven't looked so good': quoted by Auletta in NYT, December
      22, 1985
      On the stump in Harlem and receiving the Puerto Rican Minister
      in City Hall: the author was present on both occasions March 22,
      1985

CHAPTER ELEVEN   IMPERIAL, BUT POTHOLED

313   lived on East 21st: Goldberger introduction to 1983 facsimile
      edition of Chase, v
      'the owner of several companies': Chase, 41
      'synonym for big': Chase, 3
314   100 SENSATIONAL: Chase, 11
      'not elsewhere': Chase, 30
      'taken all in all': Chase, 21
      100 OUTSTANDING: Chase, 86
      Waldorf-Astoria: Chase, 129
315   'New York's chorus girls': Chase, 41

315 his innocence: see Goldberger introduction, op cit
'The Wonder Building': Chase, 211
'It is the icing': H. L. Mencken, *Prejudices*, Sixth Series, 1928,
quoted Marqusee, 3
'the incomparable, the brilliant': Gunther, op cit, 549
316 'unique in the history': Koch quoted by Auletta/*Streets*, 254
'the greatest city in the world': Mailer in *Running Against the
Machine* (NY, 1969, ed Peter Manso), 9, quoted Hacker, 143
'at the centre of the universe': introduction to WPAG, xxxii
'like a great novel': Auletta/*Streets*, xii, 8, 133
'Titan of cities . . . the civilised world': Caro, 5, 774, 830, 837, 991
'the cultural capital': Glazer, 6
317 'that rich diversity': NYCCI, op cit (foreword to)
'I do not propose': quoted Auletta/*Streets*, 30
Transit strike: ibid, 59
318 1970 education bill: NYT, July 2, 1985
water charges and 364-day year: Auletta/*Streets*, 99
319 'The market for New York City obligations': NYT, July 2, 1985
spending $12.8 billion: Auletta/*Streets*, 29
$400 million state loan: NYT, July 2, 1985
MAC set up: Auletta, 90
321 MAC bond sales, deadline and deliverance: NYT, July 2, 1985
Western economy might collapse: Auletta, 90
'a Republican president': quoted NYA, 1983, No 4, 165
322 After-effects of crisis: NYT, June 30, 1985
Paris and London subways: NYA, 1983, No 4, 165
North American subways: NYA, 1981, No 4, 1979
323 3,264 trains cancelled: MI, September 1985, 77
Subway expenditures: NYA, 1982, No 3, 53
Farebeating: ibid, 101
Abandoned subway carriages: NYA, 1981, No 4, 91; also
Fischler, 70 and Starr, 63
324 Grumman buses: NYA, 1981, No 4, 90
Sinking of *Normandie* and Grace Line pier fiasco: Starr, 14. See
also Feininger, 25
Bank mislays bonds: MI, May 1985, 97
warehouse disaster: MI, July 1985, 60
325 Pothole Corporation: Fishlock, 116
'Typical New York pothole': quoted MI, May 1985, 77
326 50 miles of steam pipes: AIA, 583
327 manhole covers: MI, January 1986, 59
raw sewage in Hudson: NYA, 1985, No 4, 40

327   Geddes: quoted WPAP, 399
      'fascinated by Calcutta': Paul Theroux in *The Imperial Way*
      (London, 1985), 23
      'a combination of freak technical failures': Newfield, 268
      Edison: Boorstin, Vol 3, 377 passim
328   Con Ed and other charges: Boyer, 114 (based on 1983 Depart-
      ment of Energy figures)
      Federal Power Commission's conclusion: Newfield, 268
329   The Great Blackout: NYT, November 11 and 12, 1965

      CHAPTER TWELVE   IT'S A HELLUVA TOWN
335   'there are two things': Professor Ronald Steel, University of
      Southern California, NYT Book Review, November 2, 1986
336   'merely the loudspeaker': WPAP, 79
      Capital City of the World: oil on linen 1982 by Robert Donley
      'When it's 9.30': quoted Marqusee, 3
337   'the tradition of hating': Mike Royko of *Chicago Sun-Times*
      quoted Boyer, xii
      'there is nothing that unites': Roger Angell, *New Yorker*, Decem-
      ber 8, 1986
      Gotham: Washington Irving, *Salmagundi*, November 11, 1807
338   'Pittsburgh Bemused': NYT, March 29, 1985
      white mobs: Morris, Charles R., 149
      citizen views in 1985 campaign: NYT, September 10, 1985
339   'highly diverse, incredibly complex': NYA, 1983, No 4, 19
      'too often life in New York': quoted by Caro, 358
      Ulysses in New York: Edmiston, 62
      Moby Dick: Edmiston, 28
      Sister Carrie: Edmiston, 66
      'A hundred times': quoted Marqusee, 4
340   'it can destroy an individual': White, 11
      'government of the people': quoted Newfield, 205
      Theodore Roosevelt and muckrakers: see Morison, Vol 3, 135,
      also Mencken *The American Language: Supplement One* (NY,
      1945), 302
      'one is glad to slip away': Vincent Patrick in NYT Book Review,
      January 11, 1987
341   The figures for casualties in Northern Ireland were compiled by
      the private Irish Information Partnership, whose assessments
      have been regarded as reliable by, among others, the Irish
      Government in Dublin.

341   Russia favours America for UN: NYT, September 24, 1985
342   Moses et al. in lobby: Caro, 771
      UN moving round New York: NYT, op cit
343   preference for Connecticut: ibid
      origins of Turtle Bay and Welfare Island: WPAG, 208 and 421,
      AIA, 301
344   UN architects: Goldberger/*Observed*, 132 and AIA, 158
      designer laureate: Collier, 213
      Senator McCarthy: NYT, September 24, 1985
345   1977 study of UN income: Auletta/*Streets*, 134
      lavish UN expenditures: MI, December 1985, 14
346   Spanish delegate kicked: NYT, op cit
      Saudi diplomat rebuffed: ibid
      New Yorkers and UN vote on Israel: Starr, 206
347   Koch at UN: NYT, September 20, 1985
348   UN birthday celebrations: NYT, September 15, 1985 et seq.
350   Pension rights: Auletta/*Streets*, 50
      LaGuardia's insurance plan: Garrett, 198: see also NYA, 1985,
      No 2, 62
351   Astor House experiment: *Evening Post*, March 4, 1863 quoted
      Spann, 98
      Cocktails: Mencken, *The American Language*, 149; also
      Moscow, 121
352   Irene Castle: Anderson, 75
      Ginsberg: Edmiston, 125
      'Somewhere along the line': *On the Road* by Jack Kerouac
      (1976), 14
      'most non-American skyscrapers': Goldberger/*Skyscraper*, ix
      Ten subway fan clubs, etc.: Fischler, 207–16
      Music under New York: NYT, August 24, 1985
353   Nancy Reagan: MI, February 1986, 96
      LaGuardia's air ticket: Morris/*Port*, 80
354   'Anti-Americanism Grows New Roots': NYT, June 11, 1986

INDEX

Abbey Theatre, Dublin, 79
Abraham & Straus, Brooklyn (store), 120
Abyssinian Baptist Church, Harlem, 138–9, 151, 155
Act of Consolidation (1898), 61
Adam Clayton Powell Boulevard, Harlem, 137
Adam, Robert, 49
Adams Street, 17–18
African-American Day, 81
African Grove (Black theatre), 143
Agee, James, 52
Albanians, 95
Alexander III, Tsar of Russia, 85
Algonquin Indians, 38–9
Ali, Muhammed (*formerly* Cassius Clay), 162
Allende, Salvatore, President of Chile, 293
Amalgamated Clothing Workers of America, 119
Ambrose Light and Channel, 31, 73
America (liner), 70
America (yacht), 205
American Civil War, 142–3
American Jewish Committee, 116
American Stock Exchange (*formerly* Curb Exchange), 170, 170n

American Telephone and Telegraph Building, 49–50
America's Cup, 205
Amish sect, 131, 132
Anastasia, Albert, 254
Anchorage Channel, 25
Andersen, Hans Christian: statue, 353
Anne, Queen of Great Britain, 171n
anti-Semitism, 114–15, 125–6; *see also* Jews
Aquarium, 227, 303
Aqueduct (racecourse), 58
Arbiter Ring see Workmen's Circle
Arlen, Harold, 149
Armstrong, Louis, 148
arson, 267–8
art: and big corporations, 184–5; study, 210
Arthur, Chester A., President of USA, 21
artists: studios, 249
Asians, 90–1, 94–5
Association for a Better New York, 199
Astor House Hotel, 351
Astor, John Jacob, 205–6, 240, 283–4
Astor, John Jacob II, 238
Astor Place Riot (1849), 258–9, 269

Astor, Mrs William Waldorf, 203, 284

Astoria (district), 248

Atkins, Charles Agee, 220–1

Attica prison riot, 295, 295n

Auchincloss, Louis, 232

Auden, W. H., 20

Babson, Roger W., 189

Baker, George (Father Divine), 153–4

Baker, George F., 65

Baldwin, James, 147–8, 157, 159

Ball, George, 321

Bank of Manhattan Building, 32, 46

Bank of Boston, 182–3

Barnum, Phineas T., 23, 226–8

Barrio, El, 141

Barsimon, Jacob, 85, 113

Bartholdi, Frédéric Auguste, 26

Basie, Count, 148, 294

Battery, The, 28–9

Beame, Mayor Abraham, 306, 310, 317–21, 346

Bean, L. L., 92

Beat Generation, 352

Bedford-Stuyvesant, Brooklyn, 240–1, 264–5

Bedloe Island (Liberty Island; *formerly* Minissais, *then* Great Oyster Island), 26–8

beggars, 269–70

Bensonhurst, 104

Berkowitz, Sol, 329

Berlin, Irving, 121

Bhopal (India), 184, 185

Biaggi, Congressman Mario, 80–1

'Big Apple': term explained, 349

Big Apple Pothole and Sidewalk Protection Corporation, 325

Big Z Two-Way Radio Inc., 219

Black Muslims, 160–4, 194

Black Spades (gang), 268

Black Star Shipping Line, 152–3

Blackbirds (show), 149

Blackout, Great (1965), 328–34

blacks, 81; and racial antipathy and discrimination, 106, 157–60, 165; and Jews, 125–6, 159–60; life in Harlem, 135–40, 146–7; slave origins, history and development of, 141–7; in armed forces, 146–7; as entertainers, 148–50, 155; militancy and racial awareness, 150–5; in Depression, 155; influx of, 155–6; employment, 165; university courses on culture of, 209; migrate, 240–2

Bonanno gang, 255

Bonwit Teller (fashion house), 176

Boston, Mass., 20, 342

Bourke-White, Margaret, 46

Bowery Boys (gang), 261

Brasco, Congressman Frank, 274

Breezy Point, 74

bridges: Moses builds, 301; *see also* individual bridges

Brighton Beach (Little Odessa), 96–8

Bristol (destroyer), 332–3

Broadway: as Indian trail, 146

Bronck, Jonas, 60

Bronfman, Edgar Miles, 207

Bronx: few skyscrapers, 56; clapboard houses, 57; character, 58–60; blacks in, 156; Expressway, 301–2

Brookhaven National Laboratory, Long Island, 302

Brooklyn: single skyscraper, 56; character, 61–4; cosmopolitanism, 91; blacks in, 156, 165; expansion, 232
Brooklyn, USS, 64
Brooklyn Bridge, 17–23, 29–30, 34–5
Brooklyn Dodgers, 63–4, 157, 158
Brooklyn Heights, 20, 24, 230
Brooklyn Manhattan Transit System (BMT), 239
Brooklyn Museum, 195n.
Brooklyn Navy Yard, 24, 110–12
Brooks, Mel, 355
Brownsville, Brooklyn, 165, 241
Brunswick Hotel, 226n
Buckley, William F., Jr., 304
budget, city, *see under* New York
building and development, 223–231; protection orders, 231–2; *see also* rent control; skyscrapers
Bunche, Ralph, 59
Buntline, Ned, 258–9
Bureau of Naval Intelligence, 256
bus services, 324; kneeling bus, 350–1

Calcutta, 327
Calgary (Canada), 20
Calloway, Cab, 155
Canarsie, Brooklyn, 64, 104, 106
Cantor, Eddie, 121, 190n
Capital City of the World (painting), 336
Capone, Al, 262
Capote, Truman, 20
Carey, Governor Hugh, 306, 319
Caribbean Cultural Center, 165
Carson, Johnny, 222
Caruso, Enrico, 104

Castellano, Paul, 253–4, 257
Castle Garden (Castle Clinton), 212–13, 226–7
Castle, Irene, 352
Catholicism *see* Roman Catholicism
Caughnawaga Indians, 39
Cavanagh, James A., 320n
Cavitt, Dick, 277
Celanese building, 49
Cement and Concrete Workers' District Council, 255
cemeteries, 59, 272
Central Park, 42, 55, 235; Zoo, 96, 303; H. C. Andersen statue, 353
Center for Ethics and Corporate Policy, 171
Chase Manhattan Bank, 172, 182, 183, 184, 292–3, 295
Chase, W. Parker: *New York, the Wonderful City*, 313–16
Chevron (company), 182
Chicago, 43–4
Chicago Tribune, 45
Chinatown, 87, 106
Chinese Exclusion Act (1882), 87
Christian Endeavour Society, 228
Chrysler building, 20, 31, 45–6, 51, 55–6
Chrysler, Walter, 45
Churchill, Winston S., 190, 296
Citibank, 293, 295
Citicorp, 181, 194
Citicorp Centre, 49
City College (University), 91, 119–20, 322
City Hall, 33; and corruption, 274–5
Civic Center, 33
civil rights, 158

class (social), 203–4
Clearinghouse Interbank Payments System, 194
Clinton, De Witt, 68
Cloisters, The, 290
clubs, 204–5
Coalition for the Homeless, 271
Cobble Hill, 248
cocaine, 265–6
cocktails, 351
Cohn, Roy, 354
Coleman, John, 170
Coliseum, 54–5
Colombo gang, 255
Colombo, Joseph, 254
Colored Orphan Asylum, 143
Columbian Order (Society of St Tammany) see Tammany
Columbus Circle, 55, 180
Commentary (journal), 116
Commissioner of Sanitation, 110
Communist Manifesto (Marx & Engels), 83
commuting, 64–5, 196–8
Coney Island: character, 62–3; Parachute Jump, 231
Consolidated Edison Company, 327–9, 334
Cooke, Alistair, 287
Cooke, Cardinal Terence, 78, 268
Coolidge, Calvin, President of USA, 188
Corallo, 'Tony Ducks', 264
Corbett, James J., 62
corporate raiding, 181–2
corruption (civic) and scandals, 274–7, 306–7
Costa Rica, 285n
Costello, Frank, 263
Cotton Club, 149
Crane, Hart, 20

crime: gangs and gangsters, 100, 261–2; and Prohibition, 262–3; organised, 262–5; see also Mafia
Croatians, 85
Cross-Bronx Expressway, 301–2
Croton River and Reservoir, 225
Cummings, Robert, 28
Cunard, Nancy, 149
Cuomo, Governor Mario, 80
Curb Exchange see American Stock Exchange

Dakota building, Central Park West, 123
Danes, 84
Dead Rabbits (gang), 261
Declaration of Independence, 33–34, 341
Democratic Party, 120; see also Tammany
demolition, 223–32
demonstrations, 106–7, 109–12; see also parades
Dempsey, Jack, 228
Depression, Great, 46–7, 155, 191–2, 219–20
DeSapio, Carmine, 102, 275
Dewey, Thomas E., 90, 120, 263, 309
Diabo, John, 39
Dice, Professor Charles Amos, 188
Displaced Persons Act, 89
Divine, Father see Baker, George
Dominicans, 90, 95
Dopey Benny Fein Gang, 262
Dos Passos, John, 20
Dow, Charles H., 192n
Dow Jones index, 192, 192n
Draft Riots (1863), 261

Dreiser, Theodore: *Sister Carrie*, 339

drugs: and crime, 265–6; and police corruption, 276

Du Bois, W. E. B., 150, 152, 161, 162, 209

Du Pont, Pierre, 226n

Dubuffet, Jean, 185

Dulles, John Foster, 114, 296

Duvall, Robert, 257

Dwyer, Big Bill, 262

earnings (income), 216–17

East River, 20–4, 68–9, 73–4, 236

Eastman, Max, 277

Ebbets Field, Brooklyn, 63–4

Edison, Thomas Alva, 327–8

education and study (adult), 208–211

electricity supply, 327–8, 328n; *see also* power failures

elevated railroads, 236–8

Ellington, Duke, 149, 198n

Ellis Island, 27–8; and immigrants, 85–7, 213–14

Elmshurst, 243

Embargo Act (1807), 283

Emerald Societies, 100; *see also* Irish, The

Empire State: name adopted, 34

Empire State Building, 20, 32; construction, 40–1, 46–7, 226; and city laws, 48; windows, 51; struck by aircraft, 53–4; ownership, 177; fame, 199, 317; lacks tenants, 315; in 1965 power failure, 331, 334

Encyclopaedia Judaica, 113

Equal Employment Opportunity Commission, 165

Equitable Life Assurance Building, 43–4, 48

Equitable Life Assurance Society, 177, 184n

Erie Canal, 68, 83

Esplanade, Brooklyn, 24

Europe: immigration from, 83–9, 90

Europe, James Reese, 148

Exxon (company), 174

Exxon building, 49

Fabius, Laurent, 94

Family Court building, 17

family life, 245–6

Farrad, Mr, 161

Federal Bureau of Investigation, 256

Federal Reserve Bank, 188

Federal Writers Project, 335

Feininger, Andreas, 69

ferry services, 236

fire-escapes, 56–7

Fitzgerald, Scott, 66

Fitzgerald, Thomas, 275

Fitzsimmons, Bob, 62

Flannery, Grand Marshal Michael, 78

Flatiron Building, 44

Flinn, John J., 43

Florida, 136

Flushing Meadows, 58; UN at, 342

food: national and ethnic, 92–3

Forbes Four Hundred, 206–7

Ford Foundation, 125

Ford, Gerald, President of USA, 294, 319–20

Forest Hills, 58, 243, 338

Forrest, Edwin, 258–9

Fortune 500, 174

Forward see *Jewish Daily Forward*

foundation garments, 352

Franklin D. Roosevelt Drive, 24, 33

Franz Josef II, Emperor of Austria-Hungary, 128

Fraunces, 'Black Sam', 143

Fred F. French Building, 39

Frederick Douglass Boulevard, Harlem, 137

Free Workers' School, 83, 119

Freedom's Journal, 143

French, The, 93–4

French Connection, The (film), 238

Freud, Sigmund, 123

Fribourg, Michel, 207

Frick, Henry C., 66

Fulton Ferry, 22

Fulton Fish Market, 30

Fulton, Robert, 236

Fulton Street, 30–1

Galante, Carmine, 254

Galbraith, John Kenneth, 187, 189, 191n

Gallo brothers, 257

Gallo, Joey, 105, 254

Gambino gang, 255, 257

gangs and gangsters *see* crime

garbage, 110

Garbo, Greta, 201

Garibaldi, Giuseppe, 61

Garment District, Manhattan, 95, 242

Garvey, Marcus, 151–3, 161

Gaynor, Mayor William Jay, 200

Geddes, Sir Patrick, 327

General Electric Company, 187, 190

General Motors (company), 174, 187, 188

General Slocum (steamship), 243–4

Genovese gang, 255

gentrification, 245–51

geology, 42–3

George III, King of Great Britain, 25, 33

George Washington Bridge, 71

German-American Bund, 287

Germans: parade, 81; immigrants, 83, 87; colony, 98

Gershwin, George, 121

Gershwin, Ira, 114, 121

Gest, Morris, 217

'Ghetto, The', 117

GI Bill of Rights, 242

Gilbert, Cass, 45

Ginsberg, Allen, 352

Giscard d'Estaing, Valéry, 320

Glazer, Nathan, 113, 123–4; *Beyond the Melting Pot* (with Daniel P. Moynihan), 141n

Glorious Revolution, 1688 (Britain), 98

Godfather, The (film), 257

Goetz, Bernhard, 277–8, 278n

'Golden Ghetto', 122

Goldman, Sol, 176–7

Goldwater, Barry, 162

Gonzales, Juan, 280

Gooden, Dwight, 355

Goodson, Mark, 207

Gophers (gang), 100, 261–2

Gorbachev, Mikhail, 179

'Gotham': as name for New York, 337, 337n

Gould, Jay, 59

Governors Island, 25–6

Graham, Billy, 151, 290

Gramercy Park East, 54
Grand Army Plaza, Brooklyn, 61
Grand Central Station, 64; Jewish proselytising at, 131; Merrill Lynch booth at, 194, 196; character, 195–7, 227; protected, 231; and homeless, 272; in power failure, 330
Grand Concourse hotel, 273
Greeks, 95–6
Greeley, Horace, 83
Greenberg, Clement, 116n
Greenwich Village, 230, 233, 249
Greyhound buses, 198
Gromyko, Andrei Andreyevitch, 348
Groves, Brigadier-General Leslie R., 288n
Guccione, Bob, 201
Guevara, Ché, 348
Guinness, (Sir) Alec, 66–7
Gulf Oil, 182, 183
guns and gun licences, 277–8
Gunther, John, 315

Haas, Rev. George, 243–4
Hackman, Gene, 238
Hammerstein, Oscar, 146
Handy, W. C., 162
Hanff, Helene, 350
Harkness, Stephen C., 65
Harlem: parades, 81; sightseeing tours, 135–41; Spanish, 140–41, 156–7; history and development, 141–7, 241; Railroad, 146; Opera House, 146; Italian, 146; modern character, 164; and expansion of New York, 234, 240–1; see also blacks
Harlem Hellfighters (369th Infantry), 147

Harper's Monthly, 225
Harrison, Wallace K., 344
Hart's Island, 272
Harvard Club, 204
Harvey, Charles, 236–7
Hasidim see under Jews
Hawkins, Coleman, 148
Heinrichs, Dutch, 261
Hell Gate Bridge, 39
Hell's Kitchen, 250
Hell's Kitchen Gang, 261
Helmsley, Harry, 177, 206
Helmsley, Leona M., 177, 206
Helmsley Palace Hotel, 177
Hemingway, Ernest, 277
Henry, O., 224
Hepburn, Katharine, 201
heroin, 265
Hester Street, 117
Hine, Lewis, 40–2
Hines, Earl, 148
Hispanics, 90, 103; see also Puerto Ricans
Hitchcock, Alfred, 28
Hill & Knowlton (PR agency), 183
Holland tunnel, 71
Hollander, Eugene, 275
Home Insurance Building, Chicago, 43–4
homelessness, 271–3
Hone, Philip, 224
Hoover, Herbert, President of USA, 188
Horne, Lena, 149
Hospitality Committee for UN Delegations, 348–9
housing: brownstone, 57, 247–8; clapboard, 57, 136; and population density, 232–3; and gentrification, 245–51; see also building; homelessness; property

Hudson Dusters (gang), 100, 261

Hudson, Henry, 67

Hudson River, 25, 69–70, 236

Hughes, Archbishop John Joseph, 101

Hughes, Langston, 154

Hungary, 128, 129

Hyde Park (*formerly* Stoutenburgh), 65

I. G. Farben company, 296

immigrants and immigration, 82–91; control of, 86–9; postwar, 90–1; illegal, 91n; exploitation of, 211–14; success stories, 217–19

Impelliteri, Mayor Vincent R., 305

Imperiale, Tony, 158

incomes *see* earnings

Independence, Declaration of *see* Declaration of Independence

Independent Subway (IND), 239–40

Indians (American) *see* Algonquin Indians; Caughnawaga Indians; Mohawk Indians

Indians (Asian), 94–5

Interborough Rapid Transit Company (IRT), 238–40

International Association of Bridge, Structural and Ornamental Ironworkers, 39

International Fur Workers' Union, 119

Irish, The: national consciousness, 80, 98–9; immigrants, 83, 89; and Catholicism, 100–1; political influence, 99–100; and police, 100, 101; mobsters and criminals, 100, 255n, 261–3; success, 101–2; numbers, 105; racialism, 106, 158; migrate to suburbs, 240; and Northern Ireland, 79–80, 340

Irish Republican Army, 79–80

Irving, Washington ('Diedrich Knickerbocker'), 193, 259, 337n; *History of New York*, 351

Ismail Pasha, Khedive of Egypt, 26

Israel, 113, 113n, 116, 131, 346; *see also* Jews

Italians, The: immigrants, 84, 88, 102–3, 214; criminal gangs, 100; and Tammany Hall, 102; exploited by compatriots, 103; and Catholicism, 103–4; lifestyle, 103–5; numbers, 105; racialism, 106, 158; anti-Semitism, 115; migrate to suburbs, 240

Jacobs, Jane, 302

James II, King of England, 98

James, Henry, 57, 171; *Washington Square*, 251

Jarmulowsky, Sender, 118

Jaruzelski, General Wojciech, 106

Javits, Jacob, 114

Jefferson, Thomas, 283

Jeffries, James, 62

Jenney, William LeBaron, 44

Jewish Daily Forward (journal), 119, 122, 127

Jewish Defence League, 116, 126

Jews: immigrants, 85, 214–15; criminal gangs, 100, 255n, 262; numbers, 105, 112–13; and black racialism, 106, 125–6, 159; Hasidic, 111–12, 127–33;

influence and character, 113–33; discrimination against, 114; education and advance, 117–21, 122–3; political involvement, 120; and psychoanalysis, 123–4; ethnic and assimilated, 124–7; and liberalism, 126; upward mobility and colonies, 240–2; and Peter Stuyvesant, 282; and UN, 346
John F. Kennedy Airport, 66, 71
Johnson & Johnson (company), 184, 205
Johnson, Basia (née Piasecka), 217–18
Johnson, J. Seward, 204–5, 218
Johnson, James Weldon, 147
Johnson, Lyndon B., President of USA, 89, 292, 293
Jolson, Al, 60, 121, 149
Jones Beach, Long Island, 300
Jones, John Paul, 205
Joplin, Scott, 149
Joyce, James: Ulysses, 339

Kahane, Rabbi Meir, 116
Kahn, Otto, 114, 299
Karmen, Steve, 310n
Keeton, Kathy, 201
Kefauver, Estes: Senate Crime Investigation Committee, 263, 305
Kempton, Murray, 355
Kennedy, John F., President of USA, 293, 294
Kerouac, Jack, 352
Kew Gardens, 243
Khrushchev, Nikita S., 162, 348
King Kong, 51
King, MacKenzie, 296
King, Martin Luther, 161

King, Grand Marshal Peter, 77–8
Kingdom, The, West 126th Street, 153
Kissinger, Henry, 201, 296
Knapp Commission, 276
Knickerbocker family, 204
Knickerbocker Trust Company, 187
Knickerbocker, Diedrich see Irving, Washington
Know-Nothings see Order of the Star-Spangled Banner
Koch, Mayor Edward Isaac: on sale of Coliseum site, 55; at St Patrick's Day Parade, 80; and anti-incinerator demo, 111–12; and subway graphics, 279; Mayoralty, 309–12; repartee, 311–12, 325; exuberance, 316, 336; and UN, 346–7
Koreans, 95
Kossuth, Louis, 226

labour unions, 72, 86, 119, 319
Ladies Garment Workers' Union, 119
Lafayette, General, 226
LaGuardia Airport, 66, 71, 354
LaGuardia, Fiorello Henry: grave, 59; opposes Tammany, 102, 274; character, 102, 307; elected, 115, 298; and Dewey, 120; and demolition of 'El', 238; and Rockefeller, 292; Mayoralty, 307–9; on life in New York, 339; Health Insurance Plan, 350; demands city airport, 354
Landmark Tavern, 250
Landmarks Preservation Act (1965), 231
Lasker, Judge Morris, 271

Latham Hotel, 273
Lauder, Estée (*née* Mentzer), 207, 221
lawyers, 178–81; working schedule, 215–16
Lazarus, Emma, 26
Le Corbusier, 344
Lehman, Herbert, 115, 298
Lennon, John, 123
Lepke, Louis, 263
Levitt, William, 159
Levittown, 159
Liberty Hall, West 138th Street, 151
Liberty Island *see* Bedloe Island
Liberty, Statue of, 26–7, 74, 280
Lie, Trygve, 343
Lincoln Center for the Performing Arts, 291
Lincoln Theatre, 148
Lincoln tunnel, 71
Lind, Jenny, 61, 226
Lindbergh, Charles, 187, 200, 281, 287
Lindsay, Mayor John, 158, 160, 256, 305–6, 317–18, 338
Liston, Sonny, 162
Little Athens, Queens, 95
Little Italy, 81, 104–5
Little Odessa-by-the-Sea, 96–8
Little Review, 339n
London Stock Exchange, 170
Long Island, 25; character and development, 65–6; property values, 175; Moses develops, 299–301
Long Island City, 248
Long Island Sound, 66, 67, 73
looting, 269
Lost-Found Nation in the Wilderness, 160–2

Louis, Joe, 162, 281
Lower Bay, 73–4
Lower East Side, 118, 127, 241, 352
Lower Hudson Valley, The, 64–5
Lubavitcher community (Hasidim), 131
Lucchese gang, 255
Luciano, Charles ('Lucky'), 254, 256, 263
Luis Muñoz Marin Boulevard, 140
Luna Park, Coney Island, 62

McCarthy, Senator Joseph, 101, 344, 354
McCullers, Carson, 20
McEnroe, John, 202
McGrath, Captain Edward, 330
McGraw-Hill building, 49
McLellan, Mayor John, 238
Macready, William, 258–9
Macy's (store), 114, 120
Madison hotel, 273
Madison Square Garden, 228–9
Mafia: and Italian community, 102–3; killings, 253–4; rackets, 254–5; gangs and organisation, 255–6; accommodation with, 256–7; trials, 264; activities, 262–4
Mahler, Gustav, 114
Mailer, Norman, 24–5, 277, 304, 316
Malcolm X (Malcolm Little), 161–163, 194
Mandela, Winnie, 164
Manes, Donald, 275–6
Manhattan: skyline, 19–20, 31–2, 56, 238; geology, 42–3; workforce, 64; purchased from Indians, 141, 281; real estate,

175–6; population density, 232–3; development and planning, 232–6
Manhattan Bridge, 24
Manhattan Inc. (journal), 201
Manhattan Project, 288
Mansfield, Sir James (Lord Chief Justice), 142
Maranzano, Salvatore, 254
Marlowe, Brian, 201
Martin, Jimmy, 220
Martini cocktails, 351
Marx Brothers, 121
Marx, Groucho, 336
Marx, Karl, 83
Masseria, Joe, 254, 256
Mayor, office of, 304–12
Melville, Herman: *Moby Dick*, 339
Mencken, H. L., 214, 315, 351
Merrick, David, 337
Merrill Lynch (corporation), 182, 185, 194, 196
Metropolitan club, 204, 218
Metropolitan Life Building, 44
Metropolitan Museum of Art, 185
Metropolitan Opera, 114, 121
Meyerson, Michael, 332
Michelin Tyre Company, 93
Milbank, Tweed, Hadley & McCloy (law firm), 179
Miller, Arthur, 20
Mills, Florence, 149–50, 154
Minuit, Peter, 39, 67, 141, 281
Miracle, The (show), 217
Mitchell, Charles E., 188, 189
Mitterrand, François, 94
Mobutu Sésé Séko, 345
Mohawk Indians, 38–9
Mones, Conrado, 96
Monk Eastman Gang, 262
Moore, Queen Mother, 166

Morgan Guaranty Trust Company, 180
Morgan, John Pierpont, 65, 204, 221–2, 228, 286
Morgan, J. P. & Co., 187
Morgan Library, 222
Morison, Samuel Eliot, 34n
Morningside Heights, 352
Morris-Jumel Mansion, 136
Morse, Samuel, 226
Moses, Robert: activities, 297–303, 309; and UN Headquarters, 342, 343
Mount Neboh Synagogue, West 79th Street, 231
Mountbatten, Edwina, Countess, 149
Mountbatten of Burma, Louis, 1st Earl, 80
Moynihan, Senator Daniel P., 80
Muhammad, Elijah (*formerly* Poole), 161–4
Mumford, Lewis, 297
Municipal Assistance Corporation, 319–21
Municipal Building, 33
Murder Inc., 263
Murdoch, Rupert, 180
Murrow, Ed, 354
Mussolini, Benito, 103

Narcotic Act (1914), 265
Narrows, The, 25, 67, 73–4
Nash, Ogden, 58
Nassau (steam ferry), 236
Nassau County, Long Island, 242
Nathan, George Jean, 149
Nation of Islam, 160
National Association for the Advancement of Colored People, 147, 150

National City Bank, 188

National Historic Preservation Act (1966), 230

National Horse Show, 203

National Origins Act (1924), 88

Negro World (weekly), 151

New Jersey, 25, 71

New School of Social Research, 209–11

New York: zoning laws and regulations, 47–8, 173, 177; early history and development, 67–8; port facilities, 68–75, 173; population, 85, 86–91, 233; industrial and commercial activities, 172–5, 248; property and real estate, 175–8, 207; millionaires in, 189n, 205–7; in Depression, 191–2; mobility in, 232; expansion, 232–6; population and community movements, 240–6; serious crime rate, 266–7; city flag, 304; administration, 304–21; budget and financing, 317–21; dilapidations and breakdowns, 324–34; status and image, 335–41; relations with Washington DC, 335–6; generosity and compassion, 350–1; idiom, wit and style, 353–6

New York, USS, 64

New York Botanical Garden, 185

New York City Opera Company, 164

New York Democratic Party, 99; *see also* Tammany

New York Jets (football team), 322

New York Life Insurance Company, 228

New York Mets (baseball team), 58, 200

New York Police Department, 260–1, 276–7

New York Post, 121

New York Prison Association, 258

New York Public Library, 185, 225

New York School of Lie Detection, 182n

New York Stock Exchange: floor activities, 167–70; membership, 170, 190; trading operations, 170–2; expansion, 187; fluctuations, 187–9, 192–3; number of customers, 189; and Wall Street crash, 189–91; computerisation, 192–3

New York Times: Jewish proprietors, 121; biases, 123n; Sunday edition, 175; and stock market, 192; on demolition of Pennsylvania Station, 229; on Mafia, 256; on empire and ruling class, 335; on rating of cities, 337–8; on skyscrapers, 352; on anti-Americanism, 354

New York Tribune, 83

New York Yacht Club, 186, 205

New York Yankees (baseball team), 157, 202, 273

New Yorker magazine, 178n, 248 Thurber cartoons, 354

Newark (NJ) Airport, 71

Newfield, Jack & Paul Du Brul: *The Abuse of Power*, 274–5

Newhouse, Si & Donald, 206

Nicaragua, 284–5

Nieuwe Haarlem, 146

Nixon, Richard M., 292, 293, 294

Normandie (ship), 70, 324
North Gowanus district, 39
Northern Ireland, 79–80, 341n
Norwegians, 81, 84

Ocean Hill, 125–6
O'Connor, Archbishop John, 78, 101, 271
O'Dwyer, Mayor William, 305
Official New York Map to the Stars' Homes, The, 201
Oliver, Betty Lou, 54
Olmsted, Frederick Law, 235, 235n
O'Malley, Walter, 63
On the Waterfront (film), 70
Onassis, Jacqueline, 201
O'Neill, Tip, 179
OPM Leasing Services, 185–6
Oppenheimer, Robert, 288
Order of Free and Accepted Americans (Wide Awakes), 99
Order of the Star-Spangled Banner (Know-Nothings), 99
Organisation of Afro-American Unity, 163
Orwell, George, 173
Owen, Chandler, 152
Oyster Bar, 196

Paine, Tom, 20
Pan Am Building, 52, 332
parades, 77–82, 152, 199–200; *see also* demonstrations
Paris Bourse, 171
Park Slope, 248
Partisan Review, 116n
Patti, Adelina, 228
Peace Corps, 350
Peel, Sir Robert, 260n

Peerce, Jan (*born* Jacob Perelmuth), 121
Pennsylvania Station, 195, 227–9
Penny Sightseeing Company, 135–41
Penthouse (magazine), 311
Perelmuth, Jacob *see* Peerce, Jan
PepsiCo Inc., 185
Persico, Carmine, 255, 264
Petit, Phillippe, 50–1
Philadelphia: and UN, 342–3
Pickens, T. Boone, Jr., 181–2, 183
Pius XII, Pope, 101
Places Rated Almanac, 337–8
Podell, Congressman Bertram, 274–5
Podhoretz, Norman, 116, 126
Poitier, Sydney, 221
Poles, 85, 106
police, 100, 101; *see also* New York Police Department
poor, the, 269–73, 280, 322
Port Authority of New York and New Jersey, 71; Bus Terminal, 353
Post, George P., 44
poverty *see* poor, the
Powell, Adam Clayton, Sr., 138, 151, 152, 155
Powell, Adam Clayton, Jr., 138, 157, 162
power failures, 268–9; 1965 Great Blackout, 328–34
Pratt, Charles, 65
Prince George Hotel, 273
Procaccino, Mario, 158, 159
Prohibition, 262–3
property values and ownership, 175–8, 207, 246–9; *see also* building

Prospect Park, Brooklyn, 235n
Proxmire, Senator William, 310
public relations, 182–4
Puerto Ricans: parade, 81; immigrants, 89–90, 156, 242; in Harlem, 140–1; socio-economic position, 156; racial antipathy to, 158; and crime, 264
Pulitzer Building, 43
Pulitzer, Joseph, 212
Puzo, Mario: *The Godfather*, 257

Queen Elizabeth II (*QE2*; ship), 29, 71
Queen Mary (ship), 70
Queens: lacks skyscrapers, 56; name, 57; character, 58, 64; nationalities in, 91; blacks in, 156
Quota Act (1921), 87

Radzievsky, Yuri, 217
Rahv, Philip (*formerly* Ivan Greenbaum), 115, 116n
Randall, John, Jr., 234–5
Randolph, A. Philip, 152
Raskob, John J., 226n
Reagan, Nancy, 353
Reagan, Ronald, President of USA, 271, 345
'Reaganomics', 181
Reddington, Katie Mulvey, 78
Redford, Robert, 201
rent control, 247, 247n
Restaurationen (ship), 84
Rhode Island: bans slavery, 142
Rickards, Tex, 228
Rickenbacker, Eddie, 291
Riis, Jacob: *How the Other Half Lives*, 118

riots, 258–60, 269
Ripley, William Z., 188
Rizzo, Frank, 158
roads: Moses develops, 301
Robeson, Paul, 148–9
Robinson, Jackie, 38, 63, 157, 158
Rockefeller Brothers Fund, 291
Rockefeller Center, 290
Rockefeller, David, 153, 292–3
Rockefeller family, 65, 288–9, 295–7
Rockefeller Foundation, 289, 291
Rockefeller, John Davidson, 65, 190n, 288–9
Rockefeller, John D. II, 289–90, 343
Rockefeller, John D. III, 291
Rockefeller, Laurence, 291–2
Rockefeller, Nelson, 179, 293–5, 303, 342, 343
Rockefeller, Tod, 295
Rockefeller, Winthrop, 290–1
Rockefeller University (*formerly* Institute for Medical Research), 296
Rockwell International (company), 186
Roebling, Emily, 21
Roebling, John, 21–3
Roebling, Washington, 21
Rogers, Will, 257
Rohatyn, Felix, 320–1, 321n
Roman Catholicism: and Irish, 98–101; and Italians, 103; Hispanics, 103; and inter-marriage between national groups, 105; and real estate, 177
Romanians, 85
Roosevelt family, 65, 146, 285–6
Roosevelt, Franklin Delano, 47, 103, 242, 286–8, 294, 306, 309

Roosevelt Island (*formerly* Welfare Island), 344n
Roosevelt, Theodore, 199–200, 213, 286–7, 340n
Rosemary's Baby (film), 123, 220
Rosenblatt, Yoselle, 121
Rothschild, L. F. (investment bank), 180
Royal Javelins (gang), 268
Rusk, Dean, 296
Russell, Bertrand, 288
Russians: immigrants, 85, 113; colony, 96–8
Ruth, Babe, 281

St Gennaro, Festival of, 81
St Mark's Lutheran Church, 243–244
St Patrick's Cathedral, 78, 101, 330
St Patrick's Day Parade, 77–81
Salerno, 'Fat Tony', 264
San Francisco, 341, 342
Sandy Hook, 67, 73; pilots, 73–4
Sanitation, Commissioner of *see* Commissioner of Sanitation
Satmar Hasidim, 127–33
Savage Nomads (gang), 268
scandals *see* corruption
Schmidt, Helmut, 320
Schulz, Dutch (Arthur Flegenheimer), 263, 274
Schurz, Carl, 98
Seabury, Judge Samuel, 306
Seagram Building, 49
Sears, Roebuck (company), 190
Sears Tower, Chicago, 44, 50
Securities Groups, The, 220–1
Seidenberg, Theresa, 162n
Serbs, 85
Seril, Nathan, 217

Sharkey, Tom, 62
Shea Stadium, 58, 297, 322
shipping, 29–30, 68–75, 324
Shulhan Aruch (Judaic law), 128
Sicily, 256
Sinatra, Nancy, 221
Sinclair, Upton, 340n
Singer Building, 44
Singer, Isaac Bashevis, 121–2
Skadden, Arps (law firm), 180, 215
skyscrapers, 19–20, 31–3; under construction, 37–42; etymology, 42–3; history and development of, 43–8; and city zoning laws, 47–8; stunts on, 50–1; accidents, 51–4; planned, 54–5; in 1965 power failure, 331–2; characterise New York, 352
slaves, slavery, 141–2, 166
Sloppy Louie's (eating place), 30
Slovenes, 85
Smith, Al, 46, 299, 303
Smith, Joe, 148
Social Register, 203–5, 284
social welfare, 317, 322, 350; *see also* poor, the
Society for the Prevention of Niggers Getting Everything, 158
Society for the Sons of New York, 145
SoHo, 250
South Bronx: arson, 267–8
South Street, 69
South Street Seaport, 31
Spanish Harlem *see under* Harlem
Spellman, Cardinal Francis, 170
Standard Oil (company), 289
Stanislavsky, Konstantin S., 217
Starrett, Theodore, 45

398   INDEX

Staten Island, 25, 28–9, 56, 60–1, 73, 110; ferry, 236, 280
Steffens, Lincoln, 340
Stein, Andrew J., 111
Steinberg, Saul, 178n
Steuben Day, 81, 98
Stevenson (cartoonist), 248
Stone, Leonard Norman, 207
Straus, Nathan, 114
Strayhorn, Billy, 198n, 241
strikes, 317–18; see also labour unions
study see education and study
Stuyvesant, Peter, 145–6, 281–3
subway system, 238–41; defacement and pop art, 278–80; violence in, 280; decline, 322–3; in 1965 power failure, 331; fan clubs, 352
success, 197–202, 211, 217–18, 222
suicides, 190–1, 219
Sunday, Billy, 290
Sutton Place, 204, 285
Swedes, 84

T & T stock, 190
Taki, 278
Talese, Gay, 255n
Tammany, Society of St (Columbian Order), 99–102, 120, 274
Tammany Hall (Great Wigwam), 274, 274n
Tarbell, Ida, 340n
taxis, 218, 218n
Teleport, Staten Island, 71
Teller, Edward, 296
Tenderloin (district), 145, 145n
Tenth Avenue Gang, 261
Testa, Salvatore, 257

Theresa Hotel, Harlem, 162, 162n, 163
Theroux, Paul, 327
Thurber, James, 354
ticker tape, 199–200
Tiffany's (jeweller's), 226
Time Life building, 49
Titanic (ship), 75
To Tell the Truth (TV show), 222
Todt Hill, Staten Island, 25
Tombs prison, 271
Tompkins Square, 243–4
Tonight Show, The, 222
Toronto Blue Jays, 202
Toscanini, Arturo, 114
traffic, 17–18, 301–2
Transit Museum, Brooklyn, 198n
transport, 236–40; see also bus services; subway system
Tree of Hope, 155
TribeCa, 250
Trilling, Lionel, 115
Trinity Church, 22, 23, 43, 171, 225
Trotsky, Leon, 60
Troy, Matthew, 275
Truman, Harry S., President of USA, 120, 147, 305, 341
Trump, Donald, 176, 177, 180
Trump Tower, 176, 180
Tucker, Richard (*born* Reuben Ticker), 121
Turbans (gang), 268
Turtle Bay, 343
Twain, Mark, 283
Tweed, William March, 99–100, 238, 274
Tylenol capsules, 184

underwear see foundation garments

Uniformed Sanitationmen's Association, 321
Union Carbide (company), 184
Union Club, 204
Unisphere, 298
United Bamboo (gang), 264
United Federation of Teachers, 321
United Nations: building, 49, 294; established in New York, 341–8; temporary locations, 342; design, 344; costs and returns, 345; effect on New York, 345–8; hospitality extended to delegates, 348–9
United States (ship), 70
United States Business Advisory Council for the Alliance for Progress (in South America), 293
United States Coastguard, 26
United States Steel (company), 187, 190
Universal Negro Improvement Association, 151–3
Upper Bay, 25, 67

Van Alen, William, 45–6
Van Schaik, Captain, 243–4
Van Slyke, Louisa, 272
Vanderbilt, Cornelius (17th-century), 284
Vanderbilt, Cornelius (Commodore), 238, 284–5
Vanderbilt, Cornelius II, 226
Vanderbilt family, 65, 228, 284–5
Vanderbilt, Mrs William Kissam, 204, 285
Vanderbilt's Accessory Transit Company, 285
Varick, Mayor Richard, 310n

Vaux, Calvert, 235n
Verrazano Bridge, 25, 60, 61, 73, 74
Verrazano, Giovanni da, 67
Victor Emmanuel, King of Italy, 61
Vidal, Gore, 277
Vietnamese, 91
violence, 277, 280; *see also* crime; Mafia Volstead Act (1920), 262

Wade (tug), 244
Wagner, Robert, Sr., 98
Wagner, Mayor Robert, Jr., 98, 304, 305, 317
Waldorf-Astoria hotel, 225–6
Walker, A'Lelia, 154
Walker, Madame C. J. (Sarah Breedlove), 154–5
Walker, Mayor Jimmy, 100, 149, 192, 306–7
Walker, William, 285
Wall Street, 32, 37, 167, 171
Wall Street (district): as financial centre, 171–2, 193–4; and lawyers, 180; scandals and frauds, 185–6; 1929 crash, 188–91, 219; *see also* New York Stock Exchange
Wall Street Journal, 257
Waller, Fats, 148
Walters, Barbara, 201
Warhol, Andy, 220
Washington, DC, 336
Washington, George, 33–4, 136, 143, 167, 171
water supply, 225
Wayne, John, 64
Weil, Sanford, 201
welfare *see* social welfare
welfare hotels, 272–3

Welfare Island (*later* Roosevelt Island), 344, 344n
West Indians, 90, 145, 165, 242
West Side Story (musical play), 268
Westchester County, 65
White, E. B., 77, 340
White, Stanford, 228
Whitman, Walt, 20, 65, 74
Whitney, Richard, 186, 190
Whyte, William H., 316
Wide Awakes *see* Order of Free and Accepted Americans
William III (of Orange), King of England, 25, 98
Williams, Bert & George Walker ('Two Real Coons'), 148
Williams, Police Captain, 145n
Williams, William, 213
Williamsburg, 128, 131
Williamsburg Bridge, 22, 24
Williamsburgh Savings Bank Tower, 56
Wilson, Woodrow, President of USA, 45, 152
Winchell, Walter, 306
Wolfe, Thomas, 20

Wood, Mayor Fernando, 262n
Woodlawn (Bronx), 59
Woollcott, Alexander, 114
Woolworth Building, 20, 31, 45
Woolworth, Frank, 45, 59
Workmen's Circle (*Arbiter Ring*), 119–20
World, The (newspaper), 212
World Trade Center, 20, 32, 50–1, 71, 74, 316
World's Fair, 1939, 242–3
World's Fair, 1964, 297–8
Wriston, Walter, 194, 321

Yakuel, Zion, 218–19
Yale Club, 204
Yankee Stadium, 60
yellow cabs, 218, 218n
Yid, Der (weekly), 131

Zabar's delicatessen, 92
Zangwill, Israel: *The Melting Pot*, 86, 90
Zeckendorf, William, 343
Ziegfeld, Florenz: Follies, 220
Zionism, 131; *see also* Israel; Jews
Zuckerman, Mortimer, 180